W9-BDB-691

KENNETH EISENBERGER has been active in the consumer movement for the past decade. He has participated in consumer action at all levels of government and has completed graduate studies at the School of Social Work, University of Southern California.

THE
EXPERT CONSUMER

A COMPLETE HANDBOOK

KENNETH EISENBERGER

Illustrations by Joseph La Jeunesse

A SPECTRUM BOOK

PRENTICE-HALL, INC., *Englewood Cliffs, New Jersey 07632*

Library of Congress Cataloging in Publication Data

EISENBERGER, KENNETH.
    The expert consumer.

    (A Spectrum Book)
    Bibliography: p.
    Includes index.
    1. Complaints (Retail trade)—Handbooks, manuals, etc.
2. Customer relations—Handbooks, manuals, etc.
3. Consumer protection—United States—Handbooks,
manuals, etc.   I. Title.
HF5415.5.E54   640.73   77-5441
ISBN 0-13-295402-8
ISBN 0-13-295394-3 pbk.

© 1977 by Kenneth Eisenberger

All rights reserved. No part of this book
may be reproduced in any form or
by any means without permission in writing
from the publisher.

A SPECTRUM BOOK

10   9   8   7   6   5   4   3   2   1

Printed in the United States of America

Prentice-Hall International, Inc., *London*
Prentice-Hall of Australia Pty. Limited, *Sydney*
Prentice-Hall of Canada, Ltd., *Toronto*
Prentice-Hall of India Private Limited, *New Delhi*
Prentice-Hall of Japan, Inc., *Tokyo*
Prentice-Hall of Southeast Asia Pte. Ltd., *Singapore*
Whitehall Books Limited, *Wellington, New Zealand*

To you,
and to my father, mother,
Laura, Bob, Joanne, Steven,
Alberto Aguas, and Ralph Nader

CONTENTS

PREFACE

I wrote this book to give you, the consumer, a good foundation of practical knowledge and strategy to use in getting the most for your money and in protecting yourself against poor products and unfair or fraudulent business practices.

For decades, the words *caveat emptor,* or "let the buyer beware," have been shoved down the throats of consumers. You have been told to take responsibility for the products you buy. If you get a defective shaver or sewing machine, you are out of luck, and it is *your* fault for not checking the product out more thoroughly. The manufacturers of goods and the providers of services have been permitted to shun their responsibility of fair exchange—consumer dollars in return for a sturdy, good-quality product or worthwhile, effective service.

Consumers must press for laws that will help to replace *caveat emptor* with *caveat venditor*—"let the *seller* beware."

Writing this book has been for me a monumental task. I had some knowledge about consumer rights and protection before beginning, but I had no idea of the magnitude of research and persistence that would be required to complete the job. The work included the perusal of thousands of newspaper and magazine articles; press releases; local, state, and federal documents; and correspondence with every state in the country. I am glad I used my own advice about saving money on long-distance telephone calls, because I made use of direct interviews with officials in the nation's capital, as well as various state and local government administrators.

I have written this book from the standpoint of a consumer, sometimes a frustrated one. Getting the necessary information was mostly a manageable task, but on a few occasions I met with a surprisingly hostile response from some of the very people who are supposed to be helping consumers. It has been worth the effort, however, because I can now put before you all my thoughts and recommendations.

The research for this book could not have been done without the cooperation of countless agencies at all levels of government, consumer groups, and many hundreds of individuals who strongly support the consumer movement. I want to single out Virginia H. Knauer, special assistant to the president for consumer affairs; the U.S. Office of Consumer Affairs; Jay N. Pike, attorney for the FTC in Los Angeles; Federal Trade Commission; U.S. Consumer Product Safety Commission; Federal Communications Commission; and Ralph Nader-affiliated organizations for their valued assistance. I also want to thank the offices of most state governors for their cooperation.

Without the creativity, encouragement, and help of four individuals, this project could never have been completed. Howard Zager is chairman of the English Department at Culver City Junior High School in California. He is a dedicated, gifted teacher who cares about the quality of education. Even more important to me, he is a cherished friend of many years. He devoted a great number of hours in helping me to present my ideas more effectively and in editing the manuscript.

Leora Brown also helped me to express my ideas and gave me moral support when my efforts faltered. In addition, she assembled information presented in several of the appendixes.

I judged the work of several cartoonists before selecting Joseph La Jeunesse to illustrate the book. This artist is gifted with the ability to take a concept and put it into meaningful, humorous form. The more you look for details in his cartoons, the funnier they become.

The typing of the manuscript was undertaken by Kenneth J. Morris, whose cooperation I appreciated.

I am happy to be able to share the material in this book with you. We all can use it.

KENNETH EISENBERGER

Chapter 1

THE BASICS:
HOW TO UTILIZE THIS BOOK

This book offers you the opportunity to increase greatly your knowledge of how to obtain help in facing many consumer problems in daily life. It can be a constantly useful tool if you first digest its facts and philosophies, and then apply them for maximum personal benefit. Thus you may want to read the book from cover to cover to prepare for any troublesome situations that may arise. Or you may choose simply to have the book close at hand for whenever you need help with a problem suddenly confronting you. Although this book cannot cover all conceivable aspects of available assistance for every consumer problem, it is intended to give you sufficient knowledge and confidence to face up to a multitude of situations. You no longer need to feel defenseless against even the largest corporations.

It is recommended that before contacting any agency named in this book, you understand the suggested basic approach in proceeding with your complaint. In this way, you do not waste your time or the time of the person whose job is to rectify the problem.

Your complaint should be a valid one in which you can produce evidence of your claim or good reasons for your dissatisfaction. You can utilize receipts, witnesses, physical evidence, professional opinion, or your own reasonable judgment.

For example, if a newspaper ad offers certain benefits for joining a club and you send in your money, but do not receive all the membership goods or services advertised, you have a right to complain. You should be prepared to submit a copy of the ad (or specific information about its content and place of publication), to give details about what you received for your money, and to specify why you feel the advertising is false or misleading.

If the coat you take into a dry cleaner is ruined through negligence of the establishment, you must be able to produce a witness or a receipt or tag proving that the clothing was brought into that particular cleaning service.

Time may be an important factor in filing a complaint. In such areas as fraud, false advertising, and product mislabeling, thousands—maybe millions—of people may be affected if action is not quickly taken to curtail the unlawful activity. It even may be a matter of life and death! As time passes, facts can become more difficult to uncover in an investigation, and witnesses or evidence may be gone. Therefore, it is essential to report *immediately* your dissatisfaction with any situation that you feel may adversely affect other people. This is the responsibility of every consumer.

One woman who buys for her child what she subsequently discovers to be an unsafe toy may be satisfied simply to take it back to the store for a refund or exchange, while another will complain to a federal agency with the purpose of getting the dangerous plaything off the market. In the latter case the complainant has admirably chosen to protect not only her child, but all other children as well. A good general rule to follow is first to decide what type of reasonable consumer satisfaction you desire—do you want the product removed from the market or do you merely want a refund?

In cases where a refund or exchange is sought, your first responsibility is to contact the store where you made the purchase or the business whose service you employed. Since a clerk cannot always handle such problems, you may have to ask to be directed to the person authorized to make the adjustment.

Whenever possible, letters and calls should be addressed to a specific person. Letters addressed to "Complaints" or "Customer Service Department" might receive less than special attention by an overburdened clerk or be filed away until a backlog of other customer communications are answered. You can often receive faster action by calling a company or consumer office first to get the name of an individual and his or her title, and then addressing the complaint to that person.

When making a phone complaint, ask for the name of the department that handles the particular area about which you want to complain. After being connected to the department, ask for the full name of the person to whom you may relate your complaint. Then request that you be connected to that party.

Much time can be wasted, and frustration generated, by describing the entire situation to an individual whose position authorizes him or her only to transfer the call to someone else. If correspondence and conversations with customer service representatives fail, do not hesitate to contact the highest accessible office. This might be the office of the company president or regional manager or, in the case of a government agency, the office of the director or chief investigator. Even if the administrator's assistant or secretary takes the call, he or she probably will be able to effect prompt action.

After you finally get through to the proper receptive ear, speak calmly, but firmly, detailing the situation clearly without tangents and expletives. Without undue emotionalism, you should be free to express your frustration, anger, concern, or sorrow.

Keep in mind that you are dealing with fellow human beings, whether you are speaking with the janitor of a building, the president of a corporation, or a consumer bureau's field investigator. Be courteous and respectful from the beginning, while remaining determined to support your consumer rights. Being belligerent, sarcastic, or disrespectful can only hurt your case. The first company employee or government worker to whom you speak may not be able to offer a remedy for a complaint simply because he or she does not know what can be done or lacks authority to take action.

Be honest in representing your position and the circumstances leading up to the complaint. Harm can be done to the consumer rights movement by a person who decides to take action for personal gain when there is no basis for the claim. Furthermore, many consumer complaint offices, particularly those set up by government bodies, require the complainant to sign an affidavit, whereby the signer leaves him- or herself open to admonishment or even prosecution should he or she willfully make false statements.

Many companies and government offices require the consumer to detail the complaint in writing before any action may be considered. This should not be construed as a method of discouraging complaints, although some offices admit using this procedure to weed out the lesser complaints by those willing to make a phone call, but not wanting to take the time to write. Many of the complaint procedures in this book do require time and patience, and you hopefully will be encouraged enough to take the steps necessary to protect your rights as a consumer.

The written complaint should present a chronological statement of facts with photocopies of receipts, correspondence, ads, or other materials to substantiate your claim. Typing or legibly writing in ink a well-thought-out letter on good-quality stationery, preferably pre-printed with your name and address, will get your complaint acted upon more quickly and favorably than if you scribble a few nonsensical and unsupported statements on a piece of notepaper.

However, the sincerity, honesty, and factual support of a claim outweigh all else. When straightforward efforts to gain satisfaction from a sales or service representative are to no avail, enlisting the action of consumer protection specialists is another route open to you.

Most of the chapters in this book deal with specific groups of the most prevalent problems. How consumer laws are enforced and the procedure for filing complaints with various government agencies will be detailed. Areas of concern include problems around the home and in travel, banking, postal service, entertainment, and advertising (Chapters 2 to 11).

Today's consumer has access to a wide variety of local government, and sometimes private, services offering help in fighting unfair and illegal business practices. One of the most important sections of this book is Chapter 12, "Local Resources for Consumer Protection." Whether you live in New York City, Austin, Texas, or Carmel, California, this chapter will make you aware of the many consumer protection services of bureaus, regulatory bodies, policing and other law enforcement agencies, and TV and radio "action lines." It also will give you an insight into the procedures and pitfalls of small claims courts.

The offices of most state attorneys general are responsible for the statewide protection of consumers. Other state and federal departments license and regulate businesses throughout the country. An overview of how these agencies serve the public and enforce the consumer laws is given in Chapter 13.

Chapter 14 describes the latest efforts of various industries to provide their own information and complaint-handling mechanisms to deal with consumer problems. It includes details on how and when to submit your complaint.

The index provides a handy guide to specific types of problems. The additional references section will assist you in selecting books and periodicals to broaden your knowledge of consumerism and to obtain up-to-date information. The appendixes provide sample forms and comprehensive lists of names and addresses for both government and private offices dealing with consumer affairs. There is also a list of toll-free telephone numbers you can use to deal with various consumer problems, and conparisons of travel services, moving companies, and small claims courts in the United States.

Seeking help for a problem is not a difficult task when you follow the procedures outlined in this chapter and throughout the book. The necessary tools include a telephone and directory, a pen, paper, and a place to keep your records. A typewriter and quality stationery are also recommended, as previously stated.

With a telephone directory you can locate the number of a local, state, or federal government office to contact for a problem within its jurisdiction. Which government agency to select and the jurisdiction of various agencies will be detailed in later chapters. To find a list of federal government offices located in your area, look under United States Government in the White Pages of your local directory.

Persons in small towns may have to request from their telephone business office a directory for the nearest large city to obtain a more complete list of sources. When a federal or state department or agency is not listed, it generally means that there is no regional or district office in your area. In that case, or when you are having difficulty getting through to the appropriate office, ask the information operator for a listing of the nearest federal information center, federal government building switchboard, or state government switchboard. The switchboard operators at these government facilities know about the location of the various offices they serve.

To find state, county, and city office listings in the telephone directory, look under the name of the state or municipality (for example, *Hawaii* State Government, *Pennsylvania* Commonwealth of, *Denver*—City & County Government, *Los Angeles* City of, and *Los Angeles* County of). These listings are usually located alphabetically in the White Pages, but sometimes may be placed elsewhere, such as at the beginning of the directory.

That an office of a government unit is not conveniently located near your residence does not mean contact will be difficult. Sometimes an 800 toll-free number for a government office out of your area may be obtained from a "WATS line" information operator by dialing area code 800 and then 555–1212 from anywhere in the 48 contiguous states. The 800 numbers for many government offices are listed in Appendix 3 and throughout Appendix 12. (Alaska and Hawaii residents cannot yet reach WATS numbers.) Certain governmental agency regional offices even send out field representatives once or twice a year to distant areas within their jurisdiction to accept complaints. These men and women set up temporary offices to interview local residents, and their visits are often publicized in local newspapers and on radio and television.

It is of the utmost importance that you keep accurate records of all your purchases, returned checks, and other valid receipts, complaints, and phone calls or correspondence with the business or with the government office handling the complaint. You should use an envelope, file folder, or uncluttered drawer to keep the original receipt or returned check; any applicable literature or advertising on the product; any guarantee or warranty issued; correspondence to and from the manufacturer, store, or government office; and your notes regarding places you have called and action that has been taken. Always submit copies of documents rather than the originals, unless you are told that the latter are needed in pursuing the investigation.

Appendix 1 shows a Consumer Contact Sheet that you may use for recording information about your complaint at the time you initiate or receive a letter or phone call. This log, which will encourage you to keep accurate records with regard to your complaint, will save you time and money in the long run.

R. T. wanted to know whether or not she was covered by her health insurance policy for a general physical examination. She had decided to visit her doctor for an annual checkup, but could not afford the large expense unless most of the charges would be paid by the insurer. She called her insurance company and was informed that her policy did cover any type of physical exam by a medical doctor.

The woman visited her physician and then requested that the bill be sent to her insurance company. Two months later she received notification that a physical examination was not a procedure covered by her policy unless the visit was in direct connection with a past or current illness or injury.

Despite the fact that this consumer was given incorrect information at the time of her original inquiry, she could not prove that she even made the inquiry because she did not keep a written record. Had she been more careful, she could later have utilized the date of her inquiry and the names of the department and individual with whom she spoke to pressure the insurance company for compensation, or to file a complaint with the appropriate government regulatory body.

In other words, it is a good idea to maintain the recordkeeping habit as a precaution.

Too often misinformation or misrepresentation of a product or service is given by an ignorant, negligent, or disreputable company representative over the phone. Let the person with whom you are discussing a product, service, or complaint take responsibility for what he or she is telling you.

Give your name freely, and then politely ask for the name of the other party. If he or she questions your asking for a name, be more emphatic, saying that the person has *your* name and you would simply like to know with whom you have been speaking. If the representative is still reluctant to divulge his or her name, be straightforward and say that you want him or her to be responsible for information given you.

If the person still refuses to give out his or her name, do not start an argument, since many employees are instructed never to give out their names. Instead, ask to speak to a supervisor. Describe the situation, and more than likely the supervisor will give you his or her name or the name of the person who first served you.

If you have difficulty in getting anyone's name up to this point, do not hesitate to ask the supervisor for the name of his or her superior. This may sound like a rather tedious procedure, but should you ever be questioned about who gave you incorrect information, you will have a written record in your defense. This procedure can also save you unnecessary frustration and a useless, time-consuming trip to a particular merchant or government office that cannot help you. For example, if you call the neighborhood drugstore to inquire about whether it carries a particular product, the answerer may be busy and respond, "Yes, I believe we do." Often, if you will ask the name of the person making the statement, he or she will tell you to hold on while a definite check is made.

The jurisdiction for handling some consumer complaints may shift from one government agency to another as economic conditions change, programs are phased out, and new departments are set up. In some cases, you may be given an incorrect referral from one agency to another simply because government employees handling public inquiries are not always immediately aware of the changes.

Some agencies work together in accepting similar complaints and enforcing the law. Although the Federal Energy Administration currently handles complaints regarding gasoline price violations, it is the Environmental Protection Agency that requires the offering of unleaded gas at stations with a minimum volume. In cases where two different agencies on the same governmental level or different levels (federal, state, and local) handle similar types of problems, you may choose to submit your complaint to both offices. However, you should report this fact to each, since one agency may want to contact the other for joint investigation and action in order not to duplicate efforts. Furthermore, some consumer agencies require disclosure of a complainant's submission of the same facts to another government office, and if the double submission is not made known and one agency discovers it, all action on the claim by that office may be dropped.

Following up your initial contact at a customer service office or government consumer affairs unit is an essential part of the complaint process. Some offices take the initiative in keeping the consumer informed of his or her claim's status, including sending out an acknowledgment that the complaint has been received; others will not reveal the progress or even the final disposition of an investigation, especially when the complaint does not involve a simple refund or adjustment of a specific product or service for which the complainant has paid. Some agencies will report back only when specifically requested to do so by the consumer.

Always mention on the phone or in a complaint letter your desire to be kept abreast of continuing developments in the handling of your case. If you are informed that this is not possible, you should find out how long a response will take, and then follow up by phone or letter after that length of time. If no lapse time is specified, follow up after a reasonable period (usually three to five weeks).

One of the necessary ingredients in the process of seeking help for a consumer complaint is patience. Although it may sometimes be difficult to obtain speedy assistance and full satisfaction for a problem, keep in mind that the consumer offices described in this book are set up to serve you. You should protect your rights and the rights of others by demanding full justice and by working toward maintenance of a happy and safe environment. It is hoped that this book will be a useful tool in helping to achieve that goal.

One final note: There is no doubt that to be expert consumers we must continue to assert ourselves and to complain effectively and constructively when we get inferior performance from goods and services. At the same time, it is just as important to praise good service and single out those products with excellent features, qualities, and service records. In your contacts with companies, industry groups, and government offices, let them know when you are particularly pleased with a product, a service, or how you have been treated. This will show that consumers recognize and reward excellent quality when they see it; it will also help ensure that standards will not be lowered.

Chapter 2

HOUSEHOLD HASSLES

When was the last time you spent your hard-earned money on a household appliance that went ka-blooey soon after you had it installed? If it wasn't the Speed-Squash garbage disposal that thundered as if Mount Vesuvius were erupting right there in your kitchen, it was the Airgush air-conditioner that blew the cool air outside and the hot air in.

Are all of the toys, sporting goods, and appliances you own safe for family use? An electric knife is a handy device, but take one that doesn't shut off properly and your Thanksgiving dinner may include turkey à la finger. What about those utilities? If all the lights in your new house had not gone out because of that improperly installed electric meter, would you have lost one of your expensive contact lenses in your new shag carpet?

This chapter will explore some of the most common problems connected with the purchase of goods and services for your home life. It will give you pointers on how to avoid some catastrophes, as well as how to pick up the pieces and work toward a just remedy. Read on. You've only begun to fight.

HINTS ON HAZARDS

It's been an "outstanding" morning at Howard and Hannah's hazardous household. Howard was awakened an hour before his alarm was set to go off because his electric blanket, with the dial turned to the lowest setting the night before, baked his buttocks to the color of an overripe tomato. Hannah gets out the spray pain-killer and, since there are no directional markings on the nozzle, sprays the medicine into her left eye, which she quickly washes out with water.

With him barely able to sit down at the breakfast table and her half blind, they find that the batter they have placed in the waffle iron has turned into something resembling the rusted front grille of their 1968 Pontiac. While they are noting that some kind of metal coating from the appliance has come off onto the food, wails from young Howie summon the two to the nursery, where the baby's head is stuck between wooden bars of the crib. After sawing through the crib and effecting a speedy rescue, they get dressed in one minute flat, grab the infant, and get out of there and over to a safe coffee shop two miles away.

You hopefully have better luck with the things you buy, but the fact remains that of the estimated 20 million people who are injured in the United States each year by products in and around their homes, 30,000 die and 110,000 are permanently disabled. In an attempt to reduce the number of product-related injuries, the U.S. Consumer Product Safety Commission (CPSC) was established in October 1972 by the Consumer Product Safety Act and was activated in May 1973 as an independent federal regulatory agency.

The CPSC, through its research and investigations and your help, develops safety standards for products and can assist you in comparing safety among various types. It can ban or order the recall of especially hazardous items, such as a defective vacuum cleaner model that sometimes gives a shock when the user turns it on, and can require manufacturers or sellers to provide repairs, replacement, or refunds. The Commission also may enforce its mandatory standards through the courts with both civil and criminal penalties.

One area of special interest to the CPSC is the safety of anything purchased for the care of young children in the home. The Commission has estimated that each year some 40,000 infants in the United States are injured seriously—and another 150 to 200 fatally—because of unsafe cribs. It has set mandatory standards for new cribs sold in this country. The regulations limit the space between crib slats to 2⅜ inches, provide for safe and secure metal parts and locking mechanisms, and require warning labels that advise the purchaser to use only a snug-fitting mattress. The rules were made in an attempt to stop infant strangulation, cuts and bruises, and falls from the crib.

A 1975 investigation by the CPSC revealed that thousands of

cribs manufactured by the Simmons Company of Wisconsin did not meet the federal standard relating to slat spacing, and had metal brackets with hazardous edges and corners. The agency required the company to recall the merchandise for destruction or modification before it could be sold. The company also agreed to refund the purchase price of the crib to anyone making such a request.

Hazardous Playthings

Toys can be a surprising cause of injury to a child playing in the home. How long is the cord used to pull the toy train? The CPSC recommends that it not be over one foot long. Is the toy mouse tiny enough to hold on a finger? No toy should be small enough or have detachable parts small enough for a baby to swallow. The Commission also recommends that toys not have sharp edges or a composition that can break into small pieces with jagged edges, openings that may catch fingers or hair, wires or nails that may be exposed, or a surface covered with toxic paint.

According to U.S. Attorney Mark Waxman, the Consumer Production Safety Commission took its first court action against the Bradley Import Company of Los Angeles, in 1974, after the firm imported from South Korea 100,000 dolls that allegedly contained dangerous straight pins. The shipment, valued at $300,000, was seized by government agents reportedly before any of the dolls were marketed.

Out of the hundreds of toys that have appeared on the CPSC's Banned Products List are such playthings as F.W. Woolworth's "Toy Concert Xylophone" with sharp edges; "Doggie Weatherman Toy Banks" with sharp wires, from Sterling Products, Inc., of Chicago; Ideal Toy Corporation's "Toddler Thumbellina" doll with sharp springs in mechanically operated legs; the flammable "Sears Cabanna Play Tent" from the Kellwood Company of New Haven, Missouri; and the "High Chaparral Toy Rifle" from Daisy-Heddon of Rogers, Arkansas, that made a sound above 138 decibels (*loud!*).

Fire!

Children and fire definitely do not mix. In 1971 children reportedly set 46,830 residential fires, causing the loss of hundreds of lives and over $60 million in property damage. In 1974 the CPSC began studying the possibility of regulating the manufacture of book matches so that children would not be able to start a fire with them.

To protect children from burns in the home, the Commission

has set standards requiring sleepwear in sizes 0 to 6X, manufactured after July 29, 1972, to be flame-retardant. Children's sleepwear in sizes 7 to 14, manufactured after May 1, 1975, is required to be flame-resistant and must bear a label indicating such. These garments also must carry a label giving cleaning instructions so as to keep the fabric from becoming less resistant to fire.

The State of California followed the original flammability standard with a more strict regulation requiring flame-resistant material to be used for all children's outerware and girls' slips in sizes 0 to 14 by July 1, 1979. Since California consumes nearly a tenth of all the children's clothing manufactured in this country, the effect will no doubt be a total conversion to fire-resistant clothing for children by the apparel industry. There is also a good chance that California's action will spur federal legislation to ensure stricter standards nationwide.

Free Safety Information

Whether the potential hazard is in Grandpa's electric toothbrush or Jennie's pogo stick, you can help to eliminate product hazards in your home by keeping informed and reporting dangerous products to the Consumer Product Safety Commission. The CPSC will provide you, on request, with free materials for any of the following topics: crib and toy safety, prevention of poisonings, lawn mower safety, flame-resistant fabrics and laundering hints, bicycle safety (see Chapter 7), preparations for a safe Christmas, and spring and summer safety tips. Write to Public Information, U.S. Consumer Product Safety Commission, Washington, D.C. 20207.

The Commission's Banned Products List (October 1, 1973, Vol. 3, Part I, Cat. #5203-000-42) was once available from the Superintendent of Documents, but the 1973 issue is no longer in print, and as of mid-1976, the CPSC had not come out with another edition. One reason may be that the list quickly becomes outdated. Although some products are added, others on the list have been modified to make them safe, and many companies have complained about their products remaining on the list until the printing of a new edition.

Keep your eyes open for news reports in which the Commission announces hazardous and banned products. The CPSC announced in 1974, for example, that "household trouble lights" manufactured by A. L. Electric Corporation of New York, and sold by such chain stores as J.J. Newberry, Woolco, and Food Fair, could cause serious electric shocks. Approximately 300,000 of the gadgets were sold across the country, and one was reportedly the possible cause of an electrocution. During that year the agency banned vinyl chloride for use as an aerosol spray propellant in such products as paints and adhesives after the chemical was alleged to be the cause of liver cancer among industrial workers. In 1975 the CPSC accepted a consent order requiring Keller Industries, Inc., of Florida to recall some carpets and rugs that failed to meet federal flammability standards.

The CPSC has held hearings on the hazards of glass bottles and their closures. It also proposed a new safety standard designed to ban firecrackers and to require better performance and labeling of other fireworks.

Reporting Dangerous Products

The Commission has also investigated hazards and enforced laws connected with such products as household chemicals, swimming pool slides, refrigerators (no longer can one be sold that is capable of trapping and suffocating a child), carpets, and architectural glass. The agency will continue to try to protect consumers from dangerous items in the marketplace. It can use your help.

If you are injured by a product you buy or find it to be potentially dangerous, contact the CPSC at the 24-hour, toll-free hotline, 800-638-2666 (Maryland residents should dial 800-492-2937; residents of Alaska and Hawaii do not have access to the toll-free number); or complete and mail a complaint form like the one in Appendix 2 to the U.S. Consumer Product Safety Commission, Washington, D.C. 20207.

Once your complaint is received, the Commission staff will take swift action. Investigators nearest your area of residence will obtain samples of the product, and then the appropriate bureau of the agency will conduct the necessary testing. After inspection is complete and computer records are checked for any available data on similar product-related injuries, an evaluation and recommendation will be made to Commission officials.

If the product is shown to present a significant hazard, the manufacturer will be notified and may be required to take corrective actions, such as contacting purchasers; repairing, replacing, or recalling the product; or providing refunds. In a case where a company's product is found to be so hazardous that safer use cannot be assured by issuance of a safety standard, the Commission can take action to ban its sale.

Federal law now requires importers, manufacturers, distributors, and retailers to contact the Commission within 24 hours after they discover a potentially dangerous product. By mid-1975, after the CPSC was in operation for nearly two years, almost 250 such notifications involving over 15 million product units had been filed.

The safety of some household goods comes under the jurisdiction of other federal agencies. In addition to handling complaints regarding food, drugs, and cosmetics (see Chapter 4), the Food and Drug Administration (FDA) looks into safety problems with television sets, chemically treated cookware, home canning materials, microwave ovens, and medical devices such as heating pads and vibrators. Direct your complaint to the nearest FDA office or write to the Food and Drug Administration, 5600 Fishers Lane, Rockville, Maryland 20852. If you want to report a problem with an alcoholic beverage, tobacco product, or firearm, write to the Bureau of Alcohol, Tobacco, and Firearms, 1111 Constitution Avenue N.W., Washington, D.C. 20226. Pesticides can be dangerous to your health. Questions about their use or a complaint about their labeling or effect should be sent to the Environmental Protection Agency (see Chapter 7).

Electronic Injury Surveillance

An injury you receive while using a product might be more than a minor cut, bruise, or burn. If the electric mixer into which you are placing blades is accidentally turned on and you suddenly find yourself minus some of your fingers, you may have to take the problem to the emergency room of the nearest hospital.

Through the CPSC's National Electronic Injury Surveillance System (NEISS, pronounced "nice"), the circumstances surrounding many such product-related accidents are logged by personnel at over one hundred hospitals around the country, reported to the Commission, and fed into computers to determine patterns of problems associated with the use of specific consumer products as well as categories of products.

For example, it was shown that about 100,000 injuries a year are being caused by washing machine wringers, and 40 percent required hospitalization. This led to development of an "instinctive release" device, which in newer wringer washers stops the rotation and separates the rollers when any object, including a finger, hair, or clothing, becomes caught.

In fiscal year 1973, NEISS estimated that 10,863 injuries were treated in emergency rooms in connection with matches, 53,000 injuries associated with home playgrounds, and 52,000 injuries related to soda bottles. Such statistics cause scrutiny of the problem products, and often the issuance of mandatory safety standards. Other product categories that seem to have a comparatively high incidence of injury include cutting and chopping devices, beds and bedding, tables, swimming pools and associated equipment, bicycles, stairs and railings, and windows and doors.

Petition Power

One of the best ways to see that something gets done is to do it yourself. The Consumer Product Safety Commission has set up a petitioning procedure by which you can do just that. Maybe you find that the shaver pinches your skin or the hair dryer burns your scalp, and you think something should be done to eliminate the possibility of such injuries from these products. If you feel your complaint relates to a problem with only a specific product and manufacturer, a call or the sending of the completed complaint form to the CPSC will get action. On the other hand, if you feel there is a safety problem with a whole line of products or a specific *type* of consumer item, you can petition the CPSC to issue a standard.

It is a simple matter to induce the Commission to consider even strong, significant action. Put in writing your experiences and thoughts relating to the hazards you have found in a particular type of product. State causes for such dangers, if you know them. Incorporate any ideas you may have about the type of remedy needed, and request that a specific standard be set. Send your letter to the Consumer Product Safety Commission, Washington, D.C. 20207.

By law, your request must be granted or denied by the Commission within 120 days. If the petition is denied, the agency is required to state the reasons in the *Federal Register*, a daily publication of federal government proceedings. It is now established, as of October 27, 1975, that you can even appeal the decision in court.

In response to the many petitions and consumer complaints against various chemical components in household products, the Commission issued an industrywide order forcing manufacturers of soap, dishwasher and laundry detergents, aerosols, paint, varnish, fuel for fondue pots and chafing dishes, and flame-retardant chemicals to submit their secret chemical formulas by May 15, 1975. The CPSC is using the information to assess the hazardous nature of chemicals and to take appropriate action to protect the public.

Your contact with the Commission need not be limited to complaining about a particular product or requesting a new standard.

You can also use the petitioning procedure to ask the agency to revoke or amend an existing safety standard. For instance, if you feel stricter regulations should be tacked onto the new bicycle safety standard (see Chapter 7), you should request it. All new consumer product safety standards are first proposed and opened for public discussion before they are officially issued. Your comments to the Commission are important and can help to effect action in the public interest.

Be a Consumer Deputy

If you want to do more than occasionally fill out a complaint form or send a letter, you will be interested in knowing that the Consumer Product Safety Commission has instituted two programs that utilize the help of consumers. The first is the Consumer Deputy Program, which sends volunteers to retail stores to check for hazardous products, especially those included on the Banned Products List. After suitable training by CPSC, you would present a letter of introduction to the store management. You would check the shop's inventory and make out a report.

The effectiveness of the Consumer Deputy Program can be seen in examples of its accomplishments. In the last few months of 1973, 990 volunteers, who visited 1,400 stores, found 1,200 banned toys in the marketplace. In March 1974 a similar project was met by 140 volunteers, who looked for required "child-proof" closures on aspirin products and on some types of liquid furniture polish.

In May 1975 deputies were sent to retailers of children's sleepwear in an effort to ensure compliance with the latest flammability standards. They also educated store owners about regulations requiring them to segregate flame-resistant sleepwear from noncomplying garments by a minimum of three feet, with signs identifying both groups.

Although the Commission has often selected individual volunteers to be deputies, it is turning more and more to organized consumer groups to get the necessary person power. Let the CPSC know if you belong to a group that would like to participate.

Helping to Set Standards

The other CPSC program utilizes consumers to make evaluations and recommendations for proposed product safety standards. After notifying the Commission of your interest, you will be notified if you are selected to participate, and your travel expenses to official meetings and hearings may be reimbursed. If you have a technical background that would be especially useful in testing or judging safety factors in the operation of a particular type of product, you probably will be given preference. However, technical training is not mandatory.

If you are interested in becoming involved in either type of consumer program, write to the Office of the Secretary, U.S. Consumer Product Safety Commission, Washington, D.C. 20207. Include your name and address, telephone number, and occupation. State any preference you have for working on particular product areas, and relate applicable schooling or experience.

ALL THE COMFORTS OF HOME

Unless you own a two-ton truck or a jumbo-sized elephant, examine and test all heavy and bulky furnishings at the store to avoid the hassle of transporting items that you may later decide to return. And "test" does not mean politely sitting on your prospective sofa like Queen Elizabeth gracefully lowering herself on a Chippendale chair for afternoon tea. Sit down easily the first time, but then shake, slap, and even pounce on the piece of furniture. Within reasonable limits, scrape the material with your fingernail, gouge the pillow with your fist, and yank on the upholstered buttons. (In fact, this is the one time to take the kids with you.) There is no sense putting your money into a piece that will fall apart after a few weeks.

Boycott any store that will not allow you the privilege of testing appliances or furniture, because that merchant is unfairly asking you to have blind faith in the durability and operability of the items.

As good an idea as it may be, you cannot take a bunch of soiled clothes into a store and try out a washer. But you should examine such an item carefully. A television set, for instance, usually can be taken from a storeroom and demonstrated so that you can see its picture quality before the appliance is taken to your home. If you do test a new item that was taken out of its package or if you are purchasing a store demonstrator, write down the item's model number and serial number, and check them with those on the product delivered later to make sure they match. That way you can be sure of getting the same merchandise you previously examined. If the item is not the same or is defective, you can refuse the purchase or ask for an immediate replacement.

Buying a large appliance or piece of furniture with a good guarantee is one way of assuring that the product, if unsatisfactory, will be fixed or replaced at the manufacturer's expense. See Chapter 3 on guarantees and warranties to gain insight into what to look for in the statements made by the company.

Save all sales receipts, warranty slips, and literature so that it will be easy to identify model numbers or fabric colors should you later need to order a new part for an appliance or a length of material to replace that which was consumed in one bite by Rover, leaving a hole smack in the center of your beautiful couch.

Especially when you are not buying a brand-name item, find out whether or not parts or fabric will be available in the future. If not, such as in the case of a close-out sale item, you can make the decision on whether or not to make the purchase. You can go ahead and buy it, with the request to be given extra material immediately or a spare part for future use.

Store to Home

After you place an order, work out with the salesperson any details relating to receipt of your goods, such as the time and date of delivery and any charges. Most stores deliver heavy merchandise without extra cost to you, but many do charge a fee for installation, especially for appliances requiring special hookups. If you cannot be at your residence at the time of delivery, ask a family member, friend, landlord, or neighbor to be there when the merchandise arrives. If you have a cooperative landlord, list him or her on the delivery instructions just in case you have to leave your apartment unexpectedly. Inform the landlord about the delivery, even though you will be home to receive it.

Hopefully the item you have ordered has been delivered to your home in good shape. Be sure to look it over carefully, checking to see that nothing is dented, cracked, or broken; then immediately put it into operation.

Should something be wrong with an appliance, politely demand on the spot that the delivery service return the item to the store. If they refuse and demand that you sign the delivery receipt, be sure to mark on all copies that the appliance is defective and must be replaced. This will protect you from a store claim that you damaged the item after it was delivered.

Call the store and request that a new unit be brought at once. In many cases, large outfits and chain stores will provide you with a replacement if you call to discuss the problem within a couple of weeks after the purchase date, even if such an immediate replacement is not required under the terms of the warranty.

Phone Ordering

Some of the department stores for which you have charge cards or the many shops that accept Master Charge or BankAmericard also accept phone orders for your convenience. Other stores often will be willing to send out your merdhandise C.O.D.

Order merchandise by phone only when you know or can determine by talking with a salesperson exactly what you want. Common articles of clothing (underwear, socks, and such), household supplies (sheets, scissors, pencil sharpeners, alarm clocks, typewriter ribbons), and certain entertainment items (phonograph albums, blank cassettes, books) are often easily ordered over the phone.

When placing an order, always mark down for your records the clerk's name, the item you're ordering, the total price including tax, the estimated shipping charges, and the delivery date and time, if it is determinable. Sometimes the store will use both a local delivery service and the U.S. Postal Service to ship its merchandise, and it may offer you a choice. Always ask how the item will be delivered, and if one delivery method is cheaper than another. A store may charge $1.50 for a typewriter ribbon to be delivered by a local company and only 25 cents if it is sent through the mail.

Be certain you know a firm before you place an order with it. Sears is one nationally known company that provides comprehensive phone-order services to both charge account and noncharge customers. It and other firms put out catalogs that you can use for phone ordering. However, such books are sometimes available to you only if you spend at least a specified amount in phone purchases.

The return of defective merchandise you have ordered by telephone does not necessarily require a trip to the store. Sears, for example, has a nationwide policy of picking up from your home those items you cannot bring back to the store because of a problem such as size or weight of the items, your illness, or lack of transportation. Sears will replace the item either on the spot or, in the case of heavy or out-of-stock merchandise, a short time thereafter. If you want a refund rather than a replacement, the credit section or customer service office may be of help in crediting your account or mailing you a refund.

Mail Ordering

Ordering products by mail from companies within your state is also an easy way to make purchases. It is best to deal with firms within a 40- or 50-mile radius of your residence, so that if there is a problem with your purchase, communication with the sender will not be difficult, and you can, if necessary, take the item back to the seller yourself.

Most of the suggestions for phone ordering also apply to mail ordering. Knowing whom you are dealing with and exactly what you are ordering is essential in protecting yourself against disappointment over a nonreturnable or defective item or fraud. There is, however, a protective measure you can take—make a copy of the ad or mail order form and file it for future reference.

Millions of dollars are lost annually by consumers who respond to bargain ads and "once-in-a-lifetime" offers, especially from out-of-state companies. Not only will you lose your money if the recipient is a crook or in the midst of bankruptcy, but you may have a difficult time getting any governmental agency to assist you, because of jurisdictional conflicts.

If you do not get satisfaction from the dealer or store manager, the investigator at a local or state consumer bureau (see Chapters 12 and 13) may be familiar with the operation of the nearby seller from which you made the purchase, especially if the agency has received similar complaints from other consumers. Such a local source usually will be the best means for prompt, effective action.

The federal Office of Consumer Affairs, Washington, D.C., has encouraged various industries to set up consumer protection panels to help handle complaints relating to types of products. Such organizations include the Major Appliance Consumer Action Panel (MACAP), Furniture Industry Consumer Advisory Panel (FICAP), and the Automobile Consumer Action Program (AUTOCAP). Each of these organizations is described in detail along with the other industry sponsored groups in Chapter 14.

If you make a purchase in response to a mail solicitation or product or service advertisement and do not get what you pay for, send a copy of the mail order form along with your letter of complaint to the U.S. Postal Service (see Chapter 9).

TURNING ON—KILOWATTS, BTUs, MESSAGE UNITS, AND H₂O

Unless you are a hermit living 13,000 feet above sea level on a secluded peak in the Rocky Mountains, you probably have to pay for basic utilities—water, gas, electricity, and telephone. And are you paying!

Saving Money

There are some steps you can take in trying to cut down the size of those utility bills. For instance, many utilities offer a special reduced rate for low usage, but they do not particularly publicize this type of service, which could save you money, especially if you live alone. If you are a lower-than-average user of any utility, call the company's business office and ask if it has such a rate from which you could benefit. The San Francisco-based Pacific Telephone and Telegraph Company, for example, offers to many California and Nevada residents "lifeline" service, which in 1976 included 30 local calls a month for $2.50 and a charge of five cents for each additional local call.

Checking this possibility is especially important when you have new service installed, because the company may have a rule that you may not make a change in type of rate once you are billed under one particular rate.

Keeping an eye on the day and exact time that you place toll and long-distance calls will definitely trim your phone bill. A coast-to-coast call you make any day between 11:00 p.m. and 8:00 a.m. or on a Saturday or Sunday morning will cost you less than half what it would during most other times. Because of time differences, then, if you live on the East Coast, you should make most of your cross-country calls just after 11:00 p.m. or on weekends. If you are a West Coast caller, hopefully you are also an early riser so that you can punch out your number before the strike of eight—of course, you can wait until the weekend too.

Whether you want to call a federal agency, appliance company, hotel chain, or magazine publisher, there is no sense in making a long-distance call at all when there is a toll-free 800 number you can use. Appendix 3 is a small directory of these and other types of numbers you may find useful in your consumer calls. The 800 numbers for many state consumer offices are included in Appendix 12.

Telephone companies have consistently refused the author access to lists of 800 numbers that are in the exclusive possession of "WATS" information operators. Ma Bell claims that the publication and distribution to consumers of those numbers is both impractical and not in the interest of those customers purchasing the 800 phone service. The author contends that these numbers, like all other listed numbers, should be available in directory form to consumers.

Since electricity is more expensive than gas, you should think twice about buying an all-electric home or only electric appliances. Also, be open to the possible benefits in a home that incorporates wind or solar energy. In an age when higher costs, blackouts, energy shortages, and rationing never seem too far behind, a sound strategy would be to provide energy for your home from more than one source.

When you conserve energy, you are helping both the environment and your pocketbook. Air-conditioners are notorious for eating up watts. When purchasing this appliance, ask which models will give you the most capability from the least amount of electricity. You can compare energy efficiency among a group of air-conditioners by looking at a unit of measure called the Energy Efficiency Ratio (EER). The higher this number, the more product performance you will get for your energy dollar.

Unfortunately, the inclusion of the EER number has been voluntary; therefore, many manufacturers have not placed it in their marketing materials. Sears is one company that has been listing the EER, at least for its air-conditioners. The more interest that consumers and consumer groups show to manufacturers and regulatory agencies in having such information available at the purchase time, the sooner it will happen. In 1975 the Federal Trade Commission proposed a regulation requiring room air-conditioners to carry a tag disclosing the EER.

If possible, obtain a unit with an EER of 7.0 or above for more efficiency. If the manufacturer does not list the rating, you can figure it out yourself by dividing the number of BTUs the unit can handle per hour (that is, the cooling capacity) by the number of watts (the energy input). A 1,380-watt unit that handles 12,000 BTUs per hour has an EER of 8.7.

Ask your local services for any free pamphlets they have on conserving energy. Many utility companies and municipal operations offer helpful publications giving hints on insulating your home, maintaining a comfortable temperature, using automatic timers, cleaning and replacing equipment, and other ways of cutting down waste.

For example, turning off every light when you leave a room can help to save energy, but the amount of electricity needed to light a room is insignificant when compared with the real culprits that cost you—the refrigerator, stove, color TV. A room air-conditioner can raise the cost of your electric bill $10 to $20 a month or more during the summer, so use it wisely.

Southern California Edison Company will send you a free copy of their booklet, "Conservation of Energy is Everybody's Business," if you write to its Consumer Information Department, 1810 South Flower Street, Los Angeles, 90017. The publication covers equipment and gives examples of the amount of energy used by a variety of household appliances. You can also receive a free booklet dealing with gas use and conservation by writing to the American Gas Association, 1515 Wilson Boulevard, Arlington, Virginia 22209.

Keeping Electricity Safe

You have no doubt seen that bold "UL" symbol a thousand times, but you may still not know why it is stuck on appliances on their packaging. This is the symbol for Underwriters' Laboratories, Inc., a not-for-profit corporation that has evaluated electrical safety and set electrical standards for countless products over the years. Figure 2–1 shows some of the emblems to look for.

A manufacturer is granted permission to affix one of these official labels when it receives notification from the testing lab that its product has met all minimum standards for safety. The procedure involves the manufacturer's providing the lab with samples of the product. The laboratory tests the item to see if the user could be exposed to shock or fire hazard. If the sample appliances meet all the required standards, the manufacturer may display the UL label on all

Figure 2–1

manufactured products of the same model or type that continue to meet requirements.

Although UL approval is a good indication that a particular product *tends* to be safe, it is by no means a guarantee that you will never find an electrical defect. Newly marketed items that are modifications of older models may be more or less safer than those tested. Furthermore, all UL-listed products may not be of the same quality, and so, if possible, judge individual model characteristics among a group of UL-listed items.

When you do not see a UL label attached to an electrical appliance, it does not necessarily mean that the product is unsafe. Submission of products to the laboratory for testing is voluntary and not required by government regulation.

Minor Complaints

If you have a complaint about an electrical problem you have found with a product carrying the UL label, write to the Underwriters' Laboratories, Inc., 207 East Ohio Street, Chicago, Illinois 60611. Any product with inherent electrical problems—whether or not it carries the UL label—should be reported to the Consumer Product Safety Commission or the Food and Drug Administration. (See section on Reporting Dangerous Products, pp. 13–14.)

Staff persons at your local utilities can help you with problems such as billing errors, poor service, a mistake in your telephone listing, or making extended payments for a bill much higher than usual. Most utilities maintain a 24-hour phone number for emergency service problems.

Bills are based on metered usage, often assisted by computers, but errors are sometimes made, and usually no one but you will initiate an inquiry to make sure you have not been overcharged. Go over each bill and review your reported usage and corresponding charges. If you think there may be a problem with the meter measuring how much water or power you use, request that a field investigator do a precision test on the instrument. Any malfunctioning unit will be promptly replaced or repaired, and proven overcharges will be credited to your account.

Any complaint you may have about a utility's rates, policies, or handling of a problem that you have brought to the company's attention without satisfaction should be made to the appropriate regulatory agency. In the case of a municipally owned operation, your local government has probably established a regulatory division as part of a governing board or utilities department to act on such matters. On the other hand, any privately owned utility company with which you do business is regulated by your state government. (See Appendix 4 for the name and address of the regulator.)

Major Informal Complaints

All of the bodies that regulate utilities set up procedures for handling both informal and formal complaints from consumers. Informal complaints usually involve any service or billing problem that is not promptly or properly solved by the local utility.

Some regulatory agencies will accept a phone complaint; others demand a letter. In either case, the person handling your problem will contact the appropriate utility office, discuss the problem, and get you at least some type of compromise.

Major Formal Complaints

Utility regulatory agents on both the local and state level will also accept formal complaints for rising rates, and for serious service problems affecting a small group or an entire city. Another function of these agencies is to accept complaints over any other problems that are not satisfactorily handled on the informal basis of the utility staff.

Filing a formal complaint often can be as complicated as filing a court brief, however. The appropriate authority may be very picky

about who files such a complaint and whether or not an established set of procedures has been conscientiously followed.

If you want to file a formal complaint, first ask the utility's regulatory body for any necessary guidelines for preparation of the document. This is important, because an investigation into your charges may be impossible without your taking the prescribed preliminary steps.

The California Public Utilities Commission, for example, makes available a pamphlet entitled "Procedure for Filing Formal Complaints in California," which states:

> No complaint shall be entered by the Commission except upon its own motion, as to the reasonableness of any rates or charges of any gas, electric, water, or telephone corporation, unless it be signed by the mayor or president or chairman of the board of trustees or a majority of the council, commission, or other legislative body of the city or city and county within which the alleged violation occurred, or by not less than twenty-five actual or prospective consumers or purchasers of such gas, electric, water, or telephone service.

Getting the names, addresses, and signatures of fellow consumers is only part of the battle. The guidelines in California also prescribe that a complaint must be printed or typed on an 8½″ × 11″ paper, include a particular title, the names and addresses of the parties involved, signatures of the complainants, facts upon which the complaint is based, type of injury, and desired relief; and it must be filed with an original and a number of copies equal to 12 plus twice the number of named defendants (utility companies). Many other states have similar provisions. Any complaint not conforming to a required form may be returned for revision.

According to a report supplied by the National Association of Regulatory Utility Commissioners, virtually every state commission will accept formal complaints directly from consumers; some will act on a formal complaint from any one consumer or interested party; others require that the issue be submitted as a formal petition by a group of consumers numbering anywhere from 10 in Kentucky and Maine to 100 in Maryland. If you live in North Dakota, you have to get 10 percent of all rate-payers together to join you in the complaint.

Writing an effective and actionable complaint is usually no easy matter, because it can take a certain amount of research and some knowledge of state and local laws and regulations affecting utility services. Finding an attorney to draw up all the facts may be the best action. Many consumer groups on national, state, and local levels retain lawyers to handle such matters.

If you do not want to go through the time and expense of drawing up a formal complaint (or hiring an attorney to do it) and acquiring all the necessary signatures, a good alternative is to try to convince an elected local government representative that it would be in the public interest to pursue such a complaint. Nearly all state utility commissions will consider formal protests directly from mayors, city councils, county boards of supervisors, and other local government administrative or legislative agencies. These public representatives have a staff with the expertise to assemble the necessary research and formulate the complaint in what may turn out to be a complex legal matter.

Once the utility regulator receives a formal complaint, it will generally ask the utility company to answer the charges within a short period of time.

In the case of rate increases or other matters of sufficient public interest, hearings may be held in which you can testify upon request before the board of directors or commissioners to present your personal views or the views of a group you represent.

All interested parties can enter evidence, and the Commission then renders its decision. If you are unhappy with this decision, you may sometimes file a petition for a rehearing. Commission decisions often can be appealed to the state's supreme court.

The U.S. Supreme Court has ruled that a public utility has a constitutional right to try to earn a reasonable profit from investment funds allocated for public use. The utility commissions investigating rate complaints make a determination of what are "reasonable" profits, and are supposed to hold rates at the lowest possible levels that will allow such returns. Where earnings of utilities are found to be substantially in excess of the level considered just, these regulatory agencies can order reductions in rates. Although these policies should be implemented in both theory and practice, many consumer groups charge that utility boards and commissions approve rate increases without adequate concern for the burden of added expenses to customers.

The formal complaint is the only means by which consumers can file a grievance in this type of situation. It can effect significant changes in decisions of the regulatory agency.

An *unsuccessful* formal complaint was made to the Pennsylvania Public Utility Commission by Sarah T. Shore of Philadelphia. She requested that her name be listed in the telephone directory as Mrs. Zephaniahaza Sebastian Klinghoffermandellfieldson III! The commission ruled that Bell Telephone did not have to list any name that is not the one used by the subscriber for general identification.

If you decide that withholding payment of your utility bill is a good way to initiate or speed action on a complaint, you may find yourself lighting candles or picking up a dead telephone. However, many states do allow you to withhold money from a utility, at least temporarily. If you want to complain about incorrect or unfair billing or poor service, look at the back of your utility bill for instructions about depositing the money with the local or state agency that regulates the utility; or call the regulatory body directly and ask if such a system has been set up and how it works.

Chapter 3

UNCONDITIONALLY GUARANTEED! (OR IS IT?)

Let's face it—there are enough lemons for you to buy at the supermarket. You don't need to find any more hidden away in the vast selection of new products, just waiting for you to make the wrong choice.

Have you ever bought a car that turned out to be a lemon? The power steering lost its power, the left-turn signal blinked when you wanted to turn right, the brake lights went on only when you pressed so hard on the pedal that the sole of your shoe cracked, and the windshield wipers stopped in the middle of the heaviest rain of the year. And what about the typewriter roller that wouldn't roll, the blender that went beserk and plastered the pink brocade wallpaper with chocolate malt, and the alarm clock that *you* had to wake up each morning?

No matter how good the refrigerator, toaster, hair dryer, watch, or automobile looks, you cannot be positive that the item will perform for even a short period of time without problems.

This is why the guarantee or warranty (consider the two synonymous) is important. It gives you the assurance that for the specified days or years during which the item is covered, you have the opportunity to throw the product right back in the lap of the company that made it.

The guarantee *ideally* has the function of pledging to you, the buyer, that the manufacturer will stand behind the product by offering to repair or replace it or its parts, or to refund the purchase price under specified conditions. Your guarantee is a binding contract that can force the manufacturer, through court action if necessary, to make good the promises. *Realistically*, the warranty is too often a set of statements written mainly for the protection of the manufacturer, who would just as soon sell you the product and never see you again—never again, that is, until you are ready to discard the old model and purchase a new one (see Figure 3–1).

Many companies do stand behind their products, however, and prove it to you with their written guarantee. Once you can tell the difference between the worthless warranty and the one that affords you adequate—sometimes excellent—protection, you will be able to spend your dollars more wisely and more confidently.

SHOPPING HINTS

Deciding where to shop for guaranteed products is the first step. If you are one of the many consumers who base decisions generally on the price, begin considering other factors such as return privileges and servicing. All the money you think you are saving may be taken away when you return a defective item to a customer service representative who smugly points to the counter's tiniest sign: "All Sales Final—No Refunds Or Exchanges" or "Minimum $30 Service Charge." In the long run you usually will find more security and peace of mind in doing business with a store that does not establish all regular sales as final, and does not refuse to make exchanges and refunds. Discount stores that allow you to bring back merchandise, and even cooperate in making refunds, are ideal places to shop.

Even though you may pay a little more, you may consider buying some items from large department stores, especially where you have a charge account. These sellers are often more agreeable to making exchanges and refunds than a small shop that cannot afford to take a loss or does not want to spend the extra time necessary to satisfy its customers. Also, charge account customers often are given more consideration than cash patrons when it comes to returning merchandise.

Preguarantee Analysis

When you go out to buy a product, how do you decide on a particular brand? Obviously, the appearance, ease of use, versatility, effectiveness, overall quality, and durability are factors to consider. Before analyzing each warranty, examine all brands on their physical

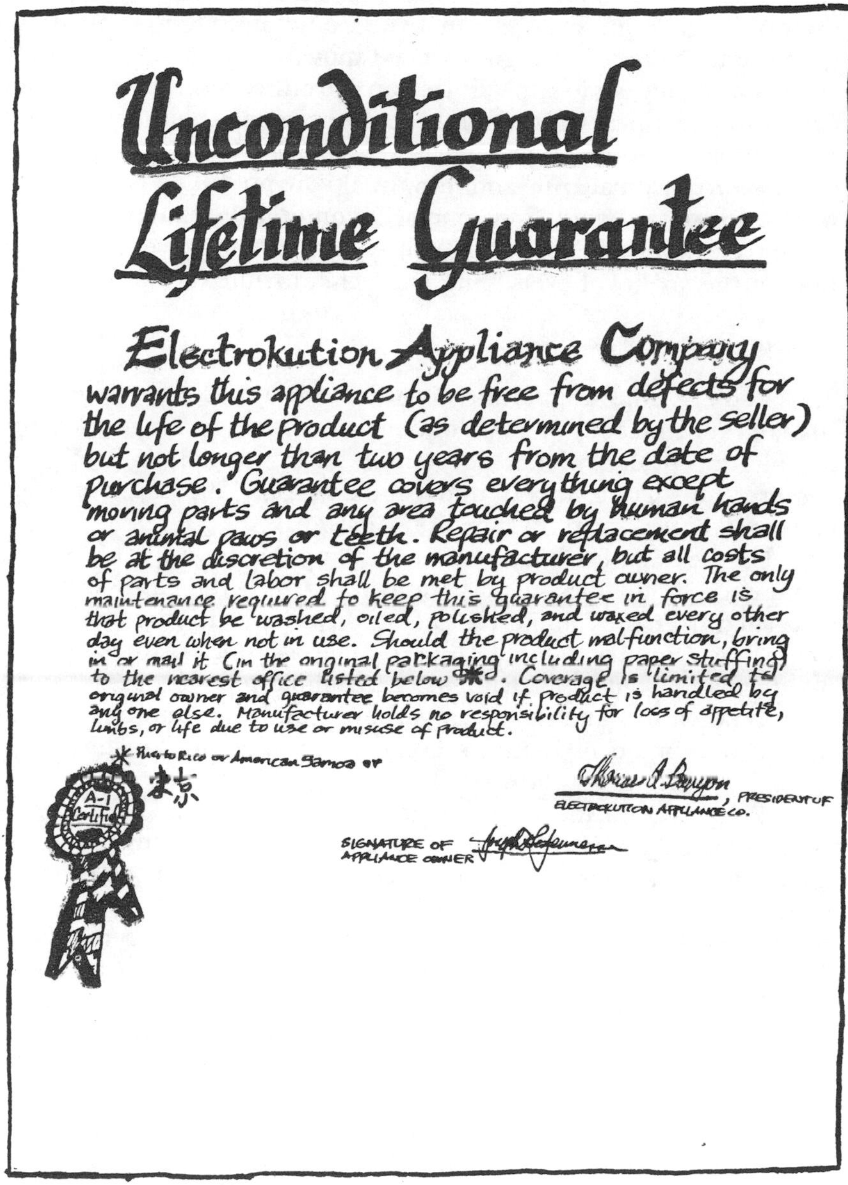

Unconditional Lifetime Guarantee

Electrokution Appliance Company warrants this appliance to be free from defects for the life of the product (as determined by the seller) but not longer than two years from the date of purchase. Guarantee covers everything except moving parts and any area touched by human hands or animal paws or teeth. Repair or replacement shall be at the discretion of the manufacturer, but all costs of parts and labor shall be met by product owner. The only maintenance required to keep this guarantee in force is that product be washed, oiled, polished, and waxed every other day even when not in use. Should the product malfunction, bring in or mail it (in the original packaging including paper stuffing) to the nearest office listed below ✱. Coverage is limited to original owner and guarantee becomes void if product is handled by any one else. Manufacturer holds no responsibility for loss of appetite, limbs, or life due to use or misuse of product.

✱ Puerto Rico or American Samoa or

_____, PRESIDENT OF
ELECTROKUTION APPLIANCE CO.

SIGNATURE OF _____
APPLIANCE OWNER

Figure 3–1

properties alone. Maybe you want a versatile blender that has many speeds and can crush ice. After ruling out the unsuitable ones, consider pricing. Perhaps you feel that you do not need the 14 speeds or juicer attachment of the higher priced model.

Comparing various products can be difficult since you cannot fully and scientifically test them before purchase. There are reliable publications, however, that report on useful and objective research. *Consumer Reports* magazine and its annual "Buying Guide Issue," both published by nonprofit Consumers Union, 256 Washington Street, Mount Vernon, New York 10550, provide excellent current information on the quality of everything from chili to automobiles.

Who Makes the Guarantee?

Look at who is guaranteeing the product. In the case of a phonograph, is it Sony or is it Wonderplay, a brand apparently known to only one dealer, who is desperately trying to unload it on you because the small company that produced only 200 of them went bankrupt 12 years ago for lack of business.

On the other hand, be aware that you might have an unfounded preference for that best-selling brand with which you have positively associated from the commercials being thrust at you 100 times in one week. If you think of TV and radio commercials not strictly as sources of information, but as persuaders, it might help you to judge products more on their own merits; and it will stop you from running out and buying one brand of mattress because you saw an attractive Hollywood star telling you how good it was.

Your faith in the name behind the guarantee is not always a reliable factor; products from even a well-known company may produce more problems than better-made items from a more obscure firm. Furthermore, just because you know that one product of a company is excellent does not mean that another model or different item from the same firm will be as good.

Narrowing down the huge number of brands to the specific name you will buy is not an easy procedure. If you are fussy when it comes to good coffee, you will want to look at more than one or two brands of electric percolators and drip makers—Sunbeam, Wards, Sears, Toastmaster, Cory, Dominion, Mary Proctor, West Bend, Penneys, General Electric, Presto, Mr. Coffee, and so on.

Forget about a snap judgment and take a little extra time in selecting an important appliance. Use as many available resources as possible: published product research, answers to questions you pose to dealers (Which do you consider the best? Is there any trouble with this brand? About which brand do you get the smallest number of consumer complaints?), and comments from friends. If you have had experience with products of a company, try to recall the quality of service you received and the attitude of the service personnel.

The Clincher

Once you have narrowed the choice down to those brands that best meet your needs, it is time to evaluate "the clincher." Any warranty that gives you better, longer, or more complete protection than those of other models and companies deserves your special notice, and it might tip the scales in favor of buying that item. Sometimes it even pays to spend a few more dollars on a model with a strong guarantee than on a cheaper item with a weak commitment from the manufacturer.

If the Federal Trade Commission has its way, consumers will be finding it easier to compare the warranties of various brands. In 1975 the FTC proposed a rule that would force stores to keep copies of all warranties on hand for your inspection. A firm would also have to give you a copy of a warranty if you request it by mail or phone.

ANALYZING THE WARRANTY

Every warranty contains a statement about the amount of time for which the product will be covered. Even the best guarantee does not have much meaning if it does not extend over a period of time that will allow you to make full and regular use of the product.

Beware of ambiguous words such as "lifetime," which should be spelled out to mean either that the guarantee remains in force until the product can no longer stand up to use (it falls apart) or that you are no longer alive to use it. The word "unconditional" when used to describe a guarantee is often a misnomer, with at least one or two conditions set forth.

A clear understanding of your guarantee and the laws affecting it will assure you of everything to which you are entitled. Seeing your calculator go haywire right in the middle of doing your taxes is bad enough. Waiting for the store to have it fixed is even worse. By the time you get the machine back, two months have passed, it is April 16, and the 90-day warranty has expired. To prevent this, California is one state that has passed a law, effective July 1, 1975, stating for any product over $50 the warranty is extended by whatever amount of time elapses from the date the purchaser brings or sends in his or her product for repairs to the day he or she receives it back.

If you think you may want to sell the product or give it away before the warranty period expires, try to select from those products that provide for coverage for the second owner. Many warranties are not transferable.

Always see what the warranty says about special maintenance that the manufacturer requires you to perform so that the agreement will remain in effect. For example, a manufacturer of an automobile may require that you have the oil changed periodically. If you fail to do so, the warranty can become void.

Replacement and Repairs

What do the guarantees you are examining state about how or where to return the product for replacement or repairs? Some manufacturers require you to bring or send the item at your expense to the factory or the closest authorized dealer or service center. (See the Yellow Pages of your telephone directory.) Many companies will have at least one such place near your home. Others may not have a repair station within hundreds of miles. You do not want to have to drive an hour or two to get to the center.

It can be rather risky relying on guarantees for lesser-known brands of merchandise you buy through the mail. After all, you cannot really expect to find a nearby authorized dealer or service shop to do warranty work on your mail-order Butterthumb toaster. A watch or pocket calculator may be easy to wrap up and mail, but having to ship a stove or console TV out of town is impractical and costly. That is one good reason why you should not buy any large or heavy item through mail order unless the company has a firmly established service facility near your home.

Provisions for Wear

A number of warranties providing for replacement because of wear for such items as automobile tires, brake linings, and batteries offer you a prorated refund or a "specially priced" replacement if the product does not give satisfactory performance to the end of the warranty period. Any money you get back will depend on a schedule based on when you bought the item and the amount of use or wear.

Some dealers set the price of the worn item's replacement at a level comparable to the amount charged in the original purchase, thus rendering that section of the guarantee virtually useless. Therefore, ask questions about what you will get should you need a replacement through the warranty, and how much, if anything, you will be charged. Don't be misled by a stipulation that the manufacturer holds no responsibility for any accidents or ill effects you may encounter in the use of its product. Courts often do not consider such a clause to be valid, especially when the injury occurred with proper use. Unfortunately, some companies do get away with taking responsibility for replacing only a defective part, even if that part has destroyed the whole product.

Save any printed advertisement that induces you to buy a product, and staple it to the printed warranty. If assurances made in the ad go beyond what is stated in the certificate accompanying the item, you may be able to use the ad to force the manufacturer to make good on its promises as if they were actually part of the original warranty. Present appropriate advertising showing such additional promises when submitting a complaint to a government agency or evidence to a court in a case where a manufacturer will not live up to guarantees implied in advertising, but not expressed in the printed warranty (see also Chapter 11).

Added Coverage

To induce you to buy a particular product (usually in higher price categories), some dealers may offer you their own guarantees, extending that given by the manufacturer, for any specified period under the same or other stipulated conditions. This arrangement, especially if it includes service, could save you some money after the manufacturer's warranty expires and the dealer's begins. Some sellers may charge an annual or semiannual fee for this extra protection, but depending on the type of product and your projected frequency of use, it could be advantageous.

As soon as you pay for the product, be sure to get a receipt showing the place of purchase, date, and amount you have spent. You may need to present this proof to show that the guarantee is in effect.

PUTTING WARRANTIES TO WORK

Before you use any new appliance, read the instructions carefully. Most guarantees become void if you abuse a product by misuse, whether intentionally or not. It is always safer to question the dealer or manufacturer before you apply complicated or unclear directions, in order not to give the seller a reason to claim customer negligence and thus refuse to honor the warranty.

Understanding how to run a particular home appliance not only will assure your protection under the warranty, but also will assure bodily protection. Many types of kitchen equipment have proved hostile to humans, and never put it past a taffymaker to try to engulf you in goo.

Validating the Warranty

Many companies require you to mail them the warranty registration card that accompanies the product. If you do not find this card and the instructions, say so, get a duplicate from the dealer or send a letter to the manufacturer. This card generally asks you to state your name and address, the brand and type of product, the item's model and serial numbers (printed or engraved on the equipment itself), and the place and date of purchase.

This procedure is often essential to validate the warranty, and many companies require your sending them notification of your purchase within 10 days or two weeks of purchase. It is important to realize this, especially when buying somebody a gift. If you purchase it too far in advance of the date you plan to give it, the warranty could be in jeopardy. In that case you should fill in the registration card with the receiver's name and address and all other pertinent information and mail the card yourself.

Your fulfilling of the specific conditions of any guarantee is essential in preparing for possible future service you may request within the warranty period. For certain products, especially new automobiles, you must assume responsibility for various types of regular maintenance, which may require the work to be done by an authorized service representative. Find this out before you have the item fixed. If the company specifies exclusive handling of service, any work that has come from another source can invalidate the guarantee.

Returning Your Purchase

Some warranties tell you to mail a small product back to the manufacturer, which may be in another state. You will be expected to pack the item well to avoid damage while the parcel is en route. Save for a month any carton, filling, and packing materials from the new

product to make the task easier should a problem appear. Be sure to insure the item at the post office or delivery service.

Although some guarantees do state a specific place for you to return the product for service, many stores will accept for repair the products they sell. Contact the place of purchase and find out their policy. If the store will fix the item or send it out to be done, you will often save time and money by letting the dealer handle it. Once you leave a product with a salesperson, the store must accept full responsibility for the care of it until it is returned to you.

Sometimes you have the opportunity to decide on either repair or a replacement. The latter alternative is recommended for any new product you buy that does not perform adequately from the outset. A new product with inherent defects often cannot perform at par with other items more perfectly made, and you run the risk that you have picked one of those lemons.

Explain to the person handling your returned merchandise that you expect a new product to work well from the very beginning and do not want to wait while it is being repaired. A dealer is not required to give you a replacement under a warranty that states the dealer or the manufacturer has the option of replacing or repairing the defective item, but if you request it, larger stores particularly will often give you a replacement.

If you leave the malfunctioning product for service, whether covered under a warranty or not, request three things from the sales-person or service representative who accepts the item:

1. An estimate of charges, if any, including both parts and labor.
2. The return to you of any bad part for which you have been charged.
3. A statement that itemizes parts installed, service completed, and the charge for each. This (and #2) will help to discourage a repair shop or department from overcharging or selling you unneeded parts or service.

If the person says that he or she cannot give you an estimate without knowing the cause of the problem, ask if the cause can be determined by a service technician while you wait. If the fix-it person is out on the usual half-hour coffee break or you do not have time to spare, ask that you be telephoned with the estimate—either regardless of what the amount may be, or only if it goes over a total dollar amount you specify—before any work is undertaken.

For service to be done, many shops require you to sign a service authorization form. Do not sign the form until the amount of the estimate has been filled in. If the estimate cannot be determined immediately and the person serving you either refuses to take your merchandise without your signature or makes it clear that no service of any kind will be performed without your signature, go ahead and sign, but write in above or below your signature a statement that this authorization is "subject to oral confirmation when an estimate or charge is determined," and list a phone number where you can be reached. Before you leave the service area, be sure to write down the name of the person taking your merchandise.

Repair Problems

When you pick up the repaired item, check it out, if possible, while still in the shop. Sometimes you may find that the defect has not been adequately fixed or something else has gone wrong with the product. This will save you another trip back to the service area, and it will give you the opportunity to assign responsibility for carelessness. Politely demand that the item be returned for further repair or that it be replaced. Accept and pay for the servicing only when you are fully satisfied.

If a dealer or service center does costly work or extra service without your authorization, hold them completely responsible and refuse to pay the full amount. Offer to pay the amount you would have been charged had the unauthorized service not been completed or a cheaper reconditioned part been installed in place of the unwanted expensive new part.

If the repairer refuses to lower the tab or give you your property back without full payment, you have two choices. You can leave the item there and try to get it back by contacting local consumer protection agencies (see Chapter 12). This might be a good way to go, but consider the added problems if you are without the use of the product for weeks or months. The alternative is to pay the full amount asked, take the item home with you, and then contact local agencies or file a small claims suit to collect the amount you were wrongfully charged. If you decide to make full payment, write the following on the back of your check or charge slip: "For Deposit Only, Pay to the order of ____(name of company)____ under protest." This will reserve your right to litigate the matter in court and will show that you disputed the bill at the time of payment.

Guarantee Complaints

Every company is legally bound by the terms of its guarantee and must provide any necessary parts or labor to which it has agreed. If a company refuses to fulfill these obligations, you can call upon local resources such as a consumer bureau (see Chapter 12) or an industry-established organization (see Chapter 14) for help. If the problem is statewide, your state attorney general's office will be of assistance (see Chapter 13). Any complaint regarding misleading advertising that contains promises the manufacturer refuses to keep should be directed to the Federal Trade Commission (see Chapter 11).

One often-untapped resource for warranty complaints relating especially to products distributed nationally is on the federal level. If you have a valid complaint about a company not living up to its guarantee, you can write or call the Office of Consumer Affairs, U.S. Department of Health, Education, and Welfare, Washington, D.C 20201. The staff either will refer your complaint to an appropriate governmental agency that has primary jursidiction on the federal level or within your state, or will write directly on your behalf to the manufacturer, requesting (or pressuring) it to resolve the problem promptly.

The FTC Role

The warranty practices of an entire industry sometimes come under examination by the Federal Trade Commission when many manufacturers or dealers are not living up to promises about quality and durability or the general service that customers will receive after purchase. An investigation of this type began at the end of 1974 after four of the largest companies in the mobile home industry were named in complaints alleging that their warranties did not fully spell out to purchasers the protection offered by the manufacturers. These companies allegedly failed to maintain an adequate system to repair, in a reasonable amount of time, the defects brought to their attention by owners.

To assure sound future practices, the FTC proposed a trade regulation rule in 1975, requiring mobile home manufacturers:

1. To make warranty-covered repairs within 30 days after being notified by an owner that there is a defect.

2. To start repairs within three business days and complete them quickly when a defect threatens safety of a mobile home.

3. To enter into a contract with any dealer handling warranty responsibilities and include a clear delineation of who—dealer or manufacturer—is to complete each type of warranty service.

4. To monitor dealers to make sure that they are fulfilling their service contracts, and terminate those who do not live up to those contracts.

5. To represent fairly the mobile home dimensions and the certification regarding construction code standards.

Another trade regulation rule proposed by the FTC in 1975 concerned unfair credit practices (see Chapter 8). The Commission also announced its investigation into deceptive practices relating to the advertising and performance of warranty services for used cars.

The issue of improved protection against all ambiguous and unfulfilled warranties is a problem that consumer groups and agencies have been tackling for decades. A 1975 federal law known as the Magnuson-Moss Warranty-Federal Trade Commission Improvement Act takes a giant step in attempting to control the use of warranties and punish companies that take advantage of consumers by not living up to promises. The new law does not require manufacturers to provide warranties for their products, but it does set mandatory standards for any warranty that a company includes with an item.

All warranties for products manufactured after July 4, 1975 must comply with FTC rules relating to clarity and content. Every warranty must be clearly labeled "limited warranty" or "full warranty," with the latter meeting federal standards providing for a refund, replacement, or repair for a defective product within a reasonable period and without charge to the consumer. Defective products or parts that are covered by a full warranty and that cannot be repaired within a reasonable length of time must be exchanged for new ones, or the purchaser must receive a full refund.

A company can no longer make exclusions or limit damages arising out of its breach of the warranty, unless those exclusions or limitations are plainly printed on the face of the warranty. Thus if your freezer goes haywire and all the food spoils, you can hold the company responsible unless it told you in the warranty that kind of problem would be totally yours.

The FTC has been given more power to deal with companies that ignore consumer interests. The Commission was once empowered only to issue cease-and-desist orders against manufacturers engaging in false and deceptive practices, but the 1975 law gives the agency the authority to represent consumers seeking redress in federal courts for injuries relating to unlawful warranty practices.

You yourself can now take the matter to either state or federal court and, if you should win, collect attorney's fees in addition to damages. In civil cases, the FTC can set penalties up to $10,000 per violation without the approval (once mandatory) from the Justice Department. With the added authority, the nearest office of the FTC will prove a good source for action on warranty violations.

MAGAZINE WARRANTIES

Many advertisers over the years have boasted about magazine recognition of their products. From infant wear and kitchen knives to laxatives and photocopy machine toner, many products and services have been "awarded" consumer guarantee seals from either of two periodicals, *Good Housekeeping* and *Parents' Magazine*. Beginning with their July 1975 issues, each magazine began labeling its seal as a "limited warranty" in an attempt to comply with new federal guidelines in the Magnuson-Moss Warranty-FTC Improvement Act.

Both publishing companies deny that their insignias are seals of approval, even though one shows on its face a star and the other

Figure 3-3

appears to be a ribbon such as those you might see displayed on prize-winning cows at the county fair (see Figure 3–3). In any case, if you read what is printed on each seal, you will see precisely what its value is to you.

Behind the Seals

Any product carrying such a seal is guaranteed by the magazine to be free from defects. If you buy a product that displays the seal, and that product is defective or its performance is poor, you can receive either a replacement or a refund. This is *your* choice, not the manufacturer's, according to both magazines.

The publishers offer these seals for use by manufacturers and providers of services for several reasons. First, consider how these seals help you, the consumer. They help you when comparing products before purchase. Remember, however, that the seals are not meant as an endorsement and do not infer that the product is of any higher quality than another model sitting next to it. The seal simply tells you that if you buy the item you will find reasonably good quality in the product: it will do what it is advertised to do, or else the magazine will make good on its promise.

Many advertised products carry no other guarantee. Both *Good Housekeeping* and *Parents' Magazine* feel confident in guaranteeing the products because of the testing that the item must undergo before earning the seal. *Parents' Magazine* hires the services of an independent laboratory named Nationwide Consumer Testing Institute, Inc., of Hoboken, New Jersey, to do most of its product testing. *Good Housekeeping* owns and operates its Good Housekeeping Institute for the same purpose.

Comparisons

Table 3-1 compares the warranty seal programs at both magazines and indicates some notable differences. *Parents' Magazine* guarantees products displaying its seal for a period of 30 days after purchase. *Good Housekeeping* does not maintain such a short time limit, and will accept a product complaint up to four years after purchase.

Another important distinction is that *Parents' Magazine* can act as

TABLE 3-1

Magazine Warranty Programs

	Good Housekeeping	*Parents' Magazine*
Paid circulation (6-month average for period ending June 1976 as filed with the Audit Bureau of Circulations)	5,312,449	1,506,103
Screens all advertising for honesty, accuracy, etc.	Yes	Yes
Requires minimum purchase of advertising before company may apply for seal	Yes	Yes
Tests all products for which manufacturer requests seal	Yes	Yes
Tests products beyond those for which seals requested	No	No
Performs most product testing with its own facilities	Yes	No
Period of seal licensing agreement	1 year	1 year
Offers "limited warranty" on *all* advertised items— with or without seal— excluding listed exceptions	Yes	No
Number of consumer complaints about advertised products (calendar year 1975)	2,300	638

Magazine Warranty Programs *(cont.)*

	Good Housekeeping	Parents' Magazine
Time limit for discovering valid product defect and reporting it to magazine	4 years	30 days
Usually sees that consumer is reimbursed for shipping of defective product	Yes	Yes
Asks manufacturer to handle complaint before magazine provides remedy	No	Yes
Types of products and services for which seals are not issued (examples)	Insurance, automobiles, realty, liquor, tobacco, depilatories, prescription drugs, high-potency vitamins, institutional advertisers, etc.	Insurance, automobiles, banks, liquor, tobacco, depilatories, prescription drugs, toy guns, projectile-type games, institutional advertisers, etc.

a middleman between you and the manufacturer. In trying to settle your valid complaint, it will ask the manufacturer to make the adjustment of your choice within 30 days of notification. If the advertiser fails to take action within 90 days, the magazine will then refund to you the price of the product or service; and the product stands a good chance of losing the magazine's seal. *Good Housekeeping*, on the other hand, makes all adjustments from the outset. It notifies the advertiser that it has received a complaint, but takes full responsibility for directly providing the remedy of your choice (replacement or refund). Apparently, *Good Housekeeping* is more likely to settle a product complaint more quickly.

Perhaps the most significant difference in the warranty policies of the two magazines concerns the scope of coverage. *Parents' Magazine*'s "limited warranty" applies only to those products and services that display the Parents' Magazine Seal; *Good Housekeeping*'s "limited warranty" applies not only for products and services displaying the Good Housekeeping Seal, but for *every* item advertised in that magazine.

Neither magazine will make an adjustment for a product with a defect or faulty performance caused by your negligence or abuse.

You may be asked to submit the product for testing so that the magazine or manufacturer can determine true liability.

Adjustments

If you have a valid gripe about a product or service that carries the Parents' Magazine Seal, send a letter of complaint within 30 days after your purchase to Consumer Service Bureau, Parents' Magazine Enterprises, Inc., 52 Vanderbilt Avenue, New York, New York 10017. Give your name, address, phone number, and place and date of purchase. State the product or service and the nature of the problem. Specify whether you want a replacement or refund. When you have a bona fide complaint against any product with the Good Housekeeping Seal or any item or service advertised in *Good Housekeeping*, address a letter with the same information to Director of the Consumer Complaint Department, Good Housekeeping, 959 Eighth Avenue, New York, New York 10019.

Do not mail your defective product unless instructed to do so. Your complaint should be handled expeditiously. In fact, *Good Housekeeping* has stated that it has the objective of satisfying your complaint within two or three weeks. If major problems develop in satisfaction from either company, file a complaint (yes, still another one) with the nearest office of the Federal Trade Commission.

HOME OWNERS' WARRANTIES

A new house is often the biggest investment that a consumer makes. It also may be quite a gamble. What can you do if you come out of the rain and into your new home to find the living room in an inch of water? How will you cope with discovering that your kitchen is slowly sliding into the driveway? If you are a smart consumer, you will have purchased a house with a guarantee.

The Home Owners Warranty (HOW) Program was initiated by the National Association of Home Builders in 1974. Modeled on a warranty program covering most homes in Great Britain, the HOW Program provides buyers with a 10-year written warranty, which is backed by insurance. In 1975, after the HOW Program had been in existence for only one year, more than 30,000 new homes were covered under the plan. Expansion of the program is continuing at a rapid rate

When you purchase a home with HOW coverage, you and the builder sign a standard Home Warranty Agreement. This document details your protection and the responsibilities of the builder during the first two years. Basically, the builder warrants the structure for the first year against defects due to faulty workmanship or materials. Also covered in the first year are appliances, equipment, and fixtures not protected by a manufacturer's written warranty. Second-year coverage continues the builder's warranty on the wiring, piping, and ductwork in the plumbing, electrical, heating, and cooling systems. It also includes protection against such problems as beam and wall failures, a weakening foundation, and structural defects in the roof.

In a case where a dispute arises in the first two years over the builder's responsibility to correct a defect, you request conciliation from your local or state HOW Council. If this procedure does not prove satisfactory, either party can request arbitration through the American Arbitration Association (or other organization following the same rules). Your request for conciliation or arbitration must be backed up by a fee, all or part of which is refundable if it is determined by the Council or arbitrator that your claim has merit. The purpose of the fee is to deter invalid complaints. If the builder refuses or is not able to fulfill warranty obligations or has gone out of business, the American Bankers Insurance Company of Florida must assume the responsibility.

In the third through tenth years after the purchase, the builder has no responsibility to handle your complaint. Major structural defects, however, remain covered under the HOW national insurance program. If a problem arises, contact your nearest HOW Council or, in some states, an insurance company representative specified in your written agreement. Arbitration remains a possible solution to disputes. The insurance company must fix the defective item, or pay you to have it fixed, if your claim is ruled valid.

One especially appealing feature of HOW coverage is that the protection plan is transferable to subsequent owners throughout the 10-year period. This is a good selling point if you decide to move.

The Home Owners Warranty Program can cover either a house or a condominium. Some builders advertise their participation in the plan. If you want further information or a list of participating housing developments, contact the nearest local or state HOW Council (see Appendix 5) or write to Home Owners Warranty Corporation, National Housing Center, 15th and M Streets N.W., Washington, D.C. 20005.

Chapter 4

IN, ON, AND AROUND YOUR BODY

This chapter will go over some fundamentals of food, drug, and cosmetic purchasing, including hints on saving money, reading labels, and complaining about mislabeled, contaminated products. Of particular interest is the section dealing with prescription drugs, and a discussion of the price and effectiveness of name-brand versus generic drugs.

EAT, DRINK, AND BE WARY

Think of all those fattening things you like to eat and drink: hotcakes with melted butter and maple syrup, orange juice, and creamy coffee for breakfast; onion soup covered with melted cheese and a huge caesar salad for lunch; duck à l'orange, baked potato with sour cream and chives, buttered baby peas, and wine for dinner. Most of us like to eat, whether it is a full-course feast at a posh French restaurant or a dime candy bar from the neighborhood newsstand.

You have the right to expect good quality food at reasonable prices. Although inflation in recent years has driven retail prices to incredibly high levels, there are ways to cut down on your food costs and still make sure that you are getting nutritious foods.

Saving Money

If you purchase food for a family—particularly a large family—you should look into the possibility of joining a food cooperative.

There are co-ops in both large and small communities, and it may be worth traveling the extra distance to save dollars instead of pennies.

Food co-ops operate on different bases. With some you buy shares or pay a small monthly or annual fee. This is in addition to, or in place of, a commitment by each member to participate in the actual buying, displaying, and distributing of the food.

If there is no co-op near where you live, you might start one of your own. You can obtain information and help by writing to the Cooperative League of the United States, 1828 L Street N.W., Washington, D.C. 20036.

Some consumer groups and at least one commercial newspaper and one cable television company have disseminated on a continuing basis the results of local food surveys, listing prices for commonly purchased meats, produce, and canned goods, and comparing the various market chains. Such a survey can help you to plan your menu economically and shop accordingly. If no such surveys are conducted in your area, consider getting together with a group of other consumers and starting one.

New computer technology is one way to help consumers save time and money at retail food stores throughout the country. The now familiar postage-stamp-sized group of vertical lines and 10-digit number found on many food packages is the Universal Product Code (UPC), a symbol that electronic scanners can read and feed into the computers that print out the prices and the totals on your sales slip, and thereby maintain effective inventory control for the store.

The new checkout system is becoming more and more popular, and is expected to be in use by all major food chains in the 1980s. Although you can expect benefits, such as faster checking, fewer errors, more information on your sales receipt, and hopefully some price savings, there are potential problems of concern to all consumers.

For one thing, many industry leaders say that the UPC does away with the need to mark a price on individual items. Consumer groups argue that this is not true and that if prices are left off products, shoppers will find it difficult to compare the costs of fresh, frozen, and canned items. In addition, it will be difficult to check on overcharging and incorrect or missing shelf prices.

The new system is fast and efficient, but try to patronize only those markets that mark prices on individual items, and take other measures to keep you fully aware of what you are buying and to assure you that you will not be charged the regular price for a sale item. Many states have been active in adopting laws to regulate the new system and protect consumers.

Many discount stores offer food at prices much lower than those at any other source. Such bargains are great unless they require you to risk eating food you would not consider feeding your dog. Never buy

cans of food with dents, leaks, or rusted tin, or those that are "blown" out of shape, even if the marked-down price is attractive.

Forget about any low-priced bagged food with holes or stains. The Federal General Accounting Office, on an investigation with the FDA and local inspectors during the summer of 1974, looked at products being sold by 30 food salvage outlets in Chicago, New Orleans, Atlanta, Los Angeles, and Seattle. Over a third of the outlets were selling filthy or insect- or rodent-infested foods. One salvager repackaged flour that had come from a warehouse in bags gnawed by rodents and stained with their urine.

Eating at your local fast-food hamburger joint can save you time and money, but be sure the food is of decent quality. One man in California was sentenced to six months in jail for selling horsemeat as beef.

When you are going to eat at an unfamiliar restaurant, call ahead and find out its price range. In this way you will not make a trip to find a menu listing its least expensive dish at $6.95, when you had planned on something less costly.

Food Labels

You no longer have to worry about whether a "diet" food is really low in calories, a particular food is appropriate for a fat-modified diet, or one brand of food is higher in vitamins than another. What happened? The Food and Drug Administration's recent labeling program was what happened, and it went into full operation June 30, 1975.

Under the program's regulations, every food product disclosing nutritional information must do so with a standard format that spells out the number and size of servings and the caloric, protein, carbohydrate, and fat content per serving. For the protein and seven specified vitamins and minerals, the label must also reveal the percentage that each contributes in relation to the nutritional standard known as RDA ("recommended daily allowance").

You have probably gone to your neighborhood market and found bread and flour labeled "enriched," or breakfast drinks, cereals, and milk labeled as "fortified" (presumably with vitamins). Any company that makes such nutritional claims or adds any kind of nutrient to a product now must comply with the established labeling guidelines.

If your doctor says you must decrease the fat or cholesterol content in your food intake, the FDA labeling system will help you to

choose appropriate foods. Companies that want to list fat and cholesterol content must provide the same complete nutritional facts as
those already mentioned. Both saturated and polyunsaturated fats
must be listed in grams per serving; amounts of cholesterol must be
stated in milligrams per serving and milligrams per hundred grams of
food. Also shown is the total fat content as a percentage of the total
number of calories in the food.

Should you decide to lose some weight, you can pick out nutritious foods that are relatively low in calories by checking the labels
on diet products. No longer can a company make false or misleading
dietary claims. FDA regulations ban the use of such statements as
those implying that a particular food can prevent some type of disease
or that a food has diet supplement properties, when in fact the special
ingredients are insignificant to human nutrition.

The word "imitation" no longer has the meaning it once did in
labeling. A company is now required to use the word only in describing a product that, when compared with the product for which it is a
substitute, has about 98 percent or less of the RDA per serving. Any
term replacing the "imitation" designation must be clear in meaning
to the shopper. Uncarbonated beverage products that falsely appear
to contain fruit juice must have a clarifying phrase on their labels. For
example, an orange drink not containing any juice must be labeled
"containing no orange juice" or a similar statement.

Even frozen dinners became a hot issue as the first category of
food for which voluntary nutritional quality standards have been set.
Under the new rules, the FDA can set desirable nutritional guidelines,
which a company may meet and thus be entitled to state on the label
that the food "provides nutrients in amounts appropriate for this class
of food as determined by the U.S. government." Such a designation
assures the consumer that minimum quantities of a variety of nutrients are in the product.

Whenever you buy canned or packaged recipe dishes, you ·.o
longer have to guess about the relative quantities of the ingredients.
Perhaps you once bought a can with the label showing a picture of
spaghetti covered with meat-rich sauce and the words "ground beef"
in large letters and "tomato sauce" in small letters underneath. When
you took the can home and opened it, you found nearly the entire
contents to be tomato sauce, with one teaspoon of meat. The latest
regulations require the common food names of the major ingredients
be listed by weight in descending order. The spaghetti sauce would

have to be labeled "tomato sauce and ground beef," and then you would know that there was more liquid than meat.

A package of ingredients for mixing with other foods to prepare a dish must have a label that mentions the name of the finished dish (such as tuna casserole) and must list those ingredients you will need to add (such as tuna). If you start reading labels carefully, you will no longer be deceived, due to the federal regulations.

Government seizures and legal action are by no means rare in cases alleging violations of labeling or packaging laws. Three products shipped by Hunt-Wesson Foods, Inc., of Fullerton, California, were seized by authorities in Phoenix, Arizona, on October 17, 1973. It was charged that combinations for Baked Chicken Italiano, Baked Chicken Western, and Baked Chicken 'n' Dressing omitted chicken, and that pictures on the packages depicting dinners containing pieces of chicken were false and misleading. Also, the can of sauce and packets of seasoning and cheese in the Baked Chicken Italiano did not show statements of ingredients and quantity of contents. Among the other alleged violations concerning the Baked Chicken 'n' Dressing was that the package and seasoning packet failed to disclose that beta carotene, one of the ingredients, was an artificial color. The subsequent consent decrees authorized donation of the seized products to charitable organizations for consumption by residents.

The Department of Agriculture had planned to adopt new guidelines for the dating of meat and poultry by December 1974. The new rules would have required processors and retailers to identify dates on packages as "sell by" date, "use before" date, or "packaging" date. So many complaints were received from trade associations, however, that the regulations were first held back and then adopted for use solely on a voluntary basis.

Food Labeling Complaints

Report any violations of the labeling rules to the nearest office of the Food and Drug Administration, or write FDA, 5600 Fishers Lane, Rockville, Maryland 20852. Include the label, if possible, or a description of the ingredients listing or format you think is in violation, along with your name, address, place of purchase, and any number coding on the can or package.

Except in connection with violations specifically related to regulations of the Food and Drug Administration, all complaints about false or misleading advertising of most foods comes under the jurisdiction of the Federal Trade Commission (see Chapter 11).

Food Complaints

Although nondeceptive packaging and labeling of foods are important to assure maximum purchasing power for your dollar, nothing is more essential than the safety of the food itself. A cast iron stomach will not save you from the aching or nausea associated with eating spoiled food or from botulism's poisonous, possibly fatal, effects.

All levels of government share the responsibility of making sure that the food sold to you is of decent quality and not injurious to your health. This is supposed to be accomplished through a system of inspection and grading.

Local health departments make periodic inspections of food establishments to see that the food is prepared and sold under sanitary conditions. These agencies have jurisdiction over food produced or prepared within your state and sold to local residents. If you have reason to believe that something edible you buy at a restaurant or grocery store could have a bad effect on your health, contact the health department of your city or county. Report the place of purchase, and do not throw away the food without discussing the matter with a health inspector, since that person may want to take a sample and test it. If you have been made sick by eating the food, the local agency may take legal action and confiscate the product under suspicion. In any case, you may decide to consult an attorney regarding a suit to recover damages from the guilty party.

State departments of health are concerned more with statewide problems resulting from distribution of unhealthy food, and with the inspection of shipments of spoiled or contaminated food to keep it from crossing state lines. Local health departments contact state officials whenever distribution of a dangerous food to other counties is suspected.

After complaints from New York consumers in 1974 that anchovies imported from Portugal and sold under three different labels were contained in swollen and leaking cans, an investigation confirmed that the food was spoiled. The food was destroyed after legal actions were set into motion by the state's agriculture department.

Most foods you buy at the supermarket are produced for distribution to more than one state. To protect others in your community, and perhaps consumers throughout the nation, you should report to the Food and Drug Administration any food you think might be mislabeled, unsanitary, or otherwise dangerous. Any product that lists on the label a company outside your state has been transported in interstate commerce, and automatically comes under federal laws and the jurisdiction of the FDA.

If there is an FDA office in your area, it will be listed in your telephone directory under U.S. Government: Department of Health, Education, and Welfare. If there is no FDA office listed or you have difficulty getting through, contact its headquarters at the Maryland address given earlier. (Phone 301-443-1240 on weekdays and 202-737-0448 on nights and weekends.)

Your complaint will be taken by letter or phone, and prompt action will follow, especially if the case involves widespread use of the suspicious product. If you call the FDA long distance, briefly explain the problem. Ask the representative to call you back if the questioning will take more than a minute or two, so that you will not be stuck with an expensive phone bill. Of course, report your experience with the product as soon as possible, so that efforts to remove it from markets will be successful.

FDA staff persons will want whatever information you can provide about the allegedly harmful food. Be prepared to give them your name, address, phone number, and directions on getting to your home or business. They may send out an agent to pick up a sample of the food, which will then be tested.

In your complaint, describe the problem. Give a description of the label and any identification letters or numbers that appear on it or on the top or bottom of the can. Give an exact or approximate date of purchase and the name and address of the store.

Notify the store or the company listed on the label of your experience and ask it to investigate the matter. If you become ill from a food, see a doctor and tell him or her about the product you ingested. Keep the remains of the product or its empty container and any unopened packages of the food, and show them to your doctor or the health authorities upon their request. While you are standing in line at the supermarket or as soon as you get home, it is a good idea to mark the date of your purchase on any cans or packages that do not show a date. This information could be helpful to you at a later time in determining if the food is still good, or to investigators who want to notify customers of a contaminated batch and take appropriate action.

Violations of the federal food laws continue to be uncovered throughout the country. For example, a shipment of eggs from the Central Carolina Farmers Egg Market contained poisonous polychlorinated biphenyls. The eggs were seized at Norfolk, Virginia, and after the company was charged with the violation in August 1971, a consent decree ordered destruction of the eggs.

The Mark Wells Distributing Company of Des Moines, Iowa, was charged in early 1974 with holding under unsanitary conditions some cake mix, which was found to contain rodent filth. Also found to contain rodent filth were shelled filberts held by Schrafft Candy Company, Inc., of Charleston, Massachusetts. The charge, entered in February 1974, ended in a consent decree allowing the filberts and other types of nuts and milk chocolate held in unsanitary conditions to be released to the dealer for salvaging.

In 1973 tuna was the subject of an intense FDA investigation into the sickness of over 200 people in the Midwest and West. A Samoan subsidiary of H.J. Heinz Company's Star-Kist Foods, Inc., and two top management personnel, were charged in August 1974 with the shipment of 173,000 cans of tuna fish alleged to contain decomposed food and a deleterious histamine, a violation of the Food, Drug and Cosmetics Act.

In 1975 thousands of cans of lobster bisque and clam bisque were recalled by the FDA because of underprocessing, which could permit dangerous microorganisms to grow in the can. The soups were marketed under such brand names as Atlantic Brand, Weathervane Farm, and Embassy Seafoods.

The only foods shipped in interstate commerce that do not come under the primary jurisdiction of the FDA are meat (except the unusual types, such as rabbit and kangaroo), poultry, eggs, and egg products. Your complaint regarding these items should be directed to the nearest office of the U.S. Department of Agriculture or to its compliance headquarters at South Building, Room 2933, Washington, D.C. 20250.

The U.S. Department of Agriculture has jurisdiction only over these areas when the food has not been utilized as part of a finished product. For example, ground beef by itself is regulated by the USDA, but if a bun is added and the food is sold as a hamburger, the law changes the food's jurisdiction back to the FDA.

Food Inspection and Grading

Your shopping expertise will be enhanced if you become familiar with the various quality grades that are used. Just because a food has a lower grade does not necessarily mean that it has a lower nutritional value or poorer taste. The lower grade generally does mean that the food will be lower in price than the higher grade.

Before food can be graded for quality, it must first be inspected for wholesomeness by the U.S. Department of Agriculture. To prevent consumption of diseased meats, the federal government tests foods and monitors farms and processing plants to assure compliance with federal standards for sanitation. After successful inspection, the circular USDA stamp shown in Figure 4–3 is affixed to the package. Also shown are the symbols used to indicate Grade A poultry and Choice beef.

Grades have been developed for about 300 farm products. Grade A turkey, chicken, or duck will have more meat and a nicer appearance than Grades B and C, which are rarely printed on the poultry label. The grade of the bird is no indication of its tenderness. Young poultry will be more tender than older fowl.

The Department of Agriculture, in an attempt to minimize confusion about the type of poultry you are buying, limits the variety of names the meat packer may use to describe the product. Young chicken, ducks, and turkeys are generally labeled as "young" or "young broiler," "roaster," "fryer," or "fryer-roaster." Young chickens also can be called "capons" or "Rock Cornish game hens." Tough and old birds are often labeled "mature," "old," "stewing," or "yearling."

The grading of foods is still mostly voluntary and done through

Figure 4–3

programs set up by the USDA. Each time new grades or revised limits for a grade are set up, the methods used to judge the quality of a particular food are supposed to be used more or less uniformly throughout the country—if you buy a product in New York City with a particular grade, the same grade of product purchased in Los Angeles should be very similar.

You will most commonly find grades on lamb, beef, turkey, chicken, duck, goose, guineafowl, eggs, butter, frozen foods, and canned vegetables and fruit. Most grading, however, is done at the wholesale level, and the processor or marketing firm often does not pass on the grading information to the consumer by means of the label, since this is not required by law. With the changes (some people consider them improvements) in the food growing and processing technologies, the grades themselves are subject to change to reflect higher qualities.

The Department of Agriculture scheduled new grading standards to go into effect in May 1975, but U.S. District Judge Robert V. Denny permanently enjoined the department from effecting the proposed change in standards. Consumer groups argued that, among other things, the new system would lower the marbling (specks of fat within the lean) requirement for Prime and Choice grade beef, thus resulting in increased prices for lower quality.

The current grades for beef, in descending order of quality, are USDA Prime, Choice, Good, Standard, Commercial, Utility, Cutter, and Canner. The meat's tenderness and flavor are judged on the basis of such factors as the age of the animal, the color and texture of the meat, and the amount of marbling.

The three lowest grades are rarely sold at the meat counter of your supermarket. They usually go into ground beef or processed meats such as hot dogs. Most meat labeled Commercial is from an older animal. It has much marbling and good flavor like the better grades, but it requires long, slow cooking with moist heat to become tender.

The top four grades are given only to meat that came from young animals. Standard and Good grades of beef are very lean and fairly tender. They lack the juiciness and flavor of the two highest grades because they have less marbling. Of all the grades, Prime has the most marbling and is the most tender, juicy, and flavorful. The Choice grade is the most common one sold in supermarkets. It is also of high quality, with slightly less marbling than Prime. These top grades are good for broiling.

Complaints about Grading

The USDA is involved in grading and the handling of grading complaints only for those products distributed in more than one state. However, the agriculture departments of many states have adopted similar standards and grades for products for intrastate consumption. These state agencies enforce their own regulations and will act on a complaint relating to any food produced and distributed exclusively within the state.

If you question the quality of any food that comes under the jurisdiction of the USDA, make your complaint promptly so that an effective investigation may be made. The law requires that most "restricted" or unacceptable eggs be destroyed, for example. Eggs not fit for human consumption are those which are dirty, leaking, or otherwise irregular.

Gather the same data mentioned for reporting a problem to the FDA. If there is no USDA office near you, or if the one you contact does not have the authority to accept the complaint, relay it to the Washington, D.C., headquarters or to any FDA office, which generally will take the complaint even though it may eventually pass the information on to the USDA.

Whenever you see a USDA label on a meat or other food, the food must conform to the grading standards set by the federal government. A supermarket cannot label or advertise a meat as Choice unless it has been graded. If you think a meat or other food has not been graded fairly, take up the matter with the USDA or state grading agency.

Corruption concerning meat grading is certainly not unknown. In 1974 three federal graders were convicted of accepting bribes from meat-packing firms in Vernon, California, and sentenced to jail. The companies allegedly bribed the inspectors to give higher grades to their meat, presumably so it would bring higher profits. Federal graders were also indicted in 1975. You can help stop unlawful activity and protect your spending power by communicating with the appropriate authorities when you think a food's grade does not match its quality.

ATTENDING TO YOUR BODY

Most of us like to think that we give our bodies tender loving care. We redecorate them when they look bedraggled, feed them when they are hungry, clothe them when they are cold, rest them after a hard day's work, and force down pills and potions when they are sick. Such devotion! But there is really no better cause.

Now look in your bathroom cabinets and drawers and see all the goo and gunk you have bought for yourself. Some of the stuff, you swear, is the best made. Other things you have never tried and, looking at them a second time, you're glad you never did.

Supposedly to help lessen the consumer's role as a guinea pig, cosmetic and drug manufacturers often set up research and development departments staffed with chemists and other trained personnel to create and test the safety, effectiveness, and marketability of new products. Such activity has created an incredibly wide range and duplication of prescription and nonprescription drugs, as well as thousands of items to clean us, disguise us, hold us together, and deodorize us.

The drug and cosmetic industries take in vast amounts of consumer dollars each year, and large sums are spent on mass media advertising and other promotions to catch your eye and make you believe that Brand X is twice as effective as Brand Y, even though they may have exactly the same ingredients.

Because most of the drugs and cosmetics you buy are distributed in more than one state, they come under such laws as the Federal Food, Drug and Cosmetics Act and the Fair Packaging and Labeling Act, which protect consumers against adulterated and misbranded products. Most states have similar laws to cover articles distributed in intrastate commerce.

Saving Money

Reading labels and prices on drugs and cosmetics can mean greater protection and more purchasing power for your dollars. This is particularly true with vitamins and common cold and pain remedies. Similar products may differ in price by hundreds of percent. The vast amounts of money spent on advertising the brand-name items from large companies must be recouped somehow, and that means passing on such costs to you, the consumer.

But paying more for a product does not necessarily mean that you are getting a better product. Small companies with less costs and no advertising expenditures can sell such items as high quality, plain aspirin at much lower costs than the well-known companies. Many chain food and drug stores can offer certain drugs and cosmetics cheaper by selling them under the store label. These products are often exactly the same as their higher priced equivalents, but without the fancy packaging.

Do not be misled by large posters and a huge supply of a well-known brand on the shelf. These are ploys of advertising, to sell the product without any appreciable discount. You should still compare the price on the item with the others sold by the store. Never mistake the words "sale price" by assuming that the item sells below equivalent products on the shelf.

Prescription Drugs

Prescription drugs have presented a special problem to consumers over the years. When you take a prescription to your local pharmacist, it is filled for a price that may be much more or less than at other drugstores. If two or more companies distribute the same drug, it is the pharmacist who often decides which brand to use, and thus how much you will pay and how much profit the store will take in.

A basic understanding of prescription drugs and how they are dispensed will prove helpful in cutting costs for medications. After a new drug has been formulated, it may be determined that the drug is for use in treating an illness that should be under the attention of a physician, or is dangerous without proper dosage or special instructions. The Food and Drug Administration may then set a regulation limiting distribution of the drug to those persons possessing a prescription.

When a drug is being evaluated before marketing, it is given a "generic" name, which is a conglomerate of chemical names or processes that best identify the new drug. This formal naming is accomplished by the United States Adopted Names Council, a triad cooperative of the American Medical Association, the American Pharmaceutical Association, and the U.S. Pharmaceutical Convention.

You might think that the generic name of a drug would become a standard for both doctors and patients, but, in fact, it often becomes obscured and known only by pharmacists. One reason is that the manufacturer of a new drug has the legal right to give it a "brand name," which is registered as a trademark. The brand name is usually easier to pronounce and remember than the generic name, and it becomes more commonly used when talking about (or ordering) the drug. (As an example, the generic name of a drug used to relieve moderate to severe pain is *meperidine hydrochloride*. It is sold under its much better-known brand name—*Demerol*—by Winthrop Laboratories of New York City.) A drug producer has a monopoly on the product for the 17 years the patent is in effect, and it can charge a high price because of a lack of competition.

During the time the original company has exclusive rights to the manufacture of the drug, it will push thousands of free samples to physicians and do much advertising to associate the drug publicly with that company's brand name rather than the generic name. Doctors, then, will prescribe the drug by the familiar brand name, and many may not even be aware of the generic name.

To further complicate matters for the consumer, many states have antisubstitution laws, which *require* pharmacists to fill prescriptions with brand-name drugs if they are specifically asked for by the physician. (By the end of 1976, some form of prosubstitution law had reportedly been enacted in Alaska, Arizona, Arkansas, California, Colorado, Connecticut, Delaware, Florida, Iowa, Kentucky, Maine, Maryland, Massachusetts, Michigan, Minnesota, New Hampshire, New Mexico, Oregon, Rhode Island, South Carolina, Virginia, and Wisconsin. Also included are the District of Columbia and Puerto Rico.) If the doctor writes a prescription using the generic name, the pharmacist may fill it by using medication with the generic name or with the higher priced brand name.

When a patent on a drug expires, the company providing the first identification for the drug continues to use that brand name, while other firms start to manufacture the product under their own brands. But by this time other brand-name companies have difficulty in competing with sales of the product under its original promoted name. Moreover, manufacturers who offer the drug under its generic name and at a lower price find competition difficult, because pharmacists may very well prefer the brand names, with bigger profit margins.

You may have heard that one brand of aspirin or decongestant is more effective than another brand. Although this is generally unlikely, a drug that contains exactly the same chemical compounds as another may be slightly different in such factors as the rate at which the drug enters the bloodstream. Interestingly, the argument that you should buy a "higher quality" brand is usually espoused by those who benefit most, the drug companies selling the higher priced drugs. The fact is that many drugs containing the same chemical compounds in equal amounts are therapeutically equivalent.

Prescription Savings

Keeping all these factors in mind, you can take several steps to bring down your expenditures for prescription medication. Since many states have not yet repealed their antisubstitution laws, the doctor has significant influence over the amount of money you will be paying for medication.

Tell your doctor that you are concerned about rising drug costs and would appreciate his or her helping by writing a prescription using the drug's generic name. Some doctors may feel uneasy about this request if they do not know the generic name. If you notice any hesitation, you might suggest that the doctor call the pharmacist to find out the generic name. A doctor should not be annoyed at such a request, and often will take the minimal trouble to find out the generic name. (Incidentally, physicians are reputed—with some justification—to have perhaps the worst handwriting of any professional group in the country, or so say many pharmacists, and trying to read your doctor's scribbling may be like deciphering hieroglyphics. Look at the prescription immediately after your doctor hands it to you and question him or her if it is unclear.)

If you have a chronic condition requiring long-term medication or an acute problem necessitating massive doses of a drug, ask your doctor to authorize the pharmacist to provide you with a large supply. This will prove more economical in the long run, as some pharmacists have a standard service charge every time you have a prescription refilled. Check the drug's expiration date to be sure that the large quantity will be used by that time.

If you or your physician is familiar with the manufacturer that sells the drug at the lowest price, it would be a good idea for the doctor to specify that firm on the prescription. Otherwise, the pharmacist may still give you a drug manufactured at a higher price.

If you are concerned about prices, do not just go to any nearby pharmacy to have a prescription filled. The cost of identical medications can vary tremendously from store to store, and sometimes from one prescription to another in the same pharmacy. In fact, in 1975 the Virginia Citizens Consumer Council reported that prices for common prescriptions can vary in one local area as much as 650 percent.

Whether your doctor has used the drug's generic name or not, you can always pick up the phone and call several pharmacies in your area. Simply tell the pharmacist that you would like to know the cost of the drug at the strength dictated by your doctor, and that, in the case where the generic name is used, you would like the least expensive source available. Then go to the pharmacy that gives you the best price.

Remember, just because one pharmacy undersells another on one particular drug does not necessarily mean the same will hold true for other drugs. One store may sell you the drug you need today at half the price that the same product is being sold for across the street. Conceivably, you could then request a different medication and be quoted a price four times as high as one by the other store.

Some stores give extra discounts to the elderly, handicapped, or other groups, and you may be able to take advantage of these savings by asking about a discount after you have already secured your original price quote. Also, especially if you buy a large quantity of medicine, ask the pharmacist the best way to store the drug so that it will remain potent until the expiration date. In this way you will avoid having to dispose of unusable medication.

Drug Surveys

If you are a more ambitious consumer with some free time or if you belong to an organized group concerned with rising costs in your community, there is even more you can do on a long-term basis to help bring down your costs of medications and to keep other consumers informed about good places to shop for drugs. The best way to get a clear picture of who is charging what for prescription drugs in your area is a well-planned, comprehensive, accurate survey.

A consumer survey of drug prices might at first seem like a difficult procedure, but the whole process is made easier by utilizing the free publication "Prescription Drug Prices Consumer Survey Handbook #2," available from the Seattle Regional Office of the Federal Trade Commission, 28th Floor, Federal Building, Seattle, Washington 98174.

If you use the sample survey form and instructions included in the FTC guide, you will find that half the work is already done for you. It lists questions about various pharmacy services and charges and contains a suggested list of 25 prescription drugs, especially emphasizing those commonly dispensed to the elderly. Guidelines de-

scribe procedures for organizing the survey and carrying it out effectively. Once the survey is completed, send a copy of your summary
work sheet and written analysis to local news media for publication
and broadcast. Once the information has spread, you may very well
see some pharmacies cutting prices to remain competitive.

The next several years will see more and more states repealing
laws that restrict the advertising of prescription drug prices and prohibit pharmacists from substituting generically labeled drugs for
higher priced, brand-name medications.

According to an FTC spokesperson, by November 1975 eleven
states—California, Connecticut, Maine, Maryland, Michigan, Minnesota, Nevada, New Hampshire, New York, Texas, and Virginia
—required pharmacies to post drug prices. Six states—California,
Hawaii, Minnesota, Nevada, South Dakota, and Washington—
required the druggist to disclose prices over the phone. The Federal
Trade Commission also proposed two regulations that would allow
the nation's approximately 50,000 pharmacies to advertise retail
prices for prescription drugs. If the new FTC regulations become
effective, any state law prohibiting the price disclosures will be invalid,
but such practices as posting prices and disseminating price information over the phone will remain enforceable by state and local laws as
long as such practices are not in conflict with the federal guidelines.

Drug and Cosmetic Labels

As a consumer, you can protect yourself and your pocketbook by
getting in the habit of reading labels on drugs and cosmetics, just as
you should for foods. Although food and drug ingredients have been
listed on labels for a long time, mandatory label disclosures of elements in cosmetics is a new development. The Food and Drug Administration regulations, which have been supported by various consumer groups and the National Organization for Women (NOW),
require manufacturers to list on cosmetic labels, in order of highest to
lowest quantities, all ingredients except fragrances, which have been
declared trade secrets.

The multi-billion-dollar cosmetic industry is not exactly smiling
about the rule that became effective November 30, 1976. This action
is, nevertheless, a step in the right direction, but there is dissatisfaction by many consumers because they say it is not strong enough,
based on the fact that the exempted category of fragrances is a main
cause for most cosmetic allergies. Therefore, perhaps the most poten-

tially harmful part of the cosmetic may remain unknown; the identifying factor in any allergic reaction you may have could be kept a secret for a long time.

Since that rule was issued, however, the FDA has come through with a new regulation that does provide some good news for anyone especially susceptible to allergies from cosmetics. A June 6, 1977 effective date outlaws a company's claim that its products are "hypoallergenic" unless that contention can be backed up with proof. Whether for suntan lotion, shampoo, lip balm, or any other cosmetic, manufacturers must do skin tests and come up with data that, to FDA satisfaction, show a product to be safer than competing products.

Drug and Cosmetic Complaints

Just as in the case of a problem with a food you buy, never throw away a drug or cosmetic that you feel has done you harm until you have communicated with health officials and receive instructions for its disposal. If the product is distributed only locally, contact your city health department. If the item is sold statewide, state health inspectors will become involved. On the other hand, if the product is sold nationwide, communicate directly with the local office of the Food and Drug Administration, or write to their headquarters at 5600 Fishers Lane, Rockville, Maryland 20852. If you are unsure whether the drug is distributed locally, statewide, or nationally, contact a local pharmacy to find out.

Especially if this is the first such report to be made on the product, the authorities will often want to examine the product itself as well as its container. The label and coding on the item will give investigators information necessary to contact the manufacturer or distributor and to determine the problem lots.

Copy all information from the label before surrendering it so that you will be able to inform any medical practitioner about the ingredients that may be causing an adverse reaction. You also may want to consult an attorney regarding the possible filing of a personal injury lawsuit. In the case of drugs, especially possible allergic reactions or overdoses, your telephone operator can connect you with the local poison control center, suicide prevention center, or general hospital emergency room.

The Food and Drug Administration has the authority to seize and ban drug and cosmetic goods introduced into interstate commerce and judged to be in violation of federal laws. Seizure actions were, for example, taken in Shreveport, New York, and Dallas, Texas, in 1973 calling for the destruction of a new drug manufactured by ICN Pharmaceuticals of Covina, California. The federal government had charged that the drug was shipped without an effective, approved New Drug Application. Another seizure action taken by the FDA, in 1974, involved rubber prophylactics called Peacocks, which were shipped by Dean Rubber Company of North Kansas City, Missouri. Some prophylactics were found to contain holes.

In 1975 the FDA took steps to ban all aerosol antiperspirant sprays containing a metallic compound called zirconium. The federal proposal, based on government findings that the ingredient can cause lung disease, resulted in ordering such spray deodorants as Secret, Sure, and Arrid-XX off the market until the manufacturers could prove their safety.

Container Safety

Drug container safety features and warning statements come under jurisdiction of the Consumer Product Safety Commission. This is the agency to contact if you want to complain that a product's label does not contain a needed or appropriate warning statement, or that the drug's container should be produced with features to keep the drug fresher or make access by children more difficult. This agency sets regulations requiring the safety bottle caps for aspirin and other products. Write to Consumer Product Safety Commission, Washington, D.C. 20207.

False Advertising

As for most other products and services in interstate commerce, false or misleading advertising for drugs and cosmetics is generally under scrutiny and subject to legal action by the Federal Trade Commission. With increasing concern over possible misleading or exaggerated ad claims by shampoo manufacturers, the FTC ordered the firms to substantiate their statements. One interesting finding was that some ad claims mentioning terrific "natural" ingredients were, in fact, referring to water!

In 1974 an FTC administrative law judge found that the Warner-Lambert Company of New Jersey had advertised false and misleading statements about Listerine mouthwash. Among deceptive claims singled out were "Listerine antiseptic kills germs by millions on contact," "for . . . colds and resultant sore throats," and "for fewer colds, milder colds." Under the order issued by Judge Alvin L. Bermin, the company was ordered to stop claiming that Listerine or any other nonprescription drug results in fewer colds or sore throats.

Sometimes the FTC may require a company to initiate advertising to rectify the false image the public has been given. The agency, for example, required Warner-Lambert in the above case to make the following disclosure in all advertising over a subsequent two-year period: "Contrary to prior advertising of Listerine, Listerine will not prevent or cure colds or sore throats, and Listerine will not be beneficial in the treatment of cold symptoms or sore throats."

The purpose of advertising is to influence you to try various products and services. One relatively new development in the field of advertising will give the consumer a clearer view of a product's attributes. This is the use of comparative advertising, which involves one company's naming the major competitor(s) in its ad and telling why its product is better. Each firm must be certain that it can prove its claims to avoid a lawsuit by the competitor. A full discussion of false and deceptive ad claims and the agencies that investigate them will be found in Chapter 11.

Chapter 5

THE UNPROFESSIONAL PROFESSIONALS

Graduate schools, trade schools, and industry training programs throughout the country are turning out an increasing number of qualified professionals to provide you with a variety of services. The physician, the dentist, the attorney, the social worker, the accountant, the psychologist, the plumber, the auto repair person, and all others who have specialized degrees and licenses to practice their trades are trained to help the consumer with many problems.

Many professionals seem to be highly respected among the general population, and often rightly so, but the idealistic view of their seemingly altruistic service to humanity is generally outgrown and replaced with a more realistic consumer understanding that such services cost money—often too much money—and that the practitioner will no doubt prefer payment of his or her bill in full to words of gratitude.

WATCHING THOSE WHO WATCH YOU

Professional services cost money, and you should purchase them as you would any product for the home. Just as there are excellent, mediocre, and lousy refrigerators, there are excellent, mediocre, and lousy doctors. Just as a badly produced toaster slips through unnoticed by inspectors on the assembly line, a dentist who would have done better at office management will be listed in the Yellow Pages.

The monetary risk may even be higher for the services of a professional, because he or she rarely provides you with any sort of guarantee. If you buy a defective toaster, the store will replace it without charge, but if you want to replace your attorney, the odds are that you will have to pay twice.

Selecting a Professional

If you are like most consumers, you want to invest your money in products and services that will give you the greatest benefit. Although advertising of professional services is often under strict regulation by state or local laws, there are other means for finding the help most suited to your needs. Just as you consider all information you can get about the type of product you want to buy (useful features, safety, durability, test reports, recommendations from others), you should utilize any available information about a type of service or a specific professional.

The perception of what is or is not good service can vary greatly from person to person, but consulting with family members, friends, and others whose opinions you value can be helpful in selecting a professional. It is certainly better than letting your fingers do the walking through the Yellow Pages.

The local chapters of most professional associations maintain a referral service that you can call for help. Keep in mind, however, that these organizations will generally refer you only to their members, and they will not comment on competency or give detailed information about any professional's services, fees, or complaint record. Other nonprofit referral sources operate on the basis of a fee you pay. One such agency is the Los Angeles Communications Center for Therapy & Growth, which has a representative interview the client (generally in person) to help the client make contact with the most appropriate source of help.

Ralph Nader, this country's foremost authority on consumer activism, and his health research group came up in 1973 with the first model consumer guide to physicians for the residents of Prince Georges County, Maryland. A second guide was issued in 1974, to the surprise of the local medical society of Springfield, Illinois. This guide, assembled by Ron Sakolsky, an instructor at Sagamon State University, was patterned after the first, with information about doctors' hours, fees, and education. It also indicated which physicians accepted Medicare patients, and listed any doctor not responding to the questionnaire as "uncooperative." Despite the medical society's attempt to discourage its members from participating in the prepublication survey, 25 percent did submit the necessary data, and the free guide was given out at stores throughout that city.

Many more guides to finding a doctor are in the planning stages or are being published throughout the nation despite the gripes from organized medicine. Consumer groups hopefully will continue to demand more openness in distributing information about professionals and their services. If doctor directories find popularity among the general population, the publication of guides listing other professional groups, such as therapists and attorneys, can be expected.

In an attempt to create new avenues whereby persons of middle and low incomes can gain greater access to professional services, group medical plans are continuing to grow. In exchange for a monthly fee, often paid in part or full by the employer, a person can visit a doctor, laboratory, or pharmacy with little or no charge.

Group legal services are less established, but are growing in importance. The high cost of obtaining even brief advice from an attorney has deterred many consumers. Included in the annual membership fee of some nonprofit organizatons such as the California Citizen Action Group is the opportunity for free consultation and discount legal services. The California law firm of Jacoby and Meyers has set up the Legal Clinic. It charges a flat consultation fee and has some standard fees that seem to be generally lower than those of most private attorneys for such matters as an individual's bankruptcy, un-contested dissolution of marriage, and the preliminary hearings on a felony charge.

Two other organizations based in Southern California are Group Legal Services, Inc., and nonprofit Responsive Educational Projects. They charge their clients or members a small annual fee, entitling them to receive an unlimited amount of advice by staff attorneys at any time over the phone, and discounted legal representation.

Dealing with a Professional

Once you request and receive any type of professional services, you are required to pay (except, of course, for free services rendered by an agency or clinic). Your payment for services entitles you to the same satisfaction that you get when you purchase a product. Although you cannot send a doctor back to medical school to do further study on an illness that he or she doesn't know much about, you should speak openly about what you expect from a physician and any charges that seem excessive.

You are paying a professional to assist you in something you cannot do yourself, such as diagnosing an illness and prescribing medicine, or drawing up an employment contract. You have every right to a clear understanding of any action this person takes in your behalf, and if necessary you should ask for further explanation. Nothing is more unsettling than leaving a medical office without a clear diagnosis and without all the important questions answered. Many professionals run from one client or patient to the next, not even realizing that they have not given adequate help.

Overcharging

Dissatisfaction with a professional who renders services can arise out of a problem in two areas: the quality of the service itself, and the fees charged.

Professional fees are set by the practitioner, who can generally charge whatever he or she pleases within certain limits. A doctor, for example, cannot get away with charging $100 for a short office visit in which he or she diagnoses your cold and recommends the usual rest, liquids, and aspirin without drawing negative reactions from the general public, colleagues, courts, and government regulatory agencies.

Overcharging and billing mistakes can be kept at a minimum if you always demand an itemized statement. Many busy people wrong-

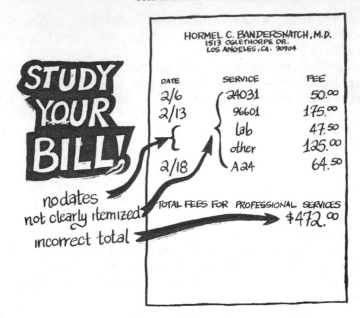

fully pay the total amount due even if they think it should be lower and the charges are not broken down.

There are several ways to respond to an unreasonably high bill. The first is simply to pay whatever you feel is correct or fair and include a letter explaining how you think you have been overcharged. This puts the burden of substantiating and collecting the balance of the bill on the provider of the service. That person will accept your money as payment in full, make an explanation, or try to collect the remainder by turning the account over to a collection agency or filing a small claims court suit. The professional may not be willing to see you again, but chances are the feeling is mutual.

One benefit of letting the professionals assume the burden of collection is that you may successfully avoid the unreasonable payment with little inconvenience. All problems connected with collecting judgments in small claims court cases (see Chapter 12) work in your favor when the circumstances involve someone's winning a case against you and then trying to collect the money. You do, however, run the risk of damaging your credit rating, and this fact deters many from not paying an unfair bill.

Another way to avoid paying unfair charges is to remit the full amount and then file your own small claims suit, requesting reimbursement for that portion of the total that you feel is not fair or correct. The professional is then required to present to the court a defense of the charges. Some professionals will settle the case before it goes to court by refunding some money to you rather than spending their time making a court appearance. If the matter does go before a judge and the decision is in your favor, you may still face the burden of collection (see Chapter 12).

Professional Negligence

Specific procedures are set up in your state for initiating an investigation into the alleged negligence or unethical or illegal conduct (including overcharging and criminal activity) by licensed professionals. Generally a detailed letter of complaint specifying dates of service and the circumstances prompting your comments will be sufficient. Send one copy to the local or state professional organization of which the person is a member. Such groups upon receiving a number of substantiated complaints about a member may take action to bar that person from renewing membership, but they have no power to take direct administrative action to affect the practitioner's license.

Send another copy of your letter to the state licensing authority for that particular field. All states, for instance, have a board of medical examiners and a board of legal examiners. These groups not only issue licenses to physicians and attorneys, but also investigate, review, and take direct action against them on behalf of all consumers. Each action may include refunds, censures, warnings, temporary license suspension, or license revocation. Each state board will have independent status or be part of a state department of licensing or consumer affairs. In some cases the state attorney general's office will handle such a complaint, especially if criminal activity is alleged.

Fraud

If you suspect someone is practicing without a license or there is obvious criminal activity, local law enforcement agencies will look into the matter and take prompt action (see Chapter 12). Professionals involved in schemes that utilize the mails may be breaking federal laws, and complaints concerning them should be directed to the Postal Inspection Service (see Chapter 9).

BEING SURE OF YOUR INSURERS

Today nearly everyone carries some kind of insurance. In most states you are required by law to have auto insurance if you drive, unless you are wealthy enough to pay a substantial claim yourself. You can also take out policies for everything from fire and theft to kidnapping. In fact, the Maryland Casualty Company (through Winchester Insurance Agency, 3033 Moorpark Avenue, San Jose, California 95128) offers renters a $100,000 policy to cover property damage from waterbeds, and Lloyds of London is famous for reportedly insuring nearly anything.

An insurance policy is your legal agreement with the insuring company and must be treated like any other legal document. Read it carefully before signing, and make certain it states the amount of coverage you requested. Demand clarification on any vague or confusing points. Although unnecessary technical jargon has thoroughly confused most consumers over the years, some companies are now showing that policy language can be brought back to clear, common English. Taking the lead is Nationwide Mutual Insurance Company of Columbus, Ohio, the nation's fifth-largest auto insurer. Its 1975 policy replaced the legalese and fine print with an index, illustrations, and a glossary of definitions. Sentry Insurance of Wisconsin has marketed a plain-talk policy with large type, short sentences, a list of definitions, and a "policy-at-a-glance" page.

Ask for any amendments in your policy that you feel are necessary. All additions should be added in ink or typed and carry your signed initials and those of the insurance agent. Noticing the information on exclusions can prevent the burden of your incurring expenses for a problem you mistakenly thought was covered.

Picking an Insurance Company and Policy

Check out the accessibility of each insurance company. Insurance is a service, and a company without a local phone number and an answering service for evenings and weekend emergency calls, may not be a good one to deal with.

Never buy insurance from an organization completely unknown to you. Look into the reputation of a company you are considering. Are claims handled promptly and fairly? Does the firm have a history of rapidly rising rates? Does the company pay out money exactly as promised in its policies? You can find some answers by asking friends and coworkers about the insurers they use and by calling the nearest Better Business Bureau, Chamber of Commerce, or consumer bureau. A particularly good source may be your state's department of insurance or commerce. The insurance regulatory body in many states will give information by phone in answer to questions about specific companies' health plans.

Shop around by calling or visiting several companies to get the best deal on the coverage you specify. Auto insurance rates are known to vary greatly from one company to another. Do not be misled into believing that a nonprofit automobile association is, by its nature, the lowest in rates. Many costs, including member services, can jack up the premiums to higher levels than you might initially expect.

Although insurance companies use promotional gimmicks like any other industry, valid discounts are often available for nonsmokers, students who have completed driver training or maintained a minimum grade average, and others. Ask about special policies, but keep in mind that a company's offer of a discount does not necessarily mean that its policy will be less expensive than one with the same coverage at another firm.

Settlement of claims is another significant area of comparison. You should be certain that the company you select has a good record of paying off the insureds' bills. In the case of auto insurance, contact several car repair shops and ask the managers if they are familiar with the companies you list; ask which pay off claims without extreme delays or other hassles. Should you later have an accident, this factor may be paramount. Doctors can tell you which companies handle medical claims most satisfactorily.

Good coverage at reasonable rates is not easy to find. Generally, the best deal is a group policy that allows you to buy insurance at lower rates as part of a company or association. Sometimes it is worthwhile to pay annual dues to an organization to get good coverage. For example, if you work full-time in a technical, professional, temporary position, from secretary to chemist, and cannot obtain adequate coverage through your employer, you may want to join the National Association of Temporary and Technical Employees (NATTE), P.O. Box 24791, Los Angeles, California 90024. You would then be eligible (except if you live in one of a few states such as Nevada) to apply for group health insurance through Blue Cross of California.

If you are retired, look into group health insurance benefits available through membership in the American Association of Retired Persons (AARP), 1909 K Street N.W., Washington, D.C. 20006. By joining a Ralph Nader organization, such as the California Citizen Action Group or other public-interest groups, you can sometimes also receive lower cost group legal services.

Claims

To be sure your insurance company does not take advantage of you, find out the firm's method of computing acceptable claims. Many times an insurer will use confusing codes to indicate medical diagnoses or types of loss. Understanding the meaning of these codes is not always necessary, but knowing how they affect the claims procedure is very important.

For instance, many health insurance policies in California provide for computation of claims based on a standard Relative Value Schedule (RVS) code that has been set—and is revised only about every five years—by the California Medical Association. With the rising rate of inflation, payments based on this often-outdated code many times fall short of what policies seem to represent.

One California company, for example, contracts with doctors to accept less money from patients insured by it than from other patients for full payment of medical charges. One policy from that company provides, after satisfaction of a deductible, for about 80 percent of the insured medical expenses based on a diagnostic code supplied by the doctor. If both the physician and patient are under contract with that company for insurance coverage and the doctor charges $20 for one type of office visit, the insurer may make the judgment to allow only $15 for such visit. Then the insurance company would pay for 80 percent of the total allowed (or $12) and not the remaining 20 percent (or $3, to be paid by the patient). Although the original bill might have been for $20, the insurance company by contract requires the physician to accept the $15 total allotment as payment in full.

In the above example, let's say the patient has his or her insurance through that company, but is going to a doctor who has not signed a contract with the company. (This is foolish because that patient is losing a money-saving benefit of the policy.) In that case, the insurer would still pay the 80 percent (or $12) based on its standard code, but the patient would be required to pay the full balance of the $20 fee (or $8). Many insured people do not even know that they

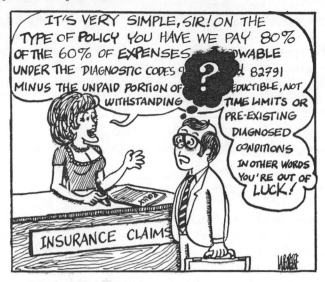

would save money by obtaining medical services from such a member doctor.

Documenting a health insurance claim is simple because your doctor can either bill the insurance company directly or provide you with an itemized statement of charges containing appropriate codes or diagnoses. It is quite another matter if you try to collect on your homeowner's or renter's policy should you be a victim of fire or theft. To avoid having such a claim unfairly cut down to a small percentage of the actual loss, you would do well to plan now for a possible misfortune. Take a physical inventory of your possessions covered by the insurance policy. Go from room to room in your residence and mark down each item, date and amount of purchase, and the present value (realistically taking depreciation into account). Many insurers have blank inventory sheets free for the asking.

Attach appropriate documentation such as sales slips or canceled checks to your inventory record. As a further safeguard, particularly for the more expensive items such as antiques, paintings, or television sets, you can prepare visual verification by taking photographs. Update your inventory with a revised listing and new photos every year or two.

If you have a loss, immediately report it to the insurer's claims adjuster. The company should pay close to what you ask if you can provide evidence to support your claim. Let's say disaster hits and you do not have solid evidence of what you lost or do not even remember some of your belongings. In that case, you might consider hiring a public adjuster to do the work in dealing with the insurance company to reach the highest possible settlement. Such adjusters are licensed in the majority of states, and charge a commission of about 10 to 12 per cent of the total money reimbursed to you. You can find a list of them under "Insurance Claims Adjusters," "Insurance Adjusters," or "Adjusters" in the Yellow Pages, but ask friends or an attorney if they can recommend one.

Insurance Complaints

Since most adults carry some kind of insurance, the industry has grown tremendously over the last few decades. Also increasing has been the number of complaints about such problems as rapid rate hikes, unfair claims settlements, and delays in paying claims. To handle the volume of consumer complaints, most states have set up an insurance regulatory agency, often under their consumer affairs or commerce department. Most of these agencies license insurance agents and companies.

In the health insurance field, the regulation may vary according to the type of insurer. In California, for example, two separate agencies have jurisdiction in handling medical insurance complaints. The Department of Insurance (under the Department of Consumer Affairs) handles problems relating to insurance companies; the office of the Attorney General accepts complaints about nonprofit health plans. Check with your state's insurance department or attorney general's office to find out which has jurisdiction to deal with your insurance company, and then file your complaint.

If you do have a gripe about how your insurer is handling a claim, you will likely to be asked to complete an insurance complaint form (see the sample in Appendix 6), which is then sent by the state agency to the insurer for an answer. Sufficient pressure often can be exerted to bring you a just settlement.

You are risking more problems if you pay premiums to an out-of-state company, since the consumer protection resources in your state may claim it is not within their power to represent you individually against persons and firms outside the state. Therefore, wherever possible, stick with a company or health plan based in your state or with permanently established representatives in your state rather than responding to a mail order insurance company hundreds of miles away. The only exceptions should be well-known, large companies or any firms known by you to be stable and with good reputations.

If you order your insurance through a mail offer—out-of-state or not—and you suspect fraud or misrepresentation, write down all the facts and turn the matter over to federal authorities at the nearest office of the Postal Inspection Service (see Chapter 9).

The small claims court may or may not allow you to file a suit to collect money on an insurance claim. In any case, this route is not recommended, and it is totally discouraged for dealing with out-of-state insurers. An alternative to getting help from your state agency might be one of the local consumer protection agencies described in Chapter 12.

THE OLD FOOT-IN-THE-DOOR ROUTINE

You are not alone if you are peeved by that "animal" who is always on the prowl: the swift and cunning boar (*bore* would be more like it) with its foot in the door ready to charge into your home at any hour of the day or night, the laughing hyena that is the only one laughing, the squawking parrot that will not shut up until it gets its cracker (your attention).

The salespersons doing this type of pushing vary as much as the products or services themselves. They range from a neighborhood kid selling cookies to make money for a trip to camp, to the strange person with the Mona Lisa smile and low voice who was just passing and thought you might be interested in selecting and beginning to make payments on your own future gravesite and tombstone. Even if the intruder does not put a foot in the door, the voice still gets through the keyhole in an attempt to reach your ear and deliver a sales pitch.

Deceptive Selling

Many unscrupulous companies use deceptive methods for selling their products. One common scheme is to inform you that you have won a contest entitling you to purchase portraits, furniture, a recreational vehicle, or other item "at cost." Another approach is the charming youngster who, before telling you about the magazines you should buy, goes into a sympathy-inducing monologue about how you can help him or her go to camp or win a bicycle by "voting" for him or her "without obligation."

Deceptive selling practices are not limited to small and unknown companies or one-person, fly-by-night operations. In January 1975, Federal Trade Commission Administrative Law Judge Ernest G. Barnes issued a cease-and-desist order against Encyclopaedia Britannica, Inc., and its subsidiary, Britannica Home Library Services, Inc., both of Chicago. Evidence showed that company salespersons deceptively gained entrance to the homes of prospective customers through the guise of delivering prizes and free booklets, and without identifying their true purpose and product.

Judge Barnes stated, "One ploy used to gain entrance into prospects' homes is the Advertising Research Analysis questionnaire. This form questionnaire is designed to enable the salesman to disguise his role as a salesman and appear as a surveyor engaged in advertising research. Encyclopaedia Britannica fortifies the deception by the questionnaire with a from letter from its Director of Advertising . . . for use with those prospects who may question the survey role. These questionnaire with a form letter from its Director of Advertising . . . of the questionnaires are thrown away by salesmen without being analyzed for any purpose whatsoever. . . ." Such sales practices attempt to catch you off guard and pressure you into buying something you can get anytime at the "bargain" price, and may not even want.

The initial decision, which was subject to appeal, prohibited the unlawful practices named and required the companies, among other things, to provide all sales job applicants with pertinent provisions of the ruling and inform them that they were required to follow these provisions. Sales representatives were required to give to the prospective customer a card clearly showing the purpose of their visit and to allow the consumer time to read the card before any sales presentation.

Confronting the Beast

The fastest way to find out what a salesperson wants to sell you is to ask directly and emphatically. Most sellers will get to the point if you demand it. Then you can make your decision about the purchase, and no more of your time will be wasted.

Most telephone and door-to-door sales are made without the salesperson's having an appointment, and so field selling involves catching you in the right mood and when you have some money to spend. It also involves pressuring you to make a decision, since the salesperson may tell you that his or her stock is running out or he or she will not be in your neighborhood again until next year.

Avoiding Unwanted Purchases

Many consumers set for themselves a policy of never buying merchandise from a person soliciting at their home or by phone to avoid being cheated or buying something they do not need. However, consider the convenience of not having to go to a store to buy the same thing.

One easy way to avoid negative consequences of spur-of-the-moment buying in your home is to ask yourself a few simple questions. Do you need the item being offered? Will you use the item now rather than storing it away for months? Do you know the person or company selling the product? Does the item have a guarantee equivalent to that of products you can purchase at the store? Will you be able to get service if necessary? Will the sale really be a bargain? If your answer to any of these questions is no, you had better give a second thought to spending your money.

No matter how hard you try to spend money wisely, there may be a few occasions when you make a rotten decision. Perhaps a salesman visits your home with color brochures and written endorsements from top educators about the encyclopedia he is selling at a very low price "for a limited time only." He does his song-and-dance and virtually everything else except pay you to take the books. You feel that you cannot pass up this never-to-be-repeated opportunity, so you sign a contract requiring you to make monthly payments over three years. Later, your children come home and tell you that the encyclopedia you ordered is too technical, too general, or too childish, and not of much use to them. To top off the blunder, your husband or wife comes home and raises the roof at not being consulted.

Returning Unwanted Merchandise

If in the future such an incident happens or you simply change your mind about the purchase, don't resort to pulling your hair out before looking into a remedy from the Federal Trade Commission. According to a federal law that became effective in June 1974, you have a right to cancel any door-to-door sales purchase if the cost, including any interest and service charges, totals $25 or more and you give written notice of your decision to cancel within three business days of the purchase. Sundays and most legal holidays are not considered business days even if your purchase is made on one of those days. Saturdays, on the other hand, are counted as business days.

Try to be aware of certain rules that the door-to-door salesperson must follow in collecting or contracting for payments totaling $25 or more. The seller must provide you at the time of the purchase with a completed receipt or contract in the same language used in the sales presentation. For instance, if the sales pitch is made in Spanish, the receipt or contract must be in Spanish. This is to prevent deceiving the purchaser by telling him or her one thing and providing a contract contradicting the oral statements or adding conditions which, if the person could read them, might cause him or her to forgo the purchase.

The seller must also attach to the receipt or contract an easily readable statement entitled "Notice of Cancellation" which spells out your right to cancel the transaction. If the seller receives this dated notice postmarked within the three-day period after purchase, he or she must refund to you within 10 business days any money you have paid and cancel any other obligations under the terms of the sale or agreement.

You have certain responsibilities too if this law is to work in your favor. Besides notifying the salesperson within the specified amount of time, you must see that any delivered goods you are planning to return remain in good condition.

Upon your cancellation, you must make the goods you are returning available to the seller at your place of residence. Or you may, at the seller's risk and expense, ship the goods back according to the seller's instructions. If, after you have made the goods reasonably available, the company representative fails to pick them up within 20 days of the date of your written notice of cancellation, the law provides you with the right to retain or dispose of the goods without any payment or other obligation. If you do not make the merchandise available to the seller or do not keep a promise to return the goods, this rule will favor the seller, and you will be fully responsible for all obligations to which you agreed in the original sales contract.

The "in-home" sales *not* subject to this trade regulation include those based on your prior visit to a store with a fixed location and those made exclusively by mail or telephone with no physical contact between you and the seller before delivery. Also exempted from the rule is the rental or sale of real property, the sale of insurance, and your purchase of commodities or securities through a broker or dealer registered with the Securities and Exchange Commission.

If you initiate contact with someone who then comes to your residence to repair an item of personal property, the work performed and any necessary replacement parts sold to you do not come under the FTC regulations. However, if at the same time you are sold other goods or services not related to the specific repairs you previously requested, you are entitled to full protection under the trade rule.

Sales Complaints

When you come across someone who you think is using illegal sales methods, there are two possible options open to you.

First, if the salesperson commits a violation of the law previously mentioned, go directly to the nearest office of the Federal Trade Commission. The FTC will investigate the practices of the individual or firm and file a formal complaint if necessary.

Second, your state has its own business code regulating door-to-door sales, so a local consumer bureau or law enforcement agency should be able to assist you in getting a refund or forcing the parties to comply with city or county ordinances regulating sales.

Chapter 6

THE WORST CHORE IN THE WORLD— MOVING

Moving your residence is a time-consuming, painstaking, exhausting activity. You have to find a place to live, negotiate the rental or buying agreement, select a reliable moving company, and make all kinds of arrangements, from setting up a phone referral to submitting a mail-forwarding order. This chapter will give you ideas to help you better plan this momentous task and to assist you in dealing with many major problems. Discussion in the first section will be limited to the problems of apartment renters, although many of the ideas presented are also applicable to renting and moving into a home. If you intend to purchase a home, be sure you have read the section on home owners' warranties in Chapter 3.

YOU VERSUS THE LANDLORD

The sweet-talking Dr. Jekyll who accepted your first month's rent and security deposit may turn into Mr. Hyde the moment you notify him that your heater is not working or the ceiling leaks. Do not be suckered into signing a lease that waives most of your rights and fully protects the lessor. There are enough vacant apartments in more areas so that an owner usually will be somewhat flexible in yielding to the wishes of prospective tenants.

The person who shows you the apartment has the job of renting it as soon as possible with the least complications, such as demands to

redecorate and move furniture in and out. He or she will obviously not be pointing out all of the negative aspects of living in that apartment, building, and neighborhood. You, then, must take on the responsibility for determining and weighing any possible obstacles to your carefree living.

Tenant Groups

Some local and state laws now provide good protection to renters, but some states have few effective statutes enabling you to take action against a negligent landlord. Keep informed about current and proposed landlord-tenant laws by contacting your local tenant association.

You can write to the National Tenants Organization, Inc., 1346 Connecticut Avenue N.W., Room 202, Washington, D.C. 20036, for help in locating the group nearest to your residence or for answers to specific questions. The NTO also may be able to provide the guidelines necessary for you to set up your own affiliate association. This national organization was begun in 1969 and now has close to 500 affiliate groups in nearly every major city across 47 states. NTO is a self-sustaining, nonprofit group that circulates bulletins on tenants' rights, helps to bring together tenants with common problems, and initiates changes in laws that will benefit all renters.

The staffed offices of local and state legislators are excellent sources for finding out about laws relating to rentals in your state. Several other sources for securing this type of information are given in Chapters 12 and 13. Besides keeping abreast of the rights guaranteed to you by applicable ordinances, you can best protect yourself by understanding the points raised in this section and implementing appropriate suggestions.

Be Your Own Private Eye

Before you make a decision to rent a particular apartment, equip yourself with a tape measure; pencil and pad; list of your "musts" such as garbage disposal, air conditioning, low street noise level; a magnifying glass; and any other paraphernalia that will aid you in scrutinizing and evaluating every square foot of each room.

This is your chance to play Sherlock Holmes. The apartment is now, or soon will be, vacant. Why? Yes, it may be true that the latest tenant has bought a house or is moving to another city. Or it may be that the landlord raises the rent every two months, or vibrations from a pipe organ in the manager's apartment next door have caused four nervous breakdowns and a repeated sell-out of aspirin at the corner drugstore. You cannot trust the word of the landlord, who might say almost anything to rent the apartment.

The tenant vacating the premises, if he or she is still around, may have witnessed several recurrent annoyances that you might shudder to think of bearing. This person might be telling you about a divorce just so you will rent the apartment, and so he or she can quietly slip out of the lease.

If you are seeing the apartment while the tenant is there, don't blow your chance. Nonchalantly give him or her the third degree. Why is the person leaving? What are the things he or she dislikes about the apartment? Is it quiet during the evening? How much rent is he or she paying? When was the last time the rent was raised?

Once you have gotten this feedback about the apartment, forge on. Do not assume anything. After receiving permission from the rental agent or tenant, check out everything in sight. Try the doorbell. Turn on the stove burners, the oven, the heater, the air-conditioner, the water faucets, the lights, the dishwasher, and the garbage disposal. Flush the toilet.

Try to get a good idea of what living there would be like. The simplest problems can turn out to be the biggest headaches. There may not be much you can do after you move in and discover that one room does not have any electrical outlets, the temperature of the water in the shower wavers between extremes, or the refrigerator you were led to believe was of the no-frost variety has suddenly provided you with an igloo.

One irate Los Angeles man residing in an old building found it necessary to move because he needed a second telephone line. The phone company said it was absolutely impossible to install another phone because of the insufficient wiring available.

First Impression Foul-ups

It never hurts to talk to your prospective neighbors or others in the building. This idea really hit home when I was looking for a two-bedroom apartment in Hollywood. I came across a vacancy that appeared to be just the thing: front apartment, large rooms, good view of trees and flowers, quiet, convenient to shopping, cable TV wiring, very reasonable rent, and tenancy on a month-to-month basis.

Before putting down a deposit, I thought, I would just meet some of the people living in the building. I met one smiling neighbor outside and asked her to tell me how she liked living there. Her eyes caught fire, and she gnashed her teeth so hard you would have thought they were going to crumble. She spouted out that she was moving because of some of the unbearable goings-on, such as the landlady's frequent shouting at the tenants' children, ordering them not to play outdoors, and offering them candy as a reward for staying inside their apartments.

Since I had talked with the landlady and gotten a first impression of her as a pleasant and reasonable person, I was a little surprised and uncomfortable, but I rationalized the tenant's comments by thinking she must be grossly exaggerating.

An older woman, passing by, overheard the conversation and felt that she had to put in her two cents. Equally angry, she said she was also planning to move out as soon as she could find another place. She confirmed the first woman's story and added that the landlady demanded cash—no checks—from all the tenants, and if anyone did not pay at least one day *before* the rent was due, the landlady would bang on the door at all hours of the day and night until she had the cash in her hands.

Believe it or not, if that wasn't enough, a third woman, shaking out a blanket over her balcony, also heard the conversation, now getting louder and louder, and yelled, "If you want to know about that so-and-so that runs this place, I can tell you plenty of stories." As soon as she told about how the landlady rented out her paid-up apartment with all her furniture and personal belongings there while she was away on a few weeks' vacation, I sincerely thanked the three for helping me save my sanity, clutched my checkbook, and scurried away.

Preparing to Move In

Before taking an apartment, make sure that you have the landlord's commitment to repair any broken appliances and get the rooms in top shape. You may have to give a small deposit to hold the apartment—make it as small as possible—and never give the first month's rent without getting the landlord's promises in writing.

Do not move in or make any substantial payment before preparing your list specifying anything you want done and indicating anything worn or damaged before your occupancy. This has a dual purpose. In addition to getting the landlord to agree in writing to fix specified items, it obtains his or her acknowledgment of any poor conditions for which you are not responsible. This will protect you from a future false accusation and can take away the lessor's grounds for withholding your security deposit when you decide to move.

Try to have a friend or family member go with you to witness the condition of the apartment and its furnishings. List all the damaged, missing, and worn objects, and note the condition of each. For example, you might write down "bathroom wall—chipped tiles" or "green upholstered chair—cigarette burn on arm." Then show which of those, if any, the lessor agrees to replace, repair, or remove. Attach one copy to each copy of the lease or rental agreement, or have the landlord sign and date the list as a separate document, prefaced by the statement: "The lessor acknowledges said condition of the apartment before (your name) assumes tenancy, and agrees to make any necessary improvements indicated herein during the first month (or week) of the above-named tenant's residence at (print full address)."

To Lease or Not to Lease

Some landlords offer their rentals on a month-to-month basis without any written agreement, as long as you pay for the first and last months in advance. Renting without a lease can have its advantages, such as the opportunity to move at will, but it can also enable the landlord to raise the rent any amount at any time (without a signed statement to the contrary), impose new restrictions on the use of the dwelling, and evict you with short notice.

Any written agreement you make with an apartment manager or

rental agent is legally binding. This person acts on behalf of the owner as his or her legal representative, and any contract you have with the rental agent becomes in effect a contract with the owner. Signing such an agreement is the most important step in renting your apartment.

It is in this document that you should acquire the written permission for possible special circumstances, such as introducing children into the household, keeping a pet alligator, or bringing in an unrelated person of either sex. Taking such liberties for granted by omitting appropriate statements from the legal agreement or accepting the landlord's oral permission, which he or she later so innocently forgets, can cause you to move prematurely. Keep in mind that your landlord will often not be required by law to accede to your very reasonable demand unless you can produce a signed statement listing that demand or prove that such an agreement was made orally.

The "Straitjacket" Lease

The lease that the landlord or rental agent gives you to sign will probably try to overprotect the owner. If you are not careful, it can put a straitjacket on your life-style. You have no one to blame but yourself if you skim over such an important document without considering all the consequences.

Never sign a lease on the spot. Take a copy with you and study it thoroughly. If there are parts with legal jargon that you do not understand, visit the local office of a tenant organization, get a law student to explain them, or call the housing office at a nearby college or university and ask if it has a legal adviser who can answer a question or two. It may even be worth paying a small fee for a 10-minute visit with the legal aid society or a private attorney.

You might be under the gross misconception that you do not need to worry about signing a standard lease form as long as it does not have a lot of additions or deletions that might show the landlord wants to change clauses for his or her benefit. On the contrary, some of the worst leases that one-sidedly protect the landlord are printed forms without changes written in. Although a court in your state may not uphold some of the provisions listed, the judge may also take into consideration the fact that you presumably did read the document and did sign it.

Leasing Safeguards

Every lease should describe the rental and its location, give the dates of your proposed occupancy, and list the amounts of deposits and amount and frequency of rent payments. If some of your deposits are refundable, be sure a statement saying just that (along with any conditions of the lessor) is included.

In some places, you may be able to, if you wish, remain in the apartment on a month-to-month basis at the expiration of the lease. If so, include in the document a clause stating that right or the option to renew the lease, along with the provision that, in either case, all specified conditions remain in effect as long as you remain a tenant. (The landlord may go along with this, but will undoubtedly include in this provision one exception—his or her right to raise the rent at the end of the lease period.)

If the lease states that you accept the apartment exactly as it is, this means that the landlord may not legally be required to fix the sliding door that sticks or replace a missing windowpane, unless you write those in as exceptions. If you have prepared your list of necessary repairs as previously suggested, you can incorporate it by indicating on the lease itself that exceptions are listed on the attached sheet.

Many leases make certain types of your additions or improvements to the dwelling the property of the owner. Therefore, if you do not want to give up the expensive shutters you will add at a window or the wooden shelves you will install on a wall, you had better write in a statement that you will retain ownership of the shutters, bookshelves, and any other fixtures or objects you attach to a ceiling, wall, or counter. Other leases just require you to repair any wall damage if you remove such things as bookshelves.

Never assume that your painting the bathroom yellow or replacing the medicine chest with an aquarium will be acceptable to the landlord. Discuss major decorating plans with him or her and include a statement in the lease giving you the okay. This will prevent a future court action claiming that you have damaged the rental or altered its appearance without authorization.

You may assume that the quoted rent is for the entire term of your lease period, but many leases provide for increases should there be raises in taxes, utility rates, or the cost of living. Try to get the landlord to agree to a constant rent with no such exceptions.

Consider requesting that you be permitted the option of renewing the rental agreement at least once under the same terms (somewhat unlikely today), or that the payment of rent will go on a month-to-month basis after expiration of the lease unless another lease is negotiated before the current expiration. The former type of request offers the security that you can stay for a long time; the latter allows you to move at any time without financial penalty after the lease expires (unless you make a later decision to enter into another lease).

If something goes wrong with your heating unit, electrical wiring, or other facility after you move in, you may not be able to force a stubborn landlord to fix it if your lease includes a statement freeing him or her from responsibility for future repairs. See to it, if possible, that the lease does cover future repairs. It should also allow you to hold the owner responsible for injuries to you or your property sustained as a result of the lessor's negligence. For example, if the landlord does not fix a cracked ceiling, a chunk of which then falls on your head and causes a concussion, you will want to sue for damages.

You should definitely prepare for the possibility—however unlikely it may seem at the time—that another person will at some future date move in with you. Imagine that happening and then being told by the landlord that you can have no additional occupants!

Most leases state that only those persons named therein may reside in the house or apartment. If you are a single person who signs a rental agreement with such a clause, you may find that you must move when you get married, want to live with a friend or lover, or take in a sick relative. The same thing can happen if you have a child. Assure yourself of this option by asking the landlord to agree in writing not to withhold permission unreasonably to add an additional occupant(s) at a later time.

Some statements in leases may con you into paying for any legal fees connected with action taken by the owner to evict you or seize your property for nonpayment of rent. A clause may be included to get you to waive your right to a jury trial. This will favor the lessor since juries tend to be more sympathetic than judges to the tenant's point of view. Try to delete such clauses.

The landlord's right of entry should be restricted except in the case of an emergency. Provisions in some leases legally allow the landlord to barge in unannounced at any hour of the day or night for a variety of reasons, such as making a repair or showing your place to a prospective tenant. This could prove startling if you are awakened from a nap or walk out of your shower to find strangers wandering from room to room. Try to get a commitment that the landlord will give notice (say 24 hours ahead) before entering without a real emergency.

Frequently included in a leasing agreement is the statement that you will abide by all regulations. If these rules are printed on a separate page, they should be attached to the lease. Never sign a lease with such a general clause without having a written list of the regulations. The stipulations may include such areas as having guests and playing music during certain hours. Try to have deleted any condition that you feel will jeopardize your freedom.

One of the most unfair conditions still found in some leases is that you agree to comply with housing rules established by the owner or landlord at any future time. This means that after you have moved in, the lessor can arbitrarily dictate, for example, that neither using the pool after dusk nor having parties that last later than midnight will be allowed. If the lessor will not delete such a clause from the rental agreement, try to get him or her to provide for some type of arbitration in case you judge a future rule to be unfair.

The American Arbitration Association maintains offices in over 22 major cities across the nation. Contact the nearest one for guidelines on including an arbitration clause in your leasing agreement, or write to its headquarters at 140 West 51st Street, New York, New York 10020.

Just because a family member becomes seriously ill and you want to move closer to him or her, or the new job you got is 60 miles from your current residence, does not mean that you can automatically terminate your lease. To protect yourself from an insensitive landlord who holds that money is more important than compassion, you should request a clause stating that you have the right to terminate the agreement under certain emergency conditions, such as relocation of your job to another city or the death or severe illness of a family member.

In case you lose your income or must later leave your area for an extended period, but may not want to give up your residence, try to get a clause allowing you to sublet the rental.

After thoroughly going over the lease, discuss all proposed changes with the landlord. Every deletion and addition on a printed form agreement or every supplemental page should be accompanied by the signed initials of both you and the owner or his or her representative. If more room is necessary to add stipulations not found on the form agreement, attach an additional page headed "Addendum to Lease of (specify address); Dated (specify date of signature)."

Also make a notation on the first page of the lease that the addendum is agreed to by all signatories. Reasonable landlords will usually allow you to amend their prepared form to some degree. Be especially cautious of the totally inflexible lessor, who will probably be difficult to deal with on all future occasions.

Writing Your Own Rental Agreement

When there is no printed lease for the rental you want, draw up a simple agreement of your own, spelling out whatever you have gotten the landlord to agree to orally, including such statements as (1) the rent will be paid on a month-to-month basis, and not raised for any reason during the first six months (or year); (2) the landlord shall be responsible for the repair of certain furnishings (specify) and maintenance of the heater, air-conditioner, plumbing, and so on (specify); (3) the tenant shall be permitted to have children occupy the apartment and one or two pets; (4) the tenant may put hooks and brackets into any wall or ceiling for the purpose of hanging decorative or funcational objects of any kind; (5) the landlord gives permission for the tenant to order, and a company (specify) to install, cable television service in the tenant's rental at any future time; (6) the landlord approves the right of the tenant to bring in to live at any future time one (or two) additional relative(s) or unrelated person(s); and (7) the tenant shall have the right to sublet the apartment.

Many lessors will appear inflexible until they see they are losing a probable tenant. This is where some strategy can go a long way. Explain to the landlord that you feel the reasonable repairs and authorizations you have requested are absolutely necessary for your occupancy. Often this truth or bluff will work, and the landlord will sign your agreement.

With a stubborn landlord, you might decline the apartment after showing strong interest, and see if the lessor runs after you. If that does not work, go back after a short time and give him or her a second opportunity to change his or her mind. If the landlord will not concede, do not expect him or her to reverse the decision later. At this point you should consider either withdrawing some of the demands that the owner refuses to meet or looking elsewhere. It might be well to remember—depending on how much you want the apartment —that if you live in a large metropolitan area, there are probably many, many prospective tenants ready to snap up the best apartments.

After You Sign

If you have to add a condition or acquire special authorization from the landlord at any time after the lease or rental agreement has been signed, first obtain his or her oral permission and then write in the statement on the original document, date it, initial it, and have the landlord initial it. This often can be accomplished without any problem, since many landlords do try to be fair and are willing to fulfill most reasonable requests.

Assuming that you have taken some of the advice in this chapter and not blindly signed away all of your tenant's rights and protections, the lease or rental agreement is a legal document you can use to force the landlord to take certain action or prevent him or her from evicting you for an action of yours to which he or she has previously given written permission. The lease will stand up in court like any other contract; if the landlord refuses to fulfill his or her part of the agreement, the court can force compliance, and you may even collect damages.

Building Complaints

A potential problem with the landlord does not always have to be covered by a provision of the lease. Most cities or counties have some kind of housing code, a copy of which you can obtain from either the local government building department or health department. These two divisions employ investigators who are sent out in response to complaints that an apartment, home, or building does not meet minimum levels of designated health and safety standards.

Perhaps the leaky faucet, broken heater, or falling plaster that the owner refuses to fix will turn up as a law violation. If after checking the housing code or talking to an inspector over the phone, you believe that the conditions violate a local ordinance, write out your complaint detailing the poor conditions and their locations. If you can get other tenants to side with you and cosign the complaint or add one of their own, the action will have more force. Make several copies of the complaint and send one to the local regulatory body and one to the landlord.

Request that an investigator inspect the premises, and give him or her a copy of the complaint when he or she arrives. Be sure to write down the official's name, identification number (often on a badge), and telephone number.

Take the investigator around and point out all of the bad living conditions. He or she will make out a report stating which of the ordinances have been violated and then issue a repair order upon which the landlord must act within a specified time. Such problems as uncomfortable building temperature, unbearable odors, faulty elevators, unusable fire extinguishers, dirty halls, rodent infestation, and insufficient lighting often constitute housing code violations.

If the landlord does not initiate his or her own remedy or comply fully with the order, notify the office from which the investigator came. The next step will be taken by the housing code authority, which will probably ask the city attorney or district attorney to prosecute.

An increasing number of states will allow you to deduct an amount of money from your rent to cover repairs that the landlord refuses to make. In states such as New Jersey, the full value may be deducted; other states set specific limits. Massachusetts allows a maximum deduction of four months' rent, and in many states you cannot take off more than $100.

Ask the building investigator for a copy of the inspection report for your files. Armed with such findings, if your state does not allow you to pay for repairs out of your rent money, you may be able to withhold your rent legally until the owner does the required work. Consult with an attorney, legal aid society, or established tenant association in your state or city for specific guidelines.

The building investigator's report may come in handy if the landlord takes retaliatory steps to evict you and you have to go to court. At least 20 states have made an eviction based on such vengeance illegal, and the judge will not think positively of someone who tried to punish you for seeing that the law was enforced.

If the housing authority does not take decisive action and it is feasible for you to withhold your rent legally, be sure you have some proof that you can use to justify the action in case you are summoned to court. You do not necessarily have to have a signed report citing housing violations from a city or county inspector to elicit sympathy from a judge or jury. A cooperative witness who lives in your building can confirm your allegations, or plaster that has fallen from your ceiling or walls can be presented as evidence.

You also might take photographs of the affected area when no other avenues of proof are open. You also should open an "escrow account" at a bank and deposit all of your unpaid rent, so that it cannot be construed by the court that you are refusing to make payment simply to save the money or because you are financially unable to pay.

Good-bye Apartment

When a lease expires, you are expected to vacate the apartment, negotiate a new lease, or continue making monthly payments, which, if accepted by the landlord, indicates his or her agreement to allow you to remain on a month-to-month basis. All special agreements written into the lease no longer will hold unless you and the landlord sign a new lease or other written statement, or you previously have written into the lease a clause stating that conditions you specify will remain in effect after the lease expires for as long as you pay your rent. If the landlord refuses your rent after the lease expires, you may face eviction proceedings and/or loss of your security deposit if you do not move out immediately.

Getting Your Deposits Back

The security, cleaning, and key deposits often charged by a landlord may or may not be refundable depending on your leasing agreement and your fulfillment of conditions. The key and cleaning charges required by the lessor are often not refundable, but your return of the keys or complete cleaning of the rental when you move may warrant you a refund. Do not rely on verbal commitment for the return of these deposits, however.

Add stipulations to your lease or rental agreement that protect you from the landlord's possible change of heart. If the landlord is not willing to put his or her promises in writing, it is a sign that he or she may not be planning to follow through on them.

At least 13 states—California, Colorado, Delaware, Florida, Hawaii, Illinois, Louisiana, Maryland, Massachusetts, Minnesota, New

Jersey, New York, and Pennsylvania—have enacted statutes regulating the collection and refunding of security deposits. The landlord is usually required to refund your money within a specified time limit after you vacate the premises. He or she may, however, use all or a portion of this deposit to pay for necessary repairs over and above "normal wear and tear." Any money he or she does deduct, and the purpose for it, must be made known to you.

Your security deposit is usually refundable unless you have violated the conditions of the lease. If you have previously protected yourself by securing written permission to hang pictures and knick-knacks on the walls, for example, the landlord cannot legally keep your deposit because of marks left on the walls that he or she considers to be unnecessary damage to the building (unless, of course, your lease stipulates that you must repair such marks before leaving).

Although it is generally illegal to force the landlord to accept the security deposit in lieu of the last month's rent, many people do it. This is an effective way to see that the landlord does not unjustifiably withhold the refund. It also puts the burden on the landlord to sue you—rather than vice versa—if he or she feels that more money than average has to be spent to make repairs and clean the rental in preparation for the next tenant.

Many states now limit the amount that the landlord can hold as a security deposit, and some require that he or she pay you interest on these funds on a yearly basis or when the original amount is returned. If the landlord does not give you back your money within a reasonable time, you can complain to a local agency or take him or her to court.

Some states have had plenty of rental problems and are beginning to respond more systematically to resolving housing conflicts. New York City's Housing Court, for instance, was created by the New York State Legislature to hear housing cases exclusively relating to the health, safety, and general welfare of state citizens. The special court handles both civil and criminal violations and can impose fines and jail sentences on violators.

Friendly Relations

In addition to protecting yourself from an exploitative leasing agreement, the best advice you can follow is to develop friendly relations with your landlord. The greeting card at Christmas or the sharing of a book or humorous article can sometimes mean the difference in the landlord's decision to grant you permission to have a pet, return your security deposit in full, or let you out of your lease with less of a penalty. Communication and cooperation are two keys to good landlord-tenant relations. You should take a little extra effort to try to have it work for you.

LIVE WHERE YOU WANT TO

A man found a job in Elmhurst, Illinois, so he and his wife deemed it necessary to move into the general area. They found an apartment advertised to rent for $150 per month in a large complex in a suburb. After the man visited the property, the agent told him that the apartment of his choice actually rented for $160 and was not available after all. Furthermore, the agent stated that only two-bedroom apartments were vacant, renting for $200 a month.

This minority couple could have just dropped the matter, but they believed that their failure to secure the apartment was the result of racial discrimination, and they took the matter to the Leadership Council for Metropolitan Open Communities in Chicago. A Council investigator talked with the same agent about renting the apartment previously sought by the complainants, and was told there was available immediately a one-bedroom apartment for $150 per month.

A lawsuit was filed on behalf of the couple, and the case went to trial after attempts at a settlement failed. After one day's proceedings, the defendants agreed to give the couple the $150 apartment, comply with the Civil Rights Act of 1968, and place an ad, one Sunday a month in the *Chicago Tribune* rentals section, which included the phrase "Equal Opportunity Renter."

Formal Complaints

When you believe that illegal discrimination has occurred, you can obtain assistance on your complaint by contacting a local office of the U.S. Department of Housing and Urban Development (HUD) or writing to its headquarters: HUD, Fair Housing, Washington, D.C. 20410. This must be done within 120 days of the alleged act for this agency to be able to take action. Tell exactly what happened by filling out a Housing Discrimination Complaint Form (see Appendix 7) or giving all the information in a phone call or letter.

Your complaint will be taken under immediate consideration by HUD officials, who may investigate the matter to uncover additional facts to determine if the law has been broken. They may contact the party about whom you are complaining and attempt a settlement aimed at getting you the property, forcing the alleged violator to stop the illegal activity and begin an affirmative action program to try to overcome wrongful past discrimination, and obtaining a reimbursement of your expenses in pursuing the complaint and possible other compensation for your inconvenience and humiliation.

The HUD office may alternatively refer your problem to a human rights commission in your state to try to resolve the matter. If the commission does not act within a reasonable time or cannot effect satisfactory resolution, the handling of the complaint will revert to the federal agency. In cases where threats or acts of violence have occurred, HUD will quickly notify the Justice Department so that a criminal complaint can be initiated.

Sometimes HUD will recommend that you take your case to court. If you decide to pursue such legal action, you should try to get the HUD representative to help you prepare for the case, and possibly even obtain legal assistance. You also may contact the nearest local U.S. attorney, a private attorney, or a local legal aid society for help. The law enables you to pursue such civil rights action in federal court even if you have taken your complaint to HUD.

Sometimes in such cases a temporary restraining order is obtained to freeze any attempt on the part of the owner or agent to sell or rent the property in question. This will prevent the possibility of a third party, unaware of the alleged violation, from taking the property before a court action is completed.

Housing Discrimination

An act of Congress dating back to 1866 prohibits racial discrimination in the rental or sale of all housing. Newer laws supplement it by declaring illegal the practice of discrimination based on race, color, national origin, sex, religion, or marital status in most advertising of dwellings for rent or sale, actual selling or renting of housing or residential lots, financing of housing, and participating in the services of real estate firms.

You cannot legally be denied the chance to purchase or rent a dwelling, be quoted different sales or rental terms and conditions from someone else, or be misled to believe that a place of residence is unavailable when such activity is based on at least one type of discrimination covered by law. Blockbusting, also illegal, is the practice of trying to make a profit by talking owners into renting or selling

their housing by telling them that minority persons are moving into the area.

Federal law does not yet generally protect you from housing discrimination based on age, general appearance (such as a man's long hair), young children in the family, pets, military status, physical condition, sexual orientation, mental condition, or police record. A young person can do little, for example, if an elderly landlord chooses to rent only to senior citizens. The complainant is protected, of course, if he or she can show that such a legal reason for refusing to sell or rent is only a front for one of the areas of discrimination that does come under the law.

There has been growing concern in San Francisco in recent years that too much housing has been closed to families with small children. Several local legislators expressed concern that increasing numbers of families were moving out of the city. In fact, it was alleged that much state and federal support was withdrawn because public school enrollment went from 92,000 to 73,000 over a five-year period.

In June 1975 the San Francisco Board of Supervisors passed an ordinance banning discrimination against families with children (or planning to have children) in the renting and leasing of apartments and houses except by owners of buildings primarily intended for senior citizens. Similar statewide laws are now in effect in Arizona, New York, New Jersey, and Massachusetts.

To assist consumers with questions and complaints relating to housing discrimination, HUD set up a toll-free, 24-hour telephone hotline. If you live anywhere in the contiguous 48 states, except Washington, D.C., call 800–424–8590. In the Washington, D.C., metropolitan area, telephone 755–5490. The number of complaints received on the line increased from 84 in 1968 to 6,263 in 1973.

THE HYSTERIA OF MOVING

Moving can be hellish. When it comes to packing, you will probably do it yourself, but will not know where to start. Start anywhere, you say, with the confidence of a true Viking, and with the unrealistic optimism that if you just apply yourself, it will be a cinch to cram six days' work into two. Of course, you later realize you started in the wrong place, because you wake up the following morning in the usual mood for breakfast and have to assume, after a thorough search, that the silverware must have been one of the first things you packed away.

Then there are those things you plan to take over to the new residence yourself, so that the moving people can concentrate on the heavy furniture and appliances, cutting down on time and charges. But you forget that the sealed carton near the dresser is filled with books, not clothes, and you bend at the waist instead of the knees, throwing your sacroiliac out of whack. This is naturally at the very same time that your daughter gets one of those oversized lollipops stuck in her hair, causing her to cry with ever-increasing volume. After your daughter's haircut and a 10-minute break, you gather together all the remaining boxes.

On moving day, the children are off to school, everything seems to be packed up and in order, and you feel slightly calm. The movers arrive, get everything in the truck without breaking more than a dozen pieces of your finest Lennox china, and leave for the new address where you agree to meet them shortly.

You hurry out to your overstuffed Toyota, which this one time you wish were a Chevy van, and suddenly realize that all your keys are in the pocket of the jacket you had planned to wear today, but had put under the shoes and shirts and pajamas and pants at the bottom of the heaviest trunk, which took half an hour just to close, and are on their way to your new home without you. The front door of your old home is locked. The neighbors are either not talking to you or at Lake Tahoe. You don't have a dime.

Moving Hints

Although it would be an out-and-out lie to say that moving can be fun, it can be said that good planning is the key to a successful move. Following some simple suggestions for any residential move with a transfer company will help you to organize so that unnecessary troubles do not arise on that fateful day and any complaint you might later have to make will be backed up by evidence.

First, be certain that all agreements between you and the carrier are in writing. Request at least a note of confirmation, which states the date and time of the move, number of persons the company will send, rates, and an estimate of the total charges.

Prepare an inventory list of every item to be moved by the company. Boxes can be numbered so that at the destination you can quickly check off everything delivered. Note any damage you find on articles before the move so that you will not unjustly accuse the movers of negligence.

Before moving day, inquire about payment of the bill. Some companies require cash or a certified check to be given at the time of delivery, while others offer credit arrangements. This is important because a mover could withhold delivery until acceptable payment has been made.

Local Claims

Do not sign for the delivered items until you are sure everything has been received in good condition. If something is missing or damaged, mark down the lost item or describe the damage. If you do not note this information before the movers leave, the company may claim that loss or damage occurred after delivery.

Obtain a claim form from the movers before they leave or from the firm's claims office as soon as possible. Fill out the form completely and return it without delay so that processing can begin immediately. On a local claim, you should receive your money within a few weeks.

Local Moving Complaints

No matter where you move within your state, the intercity trucking company comes under regulation by your state's transportation, utility, or public service department or commission. Moving com-

panies are generally required to file tariffs with the state agency, just as intrastate commuter airlines and bus services do. Any complaint regarding poor service, fees charged, or proposed rate increases should be directed in writing to this agency.

Intrastate moving companies are often required to provide you with minimum liability insurance in case of any loss or damage to articles they transport. For example, the California Public Utilities Commission as of 1975 required a liability of at least 60 cents per pound per article to be included without extra charge to customers.

Find out what liability is furnished by the transfer company, and check this information with the state regulatory office. If you desire more coverage, you can purchase whatever extra insurance you feel is necessary.

Selecting an Interstate Mover

Consumers now have better tools than ever before to select the best mover for the job. Since February 14, 1975, every interstate moving company, upon request, has been required to give you a booklet entitled "Summary of Information for Shippers of Household Goods"—also available from the Interstate Commerce Commission (ICC)—which offers many helpful hints to assist you in a more trouble-free move.

An interstate mover also must provide you with a copy of its performance report, which includes about 15 items, such as the number of various types of complaints that have been received by the company from its customers and the number of complaints that have been settled. The report is useful in determining the mover's liability and the areas of service where customers have found the firm to be unsatisfactory.

Appendix 8 summarizes consumer information about the 20 largest moving companies. The data in this table, reprinted from *Consumer News*, the newsletter of the federal Office of Consumer Affairs, were not verified by the ICC. There has been much speculation that at least some of the data, provided to the ICC through performance reports from the moving companies, are unreliable. Therefore, consider the statistics only as general indications of the true picture. Supplement this information by asking friends and coworkers about their experiences with various movers.

Interstate Moving Hints

If you move outside your state, the interstate carrier you select to take your household goods is regulated by the Interstate Commerce Commission. This federal agency, established in 1887, is the oldest independent regulatory agency created by Congress. It makes sure that firms engaging in interstate surface transportation abide by various federal laws and Commission orders.

The ICC has set up strict rules that an interstate mover must follow in arranging for services and moving your household goods across state lines. The mover must comply with your request for a written estimate of the approximate weight of the load to be transported and total price of the move. No estimate is binding, and you will be charged for the actual weight of all articles loaded onto the truck.

Once you place your order for service with an interstate moving company, you must be provided with an order form that specifies locational information about all parties involved, the dates or approximate periods of time when pickup and delivery will be made, the location of the scale that will be used to weigh the shipment, the total estimated charges and method of payment, and whether or not you have requested special notification of charges. If the mover cannot pick up your goods on the date specified, the rescheduling must be called to your attention.

If you request before the move a special notification of charges and provide the carrier with the address and/or telephone number where you can be reached while your goods are in transit, the moving company, at its own expense, must immediately notify you or the person you designate, by telephone, telegraph, or in person, the total weight charges as soon as they are determined. You should make this request so that you will have an advance idea of the charges you will be required to pay.

When the movers arrive to pick up your shipment, they are required to furnish you with the bill of lading, a contractual agreement listing the tare (preloading) weight of the van. This certificate will contain your shipment number, dates of pickup and delivery, and a weight column. The tare weight must be entered before your goods are loaded. Be sure that the place of delivery is shown correctly and that you understand the printed liability statement. Before signing the bill of lading, list on its face any item of extraordinary value. Otherwise the company may not be liable for extra value. Take this receipt with you and have it on hand when your shipment is later weighed.

You will be required to sign an inventory list made out by one of the moving persons before the truck leaves. This list is to protect the mover from future claims. It is important that you or someone else in your household be present when the list is being compiled, so that discrepancies in the company representative's description of your belongings can be contested. Write a comment on the document for each item you dispute before signing.

The ICC makes an effort to assure that an accurate weight of the empty truck is made before it arrives to pick up your belongings. After your things are loaded on the vehicle, driven to the scale, and weighed, the total weight at that time, minus the weight of the empty van (and minus another household's articles if they are being moved in the same van), will equal the weight of the shipment for which you will be charged. Therefore, it is essential that you protect yourself from overcharging by being present when the loaded truck is weighed. There is no extra charge to you for this weighing.

The mover is obligated to let you observe the procedures at the weighing site. If there is another shipment besides yours on the truck, be sure that its weight is deducted and you are not charged for it. Some moving companies have been caught illegally increasing the weights of shipments by a variety of methods. The van's loaded weight should include the driver and all dollies, pads, and other equipment used in the move, but any other crew members may not be on the truck when it is on the scale. Make sure that no other objects are placed inside the van or driver's compartment to cause you to be overcharged. As soon as the weighing is completed, check the two weight copies given you against your bill of lading.

The operator of every van must carry a Vehicle Load Manifest, which you should request to see immediately after all weights have been taken. Compare your bill of lading number and the recorded weight information with the driver's manifest. If the figures do not match, demand that they be corrected immediately. Promptly report to the ICC any trouble or questionable activity in the weighing of the shipment or completion of documents.

If you have any reason to doubt the weighings of the truck while empty and then loaded, you have the right to request that the van be reweighed at the destination before and after it is unloaded. If you decide to order this procedure, which you may also witness, the company must base its moving charges on the lower of the two weights (assuming they are not identical). If the net weight after reweighing is at least 20 pounds below the billed net weight or at least 25 per cent over the estimated net weight, you do not have to pay for the reweighing; otherwise you do.

Whenever a certified scale is not available at any stage on the moving procedure, the transfer company is permitted to substitute the regular method of determining the weight with a calculation involving the addition of seven pounds for each cubic square of loaded van space. The mover is required to notify the ICC when forced to use this method, but you should also report such an occurrence to discourage unnecessary and wrongful substitutions.

Your interstate move is covered without any additional charge by a maximum liability of "60 cents per pound per article" if you write those words in the valuation statement on the bill of lading before you sign it. Such coverage does not afford full protection, however, so you may want to pay for the more complete protection, which, if you do not declare a total value of your goods before signing the bill of lading, amounts to $1.25 times the number of pounds in your shipment. The third option is to declare on the bill a total value of your goods that exceeds the standard valuation of $1.25 per pound. The latter two types of coverage afford reimbursement for the actual value of the damage or loss up to the insured maximum rather than the smaller limit per pound for each article. Any extra charges are for the higher liabilities only; no moving company is permitted to sell you an insurance policy.

Just as in the case of a delayed pickup date or time, the moving company must notify you of any major delay in reaching its destination and the new delivery time that has been set. It also is required to give you a reason for the delay along with information about the condition of your goods and where they are located. The mover cannot force you to accept delivery before the agreed date listed on your bill of lading. You should, however, be at the destination when the moving van arrives, since many companies will not wait to make delivery.

Get out your copy of the inventory list as soon as the goods are being unloaded, and check off each item. Do not sign any delivery papers until everything has been received. Articles that are taken apart by the movers should be reassembled at the new location, but the workers are not permitted to install fixtures or appliances.

If you find that an article is missing or damaged, note the problem on your copy as well as the driver's copy of the inventory list and any delivery receipt you are asked to sign. File your claim in writing with the company as soon as possible, and mention that the applicable notation was made on the inventory list at the time of delivery. If after the move, you discover that an item has been damaged or lost, you still have up to nine months to file a claim, but any delay may cause difficulties in reaching a fair settlement.

Interstate Claims

The Interstate Commerce Commission has received many consumer complaints accusing interstate movers of disclaiming responsibility for the damage or loss of valuable items that were moved but not listed according to the mover's instructions by the customer when signing the bill of lading. In response, an ICC proposal in 1975, now a law, requires transport companies to take responsibility for every item they move. This means that no contract can act to exempt the mover from this liability. The carrier maintains the right, however, to refuse to move any goods that are improperly packed.

The ICC has also established strict rules for the processing of interstate moving claims so that you are not left in the dark as to the status of a complaint. Upon receiving your claim, the moving company must acknowledge receipt within 30 days, and either pay, refuse to pay, or offer a compromise settlement within 120 days. If the firm cannot meet the established deadline, it must notify you in writing every 30 days thereafter of the reasons for the delay and where the claim stands. The Commission can assist you in speeding action on the handling of your claim, but it will not in any way involve itself in determining the validity of your particular claim and the mover's liability.

Interstate Moving Complaints

Tariffs, specifying such information as rates and services, are filed each year with the ICC 30 days before effective dates by these companies. Although the Commission does not set rates or consider every rate presented, it does intervene in some cases when competitors or consumers show significant dissatisfaction. Its stand is that the carriers should earn reasonable, but not excessive, profits.

If you want to protest the proposed rates of a carrier, you must submit your complaint in writing by sending the original and six copies to the ICC's Board of Suspension and one copy to the carrier. The Board will either allow the rates to go into effect or issue a suspension order that sets in motion an investigation and formal proceeding, which may include a public hearing. After all evidence is gathered, the Commission issues its final decision on whether the company may charge the fees.

No interstate mover may legally discriminate against or in favor of any customer. Once its rates are set, written onto its tariff, and filed with the ICC, they become binding. Every interstate mover is required to maintain in its office a copy of its tariff for public inspection during its business hours. If you check and find that you are being charged more than the rate limits dictate, inform the ICC.

Whether you want to make a complaint about rates, service, or any other matter, the ICC welcomes your comments in order to keep informed about industry trends and changes in company practices. You should use the postpaid questionnaire at the end of one of the booklets given to you by your interstate mover.

If you do have any complaint or question about the practices of a moving company, write or call the Commission, which is one of the few federal agencies set up to accept toll-free calls from anywhere in the contiguous 48 states. Telephone 800–424–9312 (or Washington, D.C., area residents only, 343–1100). The mailing address for the complaints office at the ICC headquarters is: Bureau of Operations, Interstate Commerce Commission, Washington, D.C. 20423.

Chapter 7

LAND, SEA, AND AIR EVERYWHERE

From the simple Egyptian cargo boats used as early as 3000 B.C. to the supersonic planes of today, means of travel have depended on human ingenuity for technological development. We have made machines to transport us along streets, over mountains and deserts, across oceans, and to the moon. We have moved ourselves and our belongings with bicycles, motorcycles, trolleys, subways, cars, buses, trains, boats, balloons, airplanes, blimps, and spaceships.

With the population explosion and an increasingly mobile society, we have found the need to organize and regulate many forms of transportation. Although it is now relatively easy for the average person to travel, problems still arise that hinder the smooth movement of people and goods. This chapter will help you to cope with the variety of problems disrupting daily travel.

All United States companies providing transportation services—by land, sea, or air—to the public for intra- and intercity travel are required to file tariffs with appropriate local, state, or federal regulatory agencies, including such information as rates, routes, and financial liability. No such firm may engage in discriminatory practices. If you feel that a transportation service is promoting unfair competition or otherwise acting outside the public interest, lodge your complaint with the appropriate government regulatory body mentioned in this chapter. Before centering on public transportation problems, let us first look at the vehicles many of us own and depend on for our daily travel needs.

THE POLLUTION-FREE VEHICLE

The bicycle has become a popular mode of intracity transportation because it requires no fuel, provides the rider with good exercise, and does not add to air pollution. The vehicle can, however, be dangerous, and the U.S. Consumer Product Safety Commission (CPSC) estimates that in fiscal 1976, 465,860 injuries associated with bicycles were treated in hospital emergency rooms nationwide. Each year about a million people are involved in bike accidents, 17 percent of which are caused by equipment failures.

Accidents have been attributed to such problems as mechanical and structural defects, loss of operator control, and entanglement of a hand, foot, or clothing in the bicycle. The Commission, in response to many complaints, issued a mandatory bicycle safety standard (which took effect in 1976) to protect children and adults.

Bicycle Safety Standards

The new regulations require manufacturers to meet certain specifications for the performance and construction of the bike frame, steering system, wheels, and brakes. Reflectors imparting higher visibility at night must be placed on both sides, the front, the back, and on the pedals. Exposed sharp edges are not allowed. There is even a mandatory "date of manufacture," which must appear on an attached label to alert the consumer as to when the bike was produced and whether or not it incorporates the new safety standards.

Bike Complaints

If you want to comment on the new regulations, to report the illegal manufacture or sale of bicycles not meeting the new standards—the CPSC has the authority to ban these—or to alert the government to other problems involving the safety of the bicycle, write to the Consumer Product Safety Commission, Washington, D.C. 20207. If you live in Maryland, you can call the Commission toll-free at 800–492–2937. If you live anywhere else in the contiguous 48 states, dial 800–638–2666. Complaints relating to the safety of tricycles, roller skates, wagons, skateboards, and other children's transportation products should also be directed to the Commission.

Bikeways

The problem of bicycling in the city is especially hazardous in densely populated areas where automobile and bus traffic dominates the streets. Students have petitioned and gotten "bikeways" at many colleges and universities, and even local governments are beginning to respond to public pressure for the accommodation of the many bicycle enthusiasts. In 1974 Los Angeles banned Sunday parking along a network of main streets to provide residents at least one day a week with a hassle-free scenic bicycle route. New York City has designated times for bicycle-only traffic in Central Park. If you and your family or friends want to use your bicycles safely more often, write or call your city manager, mayor, council, board of supervisors, or recreation department to express your community's need for bicycle parking facilities and safer access to the streets for bicycling.

DEALING WITH YOUR AUTOMOBILE, DETROIT, AND THE OIL COMPANIES

In recent years, many consumers, because of fuel shortages, have sought smaller automobiles and higher mileage. The percentage of small-car sales has increased, and some plants producing full-size "gashogs" have closed down or converted their facilities to accommodate smaller car production.

Gas Mileage

The Environmental Protection Agency issues an informative annual, "Gas Mileage Guide for New Car Buyers," which, in the first edition for 1977, listed the EPA's wide range of fuel economy test results for 465 domestic and imported car models and light-duty truck models. The Volkswagen Rabbit Diesel topped all others for combined city and highway driving with 44 miles per gallon, while the Dodge Royal Monaco, Dodge Monaco, Plymouth Grand Fury, and Plymouth Fury (all with 8-cylinder 440 engines) tied in combined city and highway driving for the lowest mileage at 11 miles per gallon. The results were obtained by testing the machines indoors on a chassis dynamometer, a machine that simulates vehicle operation under a variety of driving conditions. The reported figures are only estimates and give no guarantee as to the actual mileage you will get while actually driving the vehicle; much depends on your particular driving habits. In any case, the results of these mileage studies can be of significant help in planning your purchase of a car or truck.

You can obtain the latest edition of this guide (or one specifically for car buyers in California) without charge by writing to Fuel Economy, Office of Public Affairs, U.S. Environmental Protection Agency, Washington, D.C. 20460, or to Consumer Information, Public Documents Distribution Center, Pueblo, Colorado 81009. You will be made aware of many other worthwhile materials by requesting in your letter to the latter address that you be put on the mailing list for consumer information.

Odometer Law

Many recent and proposed laws will protect the consumer in purchasing a new or used car. The Motor Vehicle Information and Cost Savings Act of 1973 has made tampering with an automobile odometer (which indicates accumulated mileage) a federal offense. (The statute excludes cars over 25 years old, new cars sold between dealers, and large trucks.) It is illegal for a seller of a car to misrepresent the mileage by turning back, disconnecting, or in any way altering the odometer.

It is also unlawful to operate a motor vehicle that has a disconnected or malfunctioning odometer with the purpose of establishing a false mileage record. If the device must be replaced or repaired and cannot be reset to show the correct total mileage to date, it must be set to zero, with a notice showing the date of repair and previous mileage (or other date for calculating the true mileage) permanently attached to the left door post of the vehicle.

An automobile owner must also abide by this law. You, the buyer of a car—or the purchaser of a car you are selling—must be given a Disclosure Statement containing the following information: (1) the exact mileage recorded on the odometer or, if the meter is inaccurate, a statement that the correct mileage is not known; (2) the date ownership is transferred; (3) the seller's name and address; (4) the car's identification number, license plate number, year, make, model, and body type; and (5) a statement that the seller understands his or her statutory civil liability for providing false information. You should report a violation of this law to the local U.S. attorney or the National

Highway Traffic Safety Administration, U.S. Department of Transportation, Washington, D.C. 20590.

Under the law you must file a civil action in a state court or federal district court for $1,500 or three times any damages you suffer, whichever is greater, simply by establishing that the odometer reading was wrong and the seller or his or her agent made a false Disclosure Statement or failed to disclose the error with the intent to defraud. In such a suit you will not be required to prove damages.

Auto Sales

The Federal Trade Commission enforces guidelines requiring manufacturers to follow standards of model year identification for all new cars. The 1975 rules were put into effect because some of the automakers were representing new vehicles unsold at the end of the year as being the upcoming year's model. Sometimes the model year was determined by the date an automobile was sold rather than the date of manufacture. Every auto manufacturer must now affix to every vehicle a label that identifies the month and year of manufacture. If you are subjected to a deceptive sales practice relating to the model year of a new car, contact the nearest FTC office or write the Federal Trade Commission, Washington, D.C. 20580.

Auto Ads

The advertising of exaggerated gas mileage claims has necessitated state and federal regulations to protect the consumer from fraudulent and misleading sales propaganda. In 1974 the Federal Trade Commission took action to curtail alleged false advertising by some of the top names in the auto industry. It reached a negotiated settlement with General Motors, which had stated in ads that the Cadillac Eldorado was superior in gas mileage to 73 other models. Basing its opinion on Environmental Protection Agency tests, the FTC claimed that the ad was deceptive because in many cases some samples for listed cars got higher mileage than both of the Eldorados tested.

The Commission also filed a formal complaint against Ford, involving the alleged misleading of consumers by ad claims implying that the average driver might get up to 32 miles per gallon in cross-country driving of Ford and Mercury cars. The FTC charged Chrysler with advertising that one of its small car lines got higher

mileage than a Chevrolet Nova, without revealing that the comparison was unfavorable between an eight-cylinder Chrysler model and
an eight-cylinder Nova. In 1975 the FTC also began a rule-making
proceeding to establish a general trade regulation to protect the public from misleading fuel economy claims made in the advertising and
promotion of automobiles. (See Chapter 11 for information about
making an advertising complaint.)

The EPA has asked the cooperation of auto manufacturers in its
Labeling Program, designed to provide the consumer with on-the-
spot fuel economy information for each new car being considered for
purchase. The automakers have their choice of two types of official
stickers. Both types list basic information comparing weight classes,
range of miles per gallon, average miles per gallon, and fuel costs.
The "specific label," in addition, shows the actual EPA mileage test
results for the vehicle; the "comparative label" is more general and
simply shows the weight category of the car. Until use of the stickers
becomes mandatory, you should secure complete fuel economy information from the EPA annual guide before making your decision
on the purchase of a car.

Auto Safety Standards

One agency working toward the safer operation of motor vehicles is the U.S. Department of Transportation's National Highway
Traffic Safety Administration (NHTSA). It was created in 1970 and,
in addition to enforcing the odometer tampering law, is responsible
for investigating the causes of and means of prevention for traffic
accidents and setting safety standards for motor vehicles.

An important element in the fight to reduce traffic deaths is the
enforcement of NHTSA safety standards, which apply to both
American-made and imported vehicles for sale. The first standard to
go into effect pronounced specifications for the manufacture of seat
belt assemblies for cars, trucks, and buses. Since then, many more
standards have been ordered relating to such areas as windshield
wiping and defrosting, transmission shift sequence, hydraulic brakes,
reflecting surfaces, tires, hood latch systems, child seating systems,
motorcycle controls, tires provided on new cars, and accident impact
protection. Other standards require manufacturers to provide to first
purchasers of motorcycles and passenger cars information on tire
reserve load, acceleration, passing ability, and stopping distance, and

to report safety-related defects to both the NHTSA and automobile warranty holders.

Recalls

The statutory authority granted to the NHTSA (and to a former safety bureau) has directly or indirectly accounted for the recalling of over 26 million cars in the United States since enactment of the Highway Safety Act of 1966. After an investigation into an alleged defect or pattern of malfunctions, this federal agency has ordered the recall of vehicles for correction of the problem. The procedure for officially ordering such a measure is often unnecessary since, according to an NHTSA spokesman, "foreign and domestic manufacturers alike have been persuaded that voluntary vehicle recall is preferable to the adverse image of a manufacturer required by statute to notify the owner that his product was defective at manufacture."

The Department of Transportation issues a Monthly Defect Investigatory Cases Report with information about investigations opened, pending, and closed. For instance, just a few of the many subjects listed as being under investigation in the January-February 1974 report were possible problems with leaking while filling the tank of 1971 and 1972 models of the Triumph TR-6, breakage at the hub of the steering wheel in 1969 and 1970 models of the Chevrolet Impala, malfunctioning brake proportioning valve, which caused the rear wheel to lock under normal braking conditions, in 1970–72 models of the Plymouth Valiant and the Dodge Dart ("A" body), and failing brakes with the breakage of drums in 1966–74 Ford school buses. In 1974 a two-year investigation of the B.F. Goodrich Company's Space Saver Tire was ended; the NHTSA said the tire could explode and cause injury or death if the tire bead did not seat properly upon inflation. The same year saw General Motors announce that it would repair without charge damage resulting from engine overheating in as many as 1.3 million Chevy Vegas sold from 1970 to 1974. Pollution control system defects caused Ford Motor Company to recall 282,000 of its 1973 and 1974 models, and Chrysler to call back 825,000 cars. In 1976 Ford again made a recall, this time for 35,000 Mustangs, because of problems with the pollution control mechanisms. In the same year, the EPA brought to the Justice Department for appropriate legal action a case involving thousands of Chrysler Plymouths and Dodges that allegedly exceeded federal standards for air pollution emissions.

Recall Information

What if you do not hear anything about the order issued for a recall of the type of car you drive? The recall might not be well publicized, you might be vacationing in Europe, or the dealer might have only an old address with which to contact you. How about your going out to buy a used car? How can you determine if the automobile has ever been recalled and, if it has, whether or not that specific vehicle has been corrected?

A federal service now gives out recall information to anyone requesting it. Call 202–426–0670 or write the Office of Consumer Services (N40-41), National Highway Traffic Safety Administration, 400 Seventh Street N.W., Washington, D.C. 20590. Provide the year, make and model, and vehicle registration number of any automobile, and the office will inform you of any recall action that has involved that car. If the recall was ordered after January 1, 1974, this agency also will tell you if the defect in the car has been fixed.

Once a recall has been instituted, the manufacturer is legally responsible to repair the safety defects at no charge to the car owner. If you are unsure about the status of your car, play it safe by contacting the above office for more information. It could save your life!

If you drive a car and discover a safety-related problem or you have pertinent information that may be helpful in a case under agency investigation, call in or mail your comments to the nearest office of the National Highway Traffic Safety Administration (listed in the White Pages under United States Government—Transportation Department of) or contact its headquarters: NHTSA, U.S. Department of Transportation, Washington, D.C. 20590. (Hopefully, this agency will sometime set up a national toll-free hotline to accept consumer comments and complaints.)

Your providing such information is a way of helping to protect yourself, contributing to highway safety, and saving lives. The NHTSA will acknowledge your complaint letter and refer it to the Office of Defects Investigation and Standards Compliance, where a copy will be sent to the manufacturer along with a cover letter asking for a report of action taken or contemplated on your behalf. The agency thereby reminds the company of its responsibility to make sure its products perform adequately and safely in the marketplace. If no reply is received or the matter is not satisfactorily handled, the agency will initiate action.

You may obtain from the NHTSA without charge helpful Fact

Sheets giving safety and performance information on such specific subjects as tires, safety belts, hydraulic brake fluids, minibikes, and importing foreign cars.

Nonsafety Problems

Problems relating to automotive service, warranties, and dealer practices are common throughout the country. The National Highway Traffic Safety Administration also accepts these types of complaints, although it has no statutory consumer protection authority over such problems. Through its Consumer Response System, the agency claims that about 75 percent of the many thousands of safety and nonsafety complaints it handles each year are taken to a satisfactory conclusion.

Complaints of auto problems not related to safety often may be successfully handled by contacting your local or state consumer bureau (see Chapters 12 and 13), calling upon a local or state law enforcement agency, or, in a monetary dispute, filing a small claims suit (Chapter 12).

Auto Repairs

The growing number of auto repair complaints throughout California caused the formation of that state's Bureau of Automotive Repair in the Department of Consumer Affairs. Based in Sacramento, the Bureau registers car repair dealers; licenses headlights repair, brake adjustment, and vehicle pollution control stations and their repair persons; requires the posting of an official list of customer rights in all auto repair shops; and maintains a toll-free, statewide hotline (800–952–5210) for complaints to be received on any weekday. Michigan, New York, the District of Columbia, and Montgomery County in Maryland also license auto repair shops and/or mechanics. Enforcement of the laws of these and other states often involves the sending of undercover investigators to stations where alleged fraud or a pattern of negligent servicing has been found, and criminal prosecution is sometimes undertaken.

Service Directory

According to the National Institute for Automotive Service Excellence (NIASE), you can keep your car from getting into the hands of mechanics who do not know what they are doing. The Institute provides competency testing and certification to mechanics throughout the country on a voluntary basis. Certifications are given in the following categories of automobile service: engine repair, automatic transmission, manual transmission and rear axle, front end, brakes, electrical systems, heating and air conditioning, and engine tune-up.

A mechanic may become certified in any one or a combination of the above areas. If all eight tests are taken and passed, the person is certified as a General Automobile Mechanic. The Institute also certifies specialists in body repair as well as painting and refinishing. Mechanics receiving certification display it at their place of business for your inspection.

The NIASE publishes an annual directory of over 9,000 dealers, service stations, specialty shops, independent garages, and other establishments employing certified mechanics. You can obtain a copy by sending a check or money order for $1.95, payable to NIASE, to the National Institute for Automotive Service Excellence, 1825 K Street N.W., Washington, D.C. 20006. To expedite handling, print "NIASE Directory" on the face of the envelope. Keep in mind that certification indicates a level of competence and does not relate to the ethical standards of the mechanic.

Auto Insurance

The auto insurance industry is huge and not without its bunko artists and unfair business practitioners. Most states, in fact, have set up offices to investigate allegedly fraudulent operations and the inequitable handling of claims. If a company violates the terms of your auto policy, refuses to pay the full benefits you feel are due, or unreasonably delays appropriate action, contact your state's department of insurance. If there is no separate state agency for such problems, you may find an insurance division listed under your state's department of commerce, department of consumer affairs, or office of the attorney general. A civil court action is another possibility when a claim is involved and your other action has not produced satisfaction.

Be cautious about a company that advertises an offer to insure its customers at the lowest rates of any company or to accept high-risk drivers even when they have been turned down elsewhere. If you are the victim of false or misleading car insurance advertising, complain to the Federal Trade Commission (see Chapter 11). If you suspect fraud in the operations of a mail order insurance company, notify the U.S. Postal Inspection Service by letter and include a copy of any applicable correspondence and the envelope in which it was received (see Chapter 9).

Octane Ratings

Octane ratings have been the subject of much confusion among consumers. One gas station may list a "research octane" number, while another displays a "motor octane" level for a similar grade of gas, and still another dealer may not display any rating at all. An octane rating is simply the measure of a gasoline's resistance to engine knock.

Octane ratings vary in different parts of the country, since a lower octane is required at higher altitudes. Octane is generally lowest in regular or economy gas and highest in premium grades. Laboratory tests to determine the research octane of a gasoline involve running engines at low speeds, which tends to give high numbers, such as 94 for one sample of a regular grade. A motor octane rating, such as 86 for a sample of regular gas, is found by testing engines at higher speeds with resulting lower numbers. To standardize the system for rating gasoline octane, a new "octane number" (the motor octane rating plus the research octane rating divided by two) has been used.

In 1975 President Gerald Ford vetoed legislation that would have extended price and other controls on gasoline. The veto dealt a severe blow to the consumer movement. Besides allowing prices to increase in a depressed economy, the action curtailed new Federal Energy Administration regulations that required the posting of octane ratings and limited to one cent per gallon the difference in price between regular and unleaded gasoline. However, a compromise bill passed by Congress and signed by the President continues some controls over all petroleum products. These controls contain no proviso for limiting the price between leaded and unleaded gas, and they are scheduled to be phased out by 1979.

Today all gas stations throughout the country are required by federal regulation to post the octane number for each grade of gas they sell. If you find a station that does not post octane ratings, telephone the nearest Federal Energy Office or write to the Federal Energy Administration, Washington, D.C. 20461. It will send an investigator to the station to make sure the ratings are posted. Penalties will be administered to any station refusing compliance.

The Federal Trade Commission issued a trade regulation rule in 1972 that would have made the nonposting of octane ratings an unfair trade practice, but the effective date of the ruling was delayed by a court challenge. If the court upholds the rule, the FTC will assume the responsibility of enforcing octane disclosures, and your complaint should be directed to that agency. Write the Federal Trade Commission, Washington, D.C. 20580.

Unleaded Gas

Beginning with 1975 models, to meet new federal pollution control standards, many new cars have been equipped with an emission control device called a catalytic converter, which is also designed to give better mileage. Such cars are made to run only on unleaded gasoline, and repeated use of leaded gas can destroy the usefulness of the converter and necessitate its replacement at an estimated cost of at least $100.

To meet the need for increased supplies of fuel for the new cars, the Environmental Protection Agency issued an order requiring every service station that sold over 200,000 gallons of fuel in 1971, or any subsequent calendar year, to carry unleaded gas. Stations in less densely populated areas were also included, so that of the July 1, 1974 effective date, about half of all stations nationwide had in operation at least one pump containing no-lead gasoline.

Nozzles on no-lead pumps must be smaller than those on pumps dispensing leaded gas to fit the new government-ordered, small gas tank openings. This is supposed to prevent the mistake of putting leaded gas into a tank labeled "unleaded gas only," a violation subject to a $10,000 fine. You can protect consumers by notifying the nearest EPA office of alleged infractions concerning unleaded gasoline. If this agency does not have an office near you, write the Environmental Protection Agency, Washington, D.C. 20460.

Auto Traveling Tips

Many consumers are economizing by replacing plans for Caribbean cruises and trips to Europe with less expensive auto traveling. Traveling to new towns and cities can be an exciting and educational experience, and you certainly do not want anything interfering with your good time.

Good planning is the key to a successful road trip. Have an adequate selection of maps covering all the places you plan to visit, as well as the surrounding areas. Gas stations may supply travelers with state and local maps, but this service has been discontinued by many stations. If you are a member of the Automobile Association of America (AAA), that organization will indicate routes and supply maps free of charge.

Do not be fooled into thinking that you can always find accommodations at any place at any time of the day or night. Popular sites can become overcrowded during holiday weekends and the winter or summer months. It is not uncommon, for instance, to drive to the Monterey Peninsula, on the California coast, an area covered with hotels and motels, and not find a single vacancy in hours of searching.

Appendix 3 contains the nationwide toll-free reservation numbers of many hotel/motel chains. Auto clubs and travel agents also can provide you with confirmed reservations. Be sure to write down the name of the person taking your reservation. At government-owned forest and park campsites, you may be required to pay a fee and make your reservations many months in advance.

Before leaving on your trip, go into a full service gas station and have everything checked: tire tread and pressure, oil, water or coolant level, battery, and so on. Otherwise, you may need help in the middle of a desert, forest, or mountain area where there is no service station. Furthermore, if you will be traveling on many highways or freeways, a check can protect you against a blowout, and possibly a serious accident.

Many oil companies and automobile clubs provide helpful services to the traveling motorist. The nature and number of services vary from company to company and include everything from route planning to emergency roadside services and insurance. Appendix 9 is a comparison of services among some of the major firms and clubs in the United States.

One of the worst problems while traveling is the loss of your wallet or purse, luggage, eyeglasses, or other valuable items. There are several companies that register credit cards and valuables in case of loss. Some of these are mentioned in Chapter 8.

Another company that especially caters to travelers is the International Luggage Registry (ILR), P.O. Box 11860, Reno, Nevada 89510. For $5 a year (free with enrollment in the International Charge Card Registry), you get a few dozen stickers bearing your initials and a nine-digit code number. You affix these to all your important possessions, from an expensive coat to a pair of skis. When you lose something that carries the distinctive sticker, you (and hopefully the finder) call the Registry. ILR can often reunite an item with its owner in less than an hour.

You may think that you have done all the planning for your upcoming trip, and then remember you have a dog that has to be taken care of. You might consider taking the pet along with you now that there is a directory listing thousands of hotel and motel accommodations throughout the country where your dog will be welcomed. "Touring with Towser" is available for $1. from Gaines TWT, P.O. Box 1007, Kankakee, Illinois 60901. The guide also gives tips on traveling with your pet.

Some states have special regulations concerning traveling with pets. If you plan to cover areas in North Carolina, you had better reserve kennel space in advance. It is against the law in that state to bring a dog into a hotel or motel room used for sleeping purposes. You cannot bring a pet into Hawaii unless it has been quarantined for 120 days.

LEAVING THE DRIVING TO THEM

Buses, taxis, and subways have an important role in transporting many people in our nation's cities. Public transportation falls into two main categories, one in which the service has been created or is wholly owned, operated, or controlled by a local or state government body, and the other in which it is privately operated and often owned by shareholders. For either type there is always a local, state, or federal agency to handle a variety of complaints, such as rate increases, poor service, lack of service, overcharging, and unfair or inadequate handling of a liability claim.

Be sure to make notes of the date, time, and place of any problem; any witnesses; the vehicle number or license plate number; the name of the driver; and details of exactly what happened and what was said.

Intracity Travel Complaints

Companies that operate taxis, buses, and ambulances with routes primarily within the boundaries of a city or county area are often required to obtain franchises or permits, which may dictate some conditions. These firms must follow fair business practices and are sometimes subject to fines or other punishment for violations of their permits and for policies that go against the public interest. For example, the City of Los Angeles charges taxi companies a franchise fee based on a percentage of their annual gross revenues. The city may raise the percentage that a company must pay if enough complaints are received by the Public Utilities and Transportation Department to indicate that the firm has provided unsatisfactory service.

The offices of city and county departments that issue permits or regulate intracity transportation services go by many names and are often not listed in the telephone directory. If you do not get satisfaction after complaining to the company and cannot find a transportation regulatory body under local government listings, contact the nearest city hall or county switchboard for referral to the appropriate office.

Other transportation services, especially costly rapid transit systems, are created by state and local governments. These municipally operated services are often headed by an elected or appointed regulatory commission or supervisory board of directors. If you have a complaint against one of these services, you should contact the customer relations office of the system or, for a more serious matter or one involving rate increases, the board or commission office. The service's public information office or your local government's administrative offices can probably refer you to the address and phone number.

Intrastate Travel Complaints

Intrastate trucking, delivery, bus, train, and mass transit services between various cities are usually regulated by a state agency called the Public Utilities Commission or the Public Service Commission (see Appendix 4). These agencies process complaints regarding strictly intrastate carriers on such problems as crowding, reckless driving, nonadherence to schedules, and lost or delayed goods. In the case of lost or damaged property, the state regulatory body cannot adjudicate claims—this is left to the courts—but like the other local, state, and federal agencies, it can sometimes successfully exert "moral suasion."

One example of how a state agency used moral suasion and acted firmly in the public interest was related by a spokesman for California's Public Utilities Commission (PUC). The case concerned a soldier who was transferred to the Fort Ord Army Base. He purchased a Greyhound bus ticket and traveled from Los Angeles to Monterey with a duffel bag containing all his possessions. Upon reaching his destination, the soldier was told his bag could not be found. He complained to the bus company and, when his belongings were not found within a reasonable time, was forced to purchase replacements. Several months elapsed before Greyhound located the bag, which had been negligently tagged for San Luis Obispo and found in Stockton. Greyhound reportedly wanted to settle the case for $15! The soldier expressed his surprise and disgust with the company, saying that the bag and its contents were no longer of any use to him and he saw no point in even picking up the recovered property. Greyhound withdrew the $15 offer, and the soldier contacted the state's Public Utilities Commission. After an investigator contacted a company representative and told him that the matter had not been handled fairly, the claim was finally settled for a much higher amount.

The California PUC investigation of another claim against Greyhound uncovered a surprise. The investigator knew that any public transportation carrier in interstate travel is normally required to insure every piece of baggage for $50 and that the California State Legislature in 1971 passed a more strict law raising the carrier liability in intrastate travel to $250–500 per piece of luggage in case of damage or loss. He discovered that from 1971 to the time of this 1974 complaint, Greyhound had in effect ignored the state law by neglecting to correct the liability statement on tickets and by charging extra fees to California passengers requesting insurance over $50 per piece.

The Commission representative wrote to Greyhound and asked an official to change the liability statement on tickets. Greyhound stated that it was operating within the law and did not think it reasonable for the company to replace tickets used nationwide with special ones for use in California. The investigator responded that the company was not handling the matter fairly and should at least post signs at its bus terminals to insure public awareness of consumer rights guaranteed by state law. He also suggested that the company stop making allegedly illegal liability charges.

When Greyhound did not take any positive action on the Commission representative's suggestion, the Los Angeles investigator, realizing that the PUC did not have authority to enforce the state's civil code, assisted an attorney from the Legal Aid Society of San Diego in a class action suit against the company. The purpose of the suit was to effect payment of one traveler's loss plus court costs, reimbursement to those persons unlawfully charged excess insurance fees, posting of the provisions of the state law in terminals, printing of the correct liability limits on ticket stubs and envelopes (possibly in both English and Spanish), and requirements for future good-faith searches for lost baggage. (The case was still in court at the time of book publication.)

Personal Injury

If you sustain a personal injury on any form of public transportation, you should immediately notify the company and then promptly contact an attorney. Unless the injury is minor and you have no desire to pursue the claim further, do not sign any settlement statement that may later bar you from taking legal action against the carrier. Make a record of all the appropriate information, and a copy for your lawyer. The legal remedy under some circumstances may even involve a suit against the city or state having control over the service.

Routes and Rates

Persons living outside the mainstream of city traffic sometimes complain about not having access to municipally operated public transportation. Consider petitioning city officials or local politicians to effect the establishment of at least one route that will connect your district with the other city or county areas.

Formal complaints regarding high fees or rate increases by both publicly and privately owned transportation systems are accepted by the appropriate governing authority. Many agencies will accept such a complaint by any individual; others require the filing of a petition by a group of 10 to 25 consumers. If you want to file a formal complaint, call or write the appropriate regulatory office for any guidelines that should be followed in preparation of the complaint. Some agencies may require the filing of a specific form or the use of certain legal jargon.

Interstate Bus Complaints

The operations of companies providing interstate bus transportation are regulated by the Interstate Commerce Commission (ICC). When you buy a ticket for a bus ride that crosses state lines, you are automatically covered (for no extra charge) with a minimum of $50 liability insurance from the carrier for each piece of baggage.

Complaints regarding fees, scheduling, reservations, passenger comfort, and unsatisfactorily handled claims should be directed to the nearest regional office of the ICC or its headquarters in Washington, D.C. 20423. The Commission has the power to take a passenger carrier to court or levy a civil forfeiture (monetary fine) against it. Problems with regard to bus driver competence, accidents, transportation of hazardous materials, or bus carrier vehicle safety should be detailed in a call or letter to the Bureau of Motor Carrier Safety, Federal Highway Administration, U.S. Department of Transportation, Washington, D.C. 20590.

Train Troubles

Legislation passed by Congress in 1970 gave the National Railroad Passenger Corporation (AMTRAK) the authority to manage the operation of all intercity passenger trains (except commuter lines) under railroad contracts. Complaints regarding track conditions, the transportation of hazardous materials by rail, and the general safety of AMTRAK and the few other interstate passenger trains should be directed to the Federal Railroad Administration, U.S. Department of Transportation, Washington, D.C. 20590. The Environmental Protection Agency, Washington, D.C. 20460, also has jurisdiction over interstate transporting of hazardous materials.

AMTRAK trains carried 14.5 million passengers over 3.8 billion miles in 1973 alone. With the renewed interest in passenger rail travel, the Interstate Commerce Commission issued new regulations, which became effective in mid-1974, to assure convenient access to, and comfortable travel on, the nation's complete network of intercity railroads. The rules apply to all AMTRAK passenger trains (whether intra- or interstate) and all other interstate passenger trains. Except for health and safety provisions, the regulations do not hold for chartered or excursion trains and any regularly scheduled train that travels less than 500 miles in any day. The rules also do not legally apply to "stand-by" or other passengers who pay fares based on a space-available condition.

First, the ICC requires the 24-hour operation of a reservation and information system for all interstate passenger train services. Most of these services come under AMTRAK, which may be telephoned without charge from anywhere in the contiguous 48 states by using the appropriate "800" number for your area. The railroad must supply you with the accommodations for which you have paid, or else give you one of the following: (1) better accommodations on the same train without an additional charge; (2) similar arrangements on a different train to reach your destination within four hours of your originally confirmed arrival time; (3) a reservation on the next available train with equal or better accommodations, while providing you with food and shelter; or (4) some other means of relief with which you will be satisfied.

Whenever you purchase a ticket for an AMTRAK train trip or any interstate passenger train service, included in the ticket price is the carrier's liability to pay the actual cash value of any damage or loss for each piece of checked baggage.

The railroad must give you a full ticket refund if you cancel your reservation at least 30 minutes before the scheduled departure time. Without such advance notice, it can deduct from your refund a service charge of $5 or 5 percent of the ticket price, whichever is greater. (The only exception is for a ticket under $10; then the service charge is $2.50)

A substantially higher maximum service charge can be deducted from a refund if you change your reservation to a later train and then fail to cancel the revised reservation at least half an hour prior to departure. Except for very good cause, a scheduled train trip may not be canceled by the railroad.

If you are too late (less than 20 minutes before departure) for the carrier to accept your baggage for placement on the train, the company is required to forward it to your destination. In either case, if your checked baggage is not made available to you within 30 minutes of your arrival, the company at its own expense must forward your property to the address you furnish.

The regulations also require the train on which you travel to have clean restrooms, adequate food and beverage service (on trips of two hours or more), a temperature within 60–80°F (or in the case of a climate control breakdown, other accommodations or appropriate relief), sleeping car service on trips of at least six hours during the period from midnight to 8 a.m., and separately appointed and well-ventilated areas for smoking. A carrier may prohibit smoking altogether in dining cars and nonrevenue dome or lounge cars, and limit it to the lounge areas of coaches during late night and early morning hours.

The complaint procedure for intercity train travel problems is well defined by the Interstate Commerce Commission. If you are dissatisfied with any aspect of your trip from initial reservation to settlement of a claim, prepare your complaint in duplicate (or triplicate, so you can keep a copy for your records) and include all of the following information: (1) the train name, number, and station; (2) date of the alleged violation; (3) your boarding points; (4) place of departure; (5) description of your complaint; (6) the name of any employee with whom you spoke with regard to your dissatisfaction; (7) relief you requested; (8) relief offered by the carrier, if any, and why it was not acceptable; and (9) your name and address. Mail one copy to the Interstate Commerce Commission, Washington, D.C. 20423, and one copy to the railroad carrier. All interstate railroads are now required to provide complaint forms to the public and to post notices in stations and trains telling where to obtain them.

RUBBER DUCK TO OCEAN LINER

Over eight million small boats are owned by Americans, and operation of these vessels accounts for about 1,500 casualties each year. Just as the National Highway Traffic Safety Administration issues safety standards and orders the recalling of cars with defective or malfunctioning parts, the U.S. Coast Guard formulates minimum safety requirements for boats and nautical equipment and enforces compliance with federal regulations.

Recalls

The Coast Guard has initiated over 100 recall campaigns since the start of the program in 1971. Examples of problems announced in a September 1974 news release listing active recall campaigns included the steering lever in all 1973 Evinrude and Johnson 50–130 horsepower outboard motors with single remote control level, the delamination of bottom plywood planking in all 1973 boats manufactured by Broadwater Boats, and the ventilation hardware in all of Monark's 1974 Mark II and Supersport models.

Boating Safety Complaints

If you find a boat safety problem or product defect, report it to the nearest Coast Guard station or contact the headquarters: U.S. Coast Guard, U.S. Department of Transportation, Washington, D.C. 20590. The Coast Guard, which also stands ready at all times to eliminate boating hazards and help mariners in trouble, responded to 67,692 cases for help in the fiscal year ending July 1974, and prevented the deaths of 4,009 people in that same period.

The safety of passengers on harbor sightseeing cruisers and ocean liners comes under the jurisdiction of the Coast Guard's Office of Marine Inspection. Small boats and large vessels (over 65 feet) are inspected annually, with the latter also receiving quarterly follow-up inspections. Any regional Coast Guard office (or the Washington, D.C., headquarters) will accept a complaint relating to passenger vessel operation, although it may be able to take effective action only if the complaint relates to safety (overcrowding, the adequacy of life-saving equipment, competency of the skipper, and so on). Licenses of passenger vessel operators must be periodically renewed and are subject to cancellation.

As a traveler embarking at a United States port on an American or foreign vessel with accommodations for 50 or more passengers, you are now assured by law that charterers or ship owners have shown the Federal Maritime Commission proof of financial responsibility to pay any judgments arising out of personal injury or death. The company also must show evidence that it can repay ticketholders in the event a scheduled voyage is canceled.

A firm called Wall Street Cruises violated Commission regulations when it offered cruises on the SS *Independence* without submitting proof of financial responsibility and thus not qualifying for a performance certificate. In March 1972 the Commission ordered the firm to cease and desist from arranging or performing the voyage until the regulations were met. If you are not familiar with a company providing ocean travel or are suspicious about its actions, check with a Commission office to make sure that the company is operating within the law. The headquarters address is: Federal Maritime Commission, U.S. Department of Commerce, Washington, D.C. 20573.

Rates charged to passengers and conditions not related to safety

aboard ship are generally not under government regulation. Occasionally, cities and states, however, do exercise some control over
marine carriers making trips within several miles of their shores.
Some coastal cities have a harbor department that can assist you in
pursuing your complaint about a passenger carrier using the harbor
facilities.

FLYING HIGH

Whether you travel on a single-engine private plane or a massive
passenger jet, all factors related to the safety of the aircraft and your
trip come under the jurisdiction of the Federal Aviation Administration. The FAA requires all aircraft to undergo regular inspections
and all pilots to pass periodic physical examinations.

Air Safety

If you find or suspect a problem relating to the safety of a flight
you take, report the information immediately to the nearest FAA
office, or write to the Federal Aviation Administration, U.S. Department of Transportation, Washington, D.C. 20590. Investigations into
those problems may prompt the agency to issue by telegram a "factory
service bulletin" or "advisory directive," which can require an aircraft
owner to replace a part within a specific number of hours, or ground
a plane until a part replacement or specified service is performed.
Just as a driver can have his or her license suspended or revoked for

drunk driving or other serious vehicle violations, so may a pilot lose or have suspended his or her license for reckless flying or other actions within the pilot's control, which may endanger the lives of the pilot and his or her passengers.

If you are injured on the ground or in flight while in the care of an airline, in addition to reporting the existence of any safety problem to the FAA, contact an attorney immediately.

The FAA has a mailing list to try to involve consumers in the agency's planning and regulating activities. If you would like to keep informed of upcoming FAA meetings, conferences, hearings, and rule-making activities, send your name and address to the Federal Aviation Administration, Community and Consumer Liason Division—A15–400, 800 Independence Avenue S.W., Washington, D.C. 20591. If you represent a consumer group, include your title and the name of your organization.

Intrastate Carrier Complaints

The rate and service regulation of all passenger airlines operating exclusively within the boundaries of a state comes under the jurisdiction of a state agency, usually a public service or utilities commission or transportation department. This regulatory body approves the fares charged, scheduling of flights, and cities to be served. If you want to express your opinion about the establishment of a proposed new route or rate increase, or if you have a complaint regarding reservations, long delays, on-board conditions, or poor treatment by an airline, contact the applicable state office by phone or letter.

The airline regulatory body also approves an amount of maximum liability by the carrier for each piece of lost or damaged baggage. Although you will generally not be helped to collect on a claim—which might necessitate your taking a carrier to court—the state office may informally pressure the airline to deal promptly with your claim and settle it fairly. Request the state agency to provide information about your rights as a passenger on an intrastate air carrier.

Interstate Airline Hassles

Any passenger airline that flies its planes to at least one other state must comply with the rate, service, and liability requirements set by the Civil Aeronautics Board (CAB). You are covered by the federal rules for such an airline even in the case of an intrastate flight.

If you have a confirmed flight reservation and are denied boarding for any reason, the carrier is required to furnish you with a written copy of the conditions and limitations of available compensation. If you have complied with check-in requirements and the airline then denies your boarding because it has negligently overbooked your flight, you are entitled to receive a refund or credit on your unused tickets. You also must be paid an amount equal to 100 percent of the purchase price of the ticket to your first destination or stopover point, or $25, whichever is more, but not to exceed $200.

Denied boarding compensation generally does not apply to circumstances beyond the control of the airline, such as when a smaller plane is substituted for safety reasons, or when a substitute carrier enables you to arrive at your destination within a reasonable amount of time after your originally scheduled arrival. If you are offered monetary compensation, you also have the right to reject it in favor of other means of redress such as court action.

There is little you can do about a canceled or delayed flight, unless it is in violation of the airline's own tariff (a written agreement with the CAB, which is open to inspection at your request). Such tariffs do generally state that the airline will provide passengers various free services when a flight delay of four or more hours is expected. Notify the CAB if an airline violates the conditions of its tariff. Write to the Office of Consumer Affairs, Civil Aeronautics Board, Washington, D.C. 20428.

The percentage of baggage damaged or lost by airlines is small, but such an occurrence becomes a major inconvenience and loss to the individual passenger. When you buy your plane ticket, your baggage is automatically insured. The airline will usually pay the value of the damage or loss (taking depreciation into account) up to a maximum of $500 per paying passenger on a domestic flight, and a maximum amount based on baggage weight (not value) for an international flight. For an additional fee, you may insure your belongings for their value above $500.

Report any loss or damage immediately, before you leave the airport. Also, see that a report form is completed. Otherwise, the airline may claim that it is not responsible or that *you* caused the damage. If your lost baggage is not found within three days, the airline should send you claim forms, which must be filled out and returned within 45 days. You can expect payment within four to six weeks (somewhat longer during holiday travel periods).

Address any complaint concerning airline rates, services, denied boardings, and claims problems to the Office of Consumer Affairs, address above. The CAB will respond to your complaint directly or send a photocopy of your letter to the airline along with a cover letter requesting that the airline respond directly to you, with a copy to the Board. If the Board feels appropriate action has been taken, the file will be closed. If the CAB does not receive an adequate response or does not find that the complaint was acted on fairly, it will again contact the company and try to effect a solution. Send a follow-up letter to the agency if you feel the airline's initial or final action is inadequate.

Although a claims complaint can be addressed to the CAB, that agency may not be able to offer much help. In that case you should consider taking the dispute to a consumer bureau or small claims court (see Chapters 12 and 13).

Nonsmokers rejoice! The enforcement of no-smoking areas for each class of service on all flights, including charters, is now required by Board regulations.

You may request from the CAB a helpful pamphlet entitled "Air Travelers' Fly Rights," which details not only your rights as an air traveler, but suggestions for ensuring a hassle-free trip.

Charter Flights

The federal regulations affecting charter flights continue to undergo various changes, often as a result of public demand. A free pamphlet available from the CAB details the various types of charters and applicable rules for each. Independent charter organizers, including travel agents offering the charter as part of a tour package, are required to furnish you (before you make any payment) with information such as the conditions for cancellations and refunds.

Become suspicious if the organizer refuses to tell you the name of the airline under contract. If you are unfamiliar with the organizer of the charter, contact the CAB to be sure it is a legitimate operation. Your failure to take precautions could mean the loss of your money or the predicament of finding yourself stranded, with no return flight. Contact your local CAB office immediately if you suspect fraud or noncompliance with group charter rules, or write to the Civil Aeronautics Board, Washington, D.C. 20428.

Recent CAB rules, which became effective in September 1975, permit you to take advantage of inexpensive charter air travel without having to belong to a church, student organization, or other group.

You may be able to find a suitable "one-stop inclusive" charter if your trip within the United States, Mexico, or Canada will last at least four days and if you are able to purchase your tickets at least 15 days in advance. If your vacation outside North America will take a week or more and you can make plans at least a month in advance, you also may be able to find a charter flight. In addition to air travel, these one-stop charters include ground transportation, baggage handling, and hotels, and can cost as little as the basic air charter fare plus $15 a day for accommodations. Check with a local travel agent or charter group for details.

"Special events" charters are also available to conference delegations, sports fans, and others planning a short visit to a city. The travel package usually includes air fare, ground transportation, a hotel room (if you are staying overnight), and a ticket to the event of your interest.

BILLS, BILLS, BILLS—
CREDIT AND BANKING

Since the day you dropped your first penny into that lavender pig with the large pink eyes, or spent your first profits from the Kool-Aid stand on a lollipop at the drugstore, you probably have been taught the importance of wisely spending and saving your money. Now that you are older, money is even more important, and there are more sophisticated methods of spending and saving your dollars.

This chapter will guide you through the ups and downs of banking services and the sometimes wonderful, sometimes treacherous world of credit. You may think that you know it all when it comes to your money, but sit back, hold tight to your credit cards, and read on. You may have some surprises in store.

A PLACE FOR YOUR MONEY

The basic idea to understand when it comes to deciding where to place your money for safekeeping is that there are many individuals and companies who will pay for the use of that money while you are not using it. The funds will go to finance anything from a college education to a Manhattan skyscraper.

Therefore, unless you are an embezzler or bank robber, stashing your cash in the cookie jar or beneath the mattress should be a forgotten tradition. Additionally, if you are a smart consumer, you will not allow yourself to be sucked into anything like those lower interest, limitation-plagued Christmas club accounts or any layaway plan where you keep making payments for merchandise that is not even in your possession.

Decisions, Decisions

Whether you are a garbage collector or a company president, you face many outstretched hands and sales pitches to lure you into depositing your money. With the hundreds of banking institutions in your state, it may be the no-cost, three-dimensional checks you are after, or the slave more/save more premium account that catches your eye. In any case, all banking services can be grouped under the five big categories of financial institutions: commercial banks, savings and loan associations, savings banks, credit unions, and thrift and loan companies.

To determine the types of institutions and accounts best suited to your needs, and whether it is time to make a change, first consider the banking services and benefits that are available:

Savings accounts (consider the interest rates, withdrawal charges, minimum balance for free service, and avoidance of withdrawal charges)

Checking accounts (consider the minimum balance requirements, check costs, service charges)

Loans (types such as bank-card, check-overdrawing privilege, installment, small unsecured, mortgage)

Long-term, higher interest savings accounts (consider the minimum balance, withdrawal penalties, interest)

Credit cards (consider the line of credit, interest charges, loan transaction and interest charges)

Drive-up tellers

Safe deposit boxes

Automatic telephone or supermarket transfer services

Money orders

Traveler's checks

Photocopying

Fast service

Banking by mail

Detailed statements

Extended business hours

Dividends (from credit union savings)

Make a list of any of the services you now have or feel you want to utilize. If you write a lot of checks, but math is the only subject you have ever flunked, you will be better off with a checking account in which payment against insufficient funds will cost you $3 as opposed to $6. If you are in a job where you are lucky if you can take time to gulp down a cup of coffee during the lunch hour, you will want to find a place that is open late in the afternoon or on Saturdays, or pays for your banking by mail.

If you are a student and think you need a federally insured loan next fall, you had better find a bank that will lend you the full amount of money you will need. Make sure that you can meet any requirement for maintaining a banking relationship for a specified amount of time. For example, if you were a graduate student at UCLA in the 1975–76 academic year, many banks would have granted you a $1,500 loan. Some institutions would have made the loan only if you had a current account, and some would have lent the money with no special strings attached. By calling many banks, however, you might have found Wells Fargo Bank to be the only one that would lend you as much as $2,500, as long as you maintained any kind of Wells Fargo bank account for a minimum of six months prior to making out your student loan application.

Checking Accounts

At least until 1975, with three exceptions, the only place you could get a checking account was directly from a commercial bank. One exception is available to you if you write only a few checks each month. Some savings banks and savings and loan associations issue a limited number of checks made out to a depositor's few creditors, or to the depositer for endorsement over to his or her creditors. Some savings institutions do not charge for this special service as long as you maintain a specified minimum balance.

A second exception is the policy of some savings and loan associations and savings banks to give you a free checking account as long as you maintain a minimum balance in a savings account with them.

The third alternative, available only in New England states (Connecticut, Maine, Massachusetts, New Hampshire, Rhode Island, and Vermont) as of December 1976, is the negotiable order of withdrawal (NOW) account, in which the depositor can draw checks on an interest-earning savings account. This type of account will hopefully soon be permitted in other states.

By making a list of any of the aforementioned banking services you now have or want to utilize, and setting them up in a chart, you can do the necessary comparison to determine which banking institution is best for you. For instance, maybe you want both checking and savings accounts and could use an all-purpose bank credit card. Furthermore, traveler's checks are important because you do a lot of traveling, and you want drive-up tellers and fast service since you are often rushed. Since you will be concerned with keeping a minimum balance, charges for dipping below the minimum are important, but a comparison of overdraw fees is unnecessary. Because you do not want your checking account tied into any other account, comparing automatic transfer services is also unnecessary. Based on these conditions, your comparison chart might look like the one in Table 8-1.

From Table 8-1, it would seem that Pittance State Bank would be your best bet because of its fast service, lower minimum balance requirements, lower credit card transaction fees, and free checks and traveler's checks. It appears that Fort Knocks Bank might be your second choice.

If you do not travel a lot for work or pleasure, look into the smaller banks to meet your needs. They may have only one or two branches in your area, but they often try to be more competitive by offering free or lower cost services.

Many banks, especially the larger chains, offer a package plan in which you pay a set amount for unlimited check writing and "free" services. Be cautious of these arrangements. They may appear to save you money, but a minimum balance arrangement whereby you pay *no* service charge is usually more advantageous. The interest you lose by tying up some of your money (which could be put in a savings account) to cover minimum balance requirements generally will be less than the amount you would be paying for an account with service and check charges.

Too many people select a bank on the basis of location. Although it is convenient to open an account at a bank branch in your office building, the bank down the street may save you $50 or $60 a year and be worth the extra steps.

Many banks offer merchandise free or at a discount to lure new customers—pocket calculators, art prints, alarm clocks, cookbooks. You may save some money on a needed item, but be sure that the bank does not make up for its generosity by subsequently charging higher fees than other banks.

There may be a free checking account right under your nose, compliments of your savings institution. Savings banks and savings

TABLE 8-1

Sample Comparison of Local Commercial Banks

Banking Needs[a]	Bank of Amor	Securious National Bank	Pittance State Bank	Fort Knocks Bank	Bank of Greens	Squander National Bank
CHECKING ACCT.						
Min. balance	$300.00	$300.00	$100.00	$200.00	$300.00	$200.00
Checkbook costs	$ 2.35	free	free	$ 2.35	free	$ 2.00
Check service charges (when below min. bal.)	$ 2.00	$ .85 + .08/ck.	$ .75 + .11/ck.	$ .75 + .11/ck.	$ 3.00	$ 2.00
CREDIT CARD						
Type	Amorocard	Mister Charge	Mister Charge	Mister Charge	Mister Charge	Mister Charge
Transaction fee rate	4%	2%	1%	2%	3%	4%
SERVICE[b]						
Fast	yes	no	yes	yes	yes	no
Drive-up	no	no	yes	yes	no	yes
OTHER						
Traveler's check fees	1%, no min.	1%, min. $.50	free	free	1%, min. $.50	1%, min. $.50

[a]A comparison of bank savings accounts is omitted because, as discussed later in this chapter, it is not recommended under most circumstances that you place savings in a commercial bank.

[b]Speed of service is not always easy to determine. You might try going to each bank during a busy hour and observing the number of depositors waiting in line.

and loan associations in many cities offer a free checking account at a local bank provided that you maintain a balance of $1,000, $2,500, or more in your savings account.

No matter where you have your checking account, reconcile every bank statement you receive. Many banks will refuse even to discuss a possible error unless you present a series of statements you have balanced and kept up to date. Some consumers get around this chore by having two checking accounts, which they use alternately every few months. That way, all outstanding checks will clear in the inactive account and a periodic ending balance can be matched to the checkbook. The problem with this method is that finding an error may be delayed for a relatively long time, and twice as many dollars in minimum balance funds are kept from your interest-earning savings account.

Savings Accounts

Let's start with the thrift and loan companies, because the question of whether they are a good place to put your dollars can be summed up in two words—forget them! You spend years and years working with a budget and saving your extra earnings, so do not risk the loss of that money. These institutions are not backed by government funds (like the other types of banking and savings institutions mentioned in this chapter) in case of bankruptcy. They may try to guarantee your money through private corporate funds, and they may pay higher interest than other places in your area, but imagine your reaction if the company went bankrupt and you lost all or part of your deposits.

Never put your money into a commercial bank savings account. Banks pay less interest than other types of institutions, and they often charge a fee if you close your account too early or withdraw money too many times during a quarter. Some do not pay any interest at all unless an average minimum quarterly balance is maintained. The only exception should be if you *must* maintain some kind of account to apply for a loan and you already have your checking account at another bank.

Savings banks (mainly in New York, Massachusetts, and Washington), savings and loan associations, and credit unions are all better places to deposit your savings. The first question you should ask at any banking institution is whether it has a minimum balance requirement for paying interest. Many depositors are not aware that they must have at least $25, $50, $100 or more in their account before any interest will be added.

Savings and loan associations and savings banks tend to pay about one percent higher interest than regular banks on all savings, including long-term, high-yield accounts. Some of these compound interest daily; other compute it on a quarterly basis. Unless you are depositing a substantial amount of money, the monetary advantage of daily compounding is very small.

You can earn the most from your money by placing it in a "time certificate" or "time deposit" account, which requires your leaving a minimum amount (usually at least $500) untouched for a period of one to five years or more. Never commit your money to this type of account unless you are certain, barring some emergency, that you will not have to withdraw any funds for the specified period. Such withdrawals will be met with interest penalties that will leave you with less total interest than if you opened a regular passbook account.

Not only is the interest higher at savings institutions, but these firms offer many benefits that commercial banks do not. These benefits often include longer business hours (sometimes Saturdays) and free money orders, traveler's checks, safe deposit boxes, income tax preparation, and photocopy services.

Savings and loans in cities throughout the country are now offering telephone transfer services. The institution, upon your phone request, makes a withdrawal from your savings account and deposits the specified amount in your bank checking account. This saves time, energy, and worry about keeping an adequate balance in your checking account. It also allows you to receive interest on your funds until the day you will want to transfer them quickly. In extending this service, many savings and loans require that you maintain a minimum balance in your savings account of $1,000 to $5,000.

An alternate place for your savings is a credit union. Such an organization, unlike a bank or savings institution, is nonprofit and run solely for the benefit of its members. Whether you work for a large company, state or local government, or a federal department or agency (such as the Internal Revenue Service or U.S. Postal Service) that has a credit union, you can join free or by paying a nominal fee and receive such benefits as a fair return (usually 5–7 percent on your savings) and the opportunity to obtain low-cost loans. Some credit unions allow you to join immediately after becoming employed;

others permit membership only after three or six months. Many credit unions also offer free, or for a small fee, a life insurance policy.

You make deposits to your credit union savings account by buying shares (increments of $5), for which dividends (similar to interest) are paid quarterly or semiannually. You can make deposits and withdrawals, as with other savings accounts, at any time. You also may arrange for a payroll deduction.

The percentage rate of return may be fixed or may vary according to the credit union's quarterly earnings. The way in which the union computes its dividends must be spelled out in its charter. Before placing funds in a credit union, ask if there is a fixed rate of return. If not, ask to be told the percentage rate for the past four quarters. That will give you a picture of how the union has done over a year's period and will help you to predict future returns. If a local savings institution pays much higher interest than your credit union, you may as well select the former.

Unlike other institutions, credit unions levy few or no service charges for withdrawals of your funds. Furthermore, interest on credit union loans is generally much lower than at other places. Most credit unions will readily allow a member to borrow an amount equal to the full amount of money he or she has on deposit. Some unions will require you to close your account if you leave the company or employees' union; others will keep the account open for the rest of your life as long as there is some money on deposit. Some credit unions that will keep your account open under these circumstances will restrict you from borrowing.

The pension law adopted by Congress in 1974 permits you to set up a special savings account for retirement funds if you are self-employed or the company you work for does not have an employee pension plan. (The Internal Revenue Service also will allow you to place these funds in a mutual fund, an insurance annuity, government bonds, or other approved plans.)

You can deposit in your "individual retirement account" (IRA) 15 percent of your annual income (up to a maximum of $1,500) and not be required to pay any taxes on the funds until you retire sometime after the age of 59½. Although this newer type of account provides a great way to save for your old age, do not put away more than you can afford. Monetary penalties equivalent to all back taxes on the accumulated amount plus an additional charge are levied if you make any withdrawal before the minimum age.

Insurance

No matter what kind of savings account you have, as long as it is located in an institution insured by an agency of the federal government or your state government, you never have to worry about losing your money. In all federally insured banking institutions and credit unions, every savings account is covered up to a maximum of $40,000, and state insuring agencies provide alternative coverage. Over 500 banks have failed since 1933, when the Federal Deposit Insurance Corporation (FDIC) was formed. This agency claims that less than one percent of all deposits in failed banks were lost. If you have a savings account in a bank insured by the FDIC and forced into liquidation, you will be paid back your money (as long as it is under the $40,000 limit for each account) within a short period—as soon as 10 days after the bank closes.

If you unwisely keep more than $40,000 in one account and your bank fails, after all bank assets are liquidated you can file a claim along with all the general creditors for any money you were saving above the limit. There is no guarantee that a substantial portion of the excess funds will be recovered.

Of course, often one failed bank is taken over by another with the help of the FDIC. In that instance, the transition is orderly, and you continue to have access to all your funds.

All national commercial banks and savings banks are insured by the FDIC. If you have any questions regarding insurance or filing a claim, write to the nearest office of the Federal Deposit Insurance Corporation, or to its headquarters at 550 Seventeenth Street N.W., Washington, D.C. 20429. All complaints concerning accounting methods, interest, service, and other policies of these nationally chartered commercial banks and savings banks (including every bank with "national" in its name) should be directed to the nearest Regional Administrator of National Banks. Look in the White Pages under U.S. Government—Treasury Department or call your local Federal Information Center. You can also write to the following office, which will forward your complaint to the appropriate jurisdiction: Comptroller of the Currency, U.S. Treasury Department, Washington, D.C. 20220.

Insurance and claims for all federally insured savings and loan institutions are handled by the nearest office of the Federal Savings and Loan Insurance Corporation (FSLIC), or you can write to its headquarters address: 320 First Street N.W., Washington, D.C. 20552.

Banking Complaints

For all complaints concerning savings and loan services and policies, write or call the supervisory agent at the nearest Federal Home Loan Bank. If you cannot locate such a bank in your area, send your complaint to the Federal Home Loan Bank Board, 101 Indiana Avenue N.W., Washington, D.C. 20552.

Some state-chartered banks also are members of the Federal Reserve System. If you want to complain about the services or policies of this type of institution, write directly to the Federal Reserve System, 20th and Constitution Avenue N.W., Washington, D.C. 20551.

If you have problems with a state-chartered bank that is not affiliated with the Federal Reserve System, file your complaint with the FDIC or the appropriate state agency. You can find out the name and address of the latter, or seek help in determining the category into which your banking firm fits, by writing to your state attorney general's office. You also can send that office the complaint and ask them to forward it.

If you find that your credit union is employing questionable services or policies, or you want to make a claim for insured funds that have been lost, contact the closest office of the National Credit Union Administration or write to its main office in Washington, D.C. 20456.

Loans

Whether you need money to have your teeth put back in place or to plug up a ceiling leak, countless lending sources are available. In choosing the type of loan and lending institution, you should first determine how much you will need and how long you will require to repay the loan. Then shop around for the best deal.

Credit unions make loans only to their members. If you belong to such an association, that is the first place to try for any type of loan. Not only do they charge less interest than banks, but they also do not charge minimum fees for your loan or the prepayment of your loan. Credit unions often allow their members to borrow for any productive purpose, from meeting current bills or medical expenses to purchasing home appliances or real estate.

Although real estate loan rates are about the same at commercial banks, savings banks, and savings and loan associations, you still should shop around, because even a small variance when it comes to such a high principal can provide a big dollar difference. Compare not only interest rates but all kinds of lending fees that may be tacked on.

Savings institutions primarily make real estate loans; commercial banks make money available for a variety of consumer loans. Banks provide these funds through installment loans, or by cash advances through checking accounts and bank cards. If you need to borrow several hundred dollars or more for at least a year, you will generally pay lower total interest if you get a regular installment loan, where there are fixed charges and monthly payments.

Never use bank cards to make large purchases for which you plan to take many months to repay. Interest rates on these cards are high. They are a good source of credit as long as you pay the debt immediately or within a few months. Checking accounts with built-in loan reserve funds are great for short-term borrowing, but they are expensive for extended indebtedness.

Steer clear of finance companies. Although interest maximums vary from state to state, these firms generally charge an annual percentage rate of 18 to 36 per cent. Car dealers are just as high. At the other end of the scale are loans from life insurance policies, which average an annual rate of 4 to 6 per cent.

An excellent guide to banking services is *Break the Bank!*, published by nonprofit San Francisco Consumer Action, 312 Sutter Street, San Francisco, California 94108. Although the guide compares only California-based banks, it provides a detailed general discussion of many different aspects of banking and shows you how to save money and earn the most for your savings no matter where you live.

You will find a discussion of truth-in-lending laws, and where to file a complaint relating to them, later in this chapter.

CREDIT CARD MONEY

Whoever thought up the adage about words being cheap overlooked two of the most costly words in the English language: *Charge it!*

Today there is a charge card for everything. You can whip out your American Express card for a round-trip ticket to London, your Diners Club card for a posh meal at the Brown Derby, your Master Charge card for tuition at the University of Southern California, and your Sears card for anything from mittens to microwave ovens. And to think you do not have to put down one cent! All is well until that envelope with the distinct look of a bill burrows its way into your mailbox and your wallet.

Credit Card Types

Credit cards can be placed in three categories—the single vendor card, the bank card, and the annual charge card. The single vendor card allows you to make purchases from an individual store or any of a number of dealers or stores in a chain. For instance, credit cards issued by Sears, Hertz, and Texaco fall into this category.

To encourage use of these cards, many companies have at various times contracted with unaffiliated firms for the convenience of cardholders. Oil companies often let their cards cover car rental services, hotels and motels, and so on, but most discontinued such ties in the early 1970s, citing costs and the cardholders' slight use of the cards for these purposes.

In mid-1975, the card issued by Standard Oil Company of California was still good at Best Western Motels, Quality Motor Lodges, and Quality Court Motels. This was discontinued in 1975, but beginning in 1976 the card was honored at Hertz Rent A Car. In 1976 a credit card from United Airlines could be used at most Western International Hotels.

The credit card issued by a bank includes Visa card and Master Charge, and it is the most versatile type. It may be used throughout the world at thousands of member establishments. These multiuse cards can be tied to funds in your checking or savings account (for overdraw coverage, cash advances, and such) or stand in a separate account.

In the coming years all-purpose cards may take the place of many, if not all, cash transactions. Thousands of automatic tellers are already in use throughout the country. These electronic wizards take deposits and pay out on checking, savings, and credit card accounts. They even transfer funds from one account to another and provide you with information about your account, such as the current balance.

In 1975, Bank of America, California Federal Savings and Loan, and Glendale Federal Savings and Loan all began installing computer terminals at Southern California supermarkets. These and other systems in many areas of the country are already allowing customers to charge grocery bills on the scene or instantaneously to pay for their food by a computerized fund transfer system. These systems may spread to all other areas of consumer purchasing, allowing you one or two credit cards in the future to take care of all your banking and credit needs.

Single vendor and bank credit cards are usually given to the applicant without an initial or annual fee. The third type of card carries a standard annual charge, even if you rarely use it. Carte Blanche, Diners Club, and American Express fall into this category. For $20 an approved applicant could get any one of these cards in 1977 for use at establishments inside and outside the United States.

There are some major differences between the fee credit cards and the other two types. Although most cards will allow you either to pay the monthly balance or to stretch out payments by incurring finance charges on a revolving credit basis, the companies issuing fee cards require that you pay the entire monthly bill within a specified number of days. The only exceptions are if you purchase airline tickets, certain travel tours, and merchandise offered directly from the card issuer or its company-owned or -affiliated magazine.

On airline tickets that could be paid in 1976 through installments (incurring finance charges), American Express and Diners Club charged their customers a maximum annual rate of 12 percent, while in many states Carte Blanche charged 18 percent. Call or write these companies (and any others in your state) if you want to choose a credit card, and compare annual rates before you make your decision.

Interest rates quoted on a monthly basis may sound low, but they add up when accumulated over a year's time. Also, where one firm's monthly rate is just a small fraction above that of another company, the annual rate will be much higher. The following are typical rates:

Rate per Month × 12	=	Annual Percentage Rate
1/2%		6%
3/4%		9%
5/6%		10%
1%		12%
1 1/4%		15%
1 1/2%		18%

Like the oil companies, firms issuing free credit cards have tended to lose many once-participating businesses. The annual fee cards usually are helpful mainly for travel. Their scope of use, however, does not seem to compare with that of the all-purpose bank cards. In many cases, because the credit card companies have not renewed their agreements with entire chains of hotels, motels, gas stations, and such, some establishments in a chain may accept a card while others may not.

Check Versus Credit Card

Many consumers take advantage of a combination of checking services and credit cards to meet their buying needs. You may choose to pay for most merchandise by cash or check and save the credit cards for the times when your cash or bank account becomes short. On the other hand, you may want to charge everything and have fewer checks to write at bill payment time.

There are good points and bad points to using a credit card as opposed to a check. Credit cards do allow you to make purchases without having the cash on hand or in the bank. The danger, however, is that your expectation of having enough money to pay off a balance or make a monthly payment may not be fulfilled. What if your car breaks down or you get a 30-day notice to move out of your apartment? Be sure you always have some money in reserve so that you will at least be able to make a minimum payment on your credit card purchases.

Using your credit cards so that you write fewer checks each month is an advantage if you have the kind of checking account in which you pay a service charge for each check. However, unlike keeping a close tab on your spending via your checkbook balance, it is more difficult to maintain an accurate picture of how much money you have spent, and how much is left to spend, when all you do is to sign a charge slip.

Checks have big advantages too. Many establishments will accept your personal check as long as you can show a valid driver's license and perhaps one or two other pieces of identification, whereas they may accept few or no credit cards.

Stopping Payment

If you buy an item by check and find that the product is faulty, you can stop payment on the check, especially if the merchant is uncooperative in making an adjustment. Simply inform the bank in writing that you want payment stopped on a specific check. It is usually necessary to sign a stop-payment order in person rather than sending it through the mail, so as to intercept the check in time. The bank then charges you a fee, and informs the merchant that the funds are being withheld at your request.

Over the years, exercising the same power over credit card drafters has been virtually impossible. Once you sign the charge slip prepared from your bank card, for instance, the merchant is assured of getting his or her money from the credit card issuer, and you are stuck with the bill. This is true even if the piece of merchandise is unsatisfactory and the dealer will not make a refund or exchange.

Some credit card companies say that there is little they can do; others contact the merchant and act as the mediator in trying to resolve the problem. A responsible company will cancel the agreement it has with any merchant about which it receives many valid complaints.

Until 1975 the "holder in due course" doctrine in many states barred a credit card holder from asserting claims and defenses against a credit card company or anyone other than the dealer from whom he or she purchased the merchandise. Thus you could be held liable for a credit card company's bill, even though the merchandise you purchased was not serviceable. The doctrine was finally outlawed by the Federal Reserve System for all bank credit card purchasing. Hopefully the Federal Trade Commission will ban the doctrine as relating to department stores and other credit card issuers.

Some states have adopted their own laws to deal with credit card disputes. Under California's Song-Beverly Credit Card Act of 1971, for example, if a dispute arises relating to a product or service you have purchased with a credit card, you can use as a defense against paying the card issuer the same claim you have asserted against the dealer, provided that: (1) the purchase is over $50; (2) the transaction was made in California; (3) you have made a written appeal to the dealer in trying to settle the matter; and (4) you provide the card issuer with a written account of the dispute, including the dealer's name and address, the date and amount of purchase, the items or services purchased, the nature of the dispute, and details about what steps you have taken to obtain satisfaction from the retailer.

Application Procedures

Credit card applications are very similar. They ask for credit references, place and length of employment, residence address and length of stay, and often monthly income and bank account information. Generally, you must have lived at your address and worked on your job for at least one year prior to your application.

Once your application is received, assuming all answers you provide are satisfactory, the company will generally check on you with a local credit reporting firm. It will also send a form to your employer to verify your work status (position, length of stay, and so on) and income. Some companies will also ask your employer if he or she recommends you for credit.

Being self-employed for only a short time is not in your favor, because from the credit card issuer's point of view you have no track record and could go out of business tomorrow. BankAmericard, for example, generally requires at least three years of self-employment for a California resident before credit will be granted.

Credit reporting services will be discussed later in this chapter.

Establishing Credit

The easiest credit cards to obtain are issued by department stores and oil companies. Do not assume that if you are turned down by one store you will be turned down by others. One company often will judge your credit history, or lack of it, differently from another firm.

As soon as you do begin using one or more cards, you can possibly start a Master Charge or Visa card account. After you begin using all your cards and paying your bills without delinquency, your credit rating will become established. Then you can probably obtain a car loan or personal loan from the bank.

If you are a woman, you will want to take more care in your

credit dealings because of the still prevalent, rampant sex discrimination. Begin to build up your credit while you are single. If you marry, be sure that your credit cards are issued with either your maiden name or your individualized married name (that is, Mrs. Mary Cardholder as opposed to Mrs. John Cardholder). Should you become separated or divorced, you will at least have some credit security to back you up. Maintain your own telephone listing and see that utility and other bills carry both your name and your husband's name.

CREDIT DISCRIMINATION

Until 1975, if you were a woman, you had a better chance of obtaining credit in many cases if you were single. From various women's groups, such as the National Organization for Women and its Task Force on Credit, have come discrimination horror stories that seem hard to believe unless you have been through it. In fact, when it comes to credit, women have generally been discriminated against no matter what their marital or financial status.

Too often, married women have been placed by creditors in the role of housewife and mother. A woman's earning ability, even if she has had a regular income, has been considered less significant than that of her husband. This idea is based on the unfair assumption that she would probably have children, and motherhood would take her out of the job market and cut off her income and contribution to family earnings indefinitely.

Marriage Discredit

When two people have married, credit cards usually have been issued in the man's name. If an additional card was issued for the wife, it was printed as the man's name preceded by "Mrs." If a woman applied for credit on her own, she was often required to get the signature of her husband, as if she were not personally capable to make the commitment. When, on the other hand, has a man been required by a credit card issuer to get the signature of his wife before an account will be opened?

During marriage, the woman may have shared the accounts and even managed them, but this fact has remained unimportant to most creditors, who have bestowed full control on the man as "head of the household." A woman who became separated, divorced, or widowed

has been seen as a stranger to the world of credit and expected to start from scratch in trying to reestablish it.

Credit discrimination is another one of those long-standing social evils that may finally be booted out the back door. Congress took a big step forward when it passed the Equal Credit Opportunity Act, effective October 28, 1975. This federal statute bans all discrimination based on sex or marital status by a creditor against an applicant. One implementing regulation also requires creditors to provide rejected credit applicants with specific reasons for the adverse action taken.

Protection

The Federal Reserve Board proposed a set of regulations to implement the new credit law. One provision disallows creditors from stopping credit solely on the basis of marital status. If a person gets married or separates from the spouse, the creditor may require another credit application to determine whether or not the customer still has the ability to pay for purchases, but such a policy must be applied equally to both sexes.

When charge accounts are used by a husband and wife, the creditor will be required to list the account in both names by June 1, 1977. This will alleviate the problem a woman faces when she separates from her husband.

In addition to forbidding creditors from using sex or marital status as a factor in determining your credit worthiness, the regulations state that you cannot be asked for the signature of your spouse if you qualify for credit on your own merit. (Both signatures can be requested, however, in states where community property laws are in effect.) Alimony and child support payments cannot be discounted at all by the creditor as long as there is reasonable certainty that regular payments will be made.

If you apply for credit as an individual, and do not depend on the credit worthiness of your present or former spouse, the creditor cannot legally require or utilize negative information about that person in judging your case. The exceptions to this in community property states are when the spouse will be permitted to use the account; the spouse will be contractually liable in the account; the applicant is relying on community property or the spouse's income; or the applicant is relying on alimony, child support, or maintenance payments from the spouse or former spouse as the basis for repayment.

If the creditor opens a charge account for you, the account will have to be put in any legal name you request. Should your request for an account be denied, you will have the right to ask for and obtain a written statement detailing the reasons.

Reactions to these proposed regulations have been mixed, yet very predictable. The American Bankers Association and the heads of various department store chains have sharply criticized the regulations, stating that the costs and constraints involved could have serious negative effects on the industry. On the side of these and even stronger proposals have been women's groups and many consumer organizations.

Enforcement of regulations concerning credit card accounts at banking institutions will come under the jurisdiction of the same agencies listed in the previous section headed "Banking Complaints."

All nonbank credit card issuers, including department stores and other retail product and service outlets, are regulated by the Federal Trade Commission. If one of these businesses violates your credit rights, contact the nearest regional office of the FTC or write to Truth-in-Lending, Federal Trade Commission, Washington, D.C. 20580. The FTC issued its first complaint under the Equal Credit Opportunity Act in December 1976 against Montgomery Ward and Company, Inc., for allegedly failing to give reasons for the denial of credit to rejected applicants who request an explanation.

MONEY AND CREDIT SAFEGUARDS

Bank Funds

Wherever you do your banking, you can take three steps to assure safekeeping for your savings. First, unless your money is in a time certificate account imposing substantial interest penalties on withdrawals, always make at least one withdrawal or deposit a year. Most banking institutions rule an account dormant if there has been no action in it after a specified length of time. The bank can then assess handling fees just for holding your money. If a specified number of years go by without contact from you, the funds could be withdrawn by the state and converted to public funds.

Second, with respect to insurance on your savings, it is foolish to keep more than $40,000 in any one account. Set up as many different accounts as necessary to accommodate your money (leaving room for interest to be added). For example, if you have a spouse, you can insure your savings up to $200,000 by opening one account for each of you, one joint account, one account in which you are the trustee for your spouse, and another account with your spouse as trustee for you. Additional combinations can be made with relatives and children.

Third, maintain your bank credit card account in an institution separate from that which carries your checking and savings account. This will eliminate the possibility that the bank will take funds out of your other account to pay a credit card overdue balance.

One California woman lost the unemployment benefit funds she had placed in her checking account, because the bank seized the money to pay for her Master Charge balance. The California Court of Appeals ruled the seizure unconstitutional without special prior notice. Keeping your card account separate will protect you against this practice until it is outlawed in your state or by federal regulation.

Truth-in-Lending

One of the most important pieces of legislation to be enacted in the last decade is the Truth-in-Lending Law. Its purpose is to let you know the exact nature of the credit offered for any goods or services you may buy, and to give you more information with which to compare the cost of credit among sources.

The frozen-smile salesman with his lethargic dog on television can no longer whet your appetite for a new-looking, used compact car by telling you that "It takes just two dollars down, and the automobile is yours." The law forces the seller to mention all important terms of credit if he or she mentions any one aspect of it. In this case, the salesman would have to add that weekly payments of $15 must be made for a period of seven years. With this law, you can see that this special two-dollar-down deal might turn into an expensive $5,462 ripoff.

Any company giving you credit on the purchase of goods or services must clearly disclose in advertising, as well as in the various forms, account statements, and installment contracts, how much the credit will cost you. All interest, service, carrying, and other charges must be lumped together and labeled as the "finance charge."

In addition to disclosing the finance charge, the creditor must also tell you the annual percentage rate you will be charged. Many companies used to tell you only the dollar amount of interest you would be paying, but this made it difficult for consumers to compare the interest rates of several companies, and so the practice was outlawed.

The Truth-in-Lending Law also provides special safeguards to anyone using his or her home as security in a credit transaction. If you take out a second mortgage or need major remodeling or repairs, and your home is used as security, you have a legal right to change your mind and cancel your original signed agreement by informing the creditor in writing within three business days. The creditor must give you written notice of your right to cancel by using a certain type of form whose type style must be at least a prescribed minimum size that is easy to read.

Your right of cancellation cannot be applied to a first mortgage used to finance a house. This right can be waived if you write to the contractor stating that you are facing a financial crisis and must immediately finance some necessary repairs to remedy conditions dangerous to you, your family, or your property. If you do not waive your right to cancel, the contractor cannot begin any work until after the three-day waiting period.

If you decide against putting up your home as security, and you cancel your original agreement within the time limit, the creditor must return to you any money you paid as a deposit, down payment, finance charge, or fee. In addition, any security interest becomes void.

The Federal Trade Commission has filed many complaints against firms that have allegedly violated the Truth-in-Lending Act.

In 1975, for example, the FTC accepted separate agreements containing consent orders prohibiting Heftler Realty Sales, Inc., of Miami and Tony Evans Motors, Inc., of Reno from violating the act. Both complaints alleged that the company did not state the rate of the finance charge as the "annual percentage rate." The former firm also did not use required terminology in stating all terms regarding the cost of credit, while the latter announced certain credit terms in its ads without making other required disclosures.

The Truth-in-Lending Law and generally all credit regulations mentioned in this chapter are enforced for banking institutions and credit unions by the agencies listed previously under "Banking Complaints." When the creditor is an airline, address your complaint to the Director, Bureau of Enforcement, Civil Aeronautics Board, 1825 Connecticut Avenue N.W., Washington, D.C. 20428. For credit from an interstate bus, train, or moving company, jurisdiction is with the Office of Proceedings, Interstate Commerce Commission, Washington, D.C. 20523. The FTC maintains jurisdication over all credit advertising and also credit policies of retail shops, department stores, finance companies, nonbank credit card issuers, and all other creditors. Address your complaint to the nearest regional FTC office, or write to Truth-in-Lending, Federal Trade Commission, Washington, D.C. 20580.

Bank Card Disputes

New procedures have been set up for protesting an alleged billing error on your bank credit card statement. The rule, issued by the Federal Reserve System in 1975, allows you to withhold payment, but it requires you to notify the creditor within 60 days after you receive the statement. The creditor has to correct or challenge the alleged mistake within 90 days. Otherwise, it must forfeit the disputed amount. If the dispute is resolved in favor of the card issuer, however, the issuer has the right to levy finance charges on the funds you withheld during the dispute.

Credit Card Liability

Once you start establishing credit, you will obtain credit cards that can cost you money if they get into the wrong hands and are used illegally. If you do find a card missing, your first concern should be to telephone the card issuer. Note for your records the name of the person who takes the information.

Most credit card issuers provide a printed postcard or an enclosure in your bill that you can use to report lost or stolen cards. Unauthorized use of your cards is not your responsibility (beyond a possible $50 maximum that some issuers may charge) once you notify the card issuer. Always send a written statement of the problem, but also call to save time. See the list of "800" toll-free telephone numbers in Appendix 3, containing numbers for many firms that issue credit cards.

Under federal law, the maximum amount of your liability for unauthorized use of your credit card is $50, regardless of when you notify the issuer of loss or theft. Although $50 is not a great deal of money, if you carry 10 credit cards, your possible liability jumps to $500. Therefore, try to keep the number of cards you hold to a minimum and lock them away for safekeeping.

At one time a company could issue a credit card without any request by a customer. This policy has been outlawed by federal regulations, and complaints have been filed against several companies in violation. If you are issued a card without requesting it, or you are deceived into requesting it by signing a contract or sales slip that has the request in small print you may not notice, contact the Federal Trade Commission, which will investigate.

Credit Reform

To strengthen the current laws affecting credit practices, the FTC in 1975 proposed a trade regulation rule to eliminate unfair provisions of credit contracts. The new rule would ban any provision that (1) gives the creditor the right to go to court to get a judgment against you without any prior notification; (2) assesses you a penalty for making late or extended payments that would raise the annual percentage rate for the credit to a higher level; (3) forces you to give up the right to your home and household furnishings if you stop making payments; (4) gives the creditor the opportunity to claim other goods in your home if you do not pay; (5) provides for a security interest clause that does not specify each item of secured property; (6) assigns your wages; and (7) makes you responsible for payment of the creditor's legal fees should you default (refrain from making all payments on the loan).

The proposed rule would require a contract to spell out that the creditor must credit you with the fair market value of any item taken by default. Another mandatory provision would be that the creditor could contact only the consumer, the consumer's spouse, and the consumer's attorney in trying to collect outstanding payments.

The proposed regulations would require the creditor to furnish the cosigner of a loan with a statement explaining the liability at least three days before the loan agreement is executed. The creditor would have to give the cosigner a copy of any document the latter signs or the lender receives.

Protective Services

To fill the need for rapid help when a consumer finds credit cards gone, at least five companies have set up protective services. For an annual fee, these firms will register in their computer banks a list of your credit card numbers. Should your cards be lost or stolen, all it takes is a toll-free phone call to the computer center. Letters are immediately sent out on your behalf, notifying the card issuers.

Such services are offered by: (1) Carte Blanche, Instant Recall Service, P.O. Box 7768, Philadelphia, Pennsylvania 19101; (2) Credit Card Sentinel, Inc., 9701 Mason Avenue, Chatsworth, California 91311; (3) Hot-Line Credit Card Bureau of America, P.O. Box 4963, Fort Lauderdale, Florida 33338; (4) International Charge Card Registry, Operations Center, 3430 Southwest 320th Street, Federal Way, Washington 98002; and (5) Credit Card Service Bureau of America, P.O. Box 9130, Alexandria, Virginia 22304.

The firms are similar in nature. They handle customers throughout the country and charge about $6 to $12 annually. You can add or delete any card from the list by writing or phoning. They accept calls on a 24-hour, seven-days-a-week basis from anywhere in the United States. Phone numbers for these and other companies are listed by category in Appendix 3.

All of the above companies except the International Charge Card Registry state in their literature that they will notify all credit card issuers of any change in your address. It seems worth it to join for a year if you know you will be moving. Otherwise, you will have to contact many companies to let them know, and to avoid finance charges added to your accounts simply because you pay late after a delay in receiving forwarded bills.

Credit Card Sentinel and Carte Blanche Instant Recall Service also provide tags and stickers for identification of keys and luggage, so that if you lose these you have a better chance of getting them back. The finder is instructed, in the case of keys, to drop them in the mailbox. They are returned postpaid to the protection service, and forwarded to you. A label for luggage instructs the airline or individual who picks up the wrong bag or finds a suitcase to call the protection service for instructions. The International Charge Card Registry and the Credit Card Service Bureau of America advertise a luggage—but no key—registry, with the latter firm charging an extra $7 for that service. The Hot-Line Credit Card Bureau of America does not list these particular services in its brochures.

The Carte Blanche Instant Recall Service and Credit Card Sentinel will also register a list of documents, product serial numbers, and other important information you may need in case of fire or theft at your residence. If you have a chronic medical problem, you might want to consider a special service of Hot-Line Credit Card Bureau of America and the International Charge Card Registry. The former will supply you with a wallet-size card containing a microfilm copy of your medical history; the latter will store medical information in its files and, in the case of an emergency, respond to the doctor's toll-free call for medical information.

Carte Blanche, for a small additional fee, will allow you to register your pets, providing a tag to attach to the animal's color or cage for immediate identification by the finder. Carte Blanche's Instant Recall Service has been slightly cheaper than the other two companies, but use of the service requires your obtaining and paying the additional, higher annual fee for a Carte Blanche credit card.

Three of the companies offer immediate financial assistance should your credit cards be lost or stolen. Hot-Line Credit Card Bureau will make you a 60-day, interest-free loan of $100 if you are at least 100 miles from your home and have reported your cards lost or stolen at least 24 hours before you request the money. The Credit Card Service Bureau of America will provide a 30-day, $100 interest-free loan or an airline ticket home. The International Charge Card Registry will give you a 45-day, interest-free loan for $300 or an airline ticket home.

If you are concerned with getting the most protection for your money, Credit Card Sentinel is recommended over the others for one specific reason. It is the only service of those surveyed that says it will cover financial liability that may result from fraudulent card use.

Suppose your wallet is lost or stolen, and you discover the loss immediately. All of the protection services guarantee immediate notification of the card companies, so your quick call to them makes it virtually impossible for you to be charged for fraudulent use of your credit cards. But what if you do not discover the loss until the next day, or two or three days later? A Credit Card Sentinel representative has stated that as long as a member in good faith notifies that company as soon as he or she *realizes* the loss (even if days have elapsed), the company will pay all charges (within the legal limits of $50 per card) that may be assessed for fraudulent use.

If you are on a trip and lose your traveler's checks, you want to be sure they can be replaced quickly. American Express claims that it can usually replace missing checks within 24 hours. The company also provides a telephone service day and night in case of loss. This firm will provide refund or replacement of checks at thousands of pickup points throughout the world.

Lost Refunds

Now you see it, now you don't. That seems to have been the policy of some department store chains in handling customer refunds. When a customer overpaid a bill or returned merchandise and so received a credit on his or her charge account, unless the credit was used within a few months the funds would be diverted into corporate accounts without the customer's being notified.

According to the Federal Trade Commission, companies that have engaged in this practice include Associated Dry Goods of New York, which owns Lord & Taylor stores; McCrory Corporation of New York, which has the Lerner stores; Carter Hawley Hale Stores of Los Angeles, which operates such stores as Neiman-Marcus and Bergdorf Goodman; Gimbel Bros. of New York; and Genesco, Inc., of Nashville, which has the Bonwit Teller stores. It was alleged by the FTC that these five chains had taken a total of $2.8 million from customer charge accounts over a five-year period.

To protect yourself from such practices, never leave a credit balance in your account. You might as well put it in a safer place, such as a savings account, where you will earn interest. Request a cash refund when you return merchandise or discover you have overpaid your account. Some stores will provide an immediate refund; others will mail you a check. Any store that refuses to provide a cash refund to clear a credit balance is not worthy of your business.

Payment under Protest

You probably have been confronted at some time with having to pay for a product, service, or repair job that you felt was poor and deserving of no or only partial payment. For instance, suppose you bring in a broken television set, and the service representative estimates that the charges will run about $25. That amount is satisfactory because you cannot afford to spend more than $30 if you are to maintain your budget. You leave the television at the shop and request that you be called if the charges will come to more than $30.

When you pick up the set, you are told that it needed additional work. You mention that you received no call, and the servicer tells you that he or she tried to call you without success, so the repair person went ahead and fixed it. You are then handed a bill for $56.

You justifiably complain that the additional repairs should not have been done without authorization from you, and had you known about the higher amount you would not have had the set fixed. The repair person then refuses to return your television unless you pay the full amount. Withholding your property for nonpayment of the service bill is illegal in some states, but the shop owners get away with it because they know the small probability that you will take the time and money to file a lawsuit.

You now have two choices. You can either leave the set in the hands of the repair service for eventual disposal as it sees fit, or you can pay the charges and get the set back into your possession. Since in this situation the World Series or the Super Bowl always seems to be on the next day, you will probably take the latter alternative.

In that case, make your dissatisfaction known and thus protect your rights for any future complaint or lawsuit you may file against the service company. Write one of the following phrases above your check signature and, if possible, on all copies of the sales slip: "without prejudice," "under protest," "under reserve," or "with reservation of all my rights." Should you later make a complaint to a government agency or file a suit, your prior action will show that you disagreed with the bill at the time of payment and will prevent the other side from taking the false stand that you showed satisfaction at that time. This could even cause a judge to look more favorably on your case.

BIG BROTHER CREDIT— REPORTING SERVICES

If you have ever had life insurance, a charge account, a mortgage, or a loan, or if you have ever applied for a job, someone somewhere has a file on you that may contain anything from your name, address, and social security number to an alleged affair with your next-door neighbor. Consumer reporting agencies gather and sell the information in your file to a variety of businesses with which you have made contact, including creditors, insurers, and employers.

Congress passed the Fair Credit Reporting Act in 1971 to protect consumers. The law spells out guidelines attempting to assure that credit reporting services' records on consumers will be fair and confidential. It also provides procedures by which you can review your file and have corrected any erroneous and outdated information. The law covers all consumer credit, including home and automobile loans and retail credit.

You can find a list of firms maintaining credit files by looking in the telephone book Yellow Pages under Credit Reporting Agencies. Some of the listed companies handle only commercial accounts. Call each firm and ask if it maintains credit files on individual customers. If it does, ask that it check to see if there is a file on you. If so, ask how you can review the information that the file contains.

Your Credit Report

If you are turned down for insurance, a loan, or a charge account, you have a legal right to know if a credit report played any part in denying your request for credit. If so, the company refusing to extend the credit must furnish you with the name and address of the credit reporting agency.

Any time a company turns you down for employment or credit, or raises your credit or insurance rates, some of the information supplied to that firm from your credit file may be false, misleading, or outdated. After any type of negative notification, you have 30 days in which to request a free review of your file from the credit reporting agency. After 30 days, you may still make such a request, but the firm can then charge you a fee to provide the information. If you are denied credit, but the creditor states that it is not due to a credit report, or simply withholds the name of any specific agency, the credit reporting firm you contact may or may not charge you a fee to review your file.

Most agencies will fulfill your request for a file review either in person or by mail or phone. Many require that you send a letter of request as a means of identification before they will set up a phone interview.

Should you make a visit to the agency, you are allowed to have one other person with you. Although the agency is not legally required to allow you to handle your file physically or to provide you with a copy of its contents, it must tell you the substance and noninvestigative sources of all nonmedical information on you that it has accumulated. The company must also reveal the names of clients who have reviewed your report as part of a credit application within the previous six months, or as part of an employment application during the preceding two years.

Your credit file will contain standard identifying information as well as comments about current and paid loans, credit cards, charge accounts, collections, tax liens, bankruptcies, and court judgments. Carefully scrutinize all information. Challenge any item that is not currently correct and that might adversely affect a report.

The agency is required to investigate any correction you feel is warranted. If the entry is found to be inaccurate, or there is presently no way to verify it, the company must delete it from the record and fulfill any request you make to inform past inquirers of the deletion.

Should you dispute the agency's reinvestigation and subsequent decision not to change an entry, you have the right to include in your report a brief statement expressing your side. In addition to including your full personal statement or a summary of it in future requests for credit information, for a reasonable fee you can ask the agency to send a copy of your version of the dispute to specific businesses.

If you once took out a loan and faithfully paid it back, or you opened a charge account that you have kept in good standing, and such facts are not on your credit report, you can generally request voluntarily placing this information in your file. This could better your chances of obtaining credit in the future, especially if you want to try to offset some negative entries.

Under the Fair Credit Reporting Act, no credit reporting agency may divulge any information from your file to anyone who does not have a legitimate business need. No government agency can have access to your file unless you have applied to that agency for a license or other benefit. If you have gone bankrupt, such information may be reported for a maximum of 14 years. Any other adverse information must be deleted from your file after seven years.

Sometimes a creditor will request more detailed information about an applicant. This might include an interview with a third person about your life-style, reputation, or character. A creditor must inform you that this type of report is being solicited. You then have the right to request from the creditor further details about the nature and scope of the investigation. Once the investigation has been completed, you have a legal right to know the substance of the information collected, but not the sources.

Follow up any request you make to a credit reporting agency or creditor. If an agency reinvestigates some entries in your file and, as a result, deleterious data are deleted, get a corrected report, contact each company that you requested the agency to notify, and make sure the new information has been received.

Credit Agency Complaints

The FTC is responsible for the enforcement of the credit reporting law. Should you find it necessary to complain about a company's credit investigation or the operations of any credit reporting agency, contact the nearest regional FTC office or write to the Federal Trade Commission, Washington, D.C. 20580. If a credit reporting firm negligently or willfully violates the law, you also can take it to court and sue for damages and attorney's fees.

The FTC has filed many complaints against companies allegedly violating the Fair Credit Reporting Act. In 1975 the Commission accepted an agreement containing an order that forbade Checkmate Inquiry Service, Inc., of New York from violating the act. The complaint alleged that the company (1) did not make disclosures to consumers about their right to have their side of disputed information sent to companies; (2) did not furnish such statements on behalf of consumers to those persons designated by the consumers; and (3) in subsequent consumer credit reports did not label appropriate entries as disputed and provide the consumer's statement or an accurate summary of it.

In another action, the FTC accepted an agreement with a consent order prohibiting the National Credit Exchange and the National Fraudulent Check Bureau, both of Canton, Illinois, from furnishing consumer credit reports to persons not having a legally permissible purpose for receiving such information.

THE COLLECTORS

Another type of profession besides door-to-door sales that is known for big-mouth, tactless workers is bill collection.

Past Due!

When you open a charge account, the store is so accommodating. Your card is accepted with a smile, and you may even get a printed form letter from the company president welcoming you as a charge customer and asking you to bring directly to his or her attention any problem in your dealings with the establishment.

All is fine, and you pay your bills regularly. Then suddenly you need an emergency appendectomy or your 1959 Dodge has run its last mile. After not being able to pay your bills for a few months, the company smile gives way to the credit manager's bared fangs. The finance charges get larger and the "past due" ink redder. Interspersed with monthly statements are letters that get more threatening. Then come phone calls from a person who comes across innocently at first, but ends up in a threatening manner. You are told that you had better pay the money you owe or your credit rating will be destroyed, your home and car will be taken away, and you will be prosecuted as a criminal. This collection agency representative says that in addition to a lawsuit, he or she may have to use stronger tactics, implying, you think, that even your safety may be in jeopardy. The collection agency takes you to court, and you finally lose your home to pay your bills.

This is an extreme example of what can happen if you are unable to keep making payments because of unforeseen circumstances, but the practices mentioned—some of them not only intolerable but illegal—have been used to scare consumers into paying their debts.

Creditor Recourse

To gain an understanding of what to do when payment problems occur, first consider the differences between your utility and nonutility creditors. If you stop paying your electric bill, for example, the power company can take effective recourse without going to court. After a couple of warnings, you may return to your all-electric home one winter evening to find it dark and freezing. Once a utility has shut off service, it may require you to pay the bill in full before it will resume service. The reinstallation may take a full day.

Other types of creditors, such as department stores, banks, and fee credit card companies, do not have much recourse other than finally seeking a court judgment. The only exception is a creditor who finances the purchase of your automobile. Generally this creditor can repossess your car for nonpayment without going to court.

No large company is going to take the time and money to pursue the case in court for a small amount such as $50, $100, sometimes even $2,000. Even if the firm does turn the matter over to an attorney, it could take many months for the case to go to court.

If a creditor succeeds in winning a judgment against you, the court can order that your wages be garnished. Involvement in such a case can be both bothersome and embarrassing for you, not to mention the added bookkeeping required by your employer.

Federal law does prohibit an employer from firing you on the basis of just one garnishment. The Truth-in-Lending Law also sets a limit on the amount of money that can be involuntarily withdrawn from your earnings. This maximum is whichever of the following two categories is less: (1) 25 percent of disposable pay (that is, any pay that remains after all legally required deductions such as income taxes and social security are withheld); or (2) the total amount of disposable earnings over an amount equal to 30 times the current federal minimum hourly wage. (In 1976 this amount, based on a job's minimum wage of $2.30 per hour, would have been $69.)

Prepare Yourself

There are many steps you can take to protect yourself from the bill collectors. As previously mentioned, do not maintain funds for a bank charge card account and a savings or checking account in the same institution. The banking firm could withdraw money from one account to pay charges on the other without your permission.

If you own a home, you should take some simple legal steps to claim the place as your "homestead." Go to any large stationery store and request the appropriate forms. Once you have filled out these papers and filed them with the county recorder or other designated office in your state, you will be able to protect as much as $15,000 of your property from seizure or lien.

The institution of marriage can give you some protection against lawsuits. You often can transfer your property to your spouse or even your children, none of whom will be responsible for your debts. If you carry separate property from your spouse and move to a state with community property laws, such as Arizona, California, Idaho, Montana, Nevada, and New Mexico, neither you nor your spouse can be held responsible for each other's separate debts.

If you ever face a financial crisis, your first concern should be continuing payments or making special arrangements for extended credit on products and services without which your daily life would be disrupted, such as utilities and automobile. Unfortunately, some creditors will refuse you any leeway at all, even in the case of an unavoidable serious financial emergency. Others are more flexible, especially if the delinquent payments need to be deferred for only two or three months.

Stalling Techniques

Your strategy for dealing with severe financial difficulties should be to stall the bill collectors as long as it is helpful. Most collection agencies will try a few times to collect on your account or arrange a payment schedule before turning the matter over to an attorney. This will often give you enough time to get the necessary funds together. Do not stall so long that you finally are subpoenaed to defend yourself in court.

In gaining time to pay for your overdue bills, you must convince the bill collector of your sincerity in wanting to make good on the account in the near future. Stay in contact with collectors rather than evading them, because if they think you are preparing to leave town they may not wait before filing a suit. You can be less concerned about paying off any balance of $25 or less, because the creditor will almost positively not want to take the time or money to sue you. Just assure the creditor that you will pay as soon as possible.

Many professional persons such as doctors will accept a small monthly payment without resorting to court action. With your check for whatever amount you can afford, enclose a short note expressing your financial difficulty. Your payment plan will often be acceptable, and the due balance probably will not be given over to a collection agency.

Collection Deals

Despite your efforts to extend the time limit for payment of a bill, some creditors will refer your account to a collection agency. This agency works on a percentage basis, generally one-third to one-half of any amount they can get from you.

This situation actually puts you in a bargaining position that you may want to take advantage of. Explain your circumstances, and, if possible, set up a payment schedule with the agency for full or partial repayment of the debt. If you feel that you cannot pay off that particular account, offer a compromise figure or maybe half the delinquent balance. Many collectors will accept such a settlement rather than having to go to court.

Often the collection agency will ask you to set a date by which the amount agreed upon will be paid. Of course, the intimation is that the agency wants payment as soon as possible, preferably within a couple of weeks. However, take the offensive and tell the collector that you are doing the best you can and will pay off the debt in 30 (or 60 or 90) days. Some collectors will give in.

If you find yourself in a sea of bills with credit sharks circling for the kill, recognize the fact that you will need help to get out of the mess. Do not wait until you receive five notices of impending lawsuits before you realize something more than wishful thinking will be required to clear up the problem. One answer may be a credit counselor.

Credit Counseling

There is nothing to be ashamed of in going to a credit counselor. A toothache sends you to a dentist, marital difficulties may require a marriage counselor, and debt may need a credit counselor. Such a counselor is not going to scream at you or make critical judgments about how you have handled your money. The person is there to assist constructively in getting you out of debt with the least trouble.

Although there are two types of credit counselors often available to consumers—those in nonprofit community clinics and those who profit from their services—more and more states are outlawing counseling companies that primarily handle debt consolidation. Why go to a profit-making operation that will charge you much more in fees for the same service? You can find the nearest nonprofit debt counseling service (which often goes by the name of Consumer Credit Counseling Service) by looking in your telephone directory Yellow Pages under such headings as Financial Consultants or Social Service Agencies, or by writing to the National Foundation for Consumer Credit, Inc., Federal Bar Building West, 1819 H Street N.W., Washington, D.C. 20006.

Nonprofit debt counseling services do not make any loans. They function to assist you to pay off creditors and avoid losing your home, your car, and your credit in general. They offer this help either free or for a nominal charge. They will give you good advice and help you to set up the most efficient plan to end your debt. They will also expect you to cooperate in keeping your commitment to follow through on your plan of payments.

When you first go into a consumer credit counseling service, the representative will help you to work out a realistic budget. You will be assisted in totaling all your monthly expenses, including rent, food, transportation, clothing, and insurance. The amount of your debt will generally then be determined by deducting your monthly net income.

If you do not have enough money to resume full payments on current and delinquent accounts, the counseling service will contact each of your creditors and ask them to accept a reduced and extended schedule of payments. Creditors often cooperate with the service because they would rather see you commit yourself to paying what you owe rather than take the alternative of bankruptcy, where they may come out without a cent.

After the counseling service arranges your payment plan with creditors, you will pay to the service an agreed-upon portion of your earnings each month. The service will distribute the money to your creditors until they all have been satisfied. If some companies refuse to accept anything less than full payment, the counselor may recommend that you get a loan from a credit union or some source of lower interest loans.

If there seems little chance that any effective steps can be taken to help you out of debt using the above method, you may be advised

to consider an alternative such as personal bankruptcy. In that case, you should contact your local legal aid society for assistance. To locate the nearest one, ask any social service agency or your local bar association.

Bankruptcy Alternatives

One alternative to making payments through a credit counseling service or declaring personal bankruptcy is to enter into a court-administered Wage Earner Plan. This protects you from various types of unpleasant creditor recourse such as garnishment, delinquency hearings, and more finance charges, but the cost can be more than double what you might pay at a nonprofit community debt counseling service.

Under this plan, you have 18 to 36 months to pay your creditors. This will be accomplished by the court appointing a trustee to distribute debt payments from a reasonable portion of your earnings, leaving enough for you to live on. You can find out more information by calling the bankruptcy division of the nearest federal court. It will be listed in the phone directory under United States Government, with a sublisting of Courts, U.S. Courts, or Bankruptcy Judges.

If you own property, you may also consider having an attorney assign it to a trustee, who will pay your debts from the property's income. This not only gives you some control over which creditors are paid first, but may even allow you to hold onto the property once your debts have been satisfied.

Collection Abuses

Despite how mean and ugly bill collectors can be, they cannot order you to be beheaded or something equally fatal. In fact, they have no legal right to harrass you in any way at all. Their zealous efforts that turn to abuse can be effectively countered if you understand your rights and the ways in which the law protects you.

As previously stated, no bill collector can attach all your wages and leave you with nothing to live on. If you feel that too much money is being garnished from your earnings, contact your state employment office for information and assistance.

No collection agency can threaten, frighten, or otherwise harass you over the phone. If this happens even once, you should complain to two different sources. First, write a letter of complaint to the Federal Communications Commission, Washington, D.C. 20554, or call directly and explain the problem. Local FCC offices do not have the authority to intervene on your behalf. Second, call your telephone company business office and request to speak to a representative regarding abusive calls. This utility can shut off the service of anyone who abuses it in this way. Inform the collector that you will not tolerate the abuse and that you have made formal complaints to the authorities.

In addition, most states have laws to protect their residents from unruly bill collectors. Call the nearest office of your state attorney general or any local law enforcement agency for information on avenues of recourse.

FTC Help

In recent years, the Federal Trade Commission has been taking an increasing role in protecting the public against unfair and deceptive methods of debt collection. In 1975 the Commission accused the following companies of engaging in the deceptive collection practice of sending a series of threatening form letters to people with unpaid bills: Community Systems Corporation and its subsidiary, Powers Service, Inc., of Chicago; United Computered Collections, Inc., of Cincinnati; North American Collections, Inc., of St. Louis; Continental Collection Service of Clarissa, Minnesota; Trans World Accounts, Inc., of Santa Rosa, California; Continental Credit Corporation, Inc., of Willingboro, New Jersey; Continental Collection Bureau of America, Inc., of Atlanta; and Trans National Credit Corporation of Hazelton, Pennsylvania.

The FTC charged that these firms engaged in the service of selling to creditors a package of abusive letters, and were not in business to collect payments on debts as was allegedly represented to consumers. Various statements by some of the firms, which indicated that a debtor's credit rating was in jeopardy or that a lawsuit would soon be filed, were allegedly false.

In addition to alleged use of deceptive letters to induce collection, the Seattle firm of State Credit Association, Inc., was also accused by the FTC in the same year of using unfair methods, including false identities to gain information that might prove helpful in collection.

Through an agreement containing a consent order, the FTC also prohibited Inter-Continental Services Corporation and North American Credit Services, Inc., of Shawnee Missions, Kansas, from falsely representing themselves as credit reporting agencies and stating nonpayment of debts would result immediately in legal action. The firms were ordered not to make phone calls to debtors outside of specified hours for the purpose of retrieving credit cards.

In February 1975, FTC Administrative Law Judge Harry R. Hinkes struck down the policy of the Speigel, Inc., catalog order company to sue in Chicago courts debtors who in some instances lived long distances away. The company would gain many default judgments as a result of non-appearing defendants in court.

The FTC ruling states that you cannot be sued for collection of a bill in a court that is unreasonably far from your home. In the same consent order based on the aforementioned case against State Credit Association, Inc., the company was also ordered to follow a policy of bringing suit in only one of the following places: (1) the county where the debtor lives when the lawsuit is filed; (2) the county where the debtor signed the contract, or (3) if there was no written agreement, wherever the debt was incurred. If one of your creditors tries to engage you in a long-distance collection suit or participates in any deceptive tactic to collect money, complain to the nearest FTC regional office or contact the headquarters: Federal Trade Commission, Washington, D.C. 20580.

Chapter 9

POST OFFICE "EFFICIENCY"

The United States Postal Service is a vast communications network that provides many—some little known—services to the consumer. It has a budget of more than $12 billion to employ almost 675,000 people and operate over 30,000 post offices nationwide.

One of the most widespread general consumer complaints involves the amount of time required for a letter or parcel to be sent from one city to another or even to another place within the same city. The Postal Service is responsible for bettering mail service through the modernizing of its operations, but the vastness of the system, the growing mail volume, and the abundant inefficiency make it a difficult service with which to do business. This chapter will help you to keep on top of postal matters.

GETTING THE MOST FROM
THE POSTAL SERVICE

Before outlining the procedures for presenting different types of complaints, it may be helpful to provide some general mailing tips. First, mail early in the day, when most postal employees are working. Often a letter or parcel can be delivered the following day to a distant city if your mail is picked up from a letter box or post office in the morning or early afternoon.

Use a Certificate of Mailing, Postal Service Form 3817, when-

ever you may later have to prove that you mailed a letter or package, or that you placed it in the mail before a deadline date. Simply fill in your return address and the name and address of the person or firm to whom the article is addressed. Then affix 10 cents in postage, and present the form and the article to be mailed to the clerk at any post office. The form will be stamped and returned to you as a receipt with a dated postmark.

ZIP Codes and Postal Services

Always address your letter or parcel with a correct ZIP code. The equipment now used in mail distribution depends on mail having ZIP codes. A piece of mail being processed without a ZIP code or with an error in the five digits must be delayed for personal attention in routing.

The national ZIP code directory has listings for every delivery zone in the country. This directory may be consulted at any post office or library, or purchased for $7.50 from the Superintendent of Documents, Government Printing Office, Washington, D.C. 20402. A privately published, less complete paperback ZIP Code directory is now available also for less than $3 at many bookstores and newsands. You may exchange an outdated governmented-printed directory for a revised edition at any time without charge.

If you need to check or find just one ZIP code, call any local post office and request ZIP information. Mention the city and the street or box address, and the clerk will provide you with the correct code. Businesses that address mail by computer may borrow at no charge through their post office customer service a "Zip-A-List" computer tape of ZIP code listings throughout the United States.

It is important to label some outgoing mail with the postal class of your choice. A large manila envelope may not be treated as "first class" mail unless it is so labeled on both sides.

Two special postal services guaranteeing delivery the next day are Mailgram, a combination letter and telegram that you can send by calling any Western Union office by midnight, and Express Mail, a system set up only between large cities for faster delivery at higher charges. Controlpak is a mail service providing added security for the mailing of credit cards and other valuable items. Specific information about utilizing these special services, insuring mail, and sending certified and registered articles may be obtained by calling or visiting any post office. The best general guide to the use of postal services is a booklet entitled *Mailer's Guide*, available free of charge from many post offices or by writing to the Consumer Advocate, U.S. Postal Service, Washington, D.C. 20260.

Mail Collection

In an interesting, although admittedly unscientific, mid-1974 study by the Special Projects Division of CBS News, television network employees posted 10 first class and 10 airmail letters from points in six major cities. There were eight groups of such letters, totaling 160, each group addressed to its own destination and mailed from the same collection box at the same time. Of the 160 letters, 15 airmail and 12 first class arrived first, and then the other 133 letters arrived at their respective destinations as a mixed batch of airmail and first class—indicating that airmail did not achieve speedier delivery.

The report further revealed the Postal Service's own figures for the first quarter of 1974: 62 percent of the time there was overnight delivery for first class mail, while airmail letters arrived the next day only 22 percent of the time. The Assistant Postmaster General, in a televised interview, admitted not personally using airmail for possibly the past 30 years, and he said that some proposals calling for the elimination of "airmail" were being prepared. "Airmail" service was finally abandoned at the end of 1975. Today, most first-class letters go by air anyway.

Certain national minimum collection standards have been set by the Postal Service to try to ensure the regularity and promptness of mail pickup and delivery. Although collection times arc often posted on boxes, it is possible to generalize about the best way to recognize and use different types of mail boxes.

All mail collection boxes may be divided into three categories —two star, one star, and nonstar. The two star, sometimes called the "night owl," type is located outside many post offices and in business areas. It has two large white stars on the side or front of the box, with daily pickup times scheduled according to area requirements, including on weekdays at least one collection shortly after 5:00 p.m. and the last one between 6:30 and 8:30 p.m. You can expect a minimum of one Saturday collection at 6:00 p.m. or later, except when the transportation schedules necessitate earlier collection.

Mailboxes with one large star are located on main streets and in business areas. On weekdays at least two collections are made, one at 5:00 p.m. or later. One or more Saturday pickups will be made at 5:00 p.m. or later.

The third category has no stars and is generally located in residential areas. The letter carrier picks up mail from these boxes at least once on a daily basis, including Saturday.

Sunday mail collections vary greatly and depend on available transportation schedules and adequate staffing. Mail not collected from a residential box on a Sunday will be picked up on Monday even if it is a holiday.

To time your letters and parcels for faster delivery, locate each of the three types of collection boxes nearest your residence and business. When trying to get out correspondence in a hurry, this knowledge will prevent the frustration of driving around a city trying to find a box where mail will be picked up in the late afternoon or early evening.

In the states of Maryland, New Jersey, eastern New York, Pennsylvania, Virginia, and West Virginia, as well as the District of Columbia, the stars on collection boxes on main streets and thoroughfares have been replaced with numbers that measure seven inches tall. The number on each box indicates the time of the last collection for that box. The U.S. Postal Service intends to expand this program throughout the nation in 1977. Every collection box now must also designate the address of the nearest box where a later collection will be made.

Postmasters are required to maintain the national minimum

level of collection standards mentioned above. Some slight variations may exist at certain locations in some cities, but if you live in an area where these minimum standards are not met, send a letter of complaint to the Consumer Advocate, U.S. Postal Service, Washington, D.C. 20260.

Delivery Complaints

U.S. Postal Service carriers have the reputation of reliably delivering mail, undaunted by heat, rain, sleet, and snow, but you may run up against any number of problems that should be reported. First, whether at a post office box, home, or office, you may subscribe to a daily publication such as a trade paper. When it does not arrive on a particular day, either the distributor has been late in delivering the issue to the post office or, more likely today, the post office has delayed in moving the piece of mail.

Second, when you do not receive correspondence you are expecting, the mail may be addressed or forwarded in such a way that the carrier is mistakenly returning or holding it. If you have recently submitted a notice of change of address, the post office may have erred in processing it.

Third, a card announcing the attempt to deliver certified, registered, insured, or postage-due mail should never be left by the carrier unless he or she has made an honest effort to leave the mail with the addressee, who happens not to be at home, or with the office, which he or she finds closed.

When problems arise, a call to the responsible station can usually bring action. Call any local post office and ask the name and phone number of the branch that handles the delivery of mail with your ZIP code (give your street or box address if you do not know your ZIP code).

After contacting the correct post office, ask to speak to the carrier who delivers to your address, the supervisor of carriers, or (preferably) the customer service representative. In the above and some other types of problems, a commonly used PS (Postal Service) Form 1835 will be filled out by the person taking your complaint. The postal representative will record your name and address, the reason for your call or visit, eventual findings, action taken, and a designation as to whether the Postal Service was at fault or there was a "customer misunderstanding."

If you want a response to your complaint and it cannot be given before the problem is evaluated or investigated, request during the initial contact that you be notified by letter or phone of the action taken. If prompt corrective action is not taken, bring your complaint to the attention of the postmaster at the same office. If the problem is still not handled effectively, write to the Consumer Advocate, U.S. Postal Service, Washington, D.C. 20260.

When you purchase postage, you are paying for service. If you can show that reasonably good service was not provided for the moving of your piece of mail, you are entitled to a refund. For example, if you send a package by air parcel post from New York to Los Angeles and it does not arrive until two weeks later, there has been bad service and you are entitled to receive a refund on the postage. Either the receiver or sender may file an "Application and Voucher for Refund of Postage and Fees," PS Form 3533, and the sender will receive a refund in the mail. The wrapper with the departing and receiving postmarks should be saved as proof. Refunds are applicable to total postage fees paid, usually excluding special service fees for registration, certification, insurance, and C.O.D. The refund form may be obtained from, and submitted to, any post office or to the Postal Service's Consumer Advocate.

Machine Losses

The federal government is responsible for refunding any money you lose in the purchase of postage stamps, insurance, envelopes, and so on at any post office or self-service postal unit. If the loss occurs in a post office during business hours, go to any window and the clerk will process your claim. He or she will provide you with whatever you tried to get from the machine or will make an immediate refund. If window service is closed, make the complaint in person during the next scheduled business hours, or send a letter specifying the date of loss, location, type of machine, amount of loss, and your return address to the Postmaster, U.S. Postal Service, in the city where the loss occurred.

Many self-service postal centers have been set up at shopping malls and college campuses throughout the country. These units are operated by the local or regional post office and often provide a rack containing postpaid Postal Action Cards, which may be used for detailing your machine loss, suggestions about better service, or complaints. These cards should be addressed in the manner described above.

Offensive Mail

With an increasing quantity of sexually oriented advertising being distributed through the mail, laws have been passed to protect an individual and his or her family from exposure to material they consider offensive. If you, or a person under 19 living with you, receive in the mail an unwanted advertisement, which offers for sale erotically or sexually provocative matter, you may request from any post office PS Form 2150, entitled "Post Office Department Notice for Prohibitory Order Against Sender of Pandering Advertisement in the Mails." By filling out the form, including the names of any affected minors, and submitting it with the objectionable advertisement and the envelope or wrapper in which it arrived, you can stop all future mailings from that particular sender. The latter is notified of your request by the post office and has the legal responsibility to concede to your demand within 30 days.

Beginning in 1971, a more comprehensive method of dealing with the unwanted receipt of sexually oriented advertisements was made available to consumers. Under the law, you may now complete at your local post office PS Form 2201, entitled "Application for Listing Persuant to 39 USC 3010," and thereby legally prohibit anyone from sending such ads to you and any minors you list. Upon submission of this form to any postal representative, you (and those under 19 you include) will be put on a reference list, which is updated monthly and made available to companies and individuals engaged in the mailing of such advertisements. A sender who violates the law by mailing a sexually oriented ad to any person whose name has appeared on the reference list subjects him- or herself to possible civil and criminal prosecution by the United States government.

If you submit this application, you may subsequently cancel it by notifying your local post office in writing; otherwise, your name will remain on the list for five years, when a new application must be filed. Should you receive a sexually oriented advertisement after the required 30-day waiting period, you may request that a post office take further action. Follow three simple steps: (1) print on the envelope or wrapper, "I received this item on (specify date)," and sign it; (2) be sure that you open the sealed piece of mail since the law prohibits anyone except the addressee from opening first class matter, and you will want investigators to have access to the enclosed advertisement to use as evidence in any legal action; and (3) take the material in its original envelope to the clerk at any post office.

Some consumers also may find other types of mail offensive, but only the receipt of sexually oriented advertisements may be stopped unless there is some criminal intent or unlawful material being mailed. For example, if you receive a note threatening bodily injury in connection with a kidnapping or in an extortion attempt, you should immediately telephone the police department or FBI for assistance. In the case of guns, poison, or other unlawful mailings of which you are aware, follow the instructions later in this chapter under Prohibited Mailings.

"Junk" Mail

Some bulk-rate mail, consisting of advertising and other less important material, is not welcomed by consumers. Although there is no federal law prohibiting such mail, you can refuse receipt of *any* individual letter or parcel—first class, bulk rate, registered, or otherwise—for *any* reason. The procedure in refusing a piece of mail is simple. Draw a line through the address, city and state; print the word "Refused" on the face of the envelope; sign your name just beneath that word; and drop the article in any mail depository or give it to your postal carrier. Bulk rate mail is destroyed after refusal, but first class and other categories of mail are returned to the sender. In the case of certified, C.O.D., registered, and insured mail, refusal may be made only at the time of delivery, and you should not sign the delivery receipt.

If you want to reduce the amount of mail advertising you receive, the Postal Service does provide a tip: write to the Mail Preference Service, Direct Mail/Marketing Association (DMMA), 6 East 43rd Street, New York, New York 10017. By requesting and returning a completed "name removal" form, the DMMA, representing about 65 percent of the industry, will include your name on a notification list it sends to participating member companies. On the other hand, if you want to receive more mail advertising, you can request from the same organization an "add-on" form on which you can select mail-order solicitation categories of interest to you.

Recalling Mail

Sometimes a very disturbing problem could be created for you if a letter or parcel you deposited in a mail collection box reaches its destination. Perhaps you mailed a nasty note to your employer just before you found out that he or she approved a good pay raise for you. Maybe you wrote the wrong address on a package meant to arrive on time for a special friend's or relative's birthday. Whatever the case, the Postal Service can be called upon to help you retrieve the article. As soon as you discover the need to recall a piece of mail, go to the postal station or central dispatching point (usually a large main post office) nearest the place you mailed the article and ask for PS Form 1509, "Sender's Application for Recall of Mail." Be prepared to answer questions relating to how the mail was sent (certified or whatever) and when and where it was deposited. There is also a place on the form to give the approximate size and to reproduce the face of the letter or address label.

Submit this application within the shortest possible time after the mistake has been made. Once the article is picked up and taken outside the local area along with thousands of other pieces of mail, it becomes more difficult for the Postal Service to get it back. In the case of something sent to another city, state, or country, you may wish to request any special action the postal clerk can suggest. This may include telephone calls or the sending of telegrams to distribution points between you and the addressee. You must pay expenses, if any, incurred by the acting postal station before the article will be returned to you. You must also present identification to assure the post office that the piece of mail is not being surrendered into the wrong hands. Where you have simply failed to enclose something in the recall letter or parcel, you may be required to address another envelope or wrapping and affix new postage before the article can again be mailed.

Access to Information

You can go to your local post office and, for a $1 fee, utilize the "Freedom of Information Request," PS Form 1478, to examine or obtain a photocopy of two types of information cards on file with the U.S. Postal Service. The first lists the forwarding address of someone with whom you want to correspond or whose mailing address you want to update for your address book. The second kind of information available is the business street address for a company or individual receiving business mail at a specified post office box or drawer. For a higher fee ($8), you may also gain access to a record showing someone's mailing permit.

Much information, such as the residential address of a boxholder, cannot lawfully be obtained without a subpoena by anyone other than governmental law enforcement agencies. If you feel you have a right to information to which you are denied access upon application, you may appeal the decision by writing to the General Counsel, Law Department, U.S. Postal Service, Washington, D.C. 20260.

Confirmation of Delivery

You may have occasion to send an important letter or parcel, and you want to make sure that it is received by the addressee. Requesting a return receipt from the post office at the time the article is sent will, for a small fee, assure you of getting a postal card signed by the receiver.

You may have reason to believe that what you sent to someone has not been received, either because the addressee has informed you of nonreceipt, an appropriate response has not been made, or you have not received the return receipt. In that case, request action at the post office in which you mailed the article or the post office nearest the mailbox you used. Ask for PS Form 3811-A, "Request for Return Receipt," and fill it out with the date you mailed the article and the address of both you and the addressee. This request may be made for any piece of mail you send certified, registered, or insured. The return receipt will contain the signature of the addressee or his or her agent, the date of delivery, and, for an additional charge, the place of delivery. There is no charge for this follow-up if a return receipt was originally requested and the fee previously paid. Otherwise, the standard fee is charged. Upon submitting this form to any postal clerk, an "Inquiry About Receipt of Mail," PS Form 1572, is prepared by the post office and mailed to the addressee, requesting that he or she signify whether or not your letter or parcel was received.

As soon as the addressee completes this form and returns it to the receiving postal station, you will be sent a copy of the addressee's response.

Money Orders

If you purchase a money order and make it payable to the wrong company or individual, or you decide against making the payment you originally intended, return the money order to any post office clerk. Upon showing adequate identification, you will be given a full refund for the face value. Another money order can be issued for the standard fee.

Some time after you purchase a postal money order, a question may arise as to whether the remittance was lost in the mail, stolen, or credited to the wrong account when cashed. Either you or the payee may submit PS Form 6401, "Enquiry as to Payment of Money Order." The form may not be filed until at least 60 days after the original money order was issued, and it serves as the only paper work necessary in reporting a possible loss. You will receive a reply, and if the record search indicates that the money order has not been cashed, a duplicate will be issued.

You may send a money order through the mail in payment of delivered merchandise and then be notified by the company that it has not received the payment. You may discover after filing the above inquiry form that your money order has been cashed. More than likely, either the money order has been paid unlawfully by means of a forged endorsement, or the payee has deposited your remittance without giving you credit. The circumstances can be determined by submitting PS Form 6065, "Request for Photocopy of a Money Order." There is a small fee, and the form must be filed within two years after the original date of issue. The response will include a photocopy of both the front and back of the canceled money order, which you can use in the same way you use a canceled personal check as proof of payment. If endorsement indicates that payment was made to the correct party, send a copy of your photocopy to the payee. That should close the matter. On the other hand, if forgery is indicated in the endorsement, take whatever information you have compiled to a U.S. postal inspector or a postal clerk who can refer the matter to the nearest office of the Postal Inspection Service.

Domestic Loss

When suspecting that any type of letter or parcel you have sent—insured or not—has been lost in the mail, you may file PS Form 1510, "Inquiry for the Loss or Rifling of Mail Matter." The information for this all-purpose tracer often will be taken over the phone by any postal clerk and acted upon immediately. Although the "Request for Return Receipt" previously mentioned is the best document proving receipt of *special* mail by someone on a specific date, this inquiry may be used to follow up *any* piece of mail, including an ordinary letter. The information returned in response to this query will indicate whether or not the article was received, and will carry the dated signature of the respondent.

When you find out that the insured or C.O.D. article you have sent has been lost in the mail or has arrived damaged, file a claim using your mailing and merchandise receipts with PS Form 3812, "Request for Payment of Domestic Postal Insurance." If the Postal Service loses or damages your registered article, you should file PS Form 565, "Application for Indemnity for Registered Mail." After a confirming investigation, including contact of the addressee, the papers are sent by the post office to the Postal Data Center in St. Louis, where final processing is completed and payment is sent to you.

These forms also may be submitted if you are the receiver of damaged merchandise, and you are claiming partial rather than complete loss. In this case, you should bring to any post office the damaged article (if possible); the canceled check or other receipt indicating the worth of the article; and the wrapping showing your address, the sender's address, postage, and markings that designate how the article was sent.

When a receipt is not available, you may submit the wrapper with PS Form 3825, "Request for Information—Postal Claim," on which you declare an approximate value of the article even if it was handmade or homemade. Any damaged article you submit in connection with a successful claim may be retained by the post office for future sale.

The payment of a claim is rarely denied. It is made within two weeks after submission of the completed forms unless you omit information that delays the settlement.

Foreign Loss

The inquiry and claims procedure for loss or damage of an insured or uninsured article mailed to or sent from a foreign country is similar to that described above. To find out whether an article has arrived in a foreign country, submit PS Form 542, "Inquiry About a Registered Article or an Insured Parcel or an Ordinary Parcel." Along with it, fill out PS Form 530, "Facsimile Address," on which you provide the Postal Service with a facsimile of the address on the missing parcel, preferably in the same handwriting or type style used on the original. One inquiry form may be used for several articles as long as you sent them in the same category of mail (for example, insured or registered), at the same time and post office, and to the same addressee.

If you have evidence that a registered or insured article has been lost or damaged, file a "Claim for Indemnity—International Insured Mail," PS Form 2855. Foreign claims take much longer to process —sometimes longer than a year—since responses to claim forms sent to foreign post offices sometimes do not come until follow-up reminders have been sent out.

Unordered Merchandise

You cannot be held legally responsible for payment on merchandise you have not ordered. In fact, it is illegal for anyone to send you a C.O.D. article that you have not ordered. Occasionally, a business may send out calendars or other promotional items, but you receive these under no obligation of any kind to patronize that firm. If you receive some type of small gift from a nonprofit organization seeking to raise funds for charity purposes, you are entitled to keep the gift regardless of whether you make a donation.

If you receive a more expensive unordered item such as a book, record album, or piece of jewelry, you are still not legally required to purchase or voluntarily to return the merchandise. This is true even if the package is labeled with your name and address but was meant for someone else with a similar name. The honest person will notify the sender of the error, but should request postage and handling fees in advance as a condition for the return of the goods.

You can also refuse an envelope or parcel if you know before opening it that it probably contains unordered merchandise, or you can notify the sender that you are holding an unordered item until satisfactory arrangements are made for the article to be mailed or picked up. If the sender initiates action in requesting return of an item sent to you by mistake, you must comply, but you have a right to demand prepayment of fees as recommended above.

DANGERS AND RIPOFFS IN THE MAIL

The law enforcement and auditing arm of the U.S. Postal Service is the Postal Inspection Service, which employs some 1,700 postal inspectors nationwide and in Puerto Rico. One of the oldest existing federal agencies, it has the responsibility for investigating all criminal matters threatening the security and integrity of the mail and involving the protection of postal valuables, personnel, and property. The Inspection Service has jurisdiction over some 85 postal-related laws and boasts the highest federal agency conviction rate—about 98 percent—of criminal cases tried.

This branch of the Postal Service accepts consumer complaints in all of the categories below. If you suspect or have evidence that the law in any of these areas has been broken, telephone, bring, or mail the information to the nearest postmaster, who will refer the matter to the postal inspector-in-charge at the nearest regional Inspection Service facility. If you write a complaint letter, get it to the Postal Inspection Service by addressing it to the postmaster in your city. If you feel the matter is serious enough to demand immediate attention, bypass the postmaster and call or write the nearest Postal Inspection Service office listed in your telephone directory.

Prohibited Mailings

Postal laws have been enacted to protect the consumer from dangerous articles being sent through the mails. These laws have designated as nonmailable anything that may injure or kill someone, or injure the mail or any property. Except under certain restricted conditions, such as between manufacturers and dealers and between law enforcement agencies, the laws prohibit the mailing of many articles, including narcotics; information used in the transfer of dangerous drugs; "obscene" matter; explosives, including bombs and fireworks; concealable firearms, including pistols, revolvers, and short-barreled rifles and shotguns (except antiques made prior to 1899); flammable materials and strike-anywhere matches; poisons, poisonous drugs, and medicines containing narcotics; highly perishable foods; intoxicating liquors; publications violating United States copyrights; all animals (except day-old poultry), such as puppies, kittens, snakes, and parakeets; sexually oriented advertisements (prohibited only when mailed to persons listed on the official reference list); radioactive materials; interstate lottery advertising, tickets, or payments; libelous matter; literature containing false names in the conduct of unlawful business; false representations; and solicitations disguised as bills or statements of account. Some articles, such as knives and flammable liquids, are mailable only if they are adequately packaged to prevent injury to mail handlers.

Since products used by the public are modified so often and new materials are constantly being developed, it is not feasible for the Postal Service to issue advance rulings concerning mailability. Under the law, it is your responsibility to request a ruling from your local postmaster if you are doubtful about the mailability of an article. Your request will be forwarded by the post office to the Office of Mail Classification, Bureau of Finance and Administration, U.S. Postal Service, Washington, D.C. 20260.

Thousands of complaints by consumers and law enforcement agencies in connection with prohibited mailings are investigated annually by postal inspectors. During fiscal year 1976, in response to over 31,000 customer complaints, 36 dealers in commercial pornography were convicted in federal courts. $137,489 was imposed in fines connected with these offenses. The Postal Inspection Service conducted 2,589 narcotics investigations, which resulted in the conviction of over 600 individuals. In one prior case, a college student at a southern university was arrested by postal inspectors and agents of the Office of Drug Abuse Law Enforcement when he went to the Baton Rouge Post Office and picked up a package containing 2,000 LSD tablets. In another case, postal inspectors, customs agents, and Pennsylvania State Police arrested four smugglers who pleaded guilty and were given jail sentences for importing from Denmark two pounds of hashish stashed inside hollowed-out books received in two parcels.

Postal Thefts

The Postal Inspection Service receives its largest number of complaints—nearly 200,000 in fiscal year 1976—from consumers reporting letter and parcel thefts from home and apartment mailboxes. These complaints resulted in 11,280 convictions. No one may lawfully take any mail, including magazines, from your postal box without your permission, or tamper with a locked box. It is a federal offense for any person, including a postal employee, to open first class mail addressed to others. Only a postal inspector or customs inspector is permitted to open certain specified classes of mail for official inspection purposes.

If you suspect the rifling of mail at your business, residence, or post office box, complain to the Postal Inspection Service. Include any evidence and clearly specify missing pieces of mail or the article taken from an opened parcel. Never throw away envelopes or parcel wrappings that may be required as evidence in legal action pursued by the government.

One of the most persistent of letter-box thieves in recent years was arrested in mid-1975. Before discovering the criminal's identity, postal inspectors nicknamed him "Suitcase Sam," because of the many bank security photos showing him holding a suitcase while attempting to cash stolen checks. He was able to escape arrest for one-and-a-half years because he would also steal passbooks, bank receipts, and other types of identification, and maintain an unsuspicious manner with bank employees as he moved from city to city. After observing his attempt at stealing welfare checks, a special investigator made the arrest that landed "Suitcase Sam" a ten-year prison sentence.

Mail Fraud

In action taken by the Postal Inspection Service in response to about 136,000 consumer fraud complaints in fiscal 1976 alone, nearly 2,800 questionable promotions were discontinued. Mail fraud is not uncommon, but it is sometimes difficult to stop. Postal inspectors not only must be aware of a dishonest scheme, but they also must gather adequate evidence to show that false claims were knowingly made in a patterned effort to defraud.

If you suspect illegal activity, gather whatever evidence you have, and ask friends, neighbors, and coworkers if they have received, and perhaps responded to, material of a similar nature. Postal inspectors cannot act to represent one individual, as a consumer bureau might do in reaching an adjustment in an unsatisfactory transaction. They intervene on behalf of all consumers to stop the use of the mails for fraudulent purposes by investigating such matters, making arrests, and turning over evidence to U.S. attorneys for possible grand jury indictments and prosecution in the federal courts.

False representations made through the mail do not come under the legal definition of criminal activity and are referred by inspectors to proper authorities for possible civil action. The Law Department of the Postal Service can attempt to stop the offender from receiving in the mail remittances relating to the unlawful activity.

Chain Referral Schemes

With American consumers spending billions of dollars annually on everything from gum to yachts, the many opportunities for swindling the unwary citizen are often taken by individuals and companies. These types of fraud are limited only by the ingenuity of the offenders. Contact the Postal Inspection Service if you are mailed an offer of expensive merchandise that alleges items can be paid for by commissions you will receive in referring others to the same store. Such chain referral schemes are meant to entice you into purchasing something you may not be able to afford, and most people cannot get more than one or two commissions.

Something for Nothing

Be cautious when you are offered something for nothing, or a deal that seems too good to be true. It is illegal for a company to offer you through the mail an item that it has no intention of selling at the advertised price. You may use a mail order ad for a product you want that everywhere else sells at a price 200 percent higher. You (and maybe thousands of other consumers) send in your check, which is cashed, and then you never receive the ordered merchandise or a refund. This is mail fraud.

Home Improvement Frauds

Home owners with various problems are often sucked in by companies that say they want to lend a "helping hand." Sometimes the helping hand only helps itself to the victim's money. One family with many debts liked the mail offer by a contractor to complete improvements on their house and to provide them with cash in return for the signing of a reasonable repayment contract.

The "reasonable" agreement called for $400 in cash to go to the client and home improvements that cost the contractor just over $400, in exchange for a $6,125 second mortgage. The terms included small monthly payments over a period of several years, with the lump sum of nearly $2,000 due on the final month. This too is mail fraud and should be reported to postal inspectors.

Family Frauds

Some families turn to finance companies in response to offers of debt consolidation. A dishonest firm may tell you that your worries will be over if you will simply turn over everything to the financial counselor. Yet the company may stall several weeks before paying off your creditors (who are close to repossessing your furniture) until the basic fee for the loan has been paid.

One type of selling scheme involves land packages and retirement homesites, which the buyer is led to believe are a secure investment, especially at only $15 a month with nothing down. A couple may feel that there is little to lose in the unseen property of sunny Florida. Little do they know, that in some cases, they are buying uninhabited and uninhabitable desert land.

Thousands of families nationwide were involved in what the Postal Services calls the "missing heir scheme." Legal-looking documents were sent to persons with the last name of Kelly, and included the offer to provide the recipient with information to aid him or her in filing a claim on a "Kelly" estate worth $50,000. Because the cost of such information was only $10, many people decided to gamble, until postal inspectors stopped the racket.

Bad Insurance

A car owner who has an unsatisfactory accident record may, after being denied a policy by well-established companies, fall victim to a disreputable insurance firm. Such a company continuously collects new premiums by mail, while keeping confidential the diminution of the corporate claims fund. The plan is to channel company funds into private interests and eventually declare bankruptcy, leaving behind unpaid claims and angry customers. This is another example of postal fraud.

Fake Contests and Charities

One illegal selling method is through the use of fake contests aimed at exciting you into thinking that you have won something such as a stereo. This is only the bait to get you into the store and force you to buy the expensive cabinet into which the stereo is built.

Although charitable organizations, including the United Way and March of Dimes, work toward combating many of society's ills and deserve widespread support, some other groups set up local and nationwide illegitimate solicitation, the money from which is diverted to personal gain. Be sure that you know an organization or can check on its integrity before making a contribution to it.

Some cities, such as Los Angeles, require the solicitor of charitable donations to secure a permit before approaching citizens by mail or in person. The permit will usually accompany reputable door-to-door solicitors and mail appeals as a means of identification. Contact the Postal Inspection Service if you suspect that a fraudulent mail solicitation has been made.

School Schemes

Many investigations have been initiated concerning correspondence school schemes directed at the consumer seeking self-improvement. Unlawful activities have included schools with poor curriculums getting consumers to sign contracts calling for monthly payments. If the pupil loses interest or feels that there is little value to a course and drops out, the school tries to coerce him or her to continue making the contract payments. In one case, women were led to believe that they could become licensed nurses by completing a correspondence course. They later found out that their diplomas were not worth much.

Know your school before you enroll in a course. To obtain some information on a school, write either to the Department of Education in your state or to the Bureau of Higher Education, U.S. Office of Education, Washington, D.C. 20202.

Investment Frauds

Those anxious to invest some money and make their fortune in business sometimes fall prey to swindles. The types of businesses used in these schemes usually have an image of being highly successful and do not require much experience. Vending machines, franchises, and distributorships may be sold by shady individuals who misrepresent the success of their operations. Promised "good" locations or service areas may turn out to be places with little traffic, affording profits that do not even cover expenses.

One case involved the sale of flimsy hot-nut machines, which the seller unloaded with a profit of $83 per unit and the unfounded promise that profits from each machine would run up to $30 a month. A promoter of fraudulent distributorships concerns him- or herself more with selling the buyer a geographical area at a high price than with standing behind his or her product or service.

If you are ever told in searching for work that you must pay a registration fee or demonstrate without pay your ability to perform a job, proceed with caution; these may be signs of fraudulent activities. A classic case involved tens of thousands of women nationwide, who, in response to newspaper ads, wrote for information about earning money at home by sewing baby shoes. The applicants were informed that they were required to submit a small registration fee and sew one pair of shoes to exhibit their skill. Nearly every one of 60,000 people who mailed money and baby shoes to the firm did not meet the "high standards."

Unlawful business promotions in the sale of advertising have been investigated in all parts of the country. Promoters sell advertising space in a directory, newspaper, or trade journal that does not exist or that circulates only a few copies. Sometimes coercive selling involves someone who says he or she represents a trade union and promises a company or store that no labor trouble will occur if the advertising is purchased.

The business person seeking a loan from a source other than an established bank or financial institution should proceed with caution, especially when an advance fee is required. Some services that guarantee loans have been shown to accept thousands of dollars as a fee from an individual and then state that the amount of the loan must be reduced with the excuse that interest rates are rising.

"Miracle" Medical Cures

Every year hundreds of promotions are stopped that involve the sale of fake "medical" equipment, products, and cures. Promoters sometimes obtain mailing lists of chronically ill patients, elderly disease victims, or others who seek unusual cures of treatments in cases where conventional methods have failed.

The dangerous promotion of fake lab tests may adversely affect the health of many people. One scheme in Texas grossed $150,000 in the administration of a fake urine test for cancer. A lab in another state reportedly gave false positive results in pregnancy tests to women considering an abortion.

Some worthless devices and medical products are sold through the mail to consumers who respond to ads making false claims. A company in Oregon was forced to stop selling pills when it could not provide medical evidence to support the claim that the medication was effective in reducing the pain of arthritis. Hair tonics sold to bald men with the claim that regular application can start or revitalize hair growth have been the subject of other investigations.

Medical quackery sometimes takes the form of clinics that advertise free services to the elderly and uneducated. When patients are examined, they are frightened by false diagnoses and pressured into signing contracts for unneeded treatments and buying worthless gadgets or "miracle" medication.

Getting Action

If you suspect or have proof of illegal activity in prohibited mailings, unordered merchandise, postal theft, or mail fraud, you have the responsibility to make a complaint to the Postal Inspection Service. For the matter to come under the jurisdiction of this federal investigative unit, remember that there must be unlawful activity in which the mails are used either to misrepresent something or to further a fraudulent scheme. In the case of any type of illegal act mentioned above, if you *receive* at least one piece of mail anywhere along the line—from the promoter's initial contact (such as a postcard advertisement) to the final communication (such as a thank you letter, check, or receipt)—federal statutes are involved.

Be sure to save any envelope addressed to you as part of a scheme, since it may be needed for evidence. Gather any other proof you may have and turn over the information to postal inspectors.

Chapter 10

WATCHING AND LISTENING—
ENTERTAINMENT MEDIA COMPLAINTS

Rapid advancement in technology over the last few decades and increasing amounts of leisure time available to the average American have resulted in a booming entertainment industry. Mass entertainment reaches millions of people every day through radio, television, motion pictures, and phonograph records. And there are constant innovations, such as cable television and videotape cassettes.

The widespread growth of the entertainment media has prompted the enactment of local, state, and federal laws and guidelines that reflect the public interest. Regulatory bodies have been set up to protect consumers and handle a wide variety of complaints.

The regulation of interstate communication by radio and television in the 50 states and Puerto Rico, Guam, and the Virgin Islands comes under the jurisdiction of the Federal Communications Commission (FCC), an independent agency created by, and reporting directly to, Congress. Under the Communications Act of 1934, the FCC's major responsibilities include the assignment of frequencies to individual broadcast stations, the regulation and licensing of stations and their operators, and encouragement of more widespread and effective use of broadcast media.

RADIO AND TV INTERFERENCE

Poor radio and television reception in your home may have many sources. If you live in an area surrounded by tall buildings or close to mountains, some broadcast signals may be weakened or cut off before reaching your receiver. Weather conditions often play a part, and sometimes a cable system, special aerial, or rooftop antenna can make a tremendous difference.

FCC Help

Interference problems created by anything other than the common causes such as those mentioned above are under the jurisdiction of the FCC's Field Engineering Bureau. With about 52 field offices, monitoring stations, and other facilities and approximately 120 investigative mobile units, the Bureau's engineers: (1) inspect nongovernment broadcast stations to verify compliance with the Commission's technical standards; (2) monitor the broadcast spectrum to detect unlawful transmissions; (3) uncover and curtail interference; and (4) investigate and help to prosecute violators of Commission rules and the Communications Act.

Complaint Procedure

If you are troubled by radio or TV interference, it may be because a broadcast station is operating with too little power, transmitting off its assigned frequency, receiving power inflow from another licensed station, or being blocked by the unlawful operation of an unauthorized station. Immediately notify the nearest field office of the Bureau by using the number listed for the Federal Communications Commission in your telephone directory. If you cannot find a listing, write to the Federal Communications Commission, Washington, D.C. 20554.

Detail the date and time of the interference, the channel number (or preferably the name and address of the station), and the program being presented. Also include any notes you can make on the type of interference—strange noises, conversations, video irregularities. While the FCC gives priority to the investigation of interference that may jeopardize public safety (for example, interference on police car, fire engine, and airport traffic tower radios), it does try to give attention to other valid problems, especially those that prompt complaints from a number of consumers.

The FCC also has jurisdiction in the investigation of the technical quality of cable TV and cable radio services. Report the name and address of the cable company and the same information needed for broadcast station interference complaints. Problems related to cable service billing, servicing, or other daily operations are generally handled by local or state franchising authorities. Contact your local city hall for more information.

BROADCAST LICENSES AND
HOW TO CHALLENGE THEM

The licenses of the more than 950 television stations and 9,000 AM and FM radio stations nationwide come up for renewal every three years. Every broadcast station must file a new application with the FCC at the time of renewal. One part of the application describes the programming and operations standards over the past three years; the other section details a proposal of the station's plans for the next three years. After considering both past performance and promises made in the application, the FCC decides to approve or reject the renewal.

Each station is required to maintain a public file containing the last approved license renewal application and any complaint letters received by the station. These materials must be available on request for public inspection during the regular business hours (sometimes excluding the lunch period).

Getting Nowhere

A letter addressed to the FCC containing statements that a station has violated the law, runs too much advertising, or is not meeting the needs of the community is often too general and will not effect any action. This kind of letter usually will be answered with a note requesting evidence to support your claim or informing you that no law or policy prevents the activity that is the subject of your complaint. For example, some people have mailed letters to the FCC complaining that certain game shows or soap operas are worthless programs that should be kept off television. No action can be taken on this type of complaint because the Communications Act prohibits censorship (except for statutory prohibitions such as the advertising of cigarettes), leaving programming content to the discretion of each broadcast station.

Stations have responsibilities in such areas as maintaining a high level in technical operations and airing no more than the maximum amount of commercial advertising approved by the FCC. They must also present a minimum amount of public service announcements and broadcast the scope of public affairs programming they have promised to the FCC.

Challenging a License

Every station must live up to the statements it has made to the FCC through its license renewal application. Whether you are working against a license renewal or just want action taken against a particular activity of the licensee, to prepare a valid complaint you should visit the station and examine their FCC application and complaint letters. Take notes that will help you to write a letter detailing the specific areas where you feel the station has departed from its promises to the FCC. Include in your complaint letter information about the number and content of complaints on file at the station relating to the subject of your dissatisfaction.

An example might be that you witnessed a specific number of minutes of advertising on a specified station during specified hours or certain dates. This seemed excessive to you, and so you checked the license renewal application at the station and found that the station aired more advertising time than the maximum approved in its application. Perhaps you also found some letters addressed to the station that complain about excessive advertising. Include all this data in your letter to the Federal Communications Commission, Washington, D.C. 20554.

After receiving your possibly actionable complaint, the FCC might begin an investigation by sending to the station an inquiry letter requesting a response to the allegations. The licensee's letter answering the charges is then forwarded to you for rebuttal. If you are satisfied with the response, the matter may be dropped; otherwise, rebut the station's answer and request that the investigation be continued.

Actionable Complaints

Complaints that will be accepted and acted upon by the FCC cover a wide variety, including unauthorized transfer of station ownership; fraudulent operational, program, or maintenance logging (a station falsely reporting a commercial as a public service announcement, the wrong number of commercial minutes broadcast, and so on); operation of a station without an adequate number of licensed personnel; technical interference; obscenity in a broadcast; local advertising that is false, misleading, offensive, or in poor taste; overcommercialization; commercials that are too loud; prohibited commercials such as those advertising cigarettes; advertising practices in restraint of trade; distortion, falsification, or staging of news; rigged contests; lotteries in a broadcast; failure to present contrasting views for a controversial issue of public importance; "payola;" fraudulent billing (a licensee's reporting that something aired when it actually did not, or reporting the payment of more money than was actually received from a local advertiser); misrepresentation to the FCC; "hypoing" (improper use of viewer ratings); lack or slanting of coverage of a local or national issue; and broadcast station and cable company employment discrimination.

In fiscal 1976 the Complaints Branch of the FCC received over 95,000 letters containing inquiries, comments, and complaints. Some were from consumers who were dissatisfied with reruns; program crime, violence, and horror; and other areas that the Commission is actively studying, but in which no significant action has yet been taken. Another area of controversy is the "prime time access rule," which, in effect, requires stations to broadcast nonnetwork programming for a minimum number of prime time hours each week. Some people complain that good prime time shows have been replaced by low budget, uninteresting programs.

Penalties

A station found violating any Commission regulation or failing to operate substantially under the proposal approved in its permit or license is subject to the imposition of a "forfeiture," a fine up to $10,000 payable to the federal government. According to an FCC spokesman, examples of forfeitures imposed during 1971–76 included $10,000 to KCBQ in San Diego, California, for fraudulent billing of national and local advertisers; $1,000 to KCCR Radio in Pierre, South Dakota, for falsification of logs; $10,000 (reduced to $5,000) to KTXS-TV in Sweetwater, Texas, for the unauthorized moving of the station's main studio; $2,000 to KTNT radio in Tacoma, Washington, for failure to log accurately the duration of commercial time; $2,000 to KHJ-TV in Los Angeles, California, for failure to give necessary sponsor identification; and $500 to WPWC radio in Quantico, Virginia, for the broadcasting of lottery information. In fiscal 1976 the FCC issued 156 "notices of apparent liability" to stations allegedly violating federal regulations.

A broadcast company that refuses to pay a forfeiture is brought into a federal district court for civil or criminal action by the U.S.

Department of Justice. Forfeitures can apply to such criminal actions as the broadcast of lottery information; obtaining money by the broadcast of false representations, fraudulent pretenses or false promises; and the broadcast of obscene, indecent, or profane language. Although forfeitures cannot be imposed for misrepresentation to the FCC or fraudulent practices not connected with billing, these are considered serious actions and may cause a license to be refused renewal or to be revoked.

OFFENSIVE PROGRAMMING

Except for enforcing a statutory ban on the broadcast of advertising of certain products, the Federal Communications Commission has no authority over editorial or programming content and cannot censor material for broadcast. However, the FCC, Congress, and especially the broadcast stations themselves are susceptible to public opinion and pressure. If you do not like the subject matter, violence, horror, or bad taste of a specific show or series, address a letter with your comments to the broadcast station, with a copy to the FCC, Washington, D.C. 20554.

Broadcast Obscenities

Federal law makes the broadcasting of obscene, indecent, or profane language a crime for which an individual may be fined a maximum of $10,000 or imprisoned up to two years. In addition, the Communications Act states that a station commiting an obscenity violation is subject to administrative law sanctions, including the imposition of a forfeiture and possible license revocation.

Obscenity Complaints

Both the FCC and the Federal Bureau of Investigation have jurisdiction in handling broadcast obscenity complaints. The FCC may bring a civil suit in a federal district court or force payment of a forfeiture, or the FBI can pursue criminal action by consulting a U.S. attorney in the Department of Justice.

The FBI maintains a vast nationwide network of 59 district offices, countless resident agent offices, and some 8,500 investigators, all of which may accept this type of complaint, while the FCC handles this kind of problem only out of its Washington, D.C., headquarters.

Further, according to an FBI spokesman, the FBI has primary juris-diction in the area of obscenity. Therefore, in making a complaint about what you feel to be a serious violation, contact the nearest office of the FBI. Prepare statements about where you saw or heard such material, the date and time it was aired, a description, and your opin-ion as to why it was obscene. What may be obscene to a resident or federal court in Vermont or Nebraska may not be obscene to a resi-dent or federal court in New York or California. If you speak on the phone with an FBI representative who feels you have a valid com-plaint, he or she may send an agent to question you and make out a report, or you may be told to send a letter with all the facts.

As a practical matter, it is usually difficult for the U.S. attorney successfully to prosecute broadcast obscenity in a criminal action be-cause of the free speech guarantee of the First Amendment to the Constitution. Also, more lenient court decisions have been rendered upon consideration of whether or not the alleged obscenity was essen-tial to the presentation of a drama or a work of art.

Because obscenity complaints are rare in most cities, and it is not widely known that the FBI has jurisdiction in this area, some agents may not even be aware of their responsibility. If, after talking to an agent, you are told that the FBI does not handle radio or TV broad-cast obscenity complaints, insist that it does and ask to speak to a supervisor, or suggest that the agent check with a supervisor.

If you have difficulty in getting a local FBI office to handle this type of complaint, if you are told that the matter cannot be success-fully prosecuted through criminal action, or if you simply prefer not to contact the FBI in the first place, call or send a complaint letter with all the facts to the Federal Communications Commission, Washing-ton, D.C. 20554.

To find out the final disposition of your complaint, request such a reply in any letter you send to the FCC. Since the FBI is purely an investigative unit, your complaint may be transferred to the local U.S. attorney's office, which you should then contact directly.

Obscenity complaints raised by Chicago residents caused the FCC to levy a $2,000 forfeiture against WGLD-FM of Oak Park, Il-linois. The investigation involved the "Femme Forum," a talk show directed toward women, who were invited to call the station and air their comments. The subject matter was different for each program, but it included, according to an FCC spokesman, such topics as "mas-turbation," "how do you keep your sex life alive?" and "do you always achieve orgasm?" The callers discussed their sexual activities explicitly. That program was taped by the FCC as evidence for the obscenity complaint, and the station paid the fine rather than contesting the Commission ruling through court action.

If you want to complain about obscenity on any broadcast other than that emanating from a licensed broadcast radio or TV station —for example, from a shortwave radio, taxicab radio, or closed-circuit television—contact the FCC headquarters only.

Sometimes state and local statutes enable local law enforcement agencies to take action on broadcast obscenity emanating from local stations and nonpublic broadcast sources. You may wish to contact the offices of the local police, city or county attorney, or state attorney general.

Film Ratings

Content of motion pictures and recordings is not subject to censorship by the federal government. Ratings are assigned to movies by the Code and Rating Administration of the Motion Picture Association of America, a nongovernment body. If you have a complaint about a movie rating, address it to that organization at 8480 Beverly Boulevard, Los Angeles, California 90048.

Complaints about the offensive content of a motion picture or record should be sent directly to the company that produced it or to the distributor. The interstate distribution of films or recordings con-

taining obscene material is a violation of federal law and is under the jurisdiction of the FBI. Complaints about a local showing or distribution of this material will be accepted by state and local law enforcement agencies where specific ordinances covering such offenses are enforced. Only complaints about movies and recordings that are broadcast will be accepted by the FCC.

One-Sided Programming

Under the Fairness Doctrine, whenever a broadcast station airs programming on a controversial issue that is important to the public, it is required to make available a reasonable opportunity for the presentation of contrasting viewpoints. The only instance where a station is required to provide equal time is in the case of candidates running for public office. Otherwise, the amount of time allotted, selection of spokespeople, and format for presenting the opposing views are left entirely to the discretion of the station.

All complaints about alleged violations of the Fairness Doctrine are handled by the Federal Communications Commission in Washington, D.C. You may at some time want to complain that all sides of a local or national issue are not receiving adequate exposure on a station or that coverage has been slanted. The required "reasonable opportunity" for the airing of contrasting views means just that. A station, for example, cannot run an editorial on a controversial issue in prime time and then expect to fulfill its responsibility by offering a person with other views the 3:00 a.m. slot for reply.

If you and another individual request time to express similar views in contrast to those already presented, the station may select either person, both of you, or neither one, as long as it makes an effort to air some of the opposing ideas. News and editorial content are completely under the control of the broadcast station, but if you can substantiate your claim that a station's point of view is continuously emphasized without a strong effort to provide some balancing viewpoints in its overall programming, the FCC will take action toward changing the station's policy to comply with Fairness Doctrine guidelines.

In submitting a complaint of this type to the FCC, you must write a letter that strongly supports your allegations. First, you must state the name and location of the station or network. Second, you must state that you have seen programming of a certain issue and explain why you feel it is controversial. Then you have to show that the issue is of public importance. (Has there been coverage on other stations or in other media such as newspapers? Is there pending legislation that relates to the issue?) Finally, you must show that little or no effort has been made by the station or network to present contrasting views in its overall programming.

When you address a complaint to the FCC without all this information, it may reply that you must furnish more facts for any action to be taken. If, however, you support your claims with facts, the FCC will likely contact the licensee and request an answer to your complaint. You may then be asked to comment on the licensee's response. The FCC, after it rules that there has been a violation, can force the licenseee to comply with its decision or to face penalties, including license revocation.

The Fairness Doctrine applies to a broadcast commercial only when there is an obvious and meaningful inclusion of a controversial issue. The FCC ruled, for example, that certain Georgia Power Company commercials were subject to Fairness Doctrine rules because they expressed the reasons why a rate increase was needed while the issue was pending before the Georgia Public Service Commission.

Although penalties for violation of the Fairness Doctrine have often been invoked, individual cases are subject to court review, and a 1974 judicial decision seems to indicate a changing philosophy of communication. The scope of the doctrine at one time included newspapers, but that decision by the U.S. Supreme Court exempted newspapers from that set of regulations. The case involved a suit brought by Pat Tornillo, a candidate for the Florida House of Representatives, against the Miami Herald Publishing Company, which denied the plaintiff's request to answer several of the paper's editorials. The high court's ruling reversed the Florida Supreme Court's sustention of a 63-year-old state law affording political candidates the free space to reply to newspaper editorials opposing them.

CABLE TV AND RADIO OPERATIONS

Cable systems are regulated by city, county, and state franchising authorities, which oversee and accept complaints about any matter relating to a cable company's daily operations, such as billing and service.

However, some rules and regulations similar to those applied to broadcast stations licensed by the FCC are also applicable to certain aspects of cable TV and radio policy. The FCC does not license cable broadcast companies, and so has no authority to impose forfeitures, but it does authorize a cable system's carrying of broadcast signals, the basis of the company's existence.

Public Access

In the larger cable markets, each company is required to provide a "public access" channel, which is for the use of community members to present any type of programming. The cable company generally may not refuse use of this channel to anyone, although the station does have the right to establish guidelines in the presentation of material. If you are interested in presenting to the viewing audience some poetry you have written or a debate on a controversial issue, for example, make application directly to the cable company. A form for this purpose may be provided to you upon request. If you are rejected, address your complaint to the Cable Complaint Service, Cable Television Bureau, Federal Communications Commission, Washington, D.C. 20554.

Complaints

Many cable TV and radio firms present programming they produce themselves, as well as material they obtain from outside sources, for airing on their company-owned station. This channel is subject to many of the regulations under FCC jurisdiction, including those of the Fairness Doctrine and broadcast obscenity statutes. Make your complaint utilizing the guidelines previously recommended for reporting dissatisfaction with broadcast stations licensed by the FCC.

Other cable-related matters handled at FCC headquarters include subscriber fee increase complaints and alleged employment discrimination by cable companies.

OBNOXIOUS COMMERCIALS

The Federal Communications Commission has no authority to regulate the content or time placement of broadcast commercials, except to enforce statutory bans on such items as cigarettes. The Commission, however, does review the renewal application, which includes the station's proposal for the maximum number of commercial minutes it intends to allow each hour. Once approved, if the agreement is breached by the station and you see more advertising than the

amount stated in the renewal application, you should report the violation to the FCC. Misrepresentation by a station to the Commission is a serious offense.

Program-Length Ads

The FCC has a policy against the presentation of a program-length commercial whose content is so interwoven throughout the program that the viewer or listener cannot clearly see where the commercial begins or ends. Several past cases involved stations airing half-hour shows promoting the raising of chinchillas. Complaints alleged that these shows constituted 30-minute commercials, while stations logged most of the 30 minutes as being entertainment, educational, or agricultural programming and only 1 to 3 minutes as actual advertising.

Complaints

In cases where it is shown that a station violates a policy, such as airing a program-length commercial, the FCC will issue the licensee a letter of admonishment, which must remain on public file at the station. For more serious policy violations, an FCC letter is released to the press. In the example of the chinchilla programs, another FCC rule against false logging was also violated, because stations reported only a small fraction of the air time as being allocated to advertising.

The FCC will also investigate any complaint alleging that a station has cut short or altered network programming to accommodate local commercials, so that the broadcast material is left incomplete or incomprehensible.

False and misleading broadcast advertising complaints that concern only a local airing are handled by FCC headquarters and some local authorities. Complaints involving national or interstate broadcast advertising campaigns are accepted by the Federal Trade Commission (see Chapter 11).

Investigation and action against harmful products advertised in the broadcast media come under the authority of the Consumer Product Safety Commission (see Chapter 2). Dangerous drugs are investigated by the Food and Drug Administration (see Chapter 4).

CANADIAN AND MEXICAN STATION COMPLAINTS

Any complaints relating to broadcasts emanating from outside the United States are not within the jurisdiction of the Federal Communications Commission. To express dissatisfaction with a Canadian station, write to the Canadian Radio and Television Commission, Berger Building, 100 Metcalfe Street, Ottawa 4, Canada. The regulating authority for Mexican stations is the Director General of Telecommunications, Department of Frequencies, Office of Assignments, Mexico 12, D.F.

Chapter 11

ADVERTISING—
DOES IT DO WHAT THE AD SAID?

Advertising is a multi-billion-dollar industry that uses many means to get you to buy everything from beauty soap to Cadillacs. Large and small businesses employ appealing faces and bodies, fast-talking salespersons, characters with turn-on personalities, and ad agencies that come up with old and new ideas on how to sell a product or service. We are flooded with advertising wherever we look—on TV and radio shows, at motion picture theaters, on billboards, in newspapers and magazines, on cars, trucks, and buses, in puffs of smoke from airplanes, in store windows, atop tall buildings, and on bus-stop benches, T-shirts, and products themselves.

While maintaining the concepts of free enterprise and free speech, local, state, and federal legislators have established government organizations that have the responsibility of enforcing laws protecting the consumer from all forms of advertising considered false, deceptive, in restraint of trade, or otherwise illegal.

OFFENSIVE ADVERTISING

The least expensive type of advertising is that purchased by individuals and small companies for a local area. Newspapers and magazines charge various rates for classified and display ads and maintain their own set of guidelines for the acceptance and rejection of material to avoid offending their readers.

Ad Policies

According to an advertising policy statement issued by the *Los Angeles Times,* an admittedly family-oriented newspaper that claims the largest home-delivered circulation in the country, the paper will not knowingly publish any advertising that it decides "(1) is designed to mislead, deceive or defraud; (2) is indecent or offensive, or which contains text or illustrations in poor taste when judged against prevailing social standards; (3) contains attacks of a personal, racial or religious nature; or (4) is in violation of local, state or federal laws."

The *Los Angeles Free Press,* on the other hand, clearly takes a more liberal attitude in judging whether or not an ad is "indecent or offensive." A spokesperson from that paper has said that an ad may be erotic and still in good taste.

Except where there is a clear violation of law, no government body may force any medium to accept or reject a company's advertising. However, public opinion and pressure weigh heavily in the decisions of the publishers, broadcast station management, and others who depend on readers and viewers to patronize their advertisers and thus encourage these companies to continue their advertising expenditures.

Public pressure concerning the newspaper advertising of X-rated movies has caused policy changes in recent years. The *Los Angeles Times* now groups such advertising in one section and clearly labels it "Adult Movies/Entertainment." The *Los Angeles Free Press* and *The Advocate,* a gay-oriented newspaper, lump all of their sexually oriented advertising into a pull-out section, which may be easily removed by the reader without altering the editorial continuity of the paper.

A company that sells advertising generally has the right to reject an ad it does not wish to carry (or readers or viewers do not wish it to carry). Advertising is obviously an important source of revenue, so a company usually will not reject an ad unless it makes false or misleading statements or exhibits extremely poor taste.

Federal laws now prohibit the broadcast advertising of certain products such as cigarettes, and station members of the National Association of Broadcasters voluntarily comply with the industry-initiated code, which calls for a ban on broadcast ads promoting such products as alcoholic beverages (excluding beer and wine).

Offensive Ad Complaints

If you find a TV or radio commercial or a newspaper or magazine advertisement to be offensive, write directly to the station or publisher stating your objections. If enough people write, the company will think twice about continuing to run that type of advertising.

Postal laws now protect you from receiving unwanted sexually oriented advertising through the mail. The procedure involves filling out one or two forms available at any post office. Violations of postal statutes concerning obscene mail and pandering advertisements are handled by the U.S. Postal Inspection Service (see Chapter 9).

DEALING WITH DECEPTION

The Federal Communications Commission does not look favorably on a station about which it receives scores of letters from angry consumers complaining about the shady broadcast advertising they have seen or heard. A strong outcry from the public will be taken into consideration by the FCC when the broadcasting company applies for its license renewal.

Local Ad Complaints

You should not stand for advertising that causes you to spend your money for a worthless product or for an item that does not live up to the advertised claims. And advertising of a product or device that is harmful to you certainly should be stopped. The program-length commercial, outlawed by the FCC, tries to promote a product or activity over the length of a program, so that the viewer cannot see when the ad begins or concludes (see Chapter 10).

The FCC has jurisdiction to take action on any of these types of complaints against an intrastate radio or TV commercial (that is, one that is aired in only one state). Write to the Federal Communications Commission, Washington, D.C. 20554. Include the name and address of the station on which you heard or viewed the advertising, details about the contents of the ad, and any bad experience you may have had in using the product or service.

If you are uncertain as to whether or not the ad has been run in at least one other state, call the station's sales department and ask. If you are still unsure, submit your complaint. If the FCC determines that the commercial has been aired in more than one state (that is, is interstate in nature), it will refer the matter to other authorities.

You should also submit your complaint about dishonest local broadcast advertising to state, county, or local law enforcement agencies. These offices also regulate intrastate deceptive newspaper and magazine advertising. For example, in California most such actions brought by the attorney general's office are based on the California Business and Professions Code, specifically Section 17500 relating to deception in advertising.

Some actions even can be taken against companies that are located outside the state of the complainant's residence. This happened in the case brought by the California Attorney General's Consumer Fraud Unit against Credit Card Service Bureau of America. The company placed full-page advertisements scaring people into believing that they might lose their homes if anyone stole their credit cards, and into paying twice the usual price for the same type of protection service offered by other companies.

Occasionally, a local law enforcement agency will seek help from the state. For example, the Fresno County District Attorney's Office, in conjunction with the California Attorney General's Office, filed a double action against the Seaboard Finance Company and a company doing business as the Sewing Machine Center, which misled people through deceptive advertising and phony contests.

The office of the city attorney also can be an effective resource against local false advertising practices. The consumer protection office of the Los Angeles City Attorney filed a suit in July 1974 against Professional Publishers, Inc., which allegedly sold advertising and subscriptions for its *Law Enforcement News* by intimating a false affiliation with law enforcement agencies, quoting a higher circulation than it actually had, and making other false claims. In the judgment agreed to by the defendants, the company was ordered to stop the various misrepresentations, cease billing people unless they subscribed, and refund money to advertisers fooled by the unlawful sales practices.

Interstate Ad Complaints

The most widely publicized of the federal consumer protection bodies is the Federal Trade Commission, which has as part of its responsibility the acceptance and investigation of complaints dealing with false and deceptive advertising in interstate commerce. The FTC is the place to turn if you are misled or hurt by advertising that you see or hear on TV or radio (including cable stations), billboards, interstate transportation vehicles, or in newspapers, magazines, or books, and which you know or suspect has appeared or aired in at least one other state or has been placed by a company residing outside your state. You need not be certain that interstate commerce is involved in specific advertising about which you want to complain. If the FTC determines that your complaint is not within its jurisdiction, it will generally refer your correspondence to the appropriate state or local consumer protection agency.

"Bait and Switch"

One common form of deceptive advertising is called "bait and switch." You go to purchase an advertised sale item and find it to have a shabby appearance, to be less desirable than the image previously presented, or to be out of stock. The salesperson then pushes the higher priced models.

"Sale" Prices

Another unlawful practice involves deceptive pricing. An advertiser cannot show a false former price in trying to get you to buy a product or service at a new, allegedly reduced price (for example, "Was $16, now $9.95"). An advertisement cannot carry false comparisons with the prices of competitors (for example, "Retail price $25, my price $16.95"). It also may not suggest a two-for-the-price-of-one sale

when the original price has been jacked up to cover the price of two items. An advertiser cannot make false claims in comparing suggested list prices.

"Easy Credit"

It is unlawful for a company to advertise "easy credit" unless it is willing to do the following:

1. Provide the credit without determining the buyer's credit rating or ability to pay.
2. Charge prices for goods or services that do not exceed the price for similar goods or services in the same area sold for either credit or cash.
3. Impose an annual percentage rate and finance charges no higher than those applying to good credit risks.
4. Extend such credit to persons whose credit worthiness is below normal standards.
5. Arrange the same down payment and payment schedule as those for an individual with good credit.
6. Deal justly with any debtor on all matters, including a late or missed payment. In the promotion of certain credit terms, the advertiser must disclose all applicable conditions, including the annual percentage rate.

Endorsements

The Federal Trade Commission will also handle your complaint about advertising that offers false or misleading certifications or endorsements. A company cannot report the endorsement of a product unless such a statement is fully valid. An ad may not include a claim falsely implying that a product or service won a ribbon or prize while competing with similar items. A certifier, whose name must be disclosed, may not be the seller or anyone affiliated with the seller. Further, there can be no misrepresentation concerning the nature, quality, method of production, or effectiveness of an advertised product. No item that has been used or reconditioned may be advertised as "new."

Furs

In advertising fur products, the seller is required to indicate the correct English name for the animal of the fur's origin, and the name of the seller, manufacturer, distributor, or transporter. For imported furs, information as to the country of origin and the natural and artificial elements of composition must be disclosed.

It's "Free"

Regulations also cover use of the word "free" in advertising. A company may not promote a "free" estimate when, in fact, certain charges or conditions are not revealed to you before you give your okay for the estimate to be made. In offering any free product or service, the advertiser must plainly state any conditions or obligations required for the receipt and retention of such offerings.

Cures

The advertising for various health-producing or medicinal foods, drugs, cosmetics, and special services may not include false claims related to their value or curative effect. An unqualified individual may not claim the ability to diagnose illnesses in promoting products.

Untrue Trade Status

No advertiser is permitted to represent his or her trade status falsely. For example, a retail seller may not call itself a wholesaler, and a company cannot say it sells factory-direct to eliminate the middleperson when, in fact, it is not a manufacturer. A business may not talk about its "laboratory" unless it maintains such facilities, and a private business can neither represent itself as an "association" nor state that it is a "manufacturer" when it produces nothing.

FTC Complaints

The Federal Trade Commission has a standard complaint form (see Appendix 10), which will be sent to you on request, or you may make your complaint by visiting any FTC regional office. Be prepared to submit a copy of the printed ad or, in the case of a broadcast or billboard ad, some notes about the contents as well as the station or location. If you cannot locate the nearest FTC regional office, address a complaint letter with this information to the Bureau of Consumer Protection, Federal Trade Commission, Washington, D.C. 20580.

In many large cities, such as Phoenix, Arizona and San Diego, California, where there is no Commission office, the Federal Information Center will relay your message to the nearest FTC regional office. A Commission representative will then return the phone call to answer questions or discuss a possible complaint. See Appendix 10 for a sample complaint form used by the FTC's Los Angeles office. The FTC also regularly monitors newspapers, television, and radio broadcasts to protect the public.

Any complaint received by the Federal Trade Commission is first analyzed by consumer protection assistants to determine jurisdiction. If it is within the Commission's jurisdiction, the case goes to a screening committee at the regional office made up of an FTC assistant director and supervisory staff investigators, and an investigator is assigned for the gathering of more facts. The investigator reports any findings to the committee, along with a recommendation to drop the matter, refer it to another government agency, or pursue a preliminary investigation. With the last suggestion, the company may be contacted about the allegations. If investigators are assured that the poor advertising practice was just an inadvertent oversight and it will be discontinued or corrected, they may decide that no further action is necessary. If, on the other hand, alleged violations appear to be more serious, a full field investigation may be undertaken.

In cases where the FTC regional office finds that a company has engaged in flagrant false and deceptive advertising practices, it usually notifies the violator of its intention to file a complaint. Then it tries to negotiate a consent order, a legal agreement that the violator will cease and desist from engaging in specific practices without any admission that there has been a violation of law. If agreed to by the advertiser, the order is sent to Washington, D.C., where the full Commission may accept or reject the negotiated order. It may reject a proposed order, for example, when it feels that the order is not strong enough or should include additional stipulations. In that case, the company will be asked to renegotiate the order. The cease-and-desist order becomes legally binding once the Commission gives it final approval.

Sometimes a company will refuse to stop its allegedly deceptive advertising practices or will want to challenge openly the judgment of the FTC. In that case, the Commission will issue a formal complaint, which must be answered by the subject of the complaint within a short period. Both sides of the issue are heard by an administrative law judge. The judge's decision may be to drop the complaint or to issue a cease-and-desist order. Either the defendant or the FTC counsel may appeal the decision to the full Commission for review. The final FTC decision may be appealed to the U.S. Circuit Court of Appeals, and eventually to the U.S. Supreme Court.

Whether it is a negotiated or litigated order that is issued, the matter goes on public record for 60 days, and anyone from an attorney general to a citizen of a small town may write to the Commission during the specified time period to express his or her pertinent views. The FTC will consider public opinion before making an order final. Some of the Commission's orders are publicized through the news media. If you are interested in receiving news releases announcing each order, write to the following address and ask that you be put on the mailing list of the FTC: Office of Public Information, Federal Trade Commission, Washington, D.C. 20580.

Action by the FTC is taken at regional offices throughout the country. In 1974 the San Francisco office announced its intention to file a complaint against the California Milk Producers Advisory Board, which made allegedly misleading claims, such as that consumption of milk is beneficial to everyone and milk is necessary for everyone without regard to state of health. The complaint stated that milk is not beneficial to everyone and not essential to individuals with certain health problems.

The Los Angeles office of the FTC negotiated a consent order requiring Lens Craft Research and Development Company to stop making false claims for its Burnor contact lenses and to run corrective ads. The company had claimed that medical practitioners generally stated the lenses could be worn on a 24-hour basis; they could be worn without discomfort; and sleeping in them would improve the wearer's eyesight. An FTC order required the company in later advertisings, among other things, to alert consumers to the possible health hazard involved in wearing hard plastic contact lenses to sleep.

The FTC's Chicago office responded to complaints that the operator of Gloria Marshall Figure Control Salons was engaged in deceptive pricing, weight reduction, and guarantee claims. Two of the challenged ad statements were: "Call your nearest salon for figure analysis and complimentary treatment" and "Only $2.50 per 1/2 hour treatment on any program." The FTC complaint alleged that free analysis or treatment was not given to prospective customers, and rather than paying $2.50 per treatment, patrons were required to take a minimum contract of 140 treatments.

The FTC makes a special effort to deal quickly with advertising that may have serious consequences on the health of the public at large. A complaint filed against the National Commission on Egg

Nutrition, based in Park Ridge, Illinois, challenged the claim that "there is absolutely no scientific evidence that eating eggs in any way increases the risk of heart attack." Another complaint was filed against Forever Young, Inc., of Denver, a manufacturer of what was advertised as a "safe and effective" wrinkle remover. According to the FTC, the carbolic acid in the product did remove a person's outer layer of skin, causing a temporary change in appearance, but the acid can be poisonous, and one patient allegedly died from the treatment.

Not even the most powerful companies in the nation are immune from these legal remedies. The Commission initiated action against some of the country's largest auto makers—Ford, Chrysler, and General Motors—for allegedly making misleading mileage claims in advertisements aired in early 1974 at the peak of the energy crisis.

The Chicago branch of the Commission in July 1974 issued a complaint against Sears, Roebuck and Company, alleging deceptive advertising practices in the sale of higher priced household appliances. The country's largest merchandiser denied allegations that it promoted appliances worth over $50 in trying to convince customers to purchase more expensive items, and that its salespersons received a higher percentage of commission when selling more expensive appliances over the cheaper models. Salespersons at Sears allegedly described a $58 advertised sewing machine as noisy, unable to sew buttonholes, and not available for half a year in order to sell a more expensive model. In October 1976, the FTC approved an order barring Sears from using bait-and-switch tactics in the sale of major home appliances.

The Federal Trade Commission does not act on behalf of the individual consumer, but it works toward effective protection of the public. Upon acceptance by the Commission, a negotiated consent order is legally binding with the same weight as the other type of cease-and-desist order arising out of litigation. Although a company is not penalized for past questionable advertising practices, either type of order demanding the discontinuance of false or misleading advertising, requiring corrective ads, or setting up guidelines for the honoring of warranties and the payment of funds is legally binding.

A company that violates an FTC order subjects itself to civil penalties assessed by the U.S. district court in the amount of $10,000 for each violation. According to an FTC spokesperson, one of the best-known violators of a cease-and-desist order was Geritol, which once was fined several hundred thousands of dollars.

Mail Ads

False and deceptive advertising you receive in the mail is in violation of federal postal statutes and should be reported directly to your local postmaster or the nearest office of the U.S. Postal Inspection Service (see Chapter 9).

It is always best to check on a company's reputation when you are not familiar with the firm before spending money on an advertised product or service. After paying, you may not always be able to secure a refund even if you file a valid complaint with the appropriate agency.

Big Brother

Advanced technology can be a very positive force in providing a safer and more comfortable life for everyone, but care must be taken that it is not used in ways adverse to the public welfare. In 1956 promoters tried out a revolutionary technique called subliminal advertising at a New Jersey drive-in movie. The words "Hungry? Eat popcorn" were flashed many times on the screen, but too fast for the eye consciously to perceive them. The theory was that the suggestion would be received by the viewer's subconscious mind, and he or she would be more likely to make a positive response (buying popcorn) than if a direct approach were used. Popcorn sales soared, but government inquiries brought out the potentially dangerous practice, and the Federal Communications Commission stated that subliminal broadcast advertising is contrary to the public interest.

Little more was heard until 1973 pre-Christmas broadcast ads prepared by the Telecast Marketing Division of Premium Corporation of America, makers of the Husker Du memory game, were found to contain the command "Get it" quickly flashed four times. Upon discovering a staff member's insertion of the two words, the company voluntarily asked stations to withdraw the ad from broadcast or appropriately edit it. The Federal Trade Commission maintains that subliminal advertising is deceptive in nature, and it will act on any complaint alleging its use.

Chapter 12

LOCAL RESOURCES
FOR CONSUMER PROTECTION

Think of all the things you buy and use in your daily life: hot water and soap for your shower, food for meals, the newspaper at the front door, gas for your car, hair products, a telephone call to a friend, your television set. And what about all the offers of goods and services that you must decide whether to purchase: magazines sold by someone at the front door; the art lessons described in the brochure you just received; a useful home appliance advertised on the radio; an article of clothing displayed in a store window, "on sale," and perfect for the party Saturday night? As careful as you are in your transactions as a consumer, you will sometimes come up against a dishonest or unfair individual or firm.

In every state there are many law enforcement agencies set up by local governments to protect residents against everything from major consumer crime to minor misrepresentation. These agencies specialize in dealing with the problems within local communities and become involved in regulating or prosecuting those persons and companies that break local and state laws. (Government prosecutions based on federal law violations are left to U.S. attorneys, whose cases originate from the various federal agencies mentioned throughout this book.)

If you have a consumer problem that affects you or others in your community, your complaint often will be best handled by a local agency. A consumer protection office can be more efficient and responsive to the citizens it serves than a distant or federal office with concurrent or no jurisdication.

No complaint is too insignificant to report to a local agency. By not reporting, you may lose only a few dollars or be caused a little inconvenience, but your inaction may be just another boost to the confidence of a crook who continues to get away with whatever he or she is doing. In the case of a large company with an unlawful business practice, your small loss multiplied by hundreds of thousands of other consumers can add up to a very large problem.

First determine the seriousness and urgency of the complaint you feel is warranted. If it is a simple case involving a local ordinance by which a person or company is not abiding, a local regulatory office can often act on your complaint and effect swift compliance. On the other hand, you should report to your local police department or sheriff's office any local individual or firm engaging in an allegedly criminal activity such as bunco, which includes a fraud or swindle involving you or other consumers.

The office of a local government prosecuting attorney can be useful in filing both civil and criminal court actions on behalf of local consumers when significant amounts of money have been lost or actions threatening the safety or rights of consumers must be stopped. Local consumer bureaus are excellent one-stop complaint centers for nearly any type of consumer problem. They also act as sources of referral to agencies covering other areas of jurisdiction.

The power of the press has been highly successful in dealing with individual consumer problems. Radio and television stations as well as newspapers throughout the country have set up free consumer action services. The small claims court is the means through which you can try to get back money that you unfairly lose in any type of transaction. Unfortunately, this type of court is often filled with roadblocks to the collection of money that the court has ruled due you. Many local agencies, upon your request, will send helpful pamphlets describing their work and the laws and common problems affecting your area.

The following sections describe the operations of the types of local resources mentioned above.

LOCAL REGULATORY BODIES

City and county regulatory agencies are set up to monitor compliance with state and local statutes and investigate complaints alleging illegal conduct. These officials often have the power to conduct hearings, issue orders to effect correction of unfair or illegal business practices and conditions adversely affecting public health or safety, penalize a violator directly, and refer the case to a prosecuting attorney for initiation of a court action. The most common types of local regulatory agencies are described below.

Pet Peeves

Local animal control departments, for example, handle complaints concerning cruelty to animals and conditions in pet shops, kennels, and animal hospitals. If you visit a pet shop or animal boarding house and see animals that are obviously underfed or overcrowded in cages, call your local animal control office. It will see that conditions are improved, or the operator's license will be taken away.

Food

No matter where you live, your city or county has a health department that protects the public from the local sale of spoiled food and monitors conditions under which food products are prepared, packaged, and sold (also see Chapter 4). If you want to complain about such products as spoiled milk and contaminated meat or unsanitary conditions in a public eating place or restroom, report full information to your local public health regulatory body.

Weights and Measures

Many products and types of food are weighed or measured at the time of sale—gallons of gasoline, pounds of apples, ounces of candy, and so on. If a store's or gas station's mechanism for totaling the amount of food or product you are purchasing is inaccurate, you may be overcharged.

The city and county department that will promptly take action on such a complaint is commonly known as "Weights and Measures." An investigator often will be sent out to examine and test an allegedly inaccurate device. If he or she finds that customers are being charged for more than they are receiving, the department will order the device to be fixed within a certain period or removed from use until accuracy is restored. The agency also may request or require that certain refunds be made to customers showing proof of purchase from that particular merchant. Complaints regarding the labeling or packaging of a product to misrepresent its volume or weight also may be taken by this local regulatory office.

Special Regulation

Some localities have set up a licensing department to oversee, regulate, and handle complaints about certain types of businesses that cause unusual public concern. Examples of operations often under special local regulation are massage parlors, bars, talent agencies, and ambulance services. The local licensing authority has the power to revoke the business license of any firms that commit illegal acts or create a public nuisance.

CALL THE POLICE!

If you live in an incorporated city, there is usually a police department to protect you and other consumers. If you reside in an unincorporated area, or a small incorporated city that contracts services from the county law enforcement body, your protection comes from the sheriff's department. These agencies take complaints, conduct investigations, and make arrests relating to all consumer-oriented crimes.

A "consumer crime" can be defined as a violation of a criminal law in which an intentional "theft" has been committed against the consumer in any false, misleading, or otherwise unfair transaction or exchange. These illegal activities range from misrepresentation of a product or service to swindle. The common denominator for all consumer fraud is deceit. The bunco artist wants to get his or her hands on your money by whatever scheme he or she thinks will work. The target will be your gullibility, kindness, or greed. Some of the more common types of criminal deception involve your direct contact with an individual or company. These necessitate immediate action, and you should complain to the local police or sheriff's department. Following are some examples of criminal conduct against the consumer.

Unneeded Repairs

A well-groomed man may visit your residence and say that he is a city or county inspector who has come to make a routine check of the premises. He will look around and invariably find something wrong with the plumbing, wiring, heating, or roof. After telling you that the hazard must be repaired, he will just happen to have the name and phone number of a "reliable" repairman or building contractor. If you are not cautious, you may pay someone to do unnecessary work. Actual government inspectors never recommend a particular source for use in complying with a repair order.

Another scheme involves a home improvement crew, the representative for which tells you that his company has just completed a job in the neighborhood. He says that he would be happy to inspect your ceilings, fireplace, or outdoor plants without charge. After finding at least one thing he alleges to be in need of repair or improvement, he may say that the truck is outside and if the job is done immediately you can save a lot of money. Furthermore, he will not have to wait to schedule another time when he will be in the neighborhood. The crew, upon your okay, hastily makes a repair that is not needed, or fixes a leaky roof, or improves a dying lawn with the cheapest of materials that you later find to be worthless or even harmful. Not only may you be presented with a bill and asked to pay it on the spot, but the $30 estimate may end up a $130 surprise. You just may be coerced into paying the unreasonably inflated total when three men standing side by side stare at you while cracking their knuckles.

The "No-Risk" Risk

An individual or company that offers incredible "no-risk" opportunities to earn money at home by making or selling products is sometimes part of a racket to bilk the unwary. In return for a large investment in the operation, the victim may be supplied with poor products or materials, or phony leads for selling them. Similar schemes promise bonuses to participants bringing others into the clutches of the operator, and collect their illegal profits from the worthless franchises or from registration fees.

"Miracle" Cures

The chronically ill and elderly are the groups most commonly victimized by medical quacks and companies pushing equipment of questionable therapeutic value. These promoters offer "miraculous" cures for cancer, arthritis, and other diseases, and in some cases even endanger the lives of those who seek alternatives to recognized avenues of medical treatment. Some of these crooks take high percentages of senior citizens' pension money for ineffective, useless "medical" treatments.

Land Sales

Every year many people lose large sums of money to land frauds. An out-of-state, high-pressure salesperson may arrive in your area with full-color brochures, weather reports, community development project promises, and large contracts containing print that can be read only with a magnifying glass. The sales pitches may be made in a hotel executive suite or convention room to impress you with the company's supposed stability and financial success. Everything will sound good, including the unbeatable purchase price, until you later find that you have been sold a nonexistent tract or a piece of land virtually uninhabitable because of flooding, inaccessibility, or the lack of utility services.

The "New" Antiques

High prices are sometimes paid by consumers for jewelry and collection items that are not authentic as represented. A "century-old antique" may have been made a few years ago, a coin with its date altered may be represented as a rare specimen, and a piece of cut glass can be sold as a diamond. A similar imposture may involve the sale of a product bearing what appears to be a highly valued brand name, but actually the product is not made by the established, well-known company.

Investment Frauds

Investment frauds are widespread. Highly speculative bonds sold as no-risk, long-term securities may leave you with worthless pieces of paper. Some "idea development" companies have been found to be more interested in taking the investor's money than in considering the marketability of his or her invention.

Other frauds victimize investors who hope to strike it rich by buying a partnership in a mining venture. The stranger may say your money is all that is needed to buy the equipment to begin digging out a deposit of valuable ore. In return, you may actually become partners in the claim—a worthless one. There may not be any real plans for such activity, and the person in whom you have placed such trust may have included certain phrases in your contract enabling him or her to use all of your money as a nice salary for him- or herself.

Social Security Fraud

A Social Security fraud is committed when someone who poses as a government worker or investigator asks you to give him or her your check, endorsed or not. He or she explains that the check was sent out by mistake before the usual recordkeeping or authorizations had been completed. Some of these imposters have even persuaded elderly persons to pay special fees in connection with phony applications for higher Social Security benefits.

Now You See It . . .

Many lawbreakers continuously travel to different communities selling nonexistent goods and services. It may be the grateful hitch-hiker you have picked up who thanks you for the ride and says that he would like to do you a favor in return. He tells you that he has a friend who is moving and wants to sell his brand-new color TV set or stereo system for $50. Your eyes light up, and you ask the stranger to make arrangements. The deal, of course, must be cash. The crook will make up some excuse why you cannot go into the apartment building, and then will take your money with him while you wait endlessly in the car. Your money, and the person you will never see again, go out the back door. Someone representing him- or herself as a professional sales-person, whom you meet on the street, may pull a similar trick by telling you that he or she is selling out the inventory for drastically reduced prices at a nearby store.

Mail Fraud

Knowing nothing about the individual or company to which you send money can cause an unexpected loss. The addressee may go out of business after he or she has cashed or deposited your check, without any intention of sending your merchandise in the first place. Schemes involving the mails also can come under the jurisdiction of the U.S. Postal Inspection Service (see Chapter 9).

Trickery

Other schemers try, in a variety of ways, to trick their victims into withdrawing a sizable amount of cash from the bank. The funds are "to show good faith" in a wager, business transaction, or charity case. There are often two operators working together so that while one diverts the victim's attention, the other can quickly switch the real money for pieces of paper. This is discovered only after the strangers are gone.

The door-to-door seller or solicitor may be an honest person from a recognized company or valid fund-raising campaign, or a crook who will pocket as much money as he or she can get out of you. The latter may dress well and carry samples of household products, magazines, or special foods. You order an item with cash and never receive it. On the other hand, someone may dress as a clergyman or nun and collect for a church or charity that does not exist.

Protective Tips

Never let anyone into your home without making sure whom he or she is. Ask the person to show identification, or to wait outside while you call the organization he or she is supposed to represent. This information will often be printed on the sales or solicitation permit that the person should be happy to show you.

Caution and reasoning are two of the best tools to use in preventing the bunco artist (or any other type of criminal) from taking you as a victim. Keep your money to yourself. Never discuss your personal finances with a stranger in person or on the phone. Watch out for your own eagerness to close a deal that is too good to be true.

Do not believe everything you hear from a stranger. He or she may turn out to be an excellent actor. Remember, the enemy will do everything in his or her power to convince you to turn over your money. Once the crook has his or her hands on your cash, he or she often will spend it immediately. He or she also may turn it over to someone else, so that there will be no money on the crook if caught.

If you regularly get Social Security or other government checks in the mail, you may want to consult your bank about signing a power of attorney so that the checks can be delivered directly to the bank and deposited in your account. Many banks now provide this free service to their customers, and it eliminates the possibility of the money being stolen from the mailbox or acquired inside your home through some type of trickery.

The bunco artist does not have to find you at your residence, place of business, or otherwise out of public view. Some of the craftiest schemes are operated in parking lots and on street corners. The person who carries off the deception can appear very innocently as a pregnant mother, a student, or a church representative, and may even hire a child to do the dirty work for him or her.

Making Your Complaint

If you are the victim of any type of criminal activity that demands emergency attention to apprehend the violator, you can get action by contacting your local police or sheriff's office. This should be done quickly—preferably at the time of the act—so that authorities can catch the person before other consumers are hurt, and you will still have a chance to get back some money.

When you call your local police or sheriff's office with a consumer fraud complaint, the first step the officials take is to determine whether the matter should be treated as a civil or criminal case. A civil case is compensatory in nature and would arise out of your charge that a person or firm has violated a civil law, which guarantees your personal rights and the safety of your property.

If your complaint necessitates only a civil action, the local policing authorities will hardly ever handle it. Instead, they will refer you to the nearest prosecuting attorney's office or consumer bureau. On the other hand, if the department makes a determination that a crime may have been committed, it will quickly assign to the case an investigator whose job is to gather necessary facts for the possible arrest of the alleged criminal.

Many times the act committed by an individual or firm will violate both criminal and civil laws. In that case, the local policing authority will investigate and act only on the criminal aspects of your complaint. Regardless of whether any criminal prosecution is undertaken, you have the right to pursue a civil court action on your own.

After at least the preliminary investigation has been completed, if enough evidence against the violator has been accumulated, the law enforcement officers will make appropriate arrests and turn over the criminal evidence to local government attorneys for prosecution. Often the defrauded consumer is asked to testify against the violator, unless sufficient witnesses can be drawn from the investigators employed by the policing agency or local regulatory body.

If a thorough investigation does not produce enough concrete evidence to warrant an arrest, the matter will be dropped, and you will be notified that the case has been terminated. Sometimes enough evidence can be gathered to show that a consumer fraud has been committed, but a necessary element such as criminal intent cannot be proven. In that instance, the policing agency may discontinue the case until more facts are known, or transfer all evidence to another government office with the hope that the case can still be pursued along civil lines.

Although policing authorities officially handle only criminal cases, some will take the time to assist you in getting a refund or adjustment. This is done by a staff investigator, who will informally discuss your complaint with the individual or firm involved. If the subject of your complaint refuses to make any adjustment, and there is no criminal violation, the investigator will notify you that there is nothing his or her office can do.

A less urgent complaint, such as fraudulent advertising, overcharging, or any other business practice that you think might involve criminal activity by an established company, should be directed to the nearest local government prosecuting attorney. With these cases, you do not have to worry as much about the violator leaving the state and taking his or her firm along before prosecution can be initiated.

THE PROSECUTING ATTORNEY'S OFFICE

You may not think that it is appropriate to call the police to complain about an alleged crook who has been in direct contact with you. At the same time, you may feel it is necessary to demand some kind of court action to force the subject of your complaint to answer criminal charges, refund money to you and other defrauded consumers, or at least stop the illegal practices. In that case, take your complaint directly to the local prosecuting attorney's office.

Cities and counties throughout the country retain attorneys to prosecute violators of local and state laws on behalf of the public. They are generally listed under city government headings such as City Attorney, and county headings such as District Attorney.

Complaints

Serving as the last step in the chain of events leading to the local prosecution of a lawbreaker, these offices accept criminal—some also take civil—complaints from local regulatory bodies, policing authorities, and individual consumers. They have their own investigators to follow up on alleged criminal activity and to prepare evidence that will be useful in trying cases. Some offices will take your complaint over the phone, but others require that you sign a statement.

The authority and jurisdiction of these local government law offices vary throughout the country. They handle virtually all criminal matters, but many cities prosecute only misdemeanors and refer felony (more serious) cases to the county district attorney. Many local prosecuting attorneys are also given authority by their state to handle civil suits on behalf of consumers.

Any time you feel that you have been misled, or your rights have been violated in any local transaction, your nearest prosecuting attorney's office may be able to help. Following are examples of how complaints are handled in several cities.

In *New York:* The New York County District Attorney's office, for example, does not handle civil cases. (These are referred to the New York City Department of Consumer Affairs or the State Attorney General.) It does, however, act on a great variety of criminal matters affecting consumers. Some common types of complaints deal with the sale of adulterated food, the failure of landlords to make repairs required under the law, and the fraudulent sale of hearing aids and medical supplies. Many cases have involved contracts between insurance adjusters and car repair shops to install new parts after an accident. Some shops were putting in cheaper, used parts and pocketing the difference.

Many cases involving airline travel agency "bust-out" schemes also have been handled by the New York County D.A. A party unknown to the airlines will buy out a reputable travel agency and continue to sell plane tickets, even though the former owner's right to do so is not transferable. When the airline companies discover this activity, the illegal operator vanishes with blank tickets and validating stamps and continues to sell unauthorized tickets. The airlines do not receive payment for the tickets and do not honor them, and so the unlucky customer, who expected a vacation, loses his or her money.

In *Los Angeles:* The Los Angeles County District Attorney's Office is very active in consumer protection and, unlike the New York County D.A., also prosecutes civil cases. Some of the more common complaints handled out of this office include those dealing with auto and television repairs, false advertising, home buying, building contractors, swimming pools, and land sales.

One case handled satisfactorily by that office without a court action involved a consumer's complaint about a bank that promised its depositors free lifetime checking services. The institution later notified account holders that because costs to the bank were higher than anticipated, it would have to begin charging them $2 a month. After the D.A.'s office contacted the bank and discussed the complaint, the company changed its mind, and about 4,000 customers did not have to pay the new fees.

Another case under investigation by the Los Angeles D.A. involved a pyramid-type scheme in which Golden Industries and Golden Products, makers of bras, soaps, and cosmetics, were allegedly cheating persons out of money by the company's greater interest in recruiting workers than selling products. The company was forced to return about $750,000 to job applicants.

At one time the District Attorney's office in Los Angeles accepted complaints directly from consumers. Rather than acting on behalf of individual citizens, the Consumer Protection and Environment Division now only accepts consumer cases referred from other agencies and processes cases primarily involving class action suits.

In *Wichita:* In 1974 the Consumer Protection Division of the Sedgwick County District Attorney's Office in Wichita, Kansas, initiated a project to crack down on the nationwide sale of flood-damaged cars. It contended that the sale of a motor vehicle without any disclosure of flood damage to the prospective buyer was a violation of fraud laws. That office submitted to insurance commissioners of all other states a proposal for the seller's reporting requirements, and has sought the accumulation of a master list of identification numbers for such cars. With Sedgwick County citizens losing an estimated quarter million dollars to business opportunity frauds in 1973, the D.A. also began making a daily search of related newspaper ads and investigating suspicious offers. A sample copy of the consumer complaint form currently used by the Sedgwick County D.A.'s office is shown in Appendix 11.

In *Fort Worth:* Residents of Tarrant County, Texas, had ordered and paid for bedroom sets they subsequently did not receive from six Sleep-Aire Mattress Company stores. The dealers suddenly were permanently closed, and angry consumers took their complaints to the Fort Worth Office of the Criminal District Attorney. The company's main office in Oklahoma was contacted by an investigator and asked to send an agent to an auditing office that the firm was still operating. All of the claims were then processed. Appendix 11 includes a sample consumer complaint form used by the Tarrant County District Attorney's office.

In *Albuquerque:* The Consumer Protection Division of the Ber-

nalillo County District Attorney's office in Albuquerque, New Mexico, began its operations in January 1973. During its first year, the office obtained the return of nearly $65,000 to dissatisfied consumers, effected the cancellation of fraudulent and misleading contracts totaling more than $18,000, and secured the replacement of a mobile home. The Bernalillo County District Attorney's office distributes consumer complaint forms like the one shown in Appendix 11.

Consumer Law Prosecution

Many municipalities are not authorized by their state to prosecute consumer cases. For example, the State of Florida, in an apparent attempt to achieve uniformity in its legal system, began in 1974 to phase out all municipal courts. In their place came a new bipartite system of county and circuit courts in which all cases, including violations of local ordinances, are prosecuted by a state attorney. Consumer fraud complaints from citizens residing in that state are still accepted by the various city attorneys and county district attorneys, but accumulated evidence for every prosecution is transferred to the state attorney's office.

The attorney for other municipalities can pursue both criminal and civil actions on behalf of consumers. The Los Angeles City Attorney's Office worked on one case involving the Hilton Watch Company, which operated a mail order business and falsely represented the value and place of manufacture for its products. Customers were led to believe that the watches were made in Switzerland, when in fact they were from Hong Kong and the U.S.S.R. The company also did not honor a money-back guarantee. Criminal restitution in excess of $50,000 was ordered by the court for more than 1,200 victims.

Many times when the action taken by an individual or company against the consumer can constitute a criminal and/or a civil violation, the factors of culpability and total assets of the violator are considered by the prosecutor in deciding which remedy to pursue first or exclusively. For example, if the government attorney discovers evil intent on the part of the defendant, he or she will look more favorably toward a criminal prosecution than a civil one. On the other hand, a very large company with tremendous assets would be virtually unaffected by a guilty plea and small fine on a misdemeanor charge. In that case, the prosecuting attorney would be more likely to initiate a civil action (if he or she has the jurisdiction), involving thousands or even millions of dollars, to assure that the violator will "feel" the penalty and not engage in further illegal activity.

Every year prosecuting attorneys' offices set up special consumer protection divisions with staff investigators who specialize in consumer law to meet the demand of a growing number of complaints. These offices resolve most complaints without having to file

formal court actions, but they stand ready to gather evidence to pursue legal remedies.

Many local prosecutors will not pursue a case unless there are a number of victims to show a pattern of unlawful activity, or a large amount of money involved. Thus, your complaint, if not immediately investigated, could be kept on file until evidence accumulates that other consumers have been cheated by the same party. In the meantime, a small claims or higher court action may be the only alternative in getting money returned to you.

Two of the most commonly named groups in local consumer complaints nationwide are home contractors and automobile dealers/services. Some of the other most common areas of consumer dissatisfaction are advertising, door-to-door sales, mobile homes, home appliances, mail order, and guarantees and warranties. Be cautious in spending your money, and report any unresolved problem. The more you and other consumers demand action, the greater will be your chances of getting immediate satisfaction and effective future protection for your local area.

LOCAL CONSUMER BUREAUS

Whether a department store refuses to make an adjustment on the defective frying pan you bought, or the newspaper will not rerun your ad under the correct classification, your local consumer bureau probably will be in the best position to provide swift, effective action to right the injustice. From Chicago to New Orleans and from Santa Cruz County in California to Montgomery County in Maryland, municipalities and counties all over the nation have been setting up their own consumer protection offices to serve the public.

Resolving Complaints

First, and perhaps most important, these agencies mediate complaints. All you must do to initiate action is to fill out a complaint form explaining the who, what, when, where, and why of the problem. Appendix 11 includes sample forms from the Allegheny County bureau in Pittsburgh and the department operated by the County of Los Angeles. Many consumer bureaus will act on all formal (written) complaints; others do not have jurisdiction in dealing with housing, banking, or certain other types of problems. If in doubt, call your local bureau and ask if your complaint can be handled.

Most consumer bureaus will generally try to handle your complaint rather than referring you to another agency. They know that many consumers are handed from one government office to another, adding to the level of frustration, so they often attempt to handle problems that could be directed to other agencies. If a bureau investigator cannot legally investigate your complaint, or feels that the problem could be handled more effectively elsewhere, he or she will return your written complaint and ask you to write to a given address, or will forward your papers directly to another agency and inform you of the transfer.

Once your complaint is received, the bureau will contact the individual or company on your behalf and request that the matter be settled fairly. With a valid complaint, this local government office can usually pressure the other party to make the adjustment you request. Most firms cooperate with these bureaus to avoid ill will and litigation.

If a local consumer protection bureau receives many complaints against a particular company, or reviews one case that may affect many people, it may start an investigation of the firm's practices to determine if laws are being broken—intentionally or not. Investigation and further legal action may involve assistance from the city attorney's or district attorney's office.

Public response to bureau operations has been great. For example, the number of formal complaints handled by the Consumer Protection Division of the County Manager's Office in Dade County, Florida, rose from 8,162 in 1969 to 37,098 in 1975. The Department of Consumer Affairs for New York City handles an average of over 200,000 complaints each year. The most common types of complaints reported to consumer bureaus throughout the country relate to automobiles, housing and landlords, appliances, home improvements, credit, mail orders, advertising, utilities, food, and clothing.

Effectiveness of these consumer agencies can be measured in dollars and cents. Refunds and adjustments now run into millions of dollars each year. In 1975 about $264,642 was returned to complainants with the Dade County consumer office. In the same year the Allegheny County Bureau of Consumer Affairs, which serves the residents of Pittsburgh and other cities, brought about adjustments totaling $202,000.

In 1974 a consumer named Anne V. Howell showed how far-reaching an individual complaint can be. She bought a new Dodge with a loan through Chrysler Credit Corporation, the auto financing subsidiary of Chrysler Corporation. Howell paid off the loan three months early, and then was mailed a $4.12 rebate. She did not think this refund covered any of the interest, so she filed a complaint with the City of Los Angeles Bureau of Consumer Affairs. (This agency has since been replaced by the Los Angeles County Department of Consumer Affairs.)

After a thorough investigation, it was discovered that other consumers also were not being reimbursed for the total amount of prepaid interest. City Attorney Burt Pines, in conjunction with the attorney general of California, filed a civil suit against Chrysler for the company's "miscalculation of refunds on unearned finance charges." Not only did Anne Howell get back the balance of $10.30 owed to her, but the final court judgment led to $248,378 being refunded to 16,467 Californians.

Information Services

In addition to handling consumer complaints, local bureaus provide various public information services. Many offices carry extensive files and are happy to try to answer any question regarding the length of time a company has been in business, a firm's general reputation, and the type, volume, and disposition of complaints received from other consumers.

Most consumer bureaus, especially those serving large populations, provide helpful information in the form of consumer pamphlets and guides. They sometimes also sponsor lectures and workshops to inform the public about current consumer issues. If you want any type of consumer information, from buying tips to a small claims court, ask a representative of your local bureau if he or she has some free literature that can be mailed to you. If not, he or she can probably suggest a good source for such information.

A comprehensive list of names and addresses for local and state government consumer offices throughout the nation is given in Appendix 12. Use this list to find the offices closest to you. The Office of Consumer Affairs of the U.S. Department of Health, Education, and Welfare prepares an annual publication entitled *Directory of Federal, State, County, and City Government Consumer Offices.* The directory annually updates the names and addresses for most consumer protection offices throughout the country. You can obtain a copy of this excellent source book by sending a check or money order for 85 cents to the Department of Public Documents, U.S. Government Printing Office, Washington, D.C. 20402. Ask for the publication by name and give its catalog number, HE-1.502:ST2/977.

MEDIA RESOURCES

Radio and TV

The news and public service departments of many radio and television stations now provide excellent assistance to individuals with consumer complaints. These stations designate someone in their staff to be the "action reporter." This person takes responsibility for accepting your complaint and taking appropriate action on your behalf.

The action reporter contacts the store or company about which you are complaining. A prompt and fair settlement probably will be reached, because no establishment wants its reputation hurt by a broadcast story of how the firm cheated someone or treated a customer unfairly. The action reporter also may be able to speed up action from a government agency to which you have already complained.

Although most stations broadcast the results of some of their complaint handling, they will generally try to help you even if they have no interest in using your story on the air. This public service is free and deserves your wholehearted support, including a big "thank you" letter for whatever help the station representative does give you.

Call For Action

One of the most exciting attempts at combining social action with media power was begun in 1963 by Ellen Straus of WMCA Radio in New York City. Straus had the idea of training volunteers to act as resources in trying to bring persons who had complaints in contact with individuals or institutions that could resolve them. The service, named Call For Action (CFA), began expanding into a national program in 1969 with funding from the Urban Coalition.

Today, Call For Action, Inc., is a highly successful information, ombudsman, and advocacy service. This independent nonprofit organization helps consumers through its nationwide network of more than 40 radio and television stations. Appendix 13 lists cities where Call For Action offices are located, the names of sponsoring stations, and CFA phone numbers and hours of operation. (Also listed are stations not affiliated with CFA that have action reporters. These services are also effective, but most require that you send a letter stating all the facts to the address shown.)

Call For Action can be one of your most valuable local resources. There is no need to write a long detailed letter explaining the problem—trained volunteers are waiting to take your complaint over the phone. You will reach not only a receptive ear, but also an expert at solving problems in your local area.

Although the highest percentage of calls does deal with consumer problems, this service is set up to help you with *any* difficulty you may have with a merchant, company, government agency, or other organization or individuals. Your gripe may involve a school, the police, or an employer, or have to do with such areas as welfare, discrimination, rehabilitation, or pollution. Maybe your spouse has just died and you are faced with returning to the work force, caring for an infant, or some other responsibility that you do not know how to handle. If you are not at all certain about what to do next or to whom you can turn, dial Call For Action.

One significant feature of the Call For Action service is the genuine concern of volunteers for helping others. You are not a case number but a human being who requires individualized assistance. Unlike many media action reporters, Call For Action volunteers emphasize follow-up and call you back to make sure that your problem has been resolved. According to surveys by local stations, about three-quarters of the callers have their problems handled successfully.

Your local Call For Action does not only involve itself in phone talk. It assists the station in preparation of material to broadcast. This helps to promote the service by giving listeners examples of how callers have been assisted. Information about help given to you is never used without your advance permission.

Call For Action workers also keep an eye on community problems and ways to solve them. In New York City, for example, the organization was a key factor in getting City Hall to start a service to handle citizen problems and assist in referrals. The WMCA Radio group also effected constructive changes in the city's enforcement of building codes, and revealed information about an illegal ring of slumlords, which led to several indictments by a federal grand jury.

Newspaper Action

Newspapers throughout the nation also have taken up the consumer cause by establishing their own action services. Many of them publish the stories of consumers whose complaints they have helped to resolve. Appendix 14 is a directory of newspapers that have offered consumer action services to the individuals in their areas.

SMALL CLAIMS COURT

Whether you do not receive the merchandise you pay for, you unsuccessfully try to get your money back for faulty goods or services, or you are overcharged without any resulting adjustment, nearly every state now provides you with the opportunity of presenting your side of the case in a court of law set up to handle claims under a relatively small maximum dollar limit.

Do not take someone to court unless other avenues have failed, because it may be difficult to prepare your case with adequate evidence, even more difficult to serve the defendant with the papers compelling him or her to appear in court, and nearly impossible to collect the money due you if the judgment is in your favor. Furthermore, some consumer bureaus and state and federal agencies have the authority to bring civil and/or criminal proceedings, and they may not be willing to take any action if you have lost a small claims case dealing with the same issue. The investigator of your complaint may find out about the court decision from you (this information is often required on the complaint form you submit) or from the former defendant he or she contacts.

Courts handling small claims matters go by many names. For example, in most locations in California and New York, it is simply the small claims court or the small claims division of the municipal or civil court; in Arizona, the Justice of the Peace court; in Kansas, and South Carolina, the magistrate court; and in Virginia, the district court. The jurisdiction of small claims cases may vary when no uniform state guidelines exist. In Michigan these cases are handled in the district court system, except for 28 cities, which have municipal courts with small claims divisions, and the City of Detroit (Wayne County), which maintains the common pleas court. Colorado and other states have small claims courts only in some of their cities and counties. In 1975, Kentucky had only one small claims court, in Louisville, but a Consumers Advisory Council was designated to resolve cases brought to it by the state's Division of Consumer Protection. This has been done through free and confidential, legally binding arbitration by a three-panel committee.

The maximum dollar limit for a small claims suit varies from state to state and sometimes from city to city. It ranges from $200 in Utah to $500 in California, Oregon, North Carolina, and New Jersey, to $1,000 in Iowa and Pennsylvania. Tennessee has the highest limit—$3,000. In North Dakota, maximum claim amounts range from $200 to $500 depending on the type of court in which the small claims action is filed. Because of inflation, the maximum limit is often raised to accommodate a higher number of claims.

To Sue or Not to Sue

When a person or company owes you money and refuses to pay, you have the right, and the obligation to fellow consumers, to file suit if your other efforts have failed. Problems that might prompt court action are: (1) a landlord withholding your security deposit without cause; (2) not receiving reimbursement for cost of repairs on your car after a traffic accident that you think you can prove is the other driver's fault; or (3) getting no compensation for clothes ruined at a dry cleaning establishment.

In courts such as those in North Carolina, a consumer may also sue for the return of an article belonging to him or her. In states where this is not the case, if a television repair shop will not return your set until you pay disputed charges, you will simply have to pay the charges, get back your set, and then sue the shop for the return of your money.

For reasons previously mentioned, before filing suit it is often better to make your complaint to the state or local consumer bureau, the state attorney general's office, or local law enforcement authorities. You will be saving yourself time and money by letting those agencies assist you in pressuring or even filing civil or criminal charges against the unfair party to make the appropriate adjustment. You also will be helping to alert your community and state officials to possible unfair business practices, deceptive advertising, and so on by an individual or company, and thus will be protecting other potential victims.

If the problem involves an advertised product or service by a company residing in another state or advertising in more than one state, the nearest regional office of the Federal Trade Commission may accept your complaint and even incidentally effect a payment. However, the emphasis of any FTC action is to curtail unlawful advertising or trade practices rather than to assist an individual consumer in trying to achieve satisfaction in a particular transaction (see Chapter 11).

If these alternative courses of action prove unfeasible or unsatisfactory, by all means file a court suit. If the amount of your claim is under the maximum dictated by the court of jurisdiction for a small claims suit, this type of action is the most appropriate.

When your claim is for an amount substantially higher than this limit, you should hire an attorney to bring a formal court action. Be sure to consider court costs and attorney fees that you will be required to pay. If your local court's maximum is $500 and you have a claim for $600, it would not be wise to have an attorney take the matter to a higher court, since his or her fee probably would be in excess of $100.

A good idea is to consult an attorney for advice on whether the case warrants legal representation for a higher claim in a more formal hearing. Some attorneys will not charge you for this advice if your decision is to proceed in filing the small claims action; they do this with the hope that you will return to them if you need legal help for a more serious matter.

Some small claims courts allow attorneys to present cases; others do not. The hiring of an attorney creates unnecessary expense, cannot be added to the amount of your claim, and is not necessary if you follow the guidelines in this chapter.

Ideally, every individual should file a small claims suit when the collection of a small amount of money is at issue. Many people feel that they do not have the time to complain or take legal action, and as a result many individuals and companies working under unfair or illegal policies are not brought to justice until numerous people are adversely affected.

Realistically, the small claims court can be a difficult route to go (futile, in fact, if the person or a defunct company you want to sue has no assets), requiring patience and sometimes surprisingly high filing and collection fees. As the plaintiff, you must file all the necessary papers and pay the initial, usually nominal, fee. You may have difficulty in finding the correct name or street address for the defendant or in serving the papers. You must take time from your daily work to represent yourself in an informal court proceeding, which may involve much waiting until the final disposition of other cases is made. The defendant may force you to make a second court appearance by calling in sick, or claiming in court that he or she needs a continuance to gather more evidence or secure the testimony of a witness who is ill or uncooperative.

In your claim, you may usually gain compensation only for specific, documented losses or expenses, and so you may not add a monetary amount to your basic claim even for extensive inconvenience or mental anguish. If the court's decision is in your favor, only half the battle is won if the party you have sued still refuses to pay the amount awarded by the court. The arduous task of collecting the money from a stubborn loser is—unfortunately—yours. This burden has caused many court-ordered payments to go uncollected by frustrated, weary consumers. In states where appeals are accepted, the loser may take the case to a higher court, where representation by an attorney is virtually mandatory.

Even with all of the potential problems connected with initiating a small claims action and collecting money awarded to you, this type of government assistance is still a valuable tool. Reputable parties often will not evade service, try to delay court action, or refuse to pay you after losing the case. If you do decide to file a small claims suit, you may find help in the following sections, which offer general suggestions for filing papers, winning the case, and dealing with potential problems in the process. Keep in mind that specific small claims procedures are unique to your state and community. Call the nearest court or city hall and ask for information about how and where to file a small claims suit. Appendix 15 is a comparison of fees, claims limits, and other general information for small claims courts throughout the United States. The information, which the author obtained through an intensive nationwide survey in 1976, is subject to much change as the various states adopt laws to standardize and reform their present court systems.

Filing Suit

You generally must be at least 18 years old to file a suit. A person under 18 may solicit the help of a parent, relative, or friend approved by the court for representation. Your first move should be to find out the court having jurisdiction. Usually you may file suit in the judicial area where (1) the person you are suing lives or works; (2) the store or company's main or corporate office is located; or (3) the contract was signed, the repairs were made, the agreement was reached, or the injury to person or property occurred. Call the court that you think may have jurisdiction. The clerk will ask you for the address of the party you want to sue or the place where the transaction occurred. After checking the boundaries of the district, the clerk will verify that that court has jurisdiction or will refer you to another court. If you file suit in the wrong district, your case may be dismissed, and you will have to start from scratch. Be sure to file your suit as soon as possible after the injustice occurs, since a statute of limitations may later void your claim.

Filing fees vary from state to state. The amount charged may also vary among courts within a state. Sometimes it depends on the total amount of the claim. California has a statewide $2 filing fee for any small claims suit; fees range from $3 to $19 in Minnesota's courts. In Pennsylvania, the filing fee ranges from $7.50 (for a claim under $100) to $12.50 (for a case involving from $300 to $1,000).

The necessary forms can be obtained by mail or in person. Some courts require that you include a stamped, self-addressed envelope with your mail request. First, you must fill in the blank form with the name and address of the plaintiff (you) and the name and address of the defendant (person, store owner, partnership, or corporation you are suing). Be sure to put down the correct name of the party you want to sue; otherwise, the justice presiding at the hearing may dismiss the case, and your efforts up to that point will have been in vain.

For example, a company that is a corporation must be so labeled, and the "fictitious" name of a store may not by itself be appropriate for naming the defendant. If Joe Johnson is the sole owner of Joe's Cleaners and your suit is against his establishment, you should list the defendant as "Joe Johnson, doing business as [dba] Joe's Cleaners."

Your local court will help you with specific requirements and suggestions about listing the defendant and finding out the necessary information through such sources as your state's corporation regulatory agency, city or county business licensing authority, and state or local tax records. When you know only the box address of a business you want to sue, the U.S. Postal Service can help you to obtain the street address (see section in Chapter 9 entitled "Access to Information").

If you encounter difficulties in obtaining necessary facts, the local city or county attorney's offices may prove helpful in suggesting sources of information, since they generally employ investigators to look into cases that may prompt local government prosecution.

You must also state on the filing form the amount of your claim, determined by totaling the amount of all canceled checks, receipts, bills, and promissory notes or contracts connected with the case. Again, only honest claims that are completely documented are awarded in full. Inconvenience created out of the defendant's actions, although of concern to the plaintiff, is not reimbursable by the small claims court unless necessary doctor bills, taxi fare receipts, and other concrete products of the inconvenience are included.

There will be a place on the court form for you to make a statement of why the defendant should pay the claim. Be clear and concise—one or two sentences may be sufficient—and provide enough information so that the defendant will understand the reasons for your filing suit.

Although courts usually accept filing of forms by mail, it is suggested that you (or someone you ask) appear in person to submit the small claims form to the court clerk, who will look over your statements and possibly ask a few questions. If the form is correctly completed, the clerk will accept it (be sure you retain a copy), charge the standard fee, and, at the same time or by return mail, notify you of the date and place of hearing. If the form must be corrected, follow the clerk's instructions to avoid further delay.

Serving the Papers

All small claims courts prescribe rules for serving papers on the defendant. These rules generally require that the defendant receive the papers at least a certain number of days before the hearing, and that the service be completed either by mail (registered with return receipt requested) or by a third party who has no personal interest in the outcome of the case (this could be a representative of a local law enforcement office set up to handle such matters or a friend or relative who is not a witness to the damage and who would not gain financially from a court award). Many courts discourage the use of the Postal Service since the receiver can easily refuse to accept delivery of the envelope containing the court order to appear.

Many people say that this is one of the most difficult parts of the small claims procedure. If the person you want to sue is evasive and cannot be found by the server, the notification requirement is not met and your case will not be heard in court.

Some courts allow an indirect method whereby an adult in the same office or residence may be served with the defendant's papers. Although the method is not legally acceptable to many courts, once the defendant does make a court appearance, the presiding justice will effect legal service in the courtroom and request that the defendant waive the notification time requirement so that the case can be heard.

Witnesses are often valuable in presenting testimony to back up your story in court. A witness may verify the existence of an oral contract or report observations of circumstances that led to the lawsuit. Some courts limit the number of witnesses that may be presented in a small claims suit.

The reluctant witness or those who cannot voluntarily leave their jobs often can be subpoenaed by the court at your request. The small claims courts of some cities such as Seattle do not issue subpoenas for witnesses, and in those courts the plaintiff has to depend on his or her persuasion to secure the appearance of a witness. Many courts allow a witness to charge appearance and mileage fees, which are then added to the amount of the judgment (assuming the decision is in favor of the plaintiff).

Preparing Evidence

Before the trial you should fully prepare to present your case to the court. Your claim may be clearly justified in your own mind, but you may lose the case to a shrewd defendant if you do not take the time to organize your evidence. This task involves gathering all documents and relevant papers—canceled checks, receipts, bills, photographs, contracts, literature—and putting them into a logical sequence that will be easily understood by the court. Hopefully, from the very start of the problem, you will have kept all applicable papers and your notes on communications (see Appendix 1) in a file.

Some people find it helpful to make a chronological list of events leading up to the suit. This list may be brought to court and consulted to help you remember all of the pertinent facts. However, you should never prepare written testimony to read in court. You must make clear statements of fact under oath and based on your recollection of the circumstances, rather than recite carefully worded sentences. The evidence you gather should relate directly to your claim, and you should not introduce irrelevant testimony.

Check with the local court clerk and ask when and where small claims cases are presented. Then visit the court and see how cases are heard and testimony is taken. This will give you a good idea of what to expect for your day in court and should relieve some of the nervousness you may feel.

A booklet describing your rights and the procedure for taking someone to court is often distributed by local courts and city, county, and state agencies such as consumer bureaus and the office of the state attorney general. You may also ask your local library's reference desk for information about small claims court procedures in your state.

Be sure you have contacted or subpoenaed any witnesses you want to testify for you in court. You should especially contact someone who has voluntarily agreed to be there, and remind him or her of the court date, time, and place a few days in advance. Discuss the case with your witnesses, telling them why you have filed the suit and informing them of the questions you will ask before the presiding justice. Tell them not to read any statement and not to argue your case. Their job is to verify your testimony and present any additional evidence.

You should go a step further in preparing your case by putting yourself in the place of the defendant and visualizing what will be the defense. This exercise may give you some new ideas of strategy to use or evidence to include.

Court Appearance

Be on time at the assigned place on the day of your hearing. Although there are many other cases and yours may not be the first one taken, many courts call the names of the plaintiffs and defendants present, and then first take default cases (usually decided against the party not in attendance).

If you become ill on the day of your scheduled appearance or cannot be in court for any other reason, immediately notify the court by phone. Then try to reach any witnesses to save them a trip to the courtroom. If your emergency is a valid one, the court should authorize a continuance, and the matter will be rescheduled for a later date. If you notify the court that you will be late because of a car breakdown or another valid reason, it probably will not act on your case until you arrive.

No court requires parties to appear in formal dress, but it is a good idea to wear presentable clothing and to be neat.

You and the defendant will be given the opportunity to present the respective sides of the case to the court. Do not hesitate to refute testimony given by your opponent; if left unchallenged, it could be accepted by the court as fact. Never interrupt the judge or your opponent, but make your relevant statements when either has finished speaking. Use the opportunity to cross-examine the defendant if it is offered and you feel that you can clarify the facts.

If you have any questions about court procedures, feel free to ask the person presiding, because the proceedings for most small claims cases are informal and you are not expected to be an expert at presenting evidence and testimony. Sometimes cases are heard in an office rather than an actual courtroom and by a person who is not a judge, but the person's decision is nevertheless legally binding.

Never argue with the court or the defendant. Such an outburst not only will be looked upon unfavorably and could have a detrimental effect on the outcome of your case, but you could be ruled in contempt and assigned a civil penalty. Be courteous, polite, and respectful, although firm, and answer truthfully any questions asked by the person presiding. Address all of your remarks to the latter while your case is being heard, unless you have permission to address another.

Judgment and Collection

After both sides of the case have been heard, the court will immediately render its decision or take evidence under submission. In the latter procedure, the issue may be complex, with the judge waiting to check the written law or give more thought to the case, and you will be notified by mail within a short time. If there seems to be a delay in receiving the court's decision, telephone the court clerk to learn the outcome.

If you sue someone and lose the case, you can appeal to a higher court in many states, but that step can involve high filing fees, attorney's fees, and much time. If, on the other hand, you win the suit, you are entitled to receive whatever money has been awarded to you, but the defendant may also have the right of appeal (see Appendix 15).

Hopefully, the person you have successfully sued (the judgment debtor) will promptly pay what he or she owes you after receiving notification of the judgment. Be sure to notify the court on the appropriate form when the judgment has been satisfied (you have been paid in full). If the judgment debtor refuses to pay the claim, it is your responsibility, with the court's help, to collect the money.

All courts provide the means for collecting judgment funds, but the burden is clearly on the winner of the case. In fact, the procedure for overcoming a loser's refusal to pay may unfortunately afford endless frustration and the necessity of having to spend much additional time and money.

In many states, the plaintiff who wins the case (the judgment creditor) may ask the court to issue a writ of execution, which gives law enforcement officers the authority to seize the judgment debtor's property. This document must be served on the party named, and if the person or company evaded service the first time, this second service may be even more difficult. Once the court allows the seizure of property, which may then be held until the judgment is paid or may be sold after a waiting period, you must decide which of the debtor's properties you want to try to get. State or local law may allow you to seize a portion of wages or profits, money from a business or personal bank account, a car, business, or real estate. You must then find out specific information about the debtor's assets.

If you want to try to get the money through your opponent's bank account, look at any canceled check you previously made out to the debtor. The name of his or her bank and the account number may be recorded on the back. If you do not have a canceled check and the judgment debtor is a company or store or a person who owns a retail firm, you or a friend can make a small purchase with a check, which will be returned by the bank and allow you to obtain the necessary information.

Otherwise, you may have to call banks in the area of the debtor's business or residence to find out which one carries his or her account. A bank may not be willing to give out such information. To avoid that problem, tell the bank you are a creditor—which you have become by winning the suit—(if you own a store or business, give its name) and request a credit check for the account of the person or company you name (without mentioning the lawsuit). Not only will you be told about the existence of any account, but you may be given a rough estimate of how much is on deposit.

Try to obtain the exact name of the account, since your reporting to collection officers the wrong name (with even the slightest variation) may hamper their efforts. If the bank account is under a name other than the one designated in your suit or lists the depositor as both the judgment debtor and a partner you have not named in your suit, collection of funds from that account may be impossible. Another roadblock to collection may be the judgment debtor's transfer of his or her funds to another bank before their seizure.

If you try to have a car seized, you must provide law officers with the license number, description, and address where it can be located. (Some of this information may be obtained from your state's department of motor vehicles.) In California this type of collection procedure involves your prepaying a $100 deposit. This money will be reimbursed at the time that judgment is finally paid, but it may be tied up for months.

To attach someone's wages, you must first find out where the person works. This is not always easy. A business or real estate levy can be much more involved and may require searching through various government records to provide the collection officers with the required information.

You may be able to obtain some information by petitioning the court to order the judgment debtor back to court so that you can question him or her regarding personal assets. Then, assuming again that the debtor can be found and served with a subpoena, you can force him or her under oath to answer questions about assets. Ask as many questions as necessary to obtain enough information to proceed with various avenues of action. (Questions might include: What is the license number and description of your car? Under what name is your bank account? In which bank is it located? What is your bank account number? Where do you work? Do you own any real estate?)

The amount of time and money spent in trying to collect from a stubborn judgment debtor may be prohibitive. Some cases can involve hours and hours of telephoning and searching through state and local government records. In California, even to collect for a claim of only $10 or $25, it may be necessary to prepay fees (which may take weeks or months to get back) of from $8.50 plus mileage for a garnishment of wages or bank account funds, to $400 or more for a business levy.

Clearly, the small claims court has not up to now been the most effective method of consumer satisfaction. It may be best first to try other forms of recourse, at least until legislators reform the system so that the main burden of collection is taken from the consumer who wins his or her case.

LEGISLATIVE WATCHDOG

Much of the good consumer legislation comes from local government. You should communicate your views about consumer issues to local legislators. Often a huge group of individuals and consumer organizations is required to counteract strong anticonsumer forces in big business when a bill is proposed.

If you are not familiar with the names of your local elected officials, contact the nearest voting registration office, local government administrative offices, or the League of Women Voters. Add the names of your representatives to your personal telephone directory, and write a succinct letter expressing your views whenever a significant law affecting consumers is introduced, or when you feel that an existing law should be amended or abolished.

NONGOVERNMENTAL CONSUMER ORGANIZATIONS

Some of the most effective consumer legislation is initiated or influenced by nongovernmental state and local consumer groups. Many of these have annual membership fees and send out newsletters detailing consumer issues and organizational activities. They welcome your financial and/or working support.

Appendix 18 lists local consumer groups nationwide, as well as national and international consumer organizations. Call or write those you may want to join, and ask for information about their goals, current projects, and benefits of membership. Then, become involved!

Chapter 13

STATE AND FEDERAL HELP

Many localities do not provide consumer protection services for their citizens. Some new or understaffed local agencies may be too slow or ineffective in pursuing complaints. You may come up against a consumer problem that involves an out-of-town company, and find that the local agency will only investigate local firms. When state or federal laws are violated, the local agency may have no jurisdiction in the matter. Under any of these circumstances, you can find a state or federal agency to pursue your complaint.

STATE ASSISTANCE

All 50 states staff at least one department or agency to deal with consumer protection. The power and scope of these bodies vary greatly, but every office is set up to promote and enforce state consumer laws under its jurisdiction. In addition to the mediation and litigation of complaints, many state consumer departments are responsible for the licensing of professionals who provide a service to the public—doctors, lawyers, barbers, building contractors, and so on. California's Department of Consumer Affairs, for example, contains more than 40 boards, commissioners, and bureaus, which license and regulate over 850,000 businesses and individuals.

Complaints

Often state agencies will file suit against a company only if they can show that harm has been done to many people. This is because of the large volume of complaints received and the high cost of litigation. Sometimes a case will be transferred from a local consumer bureau to the state office because the local bureau does not have the funds to pursue the case in court. State agencies also work in conjunction with the local government offices to make investigations and enforce the law.

Especially if there is no local consumer bureau near your residence, you may want to obtain the assistance of a state consumer office. First check Appendix 12 for the name and location of the appropriate offices. For example, California runs a Department of Consumer Affairs, while many consumer complaints in Montana and Utah are handled by a Department of Business Regulation.

Call or write to these state-run offices and ask what types of complaints are handled by each. Some departments are limited to the handling of specific kinds of problems. Oklahoma has a Department of Consumer Affairs, but it accepts only complaints relating to credit matters. Once you know the scope of state consumer affairs, you can compare it with that of the local bureaus and make a choice about where to submit your complaint.

If both the state and local agencies have jurisdiction to deal with your problem, you can address your complaint to the office at either level of government. Remember, however, that the higher the level of government, the more complex the bureaucracy and the more difficult it may be to gain satisfaction.

There are several occasions when you should file your complaint with the state rather than, or in addition to, a local bureau. First, a local bureau perhaps does not handle a case that the state will gladly accept. Second, one state agency may have the reputation of specializing in some types of complaints. In such a case, if you check with a local consumer office, the investigator may recommend a state (or federal) agency if he or she feels that it will be more effective in dealing with the problem. Third, you should contact a state agency if you strongly suspect that consumers in state areas not covered by your local bureau are being adversely affected by the same problem. Fourth, contact the state consumer agency if you want to complain about the ethics or competence of a licensed professional. Since the state regulates the practices of the individuals it licenses, it can take strong measures, including license suspension and revocation, to protect consumers from fraudulent, incompetent, and unethical professionals.

By far the most extensive network of consumer protection representatives is in New Jersey. Its attorney general's office, through the Consumer Affairs Local Assistance Program, has 98 counties, townships, and cities that appoint consumer protection officers to mediate complaints at the local level. These officers work directly with the state office and also develop educational programs for their localities.

The Attorney General

In most states the highest, and sometimes only, state consumer protection agency is embodied in the office of the attorney general. This office may handle only those complaints of major magnitude not under the jurisdiction of other state agencies. The attorneys general throughout the nation maintain sizable budgets to answer consumer complaints, make thorough investigations, and pursue litigation that can run into hundreds of thousands of dollars for a major case. The Sacramento office of the California attorney general, for instance, receives about 300 phone complaints and 100 to 250 letters a day. The attorney general's office in Wisconsin handles nearly any type of complaint and registers reported problems in a modern computer data bank for future reference. Wisconsin residents who contact that office can receive information as to whether or not a specific firm is considered reputable.

In addition to other types of problems, most attorneys general will take any complaint you have against an out-of-state firm. A local agency does not usually have as much clout in trying to remedy such a problem. One reason is that there is much cooperation between attorneys general. If a representative of one state's office suggests to the representative of another state's office that a company in the latter's jurisdiction may be acting illegally, an investigation will be undertaken.

Sometimes the actions of one or more companies or an entire industry come under scrutiny by the attorney general of more than one state. Several states may band together on behalf of consumers and file an antitrust or other type of suit, which may include court-administered refund provisions in the settlement. One example was a class-action suit filed jointly by the attorneys general of California, Hawaii, Kansas, Oregon, Utah, and Washington against five pharmaceutical companies: American Cyanamid, Bristol-Myers, Pfizer and Company, Olin-Mathieson, and Upjohn. The suit alleged that these drug manufacturers overcharged consumers for a variety of commonly prescribed antibiotics during the period of 1954–1966. Part of the resulting settlement returned $14.5 million to some 674,000 Californians alone.

Another example is an antitrust suit filed in June 1975 by California Attorney General Evelle J. Younger against 11 major oil companies. The federal suit charged Exxon, Gulf Oil, Phillips Oil, Shell Oil, Texaco, and others with "unlawfully restraining trade in the production and pricing of crude oil and the marketing of petroleum products."

Offices of state attorneys general that handle consumer complaints are given in Appendix 12.

FEDERAL ASSISTANCE

The federal government maintains a vast network of offices located in every major city in the United States. Among the many departments, boards, bureaus, and independent regulatory agencies are divisions that handle complaints directly from consumers. Your complaint to one of the offices listed in this book will usually be against an individual or company involved in interstate commerce. For prompt consideration of your complaint, follow directions outlined in the pertinent chapter. Although federal agencies are quick to accept and make a preliminary evaluation of common complaints, they are often inefficient in their problem-solving methods. In 1975 Virginia H. Knauer, consumer adviser to the president, authorized a study of 15 federal agencies by a private company, Technical Assistant Research Programs, Inc. The study was an investigation of complaint-handling procedures, and revealed shortcomings at many of the agencies.

Shortcomings

In general the study was critical of the agencies in five areas: (1) the offices at agency headquarters do not have adequate policies for handling telephone complaints; (2) recordkeeping must be improved; (3) sometimes no formal policies exist to fix responsibility for working on complaints; (4) there is no consensus on the kind of response consumers shall receive from these agencies; and (5) the agencies are inconsistent in the way they classify complaints.

Complaints

Even though many improvements are indicated, federal offices that handle consumer complaints can be responsive to your needs. Some solid persistence on your part may be required to initiate or speed up the bureaucratic process. Correspondence is sometimes misplaced, so do not hesitate to reiterate your requests. It is best to use the procedures outlined in Chapter 1, and follow up all your complaints.

You should freely contact any of the appropriate federal agencies listed in this book. Unless otherwise indicated, all of these consumer complaint offices will deal directly with you and the subject of your complaint. Most have stronger power to deal with offenders who operate across state lines and violate federal statutes.

U.S. Attorneys

The Attorney General of the United States and the U.S. attorneys nationwide can file both civil and criminal lawsuits on behalf of the federal government against violatiors of federal law. If a federal agency concludes that litigation is necessary, it can sometimes directly bring the matter to court or else request action from a U.S. attorney. Submitting your complaint directly to a U.S. attorney's office will only delay matters, because that office will forward the complaint to the appropriate agency for review. Except in the areas of unfair discrimination and unsolicited credit cards, the U.S. attorney will usually not investigate and litigate a case based solely on your complaint and without further evidence from a federal agency of harm or possible harm to other consumers.

Consumer Offices

The only federal office that handles general consumer complaints is the Office of Consumer Affairs at the U.S. Department of Health, Education, and Welfare in Washington, D.C. (Details on submitting claims to this office are given in Chapter 3.) All other federal agencies listed in this book accept consumer complaints only in the specific areas mentioned.

For years a tug-of-war has been going on between members of Congress over the formation of a federal consumer protection agency, which would represent consumers in formal and informal proceedings of federal agencies, boards, and commissions, and also represent consumer interests in the federal courts. If a bill to establish this type of agency has not passed into law, write your federal representatives and request their support. Joining legislators on the consumer side have been such organizations as Ralph Nader's Congress Watch, the Consumer Federation of America, Common Cause, United Auto Workers, and the AFL-CIO. Siding with legislators against the proposal have been the probusiness groups, including the Chamber of Commerce, the National Association of Manufacturers, and drug and grocery manufacturers.

State and Federal Legislators

Your state and federal elected representatives can be helpful to the consumer movement. These politicians are responsible for introducing and voting on bills significantly affecting consumers. You can obtain their names and mailing addresses from your local library, registrar of voters, or the office of the political party with which you are affiliated. Make your opinion on consumer issues known to these officials and offer suggestions for legislation to deal with statewide and nationwide consumer problems.

The offices of state and federal legislators are staffed with persons who specialize in serving the needs of constituents. An office for each of your representatives is located in your state. You should approach these sources if you want to check on the status of a consumer bill or to find out how your representative(s) will vote.

These offices also can be useful in helping you to obtain assistance from a state or federal legislator. These representatives do not act as complaint mediators and will simply refer the problem to the appropriate local, state, or federal agency. If you initiate your complaint with the proper state or federal agency, however, and do not receive adequate action, submit a copy of your letter or completed complaint form to your legislator. Ask for assistance in expediting your complaint. Government offices are often quick to respond to inquiries and pressure from legislators at all levels of government.

Chapter 14

INDUSTRY SOURCES OF HELP

This book has centered mainly on what you as a consumer can do to protect yourself and what the agencies at all levels of government can do to assist you. Now we will examine some of the efforts by private industry to deal with consumers and their problems in the marketplace.

COMMUNICATION

One basic way in which some companies effectively keep open the lines of communication with consumers is through easy telephone access. Many airlines, car rental agencies, and hotel and motel chains maintain nationwide toll-free numbers for you to use in making and changing reservations (see Appendix 3). Just because the local office of a firm is closed for the day or night does not mean that you have to wait to discuss a reservation or service problem.

Whirlpool Corporation, makers of washers, dryers, stoves, refrigerators, air conditioning units, and other household appliances, became one of the first—and remains one of the few—major manufacturers to encourage communications with consumers by subscribing to WATS line interstate telephone services, which were introduced in the United States in 1967. Whirlpool began its "Cool Line" in that year to enable consumers throughout the nation to telephone the company toll-free at its headquarters in Benton Harbor, Michigan.

From its inception to the end of 1976, the "Cool Line" had received roughly three-quarters of a million calls.

Whirlpool's phone line accepts calls 24 hours a day for referrals to local sources in the case of needed emergency service. At the same number during the hours of 8 a.m. to 7:30 p.m. (Eastern Standard Time), the company maintains a staff of customer service consultants to answer general questions about Whirlpool products and their warranties, and to help purchasers with any problems concerning appliance installation and operation. The representatives also accept consumer complaints.

According to Warren Bauer, manager of customer relations for Whirlpool, over 90 percent of calls received (ranging from presale inquiries to serious complaints) are handled satisfactorily over the phone. This service enables a simple problem such as a blown fuse or a closed valve to be corrected immediately and easily through the consumer's efforts.

To facilitate communication and public relations, companies in a single industry have often banded together to form a trade association. Some of these trade groups have set product and service standards, which their member firms are asked or required to follow. Trade associations that are most responsive to consumer needs set up complaint-handling systems, through which an impartial mediator will try to solve a problem you have with an associate member or nonmember.

Before deciding whether to take your complaint to an industry-run complaint office (as opposed to government-sponsored agency or newspaper or broadcast service), you should know something about who will be judging your complaint and about the evaluation process.

THE BETTER BUSINESS BUREAU

The first Better Business Bureau was formed in the early part of this century, and today over 130 bureaus make up one of the largest networks of privately sponsored, nonprofit business organizations in the world. Your BBB is not a nationally or internationally run organization; it is a local or regional group of businesses with a board of directors, president, and office staff, who follow general directives and guidelines of the parent organization, the Council of Better Business Bureaus, Inc. Bureaus are located throughout the United States and in Canada, Mexico, Puerto Rico, Venezuela, and Israel.

Since policies and procedures vary from one bureau to another, some may be more efficient or effective than others, and one might provide a public service that another does not. There are two major functions of *all* Better Business Bureaus that can be of some value to you. The first involves collection and dissemination of general information on business practices and specific information on individual companies. The second area is complaint handling.

Information Services

One misconception that many consumers have is that the BBB keeps files only on its members. The fact is that a bureau will also maintain a file on every business about which it receives an inquiry or complaint. As new correspondence and complaints are received, they are filed with past papers. As soon as enough background information is collected and consumer correspondence received, a bureau will write a profile of the company, listing the year it began operating, general information about products or services offered, its record of handling consumer complaints, and details about legal action that has been taken against the firm. This profile is available to any consumer requesting it.

Some bureaus will report information over the phone; others require a written request. This service is free, and you should use it whenever you consider doing business with a company whose reputation is unknown to you. Send your name and address and the name, address, and nature of the company about which you are inquiring to your local bureau. If there is no listing for a bureau in your town or city, write to the Council of Better Business Bureaus, Inc., 1150 Seventeenth Street N.W., Washington, D.C. 20036, for the address of the BBB nearest you.

If you want to obtain information about a company outside the area covered by the closest BBB, you should still contact that bureau. Most bureaus have files on firms outside their areas, and some will contact the bureau located nearest to the firm to get the information. If your local bureau cannot supply you with a helpful response, you may try writing to the bureau nearest the firm to get the information. Its address can be obtained from the Council.

Whether or not you ask the Better Business Bureau to act on your complaint, you help to keep BBB files accurate and up to date. Mail to your local bureau a copy of any letter—whether it praises or complains—that you write to a company or to a government agency about a company. If more consumers did this, bureaus would be better able to recognize and deal more swiftly with firms employing questionable practices or ignoring consumer complaints. Also, inquiring consumers would not receive outdated or misleading information so often.

In addition to providing reports on individual companies, many bureaus, as well as the Council in Washington, D.C., publish free consumer and investor guides. They give tips on buying and servicing and help you to protect yourself against fraudulent business schemes. Often you can also obtain from a bureau a list of local BBB members in the specific trade category of your interest, such as insurance companies, tax preparers, or television dealers. Many bureaus request a stamped, self-addressed envelope for return of the information.

Complaint Process

All Better Business Bureaus mediate complaints against both member and nonmember firms. The process is simple. If you have purchased goods or services from a company that refuses to make a fair adjustment (repair, replacement, or refund) for a problem caused by the manufacturer, dealer, or service provider, you can file a "Customer Experience Record" form, available at any BBB office or by mail.

Bureaus will act on any problem alleging misrepresentation or irregular business practices in selling or advertising. However, they will not provide legal help and will not deal with any matter that has already been judged in court. If your complaint alleges fraud or other illegal activity, the bureau will not touch it. In that case, you should take the complaint to one of the appropriate government agencies listed in this book.

After you complete and return the form to the bureau, it will send a copy to the business about which you are complaining. The company has the choice of: (1) answering the bureau's inquiry and giving the date (or projected date) of adjustment; (2) providing an explanation of why the firm refuses to reconsider making an adjustment; or (3) ignoring the bureau's intervention altogether.

Hopefully, the company will respond quickly and positively to give you the adjustment. Whether or not that is the case, you should mail the bureau the follow-up card (originally supplied to you with the blank "Customer Service Record" form) 30 days after you mail the completed complaint form to the bureau. On it, you should check the appropriate status of the problem, notifying the bureau that the company has adjusted your complaint satisfactorily, that you and the firm have been in contact without reaching an agreeable settlement, or that the company has not made contact with you and your complaint remains unresolved.

The follow-up card should be returned immediately, so that the bureau can close out your complaint or take further action. If you are notifying the bureau that your complaint has not been resolved, request at the same time that the matter be submitted to arbitration.

Arbitration

Arbitration is a process by which your complaint is judged by an impartial third party, whose decision will be legally binding in most states. The proceeding is informal and similar to that of a small claims court. Attorneys are not needed. You and a representative of the business each present a side of the dispute, and the arbitrator decides who is right and what the terms of the settlement will be.

An arbitration decision cannot be successfully set aside in court unless the losing party can show that the award went beyond the disputed issues or that the award was made through the misconduct, fraud, corruption, or substantial partiality of the arbitrator. An award can be changed by an arbitrator without going to court if there was a factual mistake or miscalculation not known before the decision was issued.

Many Better Business Bureaus offer arbitration if their initial efforts to resolve your complaint against a bureau member or nonmember fail. (If the bureau handling your complaint does not have an arbitration service, you should take your complaint to another source mentioned in this book.)

The arbitration administrator will evaluate your complaint to determine whether the matter can be arbitrated. Five factors are considered:

1. A BBB-administered arbitration must be initiated at the bureau nearest to the business about which you are complaining. Therefore, a case being considered for arbitration is sometimes transferred to another bureau for action.

2. State laws often disallow this type of proceeding for specific kinds of parties and cases. For example, California law precludes the involvement of the Public Utilities Commission in any arbitration. Thus there can be no arbitration in that state for disputes arising out of state-regulated telephone, gas, electric, and water services.

3. If your complaint may have arisen out of an unlawful act, it

will be returned to you or referred to a law enforcement agency.

4. A case where a quick settlement is urgently needed may be rejected. It can take months for the arbitration process to be completed. The size and value of an item or service are not factors in determining eligibility or scheduling times for arbitration.

5. Both you and the business involved must agree to the arbitration. If one party refuses, your complaint with the BBB is at a dead end.

The BBB pays all the basic administrative costs of the arbitration proceedings it sets up. Lists of volunteer arbitrators are sent to both parties for an indication of any preference each may have. Arbitrators are sometimes attorneys or individuals who have completed an arbitration training program. If an agreement on one arbitrator cannot be reached, each party then selects one person. The two selected arbitrators agree on a third, and all three arbitrators hear the case, with the majority making all decisions.

If the quality or operation of a product or service is being questioned, the bureau may arrange for the arbitrator to examine and evaluate the problem beforehand. If a technical opinion is necessary, the bureau will pay reasonable costs to have the item submitted to an independent testing laboratory or to bring in an expert witness.

If the arbitrator's decision is that the company must give you a refund, the firm must make full payment. If the company refuses to pay you the amount of the judgment, you must take on the responsibility of legal action to collect it, just as if you were proceeding against a firm refusing to pay you the judgment ordered by a small claims court. The bureau will then be helpful only in pressuring the company to comply with the decision or in assisting you to prepare papers with which to file a court action.

BBB Membership

All of the reporting and complaint-handling services of the Better Business Bureau involve bureau members as well as nonmembers. A member firm has the right to display the BBB symbol on its premises or in its advertising. The symbol is known nationwide. Understanding what a company's membership in a bureau does and does not mean may keep you from making some wrong decisions, based on blind faith, about which companies to patronize.

A firm's membership in the Better Business Bureau does not necessarily mean that the company deals fairly with consumers. Any company applying for membership in a bureau must complete an application on which it agrees to meet a specific set of idealistic and practical standards. These include such areas as adhering to ethical business practices and responding to all complaints forwarded by the bureau. However, a company not complying with a standard on one or more decisions does not automatically lose its membership.

Consider the membership process. Generally, a firm must be in existence for a minimum of six months to become a member, but there are exceptions. For example, someone may own a jewelry store that has been operating for many years with a good reputation. The bureau determines this by an examination of the company's file and by staff calls to credit reporting agencies, consumer bureaus, and other government offices. If that owner opens a dry cleaning establishment, he or she can probably obtain BBB membership for the new business immediately, even though the first business was never a member and the new one has no track record at all.

Each bureau is supported by the dues of member firms. The larger the company, the more dues it must pay. Salespersons are retained to secure new member accounts. Many companies want to become members of the BBB, whether truly to support sound business practices or just to boost their image as a public relations measure. At the same time, the bureau needs the revenue from its members. Because of this mutual support, few companies are forceably ousted from membership.

According to William Fritz, president of the Better Business Bureau of Los Angeles, a decision by the bureau to cancel a firm's membership is never based on the volume of complaints alone. What is judged is the company's willingness to deal fairly with the consumer complaints it receives.

BBB Effectiveness

Although Better Business Bureaus provide some good services to consumers, the overall effectiveness of their programs should be questioned and kept in perspective. Make full use of the BBB information services, but check out other sources as well. Many bureaus are grossly understaffed, and files are often outdated. There may be no new entries in a company record over a period of several years simply because no one has gone over the bulk of the latest complaints.

Many other consumer protection offices, particularly those at government-sponsored bureaus, provide similar information services. You may also consider facts and opinions supplied by friends who may have had some experience in dealing with a particular company. You may even consider stopping strangers who are leaving the establishment and asking them how they like doing business there.

In response to your inquiry about a particular firm, the BBB will often make a statement that is too vague to understand. On a form sent to consumers by the bureau in Los Angeles, one of the answers that may be checked reads: "This company has a satisfactory record. Bureau files show we have received only infrequent reports of customer dissatisfaction. These matters have been given proper consideration when brought to the company's attention by the bureau." What is a "satisfactory" record? What is considered "infrequent"? What does "proper consideration" mean? The bureau does not define these terms adequately. Also, you can be sure that many consumers would furnish definitions quite different from the people evaluating bureau files.

Many bureaus customarily refrain from being more specific in their reporting and require employees to minimize the amount of information they provide to inquirers. No information is provided to the consumer about the *nature* of the complaints received. One ex-employee of the Los Angeles BBB claimed that she was fired for giving out too much information about companies.

Bureau reports about a company can sometimes be grossly misleading. An inquirer may be told that a firm has a satisfactory record, with no mention of serious charges filed against it. A consumer contacting his or her local bureau on a Monday night may be told that the company deals fairly with customers. Another consumer, who calls on Tuesday, may be told that the firm has been convicted of false advertising and gone out of business. Misleading reporting is sometimes unavoidable, but the nature of the reporting itself can cover up serious, negative aspects of a company's operation that may even be known by the bureau.

If you decide to submit your complaint to a local source of help, the Better Business Bureau should not be your first choice. A government or media-sponsored consumer complaints office will usually have more willingness and more power than the BBB to deal with the adverse actions of a company. Government agencies retain investigators, and Better Business Bureaus do not. No BBB has legal authority over a company, as do many government bodies.

Many complaints are settled satisfactorily with the consumer getting the adjustment he or she requests. Only a very small percentage of these cases involve arbitration. However, many cases remain unsettled. In 1974 the Better Business Bureau of Los Angeles referred 404 complaints and settled 399 complaints relating to automobile dealers. It was not able to settle 452 others. In the same year, that bureau referred 140, settled 2,533, and could not settle 1,256 complaints against mail order companies. For all complaints handled by this bureau in 1974, 5,705 were referred, 8,714 were settled, and 7,701 were not settled. In 52 of the 86 categories of businesses listed, the number of unsettled complaints was equal to or greater than the number of resolved complaints. Upon requesting more recent statistical information from the Los Angeles Better Business Bureau, the author met with what seemed to be strong resistance on the part of a bureau representative. Despite verbal agreement by the bureau's president to supply the newer figures, they were never received.

CONSUMER ACTION PANELS

Increasing the effectiveness of business complaint-handling systems has been one of the major efforts of Virginia H. Knauer in her work as special assistant to the president for consumer affairs. She has also served as director of the Office of Consumer Affairs under the U.S. Department of Health, Education, and Welfare, and succeeded in awakening various industries to their responsibilities in standing behind their products and services and dealing directly and fairly with consumers and their complaints.

MACAP

Frank McLaughlin, who has been part of Virginia Knauer's staff, coordinated the "Report of the Presidential Task Force on Appliance Warranty and Service Problems," which criticized the 1968 complaint record of the major appliance industry and threatened new legislation to deal with the problem unless suggested action was undertaken. In response to that recommendation, the Major Appliance Consumer Action Panel (MACAP) was formed in 1970.

MACAP is sponsored by three industry trade groups: the Association of Home Appliance Manufacturers, the Gas Appliance Manufacturers Association, and the National Retail Merchants Association. Its main function is to handle individual consumer complaints against appliances in any of the following categories:

Refrigerators	Room air-conditioners
Freezers	Garbage disposals
Ranges	Trash compactors
Microwave ovens	Water heaters
Dishwashers	Dehumidifiers
Washers	Humidifiers
Dryers	Gas incinerators

To take advantage of the MACAP service, you must first have contacted the dealer and manufacturer and not received satisfaction on your complaint. Then call MACAP at 800–621–0477 (in Illinois, call collect 312–236–3223) or write to the Major Appliance Consumer Action Panel, 20 North Wacher Drive, Chicago, Illinois 60606. Supply the following information: (1) your name, address, and telephone number; (2) the type of appliance, brand, model, and serial number; (3) the date of purchase; (4) the dealer's name and address; (5) the service agent's name and address (if different from that of the dealer); and (6) an accurate description of the problem and an up-to-date report of whatever service has been performed.

Once your complaint is received, MACAP will contact a senior level executive of the company involved and request a response detailing the action to be taken. If the panel staff receives a positive response, it will notify you of the promised action. MACAP will then close out your file permanently, with the assumption that your complaint has been resolved, unless you later notify the panel either that the company has not carried out any action or that the action undertaken is not satisfactory. MACAP claims that of all the consumer complaints resolved, over 90 per cent are fully handled during this initial complaint procedure.

If the panel receives a negative response from a company not willing to make an adjustment or offer a reasonable alternative, the panel members will study your complaint at one of their regular meetings and make a recommendation, which hopefully reflects an equitable solution. The final resolution may require several reviews of the file as new correspondence is received and contradictory information is clarified. Of all the complaints referred to the panel for further study, more than half are judged unjustified. Of the complaints considered justified, more than half are reported as satisfactorily resolved.

Since its inception, MACAP has processed over 20,000 consumer complaints. A majority of these have related to refrigerator/freezers, ranges, and washers. According to MACAP staff member Joyce Viso, the most difficult complaints that the panel is asked to resolve are those in which the consumer or the company has failed to keep accurate service records. Commenting at the beginning of 1975 on MACAP's success in helping consumers, Viso said: "Of the total number of complaints received by MACAP, between 90–95 percent are closed resolved. Many of these involve a 'negotiated settlement,' and so we would probably be optimistic in saying that the consumer is 'totally satisfied.' Also, because the panel receives only the most difficult problems, the frustration involved inhibits 'total satisfaction.' " A subsequent, independently conducted audit study in the latter half of 1975 confirmed the effectiveness of MACAP. Of the 1,065 questionnaires sent to consumers who had previously complained to MACAP, 845 (79.3 percent) were completed and returned. In 83.8 percent of these cases, there was an industry offer to resolve the complaint as a result of MACAP's efforts. Furthermore, that offer was acceptable to about 81.1 percent of the complainants.

MACAP's high level of success has been achieved through the cooperation of industries and consumers. Perhaps the most significant factor spurring consumer trust of this program, and assuring objectivity in the decision-making process, is that all panelists are totally independent of the appliance industry. Most are involved in consumer research or education. The panel has included, for example, Dr. Virginia F. Cutler, who has served as the panel chairperson, Dean and Distinguished Professor Emeritus at Brigham Young University, and Dr. Jason Annis, Assistant Professor of Mechanical Engineering at Kansas State University.

Panelists earn no financial remuneration for their work on behalf of MACAP. They receive only funds for travel and accommodations for about 10 meetings a year.

Carpet and Rug Institute

Virginia Knauer and her staff have used the MACAP program as an example to stimulate the institution of similar organizations by other industries. Another major program was developed by the Carpet and Rug Institute in 1973, and became known as the Carpet and Rug Industry Consumer Action Panel (CRICAP). This panel was made up of consumer educators and journalists, and operated much like MACAP.

Unfortunately, CRICAP disbanded in August 1975 because of funding problems and the fact that most of the complaints were being handled by the Institute staff, and not referred to the panel for review. It is the consumer who loses, and many of the more difficult complaints that could have been resolved will now reach a dead end.

Although CRICAP is no longer in existence, the Carpet and Rug Institute will continue to receive consumer complaints at P.O. Box 1568, Dalton, Georgia 30720. You should consider writing to the Institute if you want to complain about texture change, wear, or other problem with a rug or carpet. An executive of the appropriate carpet mill will be contacted and asked to help resolve your complaint.

With pressure from federal sources, CRICAP may go gack into operation at some future time.

FICAP

If you have a complaint dealing with manufacturing defects, quality, or delivery of furniture, another source of help is the Furniture Industry Consumer Advisory Panel (FICAP). It has included a cross section of educators, consumer advocates, and retailers. This nonprofit group was formed in 1973 by the Southern Manufacturers Association, whose members produce about one-third of the furniture made in the United States.

FICAP receives about 60 to 75 complaints a month and handles them with procedures similar to those of MACAP. The highest percentage of complaints relate to the areas of workmanship and fabric.

If you have a furniture complaint that is not satisfactorily resolved with the dealer, write to the Furniture Industry Consumer Advisory Panel, P.O. Box 951, High Point, North Carolina 27261. Include the following: (1) your name, address, and telephone number; (2) the retailer's name and address; (3) the manufacturer's name and address, if you know it; (4) the date of purchase; (5) the style, color, item number, and any other identifying information; and (6) a concise description of the problem and any service already performed. If possible, also enclose copies of any correspondence between you and the dealer or manufacturer.

ICAP

The Insurance Consumer Action Panel (ICAP) began its operations in October 1976. Cosponsored by the U.S. Office of Consumer

Affairs and the National Association of Mutual Insurance Agents, ICAP was established as a one-year pilot program to resolve rapidly and equitably disputes that could not otherwise be resolved between consumers and companies in the casualty and property insurance industry. It also has the purpose of helping the industry identify and correct those problem areas that give rise to common types of disputes.

The state insurance commissioners for Michigan, Mississippi, Montana, and Utah have agreed to forward from these test states the casualty and property insurance complaints they think are appropriate for the dispute review and resolution mechanism of ICAP.

ICAP will consider consumer complaints from any source, but it will especially concentrate on those submitted by insurance commissioners in the cooperating states. At least during the pilot period, the panel will consider only disputes that arise after the sale and that tend to involve the more common problems. The panel will not handle any complaint dealing with market availability, underwriting standards, rate adequacy, and matters of fact.

The panel's paid administrator will first attempt to resolve the problem informally. If this mediation fails, the case is then presented to the panel for its review. Those selected to serve on the panel during the one-year pilot program were Dr. Salvatore Divita (panel chairman), who heads the Department of Business Administration at George Washington University; Thomas G. Allison, staff counsel to the U.S. Senate Commerce Committee; Leonard Curry, financial writer with United Press International; Patrick Portway, manager of marketing for Systems Development Corporation; and John H. Kroll, a retired independent insurance agent.

The panel has been scheduled to meet at least four times during the first year for the purpose of evaluating cases. Based on data gathered for each case file, the panel will formulate a recommendation by consensus or a majority vote. After the recommendations are returned to both parties, the administrator will follow up by encouraging the parties to accept and carry out these recommendations. The case is then considered closed.

If your insurance problem cannot be resolved through efforts on the local or state level and if it falls within the scope of ICAP's interest, try this organization. Detail the problem in a letter, along with your name, address, and phone number, and address it to Insurance Consumer Action Panel, 640 Investment Building, Washington,

D.C. 20005. You may also obtain further information by phoning ICAP at 202–628–1300.

AUTOCAPs

According to a source at the U.S. Office of Consumer Affairs, by far the greatest amount of consumer dissatisfaction in this country is in the area of automotive sales and service. During the first half of 1974, OCA received 215 automotive complaints, nearly half of which related to service repairs. The next highest number of auto complaints involved defective vehicles and warranties.

With encouragement from Virginia Knauer and her staff, Automotive Trade Association Managers (ATAM) and the National Automobile Dealers Association (NADA) set up the Automotive Consumer Action Program (AUTOCAP). It comprises a nationwide network of state and local groups called AUTOCAPs, which act on automotive complaints from consumers. Many AUTOCAPs handle consumer complaints using some of the same company contact procedures and panel activities as developed for other industry groups already mentioned.

AUTOCAPs are sponsored by local and state automotive trade associations, which consider ATAM/NADA suggested guidelines but set their own rules. Although the two parent associations have recommended that each panel consist of at least three dealers and two consumers, many AUTOCAPs include even greater dealer representation.

Each AUTOCAP functions independently, and none is governed by one of the national associations. According to C. Alan Marlette, a NADA representative, there were 35 AUTOCAPs operating in mid-1976. Sixteen of them, however, were not officially recognized by the U.S. Office of Consumer Affairs because they do not include any consumer representation in the complaint-handling and decision-making processes.

The names and addresses of the officially recognized AUTOCAPs are given in Appendix 16. Those AUTOCAPs that consist only of an ethics committee or a single mediator are listed in Appendix 17.

The Automotive Consumer Action Program does provide a means through which consumers may make complaints about any problems relating to their vehicles. However, unlike the complaint-handling systems utilized by both MACAP and FICAP, most AU-TOCAPs are overrepresented by industry-affiliated individuals. This situation raises questions about the objectivity of the AUTOCAPs. Do AUTOCAPs without consumer representation accurately take into consideration the consumer's point of view? Are industry-affiliated panelists truly fair when judging the actions of one of their association members?

If you are considering submitting your complaint to an AU-TOCAP, ask who is on the panel and what specific procedures are used to resolve complaints. Try this avenue of recourse if you feel there is adequate consumer representation. However, keep in mind the many alternative agencies (listed in this book) that not only want to help consumers with auto complaints but have legal support (unlike the AUTOCAP) to force corrective action. Avoid AUTOCAPs that do not include any consumers in their program, unless you know the group to be fair and effective and there is no other readily accessible agency.

Other "CAPs"

The U.S. Office of Consumer Affairs is continuing its discussions with various industries working toward the development of more consumer action panels. New complaint-handling programs may soon be initiated by the home moving, health care, recording tape, photo marketing, and tire industries. Complaint systems comprising groups of florists and of opticians have already been approved.

Industry-run complaint programs are ideal because they do not cost the taxpayers money and they specialize in resolving complaints dealing with products and services from their respective industries. They are especially responsive to minor consumer problems, but they are not the place to go if you suspect that a law has been broken or that consumers need fast protection from a dangerous product.

APPENDIXES

CONSUMER CONTACT SHEET

Date	To/From	Co. or Gov't. Agency Address, Phone No.

Name, Position, Department Extension No.	Subject	Results

Appendix 2

CONSUMER PRODUCT COMPLAINT REPORT

CONSUMER PRODUCT COMPLAINT REPORT		
1. NAME OF COMPLAINANT	2. TELEPHONE NO.	3. DATE OF INCIDENT
4. STREET ADDRESS	5. CITY, STATE, ZIP CODE	
6 a. DESCRIPTION OF PRODUCT(S)	6b. Date Aquired	
7. BRAND NAME	8. MODEL/STYLE NO.	
9. SERIAL NO.	10. LOT/BATCH NO.	
11. MANUFACTURER, IMPORTER OR DISTRIBUTOR NAME AND ADDRESS	12. DEALER NAME AND ADDRESS	

13. HOW PRODUCT ACQUIRED
PURCHASED NEW ☐   SECOND HAND ☐   OTHER ☐   SPECIFY _____

14. SAMPLE AVAILABLE YES ☐ NO ☐	15. WARNING LABEL YES ☐ NO ☐	16. INSTRUCTIONS YES ☐ NO ☐
17. PRODUCT DAMAGED BEFORE INCIDENT YES ☐ NO ☐	18. PRODUCT REPAIRED BEFORE ⟶ INCIDENT ⟵ AFTER YES ☐ NO ☐ YES ☐ NO ☐	19. AGE OF PRODUCT (ESTIMATE IF NECESSARY)

IF INJURY OR ILLNESS COMPLETE ITEMS 20 - 24

20. VICTIM'S AGE	21. VICTIM'S SEX MALE ☐ FEMALE ☐	22. BODY PART(S) INVOLVED

23. TYPE OF INJURY OR ILLNESS
BURN ☐   FRACTURE ☐   CUT ☐   OTHER ☐   SPECIFY _____

24. MEDICAL TREATMENT RECEIVED
PHYSICIAN'S OFFICE ☐   EMERGENCY ROOM ☐   OTHER HOSPITAL ☐   OTHER ☐   SPECIFY _____

25. GIVE DETAILS OF COMPLAINT, INJURY, OR ILLNESS. DESCRIBE HOW INCIDENT OCCURRED. USE REVERSE SIDE IF NECESSARY.

FOR COMMISSION USE ONLY   Source:

26. RECEIVING OFFICE	27. DATE RECEIVED	28. RECEIVED BY	
29. SOURCE OF REPORT LETTER ☐ PHONE ☐ VISIT ☐ OTHER ☐ SPECIFY _____			30. DOCUMENT NO.
31. FOLLOW-UP ACTION			32. PRODUCT CODE(S)
33. DISTRIBUTION		34. ENDORSER'S NAME AND TITLE	

CPSC FORM 175   (REV. 1/75)

Source: Consumer Product Safety Commission, Washington, D.C. 20207.

Appendix 3

PARTIAL LIST OF TOLL-FREE
WATS LINE TELEPHONE NUMBERS

(National Toll-Free Number Information: 800–555–1212)

AIRLINE COMPANIES

Name of Company	Toll-Free No.	From What States Can This No. Be Used?	Alternative No. for Excepted Places
American Airlines	800–252–9023	So. Calif. only.	Call information for numbers in other parts of the country.
Trans World Airlines	800–252–9001	Western states.	
United Airlines	800–252–9147	So. Calif. only.	
Western Airlines	800–453–5330	Idaho, Colo., Ariz., N. Mex., Wyo.	

APPLIANCE COMPANIES

Name of Company	Toll-Free No.	From What States Can This No. Be Used?	Alternative No. for Excepted Places
Westinghouse Electric	800–372–6357	Calif. only.	
Whirlpool "Cool Line"	800–253–1301	Nationwide (except Mich.).	800–632–2243 from Mich. only.
White-Westinghouse (Consumer Relations)	800–245–0600	Nationwide (except Pa.).	800–242–0580 from Pa. only.

BANKS

Name of Company	Toll-Free No.	From What States Can This No. Be Used?	Alternative No. for Excepted Places
Barclay's Bank Travelers Check Division	800–221–2426 or 800–221–2427	Nationwide (except N. Y.).	Call 233–1511 collect in N. Y. only.
Crocker Bank (Customer Service)	800–652–1630	Calif. only.	
Crocker Bank (to report lost or stolen credit cards)	800–227–4256	Nationwide (except Calif.).	800–622–0980 from Calif. only.
United California Bank	800–272–3225 800–272–3530	Northern Calif. Southern Calif.	
Wells Fargo Bank (Customer Service)	800–652–1580	Calif. (except San Francisco).	San Francisco local no. (415) 396–4625. Call collect outside Calif.

CAR RENTAL COMPANIES

Name of Company	Toll-Free No.	From What States Can This No. Be Used?	Alternative No. for Excepted Places
Avis Rent A Car	800–331–1212	Nationwide (except Okla.).	800–482–4554 from Okla. only.
Budget Rent-A-Car	800–228–9650	Nationwide (except Nebr.).	800–642–9910 from Nebr. only.
Hertz Rent-a-Car	800–654–3131	Nationwide (except Okla.)	800–522–3711 from Okla. only.
National Rent A Car	800–328–4567 800–432–8790	Nationwide (except Minn.). N. J. only.	Minn. residents call 612–830–2345 collect.
Sears Rent-A-Car	800–228–2800	Nationwide (except Nebr.).	800–642–9922 from Nebr. only

CREDIT CARD COMPANIES (Including "Lost or Stolen" Services)

Name of Company	Toll-Free No.	From What States Can This No. Be Used?	Alternative No. for Excepted Places
American Express	800–528–4800	Nationwide (except Ariz.).	800–528–1500 from Ariz. only.
	800–528–1000	Western states only.	
	800–221–3000	Northeast states only.	
	800–528–4800	Midwest states.	
	800–327–9325	Southeast states only.	
Carte Blanche (Instant Recall)	800–523–4815	Nationwide (except Philadelphia).	Call 215–241–4525 collect Philadelphia residents only.
Credit Card Sentinel, Inc.	800–423–5166	Nationwide (except Calif.).	800–382–3340 from Calif. only.
Credit Card Service Bureau	800–336–0220	Nationwide (except Va.).	
Diners Club	800–525–9150	Nationwide (except Colo.).	800–332–9340 from Colo. only.
Hot-Line Credit Card Bureau of America	800–327–1284; 1285	Nationwide (except Fla.).	800–432–2096 from Fla. only.
International Credit Card Registry	800–426–8112	Nationwide (except Wash. State).	800–562–8174 Wash. State only.
	800–663–3381	Canada only.	
	206–927–1001 collect	Rest of the world.	
Master Charge	800–492–0160	Md. only.	
	800–222–8020	Miss. only.	

FEDERAL GOVERNMENT OFFICES

Name of Office	Toll-Free No.	From What States Can This No. Be Used?	Alternative No. for Excepted Places
Air Force	800–447–4700	Nationwide (except Ill.).	800–322–4400 from Ill. only.
Army	800–431–1976	Nationwide (except N. Y.).	
Coast Guard	800–424–8883	Nationwide (except D.C.).	Local call in D.C.
Federal Job Information Center or Civil Service Information	800–252–9076	So. Calif. only.	
Interstate Commerce Commission	800–424–9312	Nationwide (except D.C.)	Local call in D.C.
Marine Corps Information Center	800–423–2600	Nationwide (except Calif.).	800–252–0241 from Calif. only.
National Highway Traffic Safety Administration	800–424–9393	Nationwide.	
National Response Center for Oil Pollution (Division of Coast Guard)	800–424–8802	Nationwide (except D.C.).	Local call in D.C.
Navy	800–841–8000	Nationwide (except Ga.).	800–342–5855 from Ga. only.
U.S. Consumer Product Safety Commission	800–638–2666	Nationwide (except Md.).	800–492–2937) from Md. only.
Veteran's Administration	800–352–6592	Calif. only.	

HOTELS AND MOTELS[1]

Name of Company	Toll-Free No.	From What State Can This No. Be Used?	Alternative No. for Excepted Places
Albert Pick Hotels and Motor Inns	800–621–4404	Nationwide (except Ill.).	800–972–7200 from Ill. only.

HOTELS AND MOTELS (cont.)

Name of Company	Toll-Free No.	From What States Can This No. Be Used?	Alternative No. for Excepted Places
Americana Hotels	800–228–3278	Nationwide (except Nebr.).	
Best Western Hotels	800–528–1234	Nationwide (except Ariz.).	800–352–1222 from Ariz.
Econo-Travel Motor Hotels	800–446–6900	Nationwide (except Va.).	800–582–5882 from Va.
Holiday Inns of America	800–453–5555	West Coast and Midwest only.	Contact the toll-free information. 800–555–1212 for other regions of the U.S.
Howard Johnson's Motor Lodges	800–654–2000	Nationwide (except Okla.).	800–522–4211 from Okla. only.
Hyatt Hotels	800–228–9000	Nationwide (except Nebr.).	Nebr. residents call 402–572–9444 collect.
Marriott Hotels	800–228–9290	Nationwide (except Nebr.).	Nebr. residents call 402–571–5400 collect.
Ramada Inns	800–228–2828	Nationwide (except Nebr.).	800–642–9343 from Nebr. only.
Rodeway Inns	800–228–2000	Nationwide (except Nebr.).	Nebr. residents call 402–572–8822 collect.
Sheraton Hotels	800–325–3534	Nationwide (except Mo.).	800–392–3500 from Mo. only.
Westward Ho Hotels (reservations for Las Vegas or Palm Springs)	800–634–6651	Only from states around Nev.	
Western International Hotels	800–228–3000	Nationwide (except Nebr.).	Nebr. residents call 402–571–3366 collect.

[1]Note: If you are a student with valid I.D., ask about student rates.

MAGAZINES AND NEWSPAPERS

Name of Periodical	Toll-Free No.	From What States Can This No. Be Used?	Alternative No. for Excepted Places
Advocate* (gay-oriented)	800–325–6400	Nationwide (except Mo.).	800–342–6600 from Mo. only.
After Dark*	800–325–6400	Nationwide (except Mo.).	800–342–6600 from Mo. only.
Christian Science Monitor	800–225–7090	Nationwide (except Mass.).	
Dance*	800–325–6400	Nationwide (except Mo.).	800–342–6600 from Mo. only.
Family Health Magazine*	800–325–6400	Nationwide (except Mo.).	800–342–6600 from Mo. only.
Fortune	800–621–8200	Nationwide (except Ill.).	800–972–8302 from Ill. only.
Golf Magazine*	800–325–6400	Nationwide (except Mo.).	800–342–6600 from Mo. only.
Hunting*	800–325–6400	Nationwide (except Mo.).	800–342–6600 from Mo. only.
Money	800–621–8200	Nationwide (except Ill.).	800–972–8302 from Ill. only.
Newsweek	800–631–1040	Nationwide (except N. J.).	
New York Magazine*	800–325–6400	Nationwide (except Mo.).	800–342–6600 from Mo. only.

MAGAZINES AND NEWSPAPERS (cont.)

Name of Periodical	Toll-Free No.	From What States Can This No. Be Used?	Alternative No. for Excepted Places
New West Magazine*	800–325–6400	Nationwide (except Mo.).	800–342–6600 from Mo. only.
Oui*	800–325–6400	Nationwide (except Mo.).	800–342–6600 from Mo. only.
Outdoor Life*	800–325–6400	Nationwide (except Mo.)	800–342–6600 from Mo. only.
People Magazine	800–621–8200	Nationwide (except Ill.).	800–972–8302 from Ill. only.
Playboy Magazine*	800–325–6400	Nationwide (except Mo.).	800–342–6600 from Mo. only.
Popular Science*	800–325–6400	Nationwide (except Mo.).	800–342–6600 from Mo. only.
Prevention Magazine*	800–325–6400	Nationwide (except Mo.).	800–342–6600 from Mo. only.
Reader's Digest*	800–325–6400	Nationwide (except Mo.).	800–342–6600 from Mo. only.
Rolling Stone*	800–325–6400	Nationwide (except Mo.).	800–342–6600 from Mo. only.
Saturday Review*	800–325–6400	Nationwide (except Mo.).	800–342–6600 from Mo. only.
Sports Illustrated	800–621–8200	Nationwide (except Ill.).	800–972–8302 from Ill. only.
Teachers Magazine*	800–325–6400	Nationwide (except Mo.).	800–342–6600 from Mo. only.
Time	800–621–8200	Nationwide (except Ill.).	800–972–8302 from Ill. only.
TV Times Magazine*	800–325–6400	Nationwide (except Mo.).	800–342–6600 from Mo. only.
TV Guide	800–523–7933	Nationwide (except Pa.).	

*The phone number listed is for an answering service, which in some cases will only take subscription orders.

OIL COMPANIES

Name of Company	Toll-Free No.	From What States Can This No. Be Used?	Alternative No. for Excepted Places
Atlantic Richfield Co. (Customer Service)	800–648–3051	Nationwide (except Nev.).	Nev. residents call toll-free information
Shell Oil (Credit Card Action Line)	800–331–3703	Nationwide (except Okla.).	
Standard or Chevron Oil Co.	800–642–0262 800–227–0334	Inside Calif. only. Ariz., Colo., Idaho, Mont., Wyo., Nev., Ore., Wash., Utah (accts. *billed from* Calif. use this no.).	
	800–626–4553	For all accounts *billed from* Louisville, Ky.	
Union Oil Co.	800–572–6209	Mich. only.	

OTHER COMPANIES AND SERVICES

Name of Company	Toll-Free No.	From What States Can This No. Be Used?	Alternative No. for Excepted Places
Amtrak	800–648–3850	Western states only.	Other areas have a different no.; call toll-free information

OTHER COMPANIES AND SERVICES (cont.)

Name of Company	Toll-Free No.	From What States Can This No. Be Used?	Alternative No. for Excepted Places
BMW of North America, Inc.	800–243–6006	Nationwide (except Conn.).	
California Bureau of Automotive Repairs	800–952–5210	Calif. only.	
Equitable Life Assurance Society of the U.S.	800–223–5636	Nationwide.	
Ford Motor Co. Customer Service	800–648–4848	Nationwide (except Nev.).	800–992–5777 from Nev. only.
F.W. Woolworth Co. (Insurance)	800–558–7000	Nationwide (except Wis.).	
International Luggage Registry (Protection against lost luggage-labels)	800–648–5900	Nationwide (except Reno, Nev.).	Local call in Reno, Nev.
Major Appliance Consumer Action Panel (MACAP)	800–621–0477	Nationwide (except Ill.)	Ill. residents call 312–236–3223 collect.
National Runaway Switchboard Service	800–621–4000	Nationwide (except Ill.).	800–972–6004 from Ill. only.
Proctor & Gamble Consumer Services	800–543–7276	Nationwide (except Ohio).	800–582–3945 from Ohio only.
Western Union	800–257–2241	Nationwide (except Mo.).	800–291–1010 from Mo. only.
	800–648–4100	West Coast only.	
	800–325–5100	East Coast only.	
	800–325–5200	Middle states.	

Source: Compiled by Kenneth Eisenberger and Leora Brown, 1976. Listings of companies and services do not constitute an endorsement.

Note: WATS line numbers are highly subject to change. If the number you dial is no longer in existence, dial the information operator at 800–555–1212. Statewide toll-free phone numbers for state consumer offices are listed and underlined throughout Appendix 12.

Appendix 4

STATE GOVERNMENT
UTILITY REGULATORY BODIES

ALABAMA PUBLIC
SERVICE COMMISSION

P.O. Box 991
Montgomery 36102
Phone: 205–832–3327

ALASKA PUBLIC
UTILITIES COMMISSION

338 Denali St.
Anchorage 99501
Phone: 907–272–1487

ALASKA
TRANSPORTATION
COMMISSION

338 Denali St.
Anchorage 99501
Phone: 907–279–1451

ARIZONA
CORPORATION
COMMISSION

Rm. 216, 1688 W. Adams
Phoenix 85007
Phone: 602–271–4166

ARKANSAS PUBLIC
SERVICE COMMISSION

Justice Bldg.
Little Rock 72201
Phone: 501–371–1794

ARKANSAS
TRANSPORTATION
COMMISSION

Justice Bldg.
Little Rock 72201
Phone: 501–371–1341

CALIFORNIA PUBLIC
UTILITIES COMMISSION

350 McAllister St.
San Francisco 94102
Phone: 415–557–1487

COLORADO PUBLIC
UTILITIES COMMISSION

1845 Sherman St.
Denver 80203
Phone: 303–892–3154

CONNECTICUT PUBLIC
UTILITIES COMMISSION

165 Capitol Ave.
Hartford 06115
Phone: 203–566–2104

DELAWARE DIVISION OF
TRANSPORTATION

P.O. Box 778
Dover 19901
Phone: 302–678–4306

DELAWARE PUBLIC
SERVICE COMMISSION

Old State House Annex
Dover 19901
Phone: 302–678–4247

DISTRICT OF COLUMBIA
PUBLIC SERVICE
COMMISSION

1625 I St., N.W.
Washington, D.C. 20006
Phone: 202–727–1000

FLORIDA PUBLIC
SERVICE COMMISSION

700 S. Adams St.
Tallahassee 32304
Phone: 904–488–1001

GEORGIA PUBLIC
SERVICE COMMISSION

244 Washington St. SW
Atlanta 30334
Phone: 404–656–4501

HAWAII PUBLIC
UTILITIES COMMISSION

P.O. Box 541
Honolulu 96809
Phone: 808–548–7550

IDAHO PUBLIC
UTILITIES COMMISSION

Statehouse
Boise 83720
Phone: 208–384–3420

ILLINOIS COMMERCE
COMMISSION

527 E. Capitol Ave.
Springfield 62706
Phone: 217–782–7295

INDIANA PUBLIC
SERVICE COMMISSION

901 State Office Bldg.
Indianapolis 46204
Phone: 317–633–5359

IOWA STATE
COMMERCE
COMMISSION

State Capitol
Des Moines 50319
Phone: 515–281–5309

KANSAS STATE
CORPORATION
COMMISSION

State Office Bldg.
Topeka 66612
Phone: 913–296–3325

KENTUCKY DEPT. OF
TRANSPORTATION

State Office Bldg.
Frankfort 40601
Phone: 502–564–4890

KENTUCKY PUBLIC
SERVICE COMMISSION

P.O. Box 496
Frankfort 40601
Phone: 502–564–3940

KENTUCKY RAILROAD
COMMISSION

10th Fl., State Office Bldg.
Frankfort 40601
Phone: 502–564–4640

LOUISIANA PUBLIC
SERVICE COMMISSION

P.O. Box 44035
Capitol Station
Baton Rouge 70804
Phone: 504–389–5867

MAINE PUBLIC
UTILITIES COMMISSION

State House Annex
Capitol Shopping Center
Augusta 04333
Phone: 207–289–2448

MARYLAND PUBLIC
SERVICE COMMISSION

904 State Office Bldg.
301 W. Preston St.
Baltimore 21201
Phone: 301–383–2374

MASSACHUSETTS DEPT.
OF PUBLIC UTILITIES

100 Cambridge St.
Boston 02202
Phone: 617–727–3500

MICHIGAN PUBLIC
SERVICE COMMISSION

525 W. Ottawa St.
Lansing 48913
Phone: 517–373–3244

MINNESOTA PUBLIC
SERVICE COMMISSION

Kellogg & Robert Sts.
St. Paul 55101
Phone: 612–296–7107

MISSISSIPPI PUBLIC
SERVICE COMMISSION

Box 1174
Jackson 39205
Phone: 601–354–7474

MISSOURI PUBLIC
SERVICE COMMISSION

Jefferson Bldg.
Jefferson City 65101
Phone: 314–751–3234

MONTANA PUBLIC
SERVICE COMMISSION

1227 11th Ave.
Helena 59601
Phone: 406–449–3008

NEBRASKA PUBLIC
SERVICE COMMISSION

3rd Fl., 1342 M St.
Lincoln 68508
Phone: 402–475–2641

NEVADA PUBLIC
SERVICE COMMISSION

222 E. Washington St.
Carson City 89701
Phone: 702–885–4180

NEW HAMPSHIRE
PUBLIC UTILITIES
COMMISSION

26 Pleasant St.
Concord 03301
Phone: 603–271–2452

NEW JERSEY BOARD OF
PUBLIC UTILITY
COMMISSIONERS

101 Commerce St.
Newark 07102
Phone: 201–648–2013

NEW MEXICO PUBLIC
SERVICE COMMISSION

State Capitol Bldg.
Santa Fe 87501
Phone: 505–827–2827

NEW MEXICO STATE
CORPORATION
COMMISSION

P.O. Drawer 1269
Santa Fe 87501
Phone: 505–827–2852

NEW YORK PUBLIC
SERVICE COMMISSION

44 Holland Ave.
Albany 12208
Phone: 518–474–7080

Two World Trade Center
New York 10047
Phone: 212–488–4390

NEW YORK STATE DEPT.
OF TRANSPORTATION

1220 Washington Ave.
Albany 12226
Phone: 518–457–2345

NORTH CAROLINA
UTILITIES COMMISSION

P.O. Box 991
Raleigh 27602
Phone: 919–829–4249

NORTH DAKOTA
PUBLIC SERVICE
COMMISSION

State Capitol Bldg.
Bismarck 58501
Phone: 701–224–2400

OHIO PUBLIC UTILITIES
COMMISSION

111 High St.
Columbus 43215
Phone: 614–466–3292

Public Interest Center;
1–800–282–0198,
consumer hotline.

OKLAHOMA
CORPORATION
COMMISSION

Jim Thorpe Office Bldg.
Oklahoma City 73105
Phone: 405–521–2351

OREGON PUBLIC
UTILITY
COMMISSIONER

Labor & Industries Bldg.
Salem 97310
Phone: 503–378–6603

PENNSYLVANIA PUBLIC
UTILITIES COMMISSION

P.O. Box 3265
Harrisburg 17120
Phone: 717–783–1740

PUERTO RICO PUBLIC
SERVICE COMMISSION

G.P.O. Box 4527
San Juan 00936
Phone: 809–766–1245

RHODE ISLAND PUBLIC
UTILITIES COMMISSION

169 Weybossett St.
Providence 02903
Phone: 401–277–2443

SOUTH CAROLINA
PUBLIC SERVICE
COMMISSION

P.O. Box 11649
Columbia 29211
Phone: 803–758–3621

SOUTH DAKOTA PUBLIC
UTILITIES COMMISSION

Capitol Bldg.
Pierre 57501
Phone: 605–224–3202

TENNESSEE PUBLIC
SERVICE COMMISSION

C1-102 Cordell Hull Bldg.
Nashville 37129
Phone: 615–741–2904

TEXAS AERONAUTICS
COMMISSION

P.O. Box 12607,
Capitol Sta.
Austin 78711
Phone: 512–475–4768

TEXAS RAILROAD
COMMISSION

Drawer 12967,
Capitol Sta.
Austin 78711
Phone: 512–475–2439

UTAH PUBLIC SERVICE
COMMISSION

330 E. 4th South St.
Salt Lake City 84111
Phone: 801–328–5511

VERMONT PUBLIC
SERVICE BOARD

7 School St.
Montpelier 05602
Phone: 802–828–2321

VIRGIN ISLANDS
PUBLIC SERVICE
COMMISSION

P.O. Box 40
St. Thomas 00801
Phone: 809–774–1291

VIRGINIA STATE
CORPORATION
COMMISSION

P.O. Box 1197
Richmond 23209
Phone: 804–770–3720

WASHINGTON
UTILITIES &
TRANSPORTATION
COMMISSION

Highways-Licenses Bldg.
Olympia 98504
Phone: 206–753–6423

WEST VIRGINIA PUBLIC
SERVICE COMMISSION

Room E-217, Capitol Bldg.
Charleston 25305
Phone: 304–348–2182

WISCONSIN PUBLIC
SERVICE COMMISSION

432 Hill Farms State
    Office Bldg.
Madison 53702
Phone: 608–266–1241

WYOMING PUBLIC
SERVICE COMMISSION

Supreme Court Bldg.
Cheyenne 82001
Phone: 307–777–7315

Source: National Association of Regulatory Utility Commissioners, 1102 ICC Building, Washington, D.C. 20044, 1975.

Appendix 5

HOME OWNERS WARRANTY COUNCILS
IN THE UNITED STATES

ALABAMA

Alabama State HOW
205-265-9229

ALASKA

Alaska State HOW
907-277-4319

CALIFORNIA

San Diego—HOW
714-280-9022

COLORADO

Colorado State HOW
303-758-2889

CONNECTICUT

Connecticut State HOW
203-549-7230

DELAWARE

Delaware State HOW
302-994-2597; 2598

FLORIDA

Ft. Myers—HOW
813-334-6534

Gainesville—HOW
904-372-5649

Holiday—HOW
813-849-8425

Jacksonville—HOW
904-725-4355

Miami—HOW
305-666-5954

N. Pinellas Park—HOW
813-541-2681

Orlando—HOW
305-898-7661; 7663

Palm Bch. Gardens—HOW
305-622-0300; 428-1400

Sarasota—HOW
813-959-5151

FLORIDA (cont.)

Sebring—HOW
813-382-1304

Tallahassee—HOW
904-224-6562

Tampa—HOW
813-228-7160; 223-9304

GEORGIA

Columbus—HOW
404-322-8590

Decatur—HOW
404-373-3736

Macon—HOW
912-743-8612

IDAHO

Idaho State HOW
208-345-4842

ILLINOIS

Chicago—HOW
312-887-7575

Illinois State HOW
217-753-3950

INDIANA

Bloomington—HOW
812-339-6557

Evansville—HOW
812-479-6026

Ft. Wayne—HOW
219-483-8911

Griffith—HOW
219-838-2929

Indianapolis—HOW
317-639-9191

South Bend—HOW
219-272-4134

IOWA

Iowa State HOW
515-243-1164

KANSAS

Wichita—HOW
316-265-4226

KENTUCKY

Covington—HOW
606-431-5190

Lexington—HOW
606-269-5309

Louisville—HOW
502-637-9737

LOUISIANA

Louisiana State HOW
504-387-2714

MAINE

Maine State HOW
207-622-4990

MARYLAND

Baltimore—HOW
301-821-0880

Silver Spring—HOW
(Metro. Washington)
301-588-1977

MASSACHUSETTS

Boston—HOW
617-375-5550

East Harwich—HOW
617-432-9004

Lowell—HOW
617-454-8781

MICHIGAN

Flint—HOW
313-744-2290

Grand Rapids—HOW
616-241-3469

Holland—HOW
616-392-1834

Kalamazoo—HOW
616-381-3863

MICHIGAN (cont.)

Saginaw—HOW
517–793–1120

Southfield—HOW
313–569–0644

MINNESOTA

Minn. State HOW
612–646–3978

MISSOURI

Columbia—HOW
314–443–8622

Kansas City—HOW
816–753–6000

St. Louis—HOW
317–994–7700

NEBRASKA

Nebraska State HOW
402–477–6908

NEVADA

Las Vegas—HOW
702–878–3983

Reno—HOW
702–329–4611

NEW HAMPSHIRE

N. H. State HOW
603–228–0351

NEW JERSEY

New Jersey State HOW
201–828–6315
800–352–4873 (in state
   toll-free)

NEW MEXICO

New Mexico State HOW
505–265–3509

NEW YORK

Buffalo—HOW
716–885–6080

NORTH CAROLINA

Cabarrus—HOW
704–788–3160

NORTH CAROLINA (cont.)

Charlotte—HOW
704–376–8524

Durham—HOW
919–688–2379

Hickory—HOW
704–328–4776

OHIO

Cleveland—HOW
216–524–9490

Dayton—HOW
513–223–3213

Toledo—HOW
419–473–2507

OKLAHOMA

Okla. City—HOW
405–843–1508

Okla. State HOW
405–843–5579

Tulsa—HOW
918–628–1080

OREGON

Oregon State HOW
503–378–9066

Portland—HOW
503–288–8156

PENNSYLVANIA

Lancaster—HOW
717–299–5659

Pa. State HOW
717–234–6209

Philadelphia—HOW
215–732–1004

Pittsburgh—HOW
412–281–0882

SOUTH DAKOTA

S. Dakota State HOW
605–334–2541

TENNESSEE

Memphis—HOW
901–276–4581

TENNESSEE (cont.)

Nashville—HOW
615–244–7814

TEXAS

Dallas—HOW
214–631–4840

Ft. Worth—HOW
817–457–2864

UTAH

Utah State HOW
801–485–9624

VIRGINIA

Hampton—HOW
804–826–7679

Norfolk—HOW
804–461–9140

Richmond—HOW
804–358–0600

Salem—HOW
703–389–7135

Vienna—HOW
703–893–0770

WASHINGTON

Seattle—HOW
206–284–4114

Spokane—HOW
509–328–3602

Tacoma—HOW
206–564–8788

Vancouver—HOW
206–696–0216

Yakima—HOW
502–452–6725

WEST VIRGINIA

W. Va. State HOW
304–342–5176

WISCONSIN

Milwaukee—HOW
414–258–9850

Wisc. State HOW
608–256–4887

Source: Home Owners Warranty Corporation, October 1976.

INSURANCE REPORT FORM (SAMPLE)

INSURANCE REPORT FORM

In response to your recent request for assistance we are sending our Insurance Report Form. If you are in doubt as to the merits of your problem, we recommend you file the report. If the problem does not come under this Department's regulatory jurisdiction, we will refer it to the proper agency for review. Please complete the form (do *not* separate) and mail both copies to: Department of Insurance, State of California, 600 S. Commonwealth Avenue, Los Angeles, CA 90005. You will be hearing from an Insurance Officer, IN WRITING, shortly after we receive the completed forms from you.

INSURED:_____   NAME OF INSURANCE COMPANY:
  (Please PRINT)   (As it appears on your policy)

COMPLAINANT'S NAME: (If other than above)

_____   _____

ADDRESS:_____   POLICY NUMBER:_____

_____   CLAIM NUMBER:_____

TELEPHONE NUMBER:_____   DATE OF LOSS:_____

Please check this statement: This is the only report I have submitted to the Department of Insurance regarding this particular problem. Yes:_____ No_____

1. _____The company has unfairly rejected my claim or has not paid the full benefits to which I am entitled.

2. _____The company has delayed processing my claim and I am unable to obtain a response from them concerning it.

3. _____The company has not refunded premium monies that are due me.

4. _____I believe the company's action of cancellation or non-renewal of my policy is not justified.

5. _____Briefly and in your own words, describe your problem. If more space is needed, please add additional sheets also in duplicate:

_____

_____

_____

_____

_____

_____

_____

_____

_____

PLEASE SIGN AND DATE THE FOLLOWING STATEMENT:

To the best of my knowledge, the information contained herein is correct. I am enclosing my policy, papers and other correspondence relative to this problem. I understand they will be returned to me when you have completed your review. I further understand that a copy of this form may be forwarded to the insure company involved.

_____   _____
(Signature)   (Date)

PS-1 (REV. 4-74)   25731-905 7-74 100M DUP △W OSP

Appendix 7

HUD HOUSING DISCRIMINATION COMPLAINT FORM

<table>
<tr><td colspan="2">Form Approved OMB No. 63—R1226</td></tr>
<tr>
<td>
U.S. DEPARTMENT OF HOUSING AND URBAN DEVELOPMENT
HOUSING DISCRIMINATION COMPLAINT

INSTRUCTIONS: Read this form and the instructions on reverse carefully before completing. All questions should be answered. However, if you do not know the answer or if a question is not applicable, leave the question unanswered and fill out as much of the form as you can. Your complaint should be signed and dated and, if possible, notarized. Where more than one individual or organization is filing the same complaint, each additional individual or organization should complete boxes 1 and 7 of a separate complaint form and attach it to the original form, but the other boxes need not be completed if the information is the same as in the original. Complaints may be (1) mailed to the Regional Office covering the State where the complaint arose (see list at end of form), or to an Area Office, or to Fair Housing, HUD, Washington, D.C. 20410, or (2) filed or presented in person at HUD in Washington, D.C. or at any HUD Regional or Area Office.
</td>
<td>
FOR HUD USE ONLY
Number_____
Date _____
Filing Date_____
STATE OR LOCAL

FEDERAL COVERAGE

PRIOR ACTION

PRELIMINARY DETERMINATION
</td>
</tr>
</table>

PLEASE TYPE OR PRINT

1. Name of aggrieved person or organization (Last Name – First Name – Middle Initial) (Mr. Mrs. Miss)   Telephone Number

Street Address, City, County, State and ZIP Code

2. Whom is this complaint against?

Name (Last Name – First Name – Middle Initial)	Street Address, City, County, State and ZIP Code	Telephone Number

Is the party named above a: (Check applicable box or boxes)
☐ Builder ☐ Owner ☐ Broker ☐ Salesman ☐ Supt. or Manager ☐ Bank or Other Lender ☐ Other

If you have named an individual above and you know that he was acting for a company in this case, check this box ☐ and write the name and address (Street, City, County, State and ZIP Code) of the company, in this space.

Name and Identify Others (if any) you believe violated the law in this case

3. What did the person you are complaining against do? (Check applicable box or boxes)	4. Do you believe there was discrimination because of? (Check applicable box and write your race, color, religion, sex or national origin on the line below the box checked)	5. What kind of house or property was involved?
☐ Refuse to rent, sell, or deal with you ☐ Discriminate in the conditions or terms of sale, rental, occupancy, or in services or facilities ☐ Advertise in a discriminatory way ☐ Falsely deny housing was available ☐ Engage in blockbusting ☐ Discriminate in financing ☐ Discriminate in broker's services ☐ Other (Explain in box 6 below) When did act or acts occur? (Be sure to include most recent date, if several dates are involved)	☐ Race or Color ☐ Religion ☐ Sex ☐ National Origin	☐ Single family house ☐ A house or building for 2, 3, or 4 families ☐ A building for 5 families or more ☐ Other, including vacant land held for residential use (Explain in box 6 below) Did the owner live there? ☐ Yes ☐ No ☐ Unknown Is the house or property (Check applicable box) ☐ Being sold ☐ Being rented What is the address of the house or property? Street_____ City _____ County_____ State _____

6. Summarize in your own words what happened. Use this space for a brief and concise statement of the facts. Additional details of what happened may be provided on an attachment.

NOTE: HUD will furnish copy of complaint to the person or organization against whom complaint is made.

7. I swear or affirm that I have read this complaint (including any attachments) and that it is true to the best of my knowledge, information, and belief.

_____ (Date)   _____ (Sign your name)

8.   NOTARIZATION:

Subscribed and sworn to before me this _____ day of _____ 197__.

_____ (Name)   _____ (Title)

IF IT IS DIFFICULT FOR YOU TO GET A NOTARY PUBLIC TO SIGN THIS, SIGN YOUR OWN NAME AND MAIL IT WITHOUT NOTARIZATION. HUD WILL HELP YOU GET YOUR COMPLAINT SWORN TO.

HUD-903 (2-72) PREVIOUS EDITION IS OBSOLETE

HOUSING DISCRIMINATION COMPLAINT

WHAT DOES THE FEDERAL FAIR HOUSING LAW PROVIDE?

Title VIII *(Fair Housing)* of the Civil Rights Act of 1968 declares that it is national policy to provide fair housing throughout the United States and prohibits seven specific kinds of discriminatory acts regarding housing if the discrimination is based on race, color, religion, sex or national origin.

1. Refusal to sell or rent or otherwise deal with a person.
2. Discriminating in the conditions or terms of sale, rental, or occupancy.
3. Falsely denying housing is available.
4. Discriminatory advertising.
5. Blockbusting—causing someone to sell or rent by telling him that members of a minority group are moving into the area.
6. Discrimination in financing housing by a bank, savings and loan association, or other business.
7. Denial of membership or participation in brokerage, multiple listing, or other real estate services.

WHAT DOES THE LAW EXEMPT?

The first three acts listed above do not apply (1) to any single-family house where the owner in certain circumstances does not seek to rent or sell it through the use of a broker or through discriminatory advertising, nor (2) to units in houses for two to four units if the owner lives in one of the units.

NOTE: Coercion, threats, or other interference with an individual's rights under the law, including the right to file a complaint, are also prohibited.

WHAT CAN YOU DO ABOUT VIOLATIONS OF THE LAW?

Remember, Title VIII applies to discrimination based on race, color, religion, sex or national origin. If you believe you have been or are about to be, discriminated against or otherwise harmed by the kinds of discriminatory acts which are prohibited by the law, you have a right, within 180 days after the discrimination occurred to.

1. **Complain to the Secretary** by filing this form by mail or in person. HUD will investigate and if it finds the complaint is covered by the law and is justified, it will try to end the discrimination by conciliation. In cases where State or local laws give the same rights as Title VIII, HUD must first ask the State or local agency to try to resolve the problem.

2. **Go directly to Court** even if you have not filed a complaint with the Secretary. The Court may sometimes be able to give quicker, more effective, relief than conciliation can provide and may also, in certain cases, appoint an attorney for you *(without cost)*.

You Should Also Report All Information about violations of Title VIII to HUD even though you don't intend to complain or go to court yourself.

ADDITIONAL DETAILS

If you wish to explain in detail in an attachment what happened, you should consider the following:

1. If you feel that others were treated differently from you, please explain the facts and circumstances.
2. If there were witnesses or others who know what happened, give their names, addresses, and telephone numbers.
3. If you have made this complaint to other government agencies or to the courts, state when and where and explain what happened.

You can obtain assistance (a) in learning about Title VIII, or (b) in filing a complaint at the HUD Regional Offices listed below:

U.S. Department of Housing and Urban Development
Assistant Secretary for Equal Opportunity
Washington, D.C. 20410

Region I — Boston *(Connecticut, Maine, Massachusetts, New Hampshire, Rhode Island, Vermont)*

HUD—Equal Opportunity
John F. Kennedy Federal Building
Boston, Massachusetts 02203

Region II — New York *(New Jersey, New York, Puerto Rico, Virgin Islands)*

HUD—Equal Opportunity
26 Federal Plaza
New York, New York 10007

Region III — Philadelphia *(Delaware, District of Columbia, Maryland, Pennsylvania, Virginia, West Virginia)*

HUD—Equal Opportunity
Curtis Building
6th and Walnut Streets
Philadelphia, Pennsylvania 19106

Region IV — Atlanta *(Alabama, Florida, Georgia, Kentucky, Mississippi, North Carolina, South Carolina, Tennessee)*

HUD—Equal Opportunity
1371 Peachtree Street, N.E.
Atlanta, George 30309

Region V — Chicago *(Illinois, Indiana, Michigan, Ohio, Wisconsin)*

HUD—Equal Opportunity
300 South Wacker Drive
Chicago, Illinois 60606

Region VI — Dallas *(Arkansas, Louisiana, New Mexico, Oklahoma, Texas)*

HUD—Equal Opportunity
New Dallas Federal Building
1100 Commerce Street
Dallas, Texas 75202

Region VII — Kansas City *(Iowa, Kansas, Missouri, Nebraska)*

HUD—Equal Opportunity
Federal Office Building, Room 300
911 Walnut Street
Kansas City, Missouri 64106

Region VIII — *(Colorado, Montana, North Dakota, South Dakota, Utah, Wyoming)*

HUD—Equal Opportunity
Federal Building
1961 Stout Street
Denver, Colorado 80202

Region IX — San Francisco *(Arizona, California, Hawaii, Nevada, Guam, American Samoa)*

HUD—Equal Opportunity
450 Golden Gate Avenue
Post Office Box 36003
San Francisco, California 94102

Region X — Seattle *(Alaska, Idaho, Oregon, Washington)*

HUD—Equal Opportunity
Arcade Plaza Building
1321 Second Avenue
Seattle, Washington 98101

HUD–903 (2–72) Previous editions are obsolete
GPO 891-474

Appendix 8

COMPARISON OF THE
TOP 20 MOVING COMPANIES

Under an ICC regulation published in March 1974 (*Consumer Register*: Aug. 1, 1974), all household moving companies are required to provide ICC with these performance statistics every year. Companies must also give these statistics to all prospective customers (*Consumer News*: March 1). The 20 companies covered here have already reported to ICC. Among them, they handle 70-80% of the household moving in the U.S., according to ICC. When the remaining companies file the required reports, ICC will publish them also.*

The chart [on the following two pages] shows shipments by average consumers—individuals and families who shipped their own household goods and paid their own bills.†

Source: Consumers News, April 1, 1975.

*ICC stresses that the figures given here were submitted by the companies; these statistics have not yet been verified. However, ICC does plan to spot-check the reports for accuracy.

†ICC also has on file performance data for service families moved by Defense Dept. & for civilian families moved by other Federal agencies or by private corporations. Readers interested in these additional figures may examine them at ICC regional offices (Boston, Philadelphia, Atlanta, Chicago, Fort Worth & San Francisco) or may request them by writing to Household Goods Branch, Interstate Commerce Commission, Washington, DC 20423.

Performance data	Aero Mayflower Transit Co.	Allied Van Lines	American Red Ball Transit Co.	Atlas Van Lines	Bekins Van Lines Co.	Burnham Van Service	Engel Van Lines	Global Van Lines
Shipments delivered	56,819	83,722	7,830	13,980	40,956	2,336	1,982	9,056
Shipments estimated	42,876	47,764	5,839	8,573	18,335	1,116	1,835	8,669
Percentage of shipments on which there occurred a 10% or greater overestimation of charges	37.80%	28.24%	30.66%	28.92%	40.9%	19%	5.8%	19.9%
Percentage of shipments on which there occurred a 10% or greater underestimation of charges	23.75%	25.28%	23.71%	26.15%	23%	21%	8.1%	19.7%
Percentage of shipments picked up more than 5 days later than specified in the Order for Service	1.09%	6.05%	1.54%	1.77%	1.1%	8%	1.6%	1.8%
Percentage of shipments picked up 1 to 5 days later than specified in the Order for Service	3.83%	10.03%	3.70%	2.42%	4.8%	13%	3.2%	6.3%
Percentage of shipments delivered more than 5 days later than specified in the Order for Service	7.59%	9.33%	12.04%	10.71%	5.2%	17%	5%	6.3%
Percentage of shipments delivered 1 to 5 days later than specified in the Order for Service	11.65%	11.90%	10.88%	13.61%	7%	13%	6.6%	8.1%
Percentage of shipments on which a $50 or greater claim for loss or damage was filed	22.72%	23.70%	17.18%	13.11%	16%	17%	16%	12.6%
Percentage of claims filed for damages or expenses resulting from carrier delay	2%	.94%	1.85%	1.09%	1.9%	8%	1.3%	1.4%
Average number of days to settle claims for loss or damage (for claims settled during 1974)	42	54	40	46	18	24	52	46
Percentage of claims for the calendar year settled prior to: (a) institution of judicial process (b) completion of judicial process	99.56% .40%	99.87% .07%	99.96% 0%	100% 0%	99.3% .4%	100% 0%	99.7% .1%	100% 0%
Percentage of claims carried to the completion of the judicial process & the entering of a final decree	0%	.06%	0%	0%	.3%	0%	.2%	0%

Greyhound Van Lines	John V. Ivory Storage Co.	King Van Lines	Lyon Moving & Storage Co.	National Van Lines	Neptune World Wide Moving	North American Van Lines	Pan American Van Lines	Pyramid Van Lines	Republic Van & Storage Co.	United Van Lines	Wheaton Van Lines
7,376	3,267	5,176	7,625	4,446	1,382	56,847	2,166	209	7,665	39,932	5,457
5,901	1,972	2,727	2,887	2,311	1,243	43,135	1,750	79	5,692	18,869	3,184
21.46%	17.91%	13.5%	9.2%	20.2%	18%	29.5%	17%	30.2%	18.9%	26.1%	29%
15.52%	15.61%	24.8%	11.2%	24.7%	21%	26.9%	30%	25.3%	23.3%	25.4%	17%
4.20%	1.94%	.04%	1.3%	.1%	.01%	5.4%	2%	0%	0%	5.7%	1.2%
14.25%	9.25%	.05%	5.3%	.8%	.01%	7.4%	0%	0%	0%	10.4%	2%
10.94%	11.6%	10%	14%	12%	6%	7.6%	3%	12%	6.8%	6.1%	13%
9.67%	14.62%	9.5%	15.9%	14.5%	8.1%	7.6%	9%	13.9%	8.7%	8.6%	10.4%
14.75%	11.91%	12%	16.4%	19.9%	25.6%	16%	17%	12.9%	11.1%	12.8%	13.2%
.80%	.7%	.4%	2%	2.1%	.01%	.3%	1%	1.4%	.8%	1.2%	1.3%
45	20	26	63	44	28	50	67	24	32	31	46
86.19%	100%	100%	98.4%	98.6%	99.0%	99.53%	100%	100%	99.3%	99.31%	100%
.18%	0%	0%	.8%	1.3%	.9%	.43%	0%	0%	.8%	.63%	0%
0%	0%	0%	.8%	.1%	.1%	.04%	0%	0%	.2%	.06%	0%

COMPARISON OF TRAVEL SERVICES OFFERED
BY OIL COMPANIES AND AUTO CLUBS

	Amoco Motor Club	Arco Travel Club	Automobile Club of So. Calif. (affiliated w/AAA —services may differ in other areas of the country)	Chevron Travel Club
Membership Fees (includes all services)	$18.50 for 1 year for husband and wife. $10 additional/yr. for associate members—children under 25 yrs., living at home or at college.	Offers "classes" of membership varying from $1.50 to $4.55 for 1 month, billed to Arco credit card ($18 to $54.60 for 1 year).	$34/1st year; $22/renewal year. For $7 extra any year you may sign spouse; for $10 extra you may sign an associate member—child under 21 living in household.	Offers "classes" of membership—varying from $2.50 to $3.50 per month billed to Chevron credit card ($20 to $42 for 1 year).
Emergency Road and Towing Services	Pays up to $25 per call from any service facility, even if authorized dealer is not available.	$25 reimbursal for towing, plus $10 for emergency service & labor costs. Call any nearby towing service.	Emergency road service telephone #s all over country; provides many services from towing to nearest contract station or other repair shop en route to bringing gasoline & doing minor adjustments, battery charging, changing tires, etc. on the spot. No charge except parts & supplies. 24 hours, 7 days per week.	

Exxon Travel Club	*Gulf Travel Club*	*National Automobile Club (Calif. only)*	*Allstate Motor Club*	*Montgomery Ward Auto Club*
Offers "classes" of membership—varying from $2.25 to $3.50 for 1 month. Different classes include spouse or children or both w/member ($27 to $42 for 1 year).	$1.75 for 1 month billed annually for Gulf credit account ($21 for 1 year).	1st time only enrollment fee of $5, plus annual dues of $22 for one person or $25 for both spouses. Dependents under 25 years, living at home or college—$10/yr. extra. (multiple-year membership discount—5% for 2 years, 10% for 3).	$22.50 a year, both spouses. Can be charged on Sears credit card.	$2.25 a month on Ward's credit account ($27 a year). Covers both spouses.
Provides highway safety emergency telephone directory to enable you to find help.		Service guide listing NAC official service garages all over state. Many services available all free —gasoline delivered, towing, car starting, battery replacement—you pay for supplies. 24 hours. Out-of-state service available on a $25 reimbursal per call basis.	Pays up to $25 for cost of towing & labor to get your car running. Call nearest garage (reimbursal basis).	Pays up to $30 per service call, choose any nearby service station (reimbursal basis). Can get paid for service to disabled unattended cars, snow-bound cars, or cars in muddy fields, beaches, etc. Emergency service even if you're not there (limited to $25 in Va. or N.C.).

	Amoco Motor Club	Arco Travel Club	Automobile Club of So. Calif. (affiliated w/AAA —services may differ in other areas of the country)	Chevron Travel Club
Routing, Maps, Other Vacation Services*	Auto trip routing service for most scenic or most direct route to destination anywhere in U.S. Also offers worldwide group travel vacations.	Routing & maps with most direct route in a kit w/games for children, expense record etc. Requires 10 days notice to the club. Custom vacation offers.	Personalized routing "mile by mile," detour and law enforcement info included. Detailed info about area through which you travel— restaurants, accommodations, etc. AAA provides info on camping & trailering as well as tolls, special events, etc. World travel dept. provides complete travel agency services, domestic and international. Obtain international driving permit.	Maps marked with best routes to avoid construction & detours. Info on points of interest, trip expense record, first aid kit, etc., included.

Exxon Travel Club	Gulf Travel Club	National Automobile Club (Calif. only)	Allstate Motor Club	Montgomery Ward Auto Club
Personalized trip planning & marked maps showing direct routes. Vacation guides, group travel opportunities.	Personalized trip planning, marked maps. Group travel & inexpensive "package" trips available. Vacation guides to help you plan.	Personalized routing & strip maps w/enlarged individual sections. Reports on sports conditions. Purchase hunting and fishing licenses at all NAC offices. Camping info. Reservations at hotels & motels made if desired. Complete foreign & domestic touring packages. Can get Thomas Cook Travelers Checks, PSA tickets, Hertz Rent-a-Cars, & international driver's license at any NAC office.	Personal map routing in book form. Suggestions for accommodations & points of interest. Campsite info on request. Protection against paying increased rates at hotels & motels.	Call toll-free for complete personalized trip routing, mile by mile instructions & maps. Points of interest, mileage guide, trip estimate & expense records, car games for kids included. 10% discount through participating hotels & motels (not available to residents of Tenn.). Worldwide tour service charter rates. Motel & hotel reservations across U.S. in Mexico & Canada.

	Amoco Motor Club	Arco Travel Club	Automobile Club of So. Calif. (affiliated w/AAA —services may differ in other areas of the country)	Chevron Travel Club
Insurance (Accidental death or dismemberment insurance may not be available by law in some states.)	Periodically makes car insurance plans available through registered agents. Both spouses covered by $1,500. Traffic & travel accident insurance 1st year; increases to $1,750 the 2nd year, $2,000 the 3rd (not available to members in N.Y.).	Accidental death or dismemberment insurance pays from a basic $2,000 to $25,000 for cardholder, $12,500 for spouse, $2,500 for each eligible child depending on class of membership you select. Protects *all* year round traveling or not; a few exceptions— war, suicide, illness, childbirth, accidents while on active duty in armed forces.	Makes available insurance to members who qualify through affiliated Interinsurance Exchange, including auto, liability, boat, personal accident insurance.	Accidental death insurance covers death occurring up to 100 days after an accident—protects year round. Basic membership class provides member w/$25,000 coverage; other classes provide up to $27,400 for member, $9,900 for spouse, $3,500 each child. If both spouses die in common accident, upper limit class pays single benefit up to $37,300 plus $100 per month to each eligible child till 21st birthday. Usual exceptions—suicide, war, while pilot or crew member of an aircraft, or travel in military aircraft (besides MAC).

Exxon Travel Club	Gulf Travel Club	National Automobile Club (Calif. only)	Allstate Motor Club	Montgomery Ward Auto Club
Basic class provides member w/$20,000 accidental death insurance; up to $20,000 for member, $10,000 for spouse, $5,000 for each eligible child for upper limit class. Protects year round, at home, away, even when you fly (except as a pilot or crew member, or in military aircraft other than MAC). Other exceptions—suicide or war. Pays for deaths occurring within 100 days of accident. If both member & spouse covered & killed together, or die within 24 hours of each other, combined payment is $100,000.	Accidental death insurance pays for deaths involving motor-powered vehicles even if you are pedestrian; $5,000 for 1st year, $7,500 2nd year, $10,000 3rd year if a member. Usual exceptions—suicide, illness, infections, war, while a pilot or crew member of an aircraft, or while flying in military aircraft other than MAC.	Accidental death & dismemberment insurance, provides 24-hour all-risk protection for member & spouse to $1,500 each ($5,000 per person in event of commercial airline accident). Mexican automobile insurance policies written and issued through all NAC offices.	Accidental death or dismemberment coverage—$1,000 first year, $1,250 2nd year, $1,500 3rd year if a member, pays for each spouse. Benefit doubles if death occurs while fare-paying passenger on common carrier such as commercial plane, train, bus, taxi.	Up to $5,000 all-risk, no exclusion accidental death & dismemberment protection. Protects year round. (Not available to North Carolina residents; to replace this benefit, N.C. residents have toll-free message service available.)

	Amoco Motor Club	Arco Travel Club	Automobile Club of So. Calif. (affiliated w/AAA —services may differ in other areas of the country)	Chevron Travel Club
Accident Expense Assistance	Reimbursal for member or spouse up to $200 in expenses for car rental, local lodging, meals, or commercial transportation to destination —if you have an accident more than 50 miles from home.	Pays up to $50 for commercial transportation to hotel, home, or wherever following disabling collision or accident.		
Cash and Check Services	Credit cardholder may cash personal checks up to $25 at any Amoco dealer.		Members traveling throughout Calif. & Nevada may pay up to $150 by personal check for emergency vehicle repairs at Club contract stations.	
Bail Bond (or arrest service payment; arrest bonds are not acceptable in some states, e.g., Calif.)	If arrested for a traffic violation, membership card serves as an arrest bond up to $200 (excluding Calif.).	$200 guaranteed arrest bond certificate issued by National Surety Corp.; for more serious violations & in places where certificate not acceptable, $5,000 bail bond certificate entitles you to bond issued by agent of Nat'l. Surety. Certificates unacceptable in cases of driving while intoxicated or in the case of a felony.	Bail bond service for most traffic violations available to members for up to $5,000, 24 hours a day, all over the country. Exceptions are offenses involving intoxication, drugs, or suspended or revoked driver's license. Some states may accept member's card in lieu of cash bail (member is billed cost of retrieving card).	

Exxon Travel Club	Gulf Travel Club	National Automobile Club (Calif. only)	Allstate Motor Club	Montgomery Ward Auto Club
		Will reimburse $10 for ambulance charges from the scene of the accident for each member and immediate family.	Pays expenses incurred within 72 hours of accident over 100 miles from your home—up to $200 ($100 for Va. residents).	Pays expenses incurred up to 3 days after accident over 50 miles from home, up to $100.
	$200 emergency cash loan wired to you by calling club (over 50 miles from home).		With Allstate Motor Club membership card and Sears revolving charge account card, may cash check in any Sears retail store. Amt. at discretion of store manager.	N.C. residents may cash checks up to $25 in any Montgomery Ward store.
$200 guaranteed arrest bond through National Surety Corp.; for more serious violations or if arrest bond is unacceptable; Nat'l. Surety furnishes $5,000 bail bond service through local representative.	$200 arrest bond certificate and $5,000 bail bond certificate issued through National Surety Corp. for any violation of motor vehicle law unless intoxicated or in violation of a narcotic act.		If arrested for traffic violation, membership card can be used for bail up to $500 in most states (arrest bond certificates not acceptable in Calif., certain states limit this to $200).	$200 arrest bond & $5,000 bail bond coverage. If $200 arrest bond certificate not acceptable, contact nearest Nat'l. Surety agent to post bond. Covers motor vehicle violations except driving while intoxicated or without valid operator's permit, or for felony.

	Amoco Motor Club	Arco Travel Club	Automobile Club of So. Calif. (affiliated w/AAA —services may differ in other areas of the country)	Chevron Travel Club
Legal Defense Assistance	Pays up to $500 in scheduled legal fees for traffic violations. Choose your own lawyer.	Pays up to $500 for legal defense— choose your own lawyer. (Not available when member is charged with a felony, except manslaughter by car, or while driving under influence of liquor, narcotics.) Not available to residents in N.Y.; limited to $200 in Va.	Traffic citation service for members through all district offices. Bail determined and forwarded to proper traffic court. In some courts written facts may be presented with the bail and citation, or member's written plea of not guilty.	
Theft Protection	Pays $500 reward for information leading to conviction of anyone stealing or forcibly entering your car (warning sticker for window).		Auto Theft Bureau Service.	
Lost Key Service		Coded key tag. Arco pays postage if finder will "drop in any mail box."		Coded key tag. Chevron mails returned keys to you.

Exxon Travel Club	Gulf Travel Club	National Automobile Club (Calif. only)	Allstate Motor Club	Montgomery Ward Auto Club
	Pays for portion of trial and appeal costs, according to a schedule of fees. Choose your own lawyer.	NAC will assist in handling traffic violation citations and processing property damage claims.	Pays for the cost of your trial defense according to a schedule of fees, up to $500. Choose your own lawyer. Exceptions: drunk driving, violations including drugs, reckless driving or manslaughter.	Provides up to $500 legal defense reimbursement, choose your own lawyer. (Not available to residents of N.Y.).
Pays $500 for information leading to conviction of anyone stealing your car.	$500 reward sticker for car. Pays anyone for information leading to conviction of someone stealing your car.	Has access to the services of nationwide auto theft bureau.	Theft, hit & run warning decal offers $500 reward for information leading to conviction of anyone stealing or hitting & leaving your car.	Offers $200 reward for information leading to conviction of anyone stealing your car (warning sticker).
Coded key tags. Exxon mails returned keys to you.	See "Other Services."			Registered key tag; keys will be returned free if finder drops them in mailbox.

	Amoco Motor Club	*Arco Travel Club*	*Automobile Club of So. Calif. (affiliated w/AAA —services may differ in other areas of the country)*	*Chevron Travel Club*
Publications Available Through Club	Travel magazine, 4 times a year.	Bimonthly newsletter.	Special area maps, guides with variety of travel information, monthly travel magazines.	Travel magazine, 4 times a year. Chevron road atlas and scenic guide.
Other Services	Quality merchandise offered at a savings discount to members. Discounts on car rentals from Econo-Car & National Rent-a-Car. Safety-reflective club bumper emblem. 10% discount at Quality Inns.	Chances to purchase merchandise through the mail, pay by Arco credit card. Nationwide message center, toll-free number through which you can be reached when away.	Nationwide offices. License services: assistance in completing registration transactions for any vehicle, or use the Club's service to notify Dept. of Motor Vehicles of change of address on a vehicle registration or driver's license. Discount cards for local tourist attractions. Ticket-ron service. Vehicle code books & sample tests from DMV.	

Exxon Travel Club	Gulf Travel Club	National Automobile Club (Calif. only)	Allstate Motor Club	Montgomery Ward Auto Club
Travel magazine, 4 times a year. Travel atlas & vacation guides.	Travel magazine, 6 times a year. Travel newsletters, 4 times a year. Special reports on popular vacation areas.	Travel magazine, 6 times a year, Touring guide to help with your trips, includes maps, distances, mileage logs. Details on national & state parks.	Travel magazine, 4 times/yr. Entitled to a free Sears catalog for your personal use.	*Auto Club News*, 4 times a year.
Opportunities to purchase merchandise at members-only prices. Discount vouchers good at many points of interest in U.S. Registration of all of member's credit cards with Hot-Line Credit Card Bureau of America at no cost to member. Toll-free call reports lost or stolen cards.	Discount privileges in restaurants, hotels, night clubs in major cities & vacation areas in N.A. A few additional services, lost key & luggage protection, medical history card, lost credit card service for an additional $8.40/yr.	Travel counselors at every NAC office to help plan short or long trip. For automobiles & boats, apply for registration, renewal, ownership transfer, lost certificates.	20% discount from Hertz Rent-a-Car/ Tower Film Club Service. (Purchase and have film developed through Sears).	Toll-free # from anywhere in continental U.S. Car rental discounts, 25% from Hertz. Discounts on merchandise offered in *Auto Club News.*

Source: Compiled by Leora Brown, 1976.

*Texaco and Union Oil also provide route-marked maps to cardholders.

FEDERAL TRADE COMMISSION COMPLAINT FORM
(LOS ANGELES REGIONAL OFFICE)

Federal Trade Commission
11000 Wilshire Blvd., Room 13209
Los Angeles, California 90024

Gentlemen:

      I wish to file a complaint against the company or firm named below. I understand that the Federal Trade Commission does not represent private citizens seeking the return of their money or other personal remedies. I am, however, filing this complaint to notify your office of the activities of this company. I understand that if this matter is not within the scope of the Federal Trade Commission's regulatory activities, it will be referred to another agency, Federal, state, or local, if possible.

(PLEASE PRINT OR TYPE, IF POSSIBLE)

Name of Company
or firm_____
           (Use name appearing in telephone book, if possible)

Address_____
        Street   City   State   Zip Code
                              Name of Salesman
Telephone_____or Representative_____
                              Date you complained
Date of Transaction_____to Company or Firm__ _____

Have you contacted   If so,
a private attorney?_____Attorney's Name_____

Attorney's Address_____
                Street   City   State   Zip Code

Has a lawsuit been filed in Small Claims Court?_____In another court?_____

Name or Description of Product or Service Involved_____

_____
                        (If so, attach a copy or send us
Was a contract signed?_____the original to copy and return)

If the product or service
was advertised: When?_____   Where?_____
(Attach a copy of the advertisement or send us the original to copy and return)

Describe the events as fully as you can, in the order in which they happened, using extra sheets if you need to:

_____

_____

_____

_____

PLEASE GO ON TO THE NEXT PAGE

_____

_____

_____

_____

_____

_____

_____

_____

_____

Names, Addresses and Telephone Numbers of Other Witnesses:

First Name	Middle Initial	Last Name

Street	City	State	Zip Code	Telephone

First Name	Middle Initial	Last Name

Street	City	State	Zip Code	Telephone

Who referred you to the Federal Trade Commission?   Private Attorney_____

Legal Aid_____ Newspaper_____ Radio/TV_____ Other (specify)_____

    I hereby certify that I have read the information contained in this complaint and that all of the information which I have given herein is true, correct, and complete to the best of my knowledge, information and belief. I authorize the use of my name in processing my complaint & the referral of this complaint to the company complained about and to other regulatory agencies.

_____YES   _____NO

Check one of the above.   (signed)_____

(date)_____

Your Name_____

     First Name   Middle Initial   Last Name

Home Address_____

     Street   City   State   Zip Code

Business Address_____

     Street   City   State   Zip Code

Telephone: Home_____ Work_____

In accordance with Section (e)(3) of the Privacy Act of 1974, each individual from whom personal information is being solicited in the course of Commission investigation or any other Commission activity must be given the reasons for requesting the information, as well as other pertinent details. Therefore, it is requested that you read the "INFORMATION DISCLOSURE STATEMENT" which complies with this requirement of the Privacy Act, and should be retained by you.

INFORMATION DISCLOSURE STATEMENT - PRIVACY ACT

Title and No. of Form, if any:

Authority for collecting information:

Federal Trade Commission Act, as amended (15 U.S.C. 41 et seq)

Principal purpose(s) for which information is intended to be used:

To determine whether violations exist of the Federal Trade Commission Act and other acts and Rules administered or enforced by the Federal Trade Commission.

Routine uses which may be made of information:

For use of Commission staff in all investigative and adjudicative proceedings of every type and form; possible referral to other federal, state or local agencies for possible investigation or prosecution, criminal or civil.

Providing the information requested is: _____ mandatory

                                       X___ voluntary

Effects on the individual, if any, of not providing all or any part of the requested information:

Your complaint will not be processed.

Appendix 11

SAMPLE COMPLAINT FORMS
USED BY LOCAL AGENCIES

CONSUMER COMPLAINT FORM   DATE _____

Please fill this out as completely as possible. A copy of the form will be sent to the company involved. If you wish any information to remain confidential, please include it on a separate sheet.

1. Your Name_____ 2. Company Complaint Against_____

   Address _____   _____

   _____Zip_____   Address_____

   Home Phone_____   _____Zip_____

   Work Phone_____   Phone_____

3. Did you complain to the company?_____ How many times?_____

4. What is your complaint?_____

   _____

   _____

   _____

   _____

   _____

5. Details of complaint: Manufacturer, model number, etc._____

   _____Date of Purchase_____When did the trouble occur?_____

   _____Price?_____Place of purchase: Store of dealer_____

   Door-to-Door Sales_____Mail Order_____Telephone Solicitation_____

6. Is the product or service financed through another company?_____If so, please

   give the name and address._____

7. Check other agencies you have contacted about this problem: Better Business Bureau___

   Pa. Bureau of Consumer Protection_____, Alliance for Consumer Protection_____

   Private Attorney_____(Name:_____), Other (Name)_____

8. Check types of settlement you would accept: Refund_____, Adjustment of price_____

   Servicing_____, Replacement of item_____, Other_____

IMPORTANT: PLEASE ATTACH COPIES OF CONTRACTS, LETTERS, RECEIPTS, SALES SLIPS, CANCELLED

CHECKS, ADVERTISEMENT RELEVANT TO YOUR COMPLAINT. SEND COMPLAINT TO:

                ALLEGHENY COUNTY BUREAU OF CONSUMER AFFAIRS
                3RD FLOOR JONES LAW BUILDING ANNEX, PITTSBURGH, PA. 15219

SIGNATURE_____

LOS ANGELES COUNTY
DEPARTMENT OF CONSUMER AFFAIRS
B-96 Hall of Administration
500 West Temple Street
Los Angeles, California 90012
(213) 974-1452

For Office Use Only

CASE NO._____
Category_____S. Dist._____
Date Received _____
Assigned to _____
Date Closed _____

CONSUMER COMPLAINT FORM

Please complete both sides of this form (PRINT or TYPE), attach copies of all documents
(contracts, receipts, canceled checks, correspondence, etc.), if any. DO NOT SEND
ORIGINALS.

CONSUMER   COMPLAINT AGAINST

_____   _____
Name   Name

_____   _____
Address: Number   Street   Address: Number   Street

_____   _____
City   State   Zip Code   City   State   Zip Code

_____   _____
Telephone (from 9 a.m. to 5 p.m.) Telephone

Did you sign papers or documents?_____
                        Yes-No   _____
(If yes, attach copy)   Charge Account, Invoice or Contract No.,
                                   if any

Have you complained to the business? _____. Name(s) of person(s) with whom
                                      Yes - No

you have dealt._____ Date_____

Have you filed a complaint with another agency? _____. If yes, which one(s).
                                                  Yes - No

_____

Name and address of company you make payments to _____

_____

May we send a copy of your complaint to the company or merchant whom you are complaining
against? _____.
          Yes - No

(PLEASE COMPLETE BOTH SIDES)

(Print or Type)

As briefly as possible, please give the details of your complaint. Includes names of individuals and dates, if you remember. Use additional pages, if necessary.

_____

_____

_____

_____

_____

_____

_____

_____

_____

_____

_____

_____

_____

_____

_____

_____

_____

What do you consider a fair and reasonable settlement? _____

_____

I hereby certify that the information contained in this complaint and all of the information which I have given herein is true, correct and complete to the best of my knowledge, information and belief.

_____   _____
          Signature   Date signed

DO NOT FORGET TO INCLUDE <u>COPIES</u> (NOT ORIGINALS) OF ANY DOCUMENTS.

DCA 1

OFFICE OF THE
CRIMINAL DISTRICT ATTORNEY
TIM CURRY
DISTRICT ATTORNEY
FORT WORTH, TEXAS 76102   DATED_____

Gentlemen:

I wish to file a complaint against the company named below. I understand that the District Attorney's Fraud Division is unable to represent private citizens seeking the return of their money or other personal remedies. I am, however, filing this complaint to notify your office of the activities of this company.

PLEASE PRINT OR TYPE: OTHERWISE YOUR COMPLAINT CANNOT BE CONSIDERED

NAME OF COMPANY OR
FIRM COMPLAINED ABOUT _____

ADDRESS _____ TELEPHONE_____

                                              DATE OF
SALESPERSON _____ TRANSACTION_____

AGE _____ RACE _____ SEX _____

HAVE YOU CONTACTED   NAME OF PRODUCT OR
A PRIVATE ATTORNEY?_____ SERVICE INVOLVED _____

WAS A CONTRACT SIGNED?_____ (If so, attach copy of contract)

COMPLAINT INVOLVES MISREPRESENTATIONS:

ADVERTISED _____ , ORAL _____ , OTHER _____

EXPLAIN FULLY: The substance of your complaint must be fully summarized below. (and on the reverse side of this page if you need more room) LIST and NUMBER each fact occurred. INCLUDE DATES (or approximate dates) and attach all contracts, documents, and ads or writings (copies only, please) that relate to your complaint. (REMEMBER: YOU MUST PRINT OR TYPE AND SEPARATELY NUMBER EACH FACT.)

_____

_____

_____

NAMES AND ADDRESSES OF OTHER WITNESSES _____

_____

_____

THIS COMPLAINT MAY BE SENT TO THE COMPANY COMPLAINED ABOUT:

          YES_____   NO _____

YOUR NAME (Print or Type) _____

AGE_____   RACE _____   SEX _____

HOME ADDRESS _____

_____ TELEPHONE _____
      City   State   Zip Code

BUSINESS ADDRESS _____ TELEPHONE _____

              SIGNED _____

DA–94
GPC–0550

OFFICE OF THE DISTRICT ATTORNEY
18TH JUDICIAL DISTRICT
CONSUMER PROTECTION DIVISION
SEDGWICK COUNTY COURTHOUSE
525 N. MAIN – ROOM 503
WICHITA, KANSAS 67203

Phone
(316) 268-7405

File No._____

KEITH SANBORN
District Attorney

VERIFIED COMPLAINT

Date Filed _____

YOUR NAME_____ DATE OF BIRTH_____

YOUR ADDRESS_____ PHONE_____

CITY_____ ZIP_____ DAYTIME PHONE_____

NAME OF COMPANY OR PERSON
COMPLAINED ABOUT_____

THEIR ADDRESS_____ CO. TELE. NO._____

DATE AND PLACE ADVERTISED (ATTACH AD IF POSSIBLE)_____

NAME OF PERSON YOU DEALT WITH_____

DATE AND PLACE CONTRACT WAS SIGNED_____

NAME AND ADDRESS OF YOUR ATTORNEY_____ _____

AMOUNT OF MONETARY LOSS $_____

EXPLAIN FULLY THE CIRCUMSTANCES OF YOUR COMPLAINT. State What the Seller or Advertiser Told You Orally or Stated in Writing That Was not True. Use Reverse Side and or Extra Sheets of Paper if Necessary and Place Your Initials at the Bottom of Each. Include all pertinent dates, places, contracts, documents and other information.

SPECIFIC RELIEF YOU SEEK_____

_____

I _____, being first duly sworn, do upon my oath state that I have read the above and foregoing complaint and attachments thereto and know the contents thereof, and the same is true and correct.

_____
(Your Signature)

SUBSCRIBED AND SWORN to before me this_____ day of_____ 19_____ .

My Commission Expires:

_____
(Notary Public)

OFFICE OF CONSUMER AFFAIRS
DISTRICT ATTORNEY'S OFFICE
WESTERN BANK BUILDING
505 MARQUETTE N.W., SUITE 1400
ALBUQUERQUE, NEW MEXICO   87101

DATE _____
PROCESSED BY _____
TELEPHONE: 766-4340

    I wish to file a complaint against the company or person named below. I understand that the District Attorney's Consumer Affairs Division does not represent private citizens in court. I further understand that if this complaint cannot be settled through your office, I can seek other venues of settlement.

(THIS FORM IS SELF-CARBONING, PLEASE PRINT OR TYPE)

NAME OF COMPANY, FIRM OR
PERSON COMPLAINED ABOUT _____

ADDRESS _____ CITY, STATE & ZIP _____

TELEPHONE _____ SALESPERSON _____ DATE OF TRANSACTION _____

HAVE YOU CONTACTED A
PRIVATE ATTORNEY, IF SO, WHO? _____

NAME OF PRODUCT OR
SERVICE INVOLVED _____

HAVE YOU FILED WITH ANY OTHER AGENCY, IF SO, WHO _____

HAVE YOU CONTACTED THE FIRM COMPLAINED ABOUT? _____

WAS A CONTRACT SIGNED? _____

(If so, attach a copy of the contract or
send original for us to copy and return)

IF THE CONTRACT WAS SOLD TO A THIRD PARTY, GIVE NAME AND ADDRESS OF THE BANK OR FINANCE
COMPANY _____

COMPLAINT INVOLVES MISREPRESENTATIONS: ____ ADVERTISED ____, ORAL ____, OTHER ____

    EXPLAIN FULLY: (Describe events in the order in which they happened)
             USE SEPARATE SHEET IF NECESSARY

_____
_____
_____
_____
_____
_____
_____
_____
_____
_____
_____
_____
_____
_____
_____
_____
_____

THIS COMPLAINT WILL BE SENT TO THE COMPANY COMPLAINED ABOUT

PRINT YOUR NAME _____

ADDRESS _____ ZIP _____

CITY & STATE _____ HOME TELEPHONE _____

SIGNATURE _____ BUSINESS TELEPHONE _____

Appendix 12

DIRECTORY OF LOCAL AND STATE
CONSUMER PROTECTION OFFICES

STATE, COUNTY AND CITY GOVERNMENT CONSUMER OFFICES
LISTED BY STATE

(NOTE: Toll-free telephone numbers underscored)

ALABAMA

State Offices

Governor's Office of
Consumer Protection
138 Adams Ave.
Montgomery 36130
205–832–5936
1–800–392–5658

Consumer Services
Coordinator
Office of Attorney
General
669 S. Lawrence St.
Montgomery 36107
205–832–6820

ALASKA

State Offices

Chief Consumer
Protection Section
Office of Attorney
General
360 "K" St.
Anchorage 99501
907–279–1567

Branch Offices

Pouch K, State Capitol
Juneau 99801
907–586–5931

604 Barnette, Box 1309
Fairbanks 99701
907–452–1567

ARIZONA

State Office

Economic Protection
Division
Department of Law
159 State Capitol Bldg.
Phoenix 85007
602–271–5763

ARIZONA (cont.)

County Offices

Cochise County

Cochise County Attorney's
Office
Bisbee 85603
602–432–2291

Pima County

Consumer Protection
Division
Pima County Attorney's
Office
111 W. Congress, 9th Fl.
Tucson 85701
602–792–8668

City Offices

Phoenix

Consumer Affairs
Operation
Mayor's Citizens
Assistance Office
251 W. Washington
Phoenix 85002
602–262–7777

Tucson

Consumer Affairs Division
Tucson City Attorney's
Office
P.O. Box 5547, 180 N.
Meyer
Tucson 85703
602–791–4886

ARKANSAS

State Offices

Consumer Protection
Division

ARKANSAS (cont.)

State Offices (cont.)

Office of Attorney
General
Justice Bldg.
Little Rock 72201
501–371–2341
1–800–482–8982

Consumer Service Division
Department of Insurance
University Tower Bldg.
12th and University,
400-18
Little Rock 72204
501–371–1325

CALIFORNIA

State Offices

Department of Consumer
Affairs
1020 N St.
Sacramento 95814
916–445–1254
1–800–952–5210 (auto
repair complaints only)

Branch Offices

107 S. Broadway, Rm.
8020
Los Angeles 90012
213–620–2003

30 Van Ness Ave., Rm.
2100
San Francisco 94102
415–557–2046

Environment/Consumer
Protection Section
Office of Attorney
General
350 McAllister St.
San Francisco 94102

CALIFORNIA (cont.)

Branch Offices (cont.)

800–952–5225 (consumer comps. in California)
916–952–5225 (consumer comps. from out of state)
Consumer Affairs Division
Department of Insurance
600 S. Commonwealth Ave.
Los Angeles 90005
213–620–4639 (insurance only)

Branch Office

1407 Market St.
San Francisco 94103
415–557–3646

County Offices

Alameda County

Consumer Protection
Alameda County Office of District Attorney
125-12th St., Rm. 207
Oakland 94607
415–874–5656

Contra Costa County

Special Operations Division
District Attorney's Office
13201 San Pablo Ave., Suite 300
San Pablo 94806
415–233–7060, ext. 3511

Del Norte County

Del Norte County Division of Consumer Affairs
2650 Washington Blvd.
Crescent City 95531
707–464–2716 or 3756

Fresno County

Consumer Coordinator
Fresno County
  Department of Weights
  & Measures & Consumer Protection
4535 E. Hamilton Ave.
Fresno 93702
209–488–3027

CALIFORNIA (cont.)

Fresno County (cont.)

Consumer Fraud Division
District Attorney's Office
1100 Van Ness Ave., Courthouse
Fresno 93721
209–488–3050

Inyo County

Consumer Unit
District Attorney's Office
P. O. Box 37
Independence 93526
714–878–2411

Kern County

Consumer Unit
District Attorney's Office
1415 Truxton Ave.
Bakersfield 93301
805–861–2443

Los Angeles County

Consumer and Environment Protection Division
District Attorney's Office
540 Hall of Records
320 W. Temple
Los Angeles 90012
213–974–3974

Department of Consumer Affairs
500 W. Temple
Los Angeles 90012
213–974–2417

Madera County

Madera County Weights and Measures/Consumer Protection
902 N. Gateway Dr.
Madera 93637
209–674–4641, ext. 218

Marin County

Consumer Services Deputy
Human Relations Department
Civic Center, Rm. 276
San Rafael 94903
415–479–1100, ext. 2971

CALIFORNIA (cont.)

Marin County (cont.)

District Attorney
Consumer Fraud Division
Hall of Justice, Civic Center, Rm. 155
San Rafael 94903
415–479–1100

Mendocino County

Consumer Unit
District Attorney's Office
P. O. Box 185
Ukiah 95482
707–462–4731, ext. 231

Monterey County

Department of Consumer Affairs
1220 Natividad Rd.
Salinas 93901
408–758–3859

Consumer Fraud Unit
District Attorney's Office
P. O. Box 1369
Salinas 93901
408–758–4626

Napa County

District Attorney
810 Brown St.
Napa 94558
707–224–7967

Orange County

Office of Consumer Affairs
511 N. Sycamore St.
Santa Ana 92701
714–834–6100

Branch Offices
Monday:

Garden Grove City Hall
11391 Acacia Pky.
Garden Grove 92640
714–638–6623

Westminster City Hall
8200 Westminster Ave.
Westminster 92683
714–898–3311, ext. 257

CALIFORNIA (cont.)

Branch Offices (cont.)

Tuesday:

Fountain Valley
Community Services
Project
10200 Slater Ave.
Fountain Valley 92708
714-962-2424, ext. 241

Cypress City Hall
5275 Orange Ave.
Cypress 90630
714-828-2200, ext. 58

Wednesday:

South Orange Civic
Center
30143 Crown Valley Pky.
Laguna Niguel 92675
714-495-1650

Old Placentia City Hall
120 S. Bradford
Placentia 92670
714-993-8178

Thursday:

Fullerton City Hall
303 W. Commonwealth
Fullerton 92631
714-525-7171, ext. 217

Huntington Beach City
Hall
2000 Main St.
Huntington Beach 92648
714-536-5265, or 5266

Friday:

La Habra Administration
Bldg.
Civic Center
La Habra 90631
714-526-2227, ext.
228/229

Anaheim Social Services
Center
173 W. Lincoln Ave.
Anaheim 92805
714-956-5500

Major Fraud and Economic
Crime Division
District Attorney's Office
P. O. Box 808

CALIFORNIA (cont.)

Branch Offices (cont.)

700 Civic Center Dr. W.
Santa Ana 92702
714-834-3600

Riverside County

Consumer Unit
District Attorney's Office
P. O. Box 1148
Riverside 92501
714-787-6372

Sacramento County

Fraud Division
District Attorney's Office
P. O. Box 749
Sacramento 95804
916-440-6823

Consumer Protection
Bureau
816 "H" Street, Rm. 104
Sacramento 95814
916-454-2113 or 2417

San Bernardino County

Department of Weights &
Measures and Consumer
Affairs
160 E. 6th St.
San Bernardino 92415
714-383-1411

Branch Office

310 West B St.
Ontario 91762
714-988-1191

Consumer Fraud
District Attorney's Office
Courthouse, Rm. 200
San Bernardino 92415
714-383-1134

San Diego County

Consumer Fraud Division
District Attorney's Office
220 W. Broadway
San Diego 92101
714-236-2382

San Francisco County

Consumer Fraud Division
District Attorney's Office

CALIFORNIA (cont.)

San Francisco County (cont.)

880 Bryant St., Rm. 301
San Francisco 94103
415-553-1030

San Luis Obispo County

Consumer Unit
District Attorney's Office
302 Courthouse Annex
San Luis Obispo 93401
805-543-3464

San Mateo County

Deputy District Attorney
Hall of Justice and
Records
Redwood City 94063
415-364-5600

Santa Barbara County

Consumer Business Law
Section
District Attorney's Office
1114 State St., Suite 273
Santa Barbara 93101
805-963-1441

Santa Clara County

Department of Weights &
Measures and Consumer
Affairs
1555 Berger Dr.
San Jose 95112
408-299-2105

Deputy District Attorney
Consumer Fraud Unit
232 E. Gish Rd.
San Jose 95112
408-275-9651

Santa Cruz County

Department of Weights &
Measures and Consumer
Affairs
640 Capitola Rd.
Santa Cruz 95062
408-425-2054

Branch Offices

Outreach Consumer
Office
New International
Senior Center

CALIFORNIA (cont.)

Branch Offices (cont.)

127 E. Beach St.
Watsonville
408-728-1761

Consumer Fraud Unit
District Attorney's Office
P. O. Box 1159
701 Ocean St.
Santa Cruz 95060
408-425-2071

Solano County

Deputy District Attorney
Consumer Fraud Unit
Hall of Justice
600 Union Ave.
Fairfield 94533
707-429-6451

Sonoma County

Deputy District Attorney
Consumer Fraud Unit
2555 Mendocino Ave.
P. O. Box 1964
Santa Rosa 95403
707-527-2641

Stanislaus County

Consumer Affairs
  Coordinator
Office of Consumer
  Affairs
725 B County Center #3
Modesto 95355
209-526-6211

Deputy District Attorney
Consumer Fraud Unit
P. O. Box 442
Modesto 95353
209-526-6345

Sutter County

Assistant District Attorney
Consumer Unit
Courthouse Annex
Yuba City 95991
916-673-5058

Ventura County

Department of Weights &
Measures-Consumer
Affairs

CALIFORNIA (cont.)

Ventura County (cont.)

608 El Rio Dr.
Oxnard 93030
805-487-7711, ext. 4377

Consumer Fraud Section
District Attorney's Office
501 Poli St.
Ventura 93001
805-648-6131, ext. 2537

Yolo County

Deputy District Attorney
Consumer Fraud Division
P. O. Box 1385
Woodland 95695
916-666-8454

City Offices

Long Beach

Department of Consumer
  Affairs
222 Pacific Ave.
Long Beach 90802
213-436-7284

Los Angeles

Bureau of Consumer
  Affairs
Los Angeles City Hall
Los Angeles 90012
213-485-4682 or 5002

Consumer Protection
  Section
Deputy City Attorney
1700 City Hall East
200 N. Main St.
Los Angeles 90012
213-485-4515

Merced

Consumer Affairs Office
P. O. Box 2068
Merced 95340
209-722-3924

Redwood City

Consumer Protection Unit
Redwood City Police Dept.
P. O. Box 189
Redwood City 94062

CALIFORNIA (cont.)

City Offices (cont.)

San Diego

Consumer Protection Unit
Office of City Attorney
City Admin. Bldg.
San Diego 92101

COLORADO

State Offices

Office of Consumer
  Affairs
Office of Attorney
  General
104 State Capitol
Denver 80203
303-897-2542

Consumer & Food
  Specialist
Colorado Dept. of
  Agriculture
1525 Sherman St., Rm.
  422
Denver 80203
303-892-3561

County Offices

*Adams, Arapahoe,
Boulder, Denver, and
Jefferson Counties*

Metropolitan District
Attorney's Consumer
  Office
655 S. Broadway
Denver 80209
303-777-3072

*Archuleta, LaPlata, and
San Juan Counties*

District Attorney
P. O. Box 1062
Durango 80301
303-247-8850

*El Paso and Teller
Counties (4th Judicial
Circuit)*

Consumer Affairs Division
District Attorney's Office
303 S. Cascade, Suite B
Colorado Springs 80902
303-473-3801

COLORADO *(cont.)*

County Offices (cont.)

Pueblo County

Consumer Affairs
Specialist
District Attorney's Office
County Courthouse, Rm.
344
Pueblo 81003
303-543-3550

CONNECTICUT

State Offices

Dept. of Consumer
Protection
State Office Bldg.
Hartford 06115
203-566-4999
800-842-2649

Consumer Protection
Office of Attorney
General
Rm. 177, State Office
Bldg.
Hartford 06115
203-566-3035

Office of Consumer
Counsel
Conn. Public Utility
Commission
165 Capitol Ave.
State Office Bldg.
Hartford 06115
203-566-7287

City Offices

Middletown

Office of Consumer
Protection
City Hall
Middletown 06457
203-347-4671

DELAWARE

State Offices

Consumer Affairs Division
Dept. of Community
Affairs and Economic
Development
200 W. Ninth St., 6th Fl.

DELAWARE *(cont.)*

State Offices (cont.)

Wilmington 19801
302-571-3250

Branch Offices

New Castle County:
571-3250
Kent County: 678-4000
Sussex County: 856-2571

Deputy Attorney General
Consumer Protection
Division
Department of Justice
Public Bldg.
Wilmington 19801
302-571-2524

DISTRICT OF COLUMBIA

Director
D. C. Office of Consumer
Affairs
1407 "L" St., N. W.
Washington, D. C. 20005
202-629-2617

Office of the People's
Counsel of the District of
Columbia
1625 Eye St., N. W.
Washington, D. C. 20006
202-727-3071

FLORIDA

State Offices

Consumer Protection and
Fair Trade Practices
Bureau
Department of Legal
Affairs
State Capitol
Tallahassee 32304
904-488-4481

Branch Offices

Ass't Attorney General
Sunset Executive Center
Suite 75
8585 Sunset Dr.
Miami 33143
305-279-8700

FLORIDA *(cont.)*

Branch Offices (cont.)

Ass't Attorney General
419 Stoval Prof. Bldg.
305 Morgan St.
Tampa 33602
813-223-2561

Division of Consumer
Services
Dept. of Agriculture and
Consumer Services
107 Mayo Bldg.
Tallahassee 32304
904-488-2221
1-800-342-2176 (Fla.
only)

Director for Consumer
Protection
Office of the Comptroller
State Capitol
Tallahassee 32304
904-488-5275 or
488-8830

Branch Offices

1515 N.W. 7th St., Rm.
210
Miami 33125
305-649-8650

103 Century Twenty-One
Dr., Suite 113
Jacksonville 32216
904-724-3952

807 W. Morse Blvd.
Suite 201
Winter Park 32789
305-644-4353

Exec. Square Office Park
Suite 113, 402 Rio St.
Tampa 33609
813-272-2565

2453 N. Military Trail
W. Palm Beach 33401
305-686-8640

800 N. Reus St., Suite 5A
Pensacola 32501
904-434-0626

Bureau of Consumer
Research and Education
Department of Insurance
State Capitol, Suite 53

FLORIDA (cont.)

Branch Offices (cont.)

Tallahassee 32304
904–488–6084 (insurance
only)

Branch Offices

Call 904–488–6085 for
nearest of 21 service
offices

Office of Consumer
Affairs
Public Service Commission
700 S. Adams St.
Tallahassee 32304
904–488–7238
1–800–342–3552 (utility
complaints only)

Office of Public Counsel
Holland Bldg., Rm. 308
Tallahassee 32304
904–488–9330
(litigation only)

County Offices

*Brevard County (18th
Judicial District)*

Consumer Fraud Division
State Attorney's Office
County Courthouse
Titusville 32780
305–269–8421

Branch Office

P. O. Box 846
Sanford 32771
305–322–7534

Broward County

Office of Consumer
Affairs
200 S. E. 6th St., Rm. 202
Fort Lauderdale 33301
305–765–5307

Dade County

Consumer Protection
Division
Metropolitan Dade
County
140 W. Falgler St., 16th Fl.
Miami 33130
305–579–4222

FLORIDA (cont.)

County Offices (cont.)

Branch Offices

South Dade Gov't Center
10710 S. W. 211th St.
Miami 33157
305–232–1810, ext. 285

Model Cities Office
2741 N. W. 49th St.
Miami 33132
305–633–8447

Consumer Fraud Division
Office of State Attorney
(11th Judicial Circuit)
1351 N. E. 12th St.
Miami 33125
305–324–4800

Consumer Advocate
Office of County Manager
140 W. Flagler St., 16th Fl.
Miami 33130
305–579–4222

*DeSota, Manatee,
Sarasota Counties (12th
Judicial Circuit)*

State Attorney
2078 Main St.
Sarasota 33577
813–955–0918

Hillsboro County

Hillsboro County
Department of
Consumer Affairs
205 Marion St.
Tampa 33602
813–272–6750

Palm Beach County

Department of Consumer
Affairs
301 N. Olive Ave.
W. Palm Beach 33401
305–837–2670

Consumer Fraud Division
Office of State Attorney
County Courthouse, Rm.
430 .
W. Palm Beach 33401
305–659–4222

FLORIDA (cont.)

Branch Offices (cont.)

Pinellas County

Office of Consumer
Affairs
315 Haven St.
Clearwater 33516
813–441–8976

City Offices

Jacksonville

Consumer Affairs Officer
Division of Consumer
Affairs Dept. of Human
Resources
220 E. Bay St.
Jacksonville 32202
904–355–0411, ext. 531

St. Petersburg

Division of Consumer
Affairs
175 Fifth St., N.
St. Petersburg 33701
813–893–7395

GEORGIA

State Offices

Governor's Office of
Consumer Affairs
104 State Capitol
Atlanta 30334
404–656–1794
1–800–282–4900

Assistant Attorney
General for Deceptive
Practices
Office of Attorney
General
132 State Judicial Bldg.
Atlanta 30334
404–656–3343

Consumers' Utility
Counsel of Georgia
c/o Bryan, Ramos and
Arnold
134 Peachtree St.
310 Rhodes Haverty Bldg.
Atlanta 30303
404–681–0444 (on state
retainer basis)

GEORGIA *(cont.)*

City Offices

Atlanta

Office of Consumer Affairs
City Hall-Memorial Dr.
Annex
121 Memorial Dr., S. W.
Atlanta 30303
404–658–6704

GUAM

State Offices

Office of Consumer Counsel
Government of Guam,
Box DG
Chase Manhattan Bank
Bldg., 7th Fl.
Agana 96910

HAWAII

State Offices

Director of Consumer Prot.
Office of Governor
250 S. King St.
602 Kamamalu Bldg.
P. O. Box 3767
Honolulu 96811
808–548–2560
(administration)
808–548–2540
(complaints)

IDAHO

State Offices

Consumer Protection Division
Office of Attorney General
State Capitol, Rm. 225
Boise 83720
208–384–2400

ILLINOIS

State Offices

Consumer Advocate's Office

ILLINOIS *(cont.)*

State Offices (cont.)

Office of Governor
State of Illinois Bldg.
Rm. 2000
160 N. LaSalle St.
Chicago 60601
312–793–2754

Consumer Fraud Section
Office of Attorney General
134 N. LaSalle St., Rm. 204
Chicago 60602
312–793–3580

Branch Offices

Spec. Assistant to the Attorney General
2151 Madison-Project Uplift
Bellwood 60104

Spec. Assistant to the Attorney General
13051 Greenwood Ave.
Blue Island 60406
312–597–8984

Spec. Assistant to the Attorney General
50 Raupp Blvd.
Buffalo Grove 60090
312–537–8084

Spec. Assistant to the Attorney General
1104 N. Ashlawn Ave.
Chicago 60622
312–793–5638

Spec. Assistant to the Attorney General
4750 N. Broadway, Rm. 216
Chicago 60640
312–769–3742

Spec. Assistant to the Attorney General
7906 S. Cottage Grove
Chicago 60619
312–488–2600

Spec. Assistant to the Attorney General
800 Lee St.
Des Plaines 60016

ILLINOIS *(cont.)*

Branch Offices (cont.)

312–824–4200

Spec. Assistant to the Attorney General
901 Wellington St.
Elk Grove Village 60007
312–439–3900

Spec. Assistant to the Attorney General
Evanston Library
1703 Orrington
Evanston 60204
312–475–6700

Spec. Assistant to the Attorney General
71 N. Ottawa St.
Joliet 60434
815–727–5371

Spec. Assistant to the Attorney General
1603 North Ave.
McHenry 60050
815–384–1703

Spec. Assistant to the Attorney General
6300 N. Lincoln Ave.
Morton Grove 60053
312–967–4100

Spec. Assistant to the Attorney General
217 S. Civic Dr.
Schaumberg 60172
312–894–7771

Spec. Assistant to the Attorney General
5127 Oakton St.
Skokie 60076
312–674–2522

Spec. Assistant to the Attorney General
149 S. Genesee
Waukegan 60085
312–244–4900

Consumer Protection Division
Office of Attorney General
500 S. Second St.
Springfield 62706
217–782–1090

ILLINOIS (cont.)

State Offices (cont.)

Branch Offices

Spec. Assistant to the
   Attorney General
Alton Chamber of
   Commerce Bldg.
112 E. Broadway
Alton 62002
612–462–9201

Spec. Assistant to the
   Attorney General
103 S. Washington, Suite
   12
Carbondale 62901
618–549–3369

Spec. Assistant to the
   Attorney General
820 Martin Luther King
   Dr.
E. St. Louis 62201
618–874–2238

Spec. Assistant to the
   Attorney General
500 Main St.
Peoria 61602
309–773–3100

Spec. Assistant to the
   Attorney General
208-18th St.
Rock Island 61201
309–786–3303

Spec. Assistant to the
   Attorney General
401 W. State St.
Rockford 61101
815–965–8635

Spec. Assistant to the
   Attorney General
123-1/2 N. Garrard St.
Rantoul 61866
217–893–1401

Consumer Market Branch
Department of Insurance
215 E. Monroe
Springfield 62767
217–782–4515
   (insurance only)

County Offices

Cook County

Consumer Complaint
   Division

ILLINOIS (cont.)

Cook County (cont.)

Office of State's Attorney
Civic Center, Suite 303
Randolph at Clark
Chicago 60602
312–443–8425

Madison County

Office of State's Attorney
103 Purcell St., 3rd Fl.
Edwardsville 62025
618–692–4550

Rock Island County

Consumer Protection
   Division
Office of State's Attorney
1318 Third Ave.
Rock Island 61201
309–794–9072

City Offices

Chicago

Dept. of Consumer Sales,
   Weights & Measures
City Hall
121 N. LaSalle St.
Chicago 60602
312–744–4092

Park Forest

Consumer Protection
   Com.
Village Hall, 200 Forest
   Blvd.
Park Forest 60466
312–748–1112

INDIANA

State Offices

Chief, Consumer
   Protection Division
Office of Attorney
   General
215 State House
Indianapolis 46204
317–633–6496 or 6276
1–800–382–5516

Division of Consumer
   Credit
Dept. of Financial
   Institutions

INDIANA (cont.)

State Offices (cont.)

1024 Indiana State Office
   Bldg.
Indianapolis 46204
317–633–6297 (credit
   only)

Consumer Services
   Division
Department of Insurance
State Office Bldg., Rm.
   509
Indianapolis 46204
317–633–6338 (insurance
   only)

Office of Public Counselor
807 State Office Bldg.
Indianapolis 46204
317–633–4659 (utilities
   only)

County Offices

Lake County

Prosecuting Attorney
2293 N. Main St.
Crown Point 46307
219–923–7260

Branch Offices

Assistant to Prosecutor
Consumer Protection Div.
232 Russell St.
Hammond 46320
219–931–3440, ext. 58

Ass't to Prosecutor
Consumer Protection Div.
400 Broadway, Rm. 104
Gary 46402
219–886–3621, ext. 385

City Offices

Gary

Office of Consumer
   Affairs
City of Gary, Annex East
1100 Massachusetts
Gary 46402
219–883–8532–33–34

IOWA

State Office

Consumer Protection
Division
Office of Attorney
General
1209 E. Court
Executive Hills West
Des Moines 50319
515-281-5926

KANSAS

State Offices

Consumer Protection
Division
Office of Attorney
General
State Capitol
Topeka 66612
913-296-3751

State Insurance
Department
State Office Bldg., Rm.
129-S
Topeka 66612
913-296-3071
1-800-432-2484
(insurance only)

County Offices

Johnson County

Consumer Protection
Division
District Attorney's Office
County Courthouse, Box
728
Olathe 66061
913-782-5000, ext. 318

Branch Office

Northeast Johnson County
Office Bldg.
6000 Lamar
Mission 66202
913-384-1100, ext. 222

Sedgwick County

Consumer Protection
Division
District Attorney's Office
County Courthouse, 5th
Fl.
Wichita 67203
316-268-7405

KANSAS *(cont.)*

County Offices (cont.)

Wyandotte County

Consumer Protection
Division
District Attorney's Office
710 N. 7th St.
Kansas City 66102
913-371-1600, ext.
231-234

City Offices

Kansas City

Department of Consumer
Affairs
Municipal Office Bldg.
One Civic Plaza
701 N. 7th St., Rm. 350
Kansas City 66101
913-371-2000, ext.
230-231

Topeka

Consumer Protection
Division
City Attorncy's Office
215 E. 7th St.
Topeka 66603
913-235-9261, ext. 205

KENTUCKY

State Offices

Consumer Protection
Division
Office of Attorney
General
State Capitol, Rm. 34
Frankfort 40601
502-564-6607
1-800-372-2960

County Offices

Jefferson County

Consumer Protection
Dept.
208 S. Fifth St., Rm. 401
Louisville 40202
502-581-6280

KENTUCKY *(cont.)*

City Offices

Louisville

Department of Consumer
Affairs
MSD Bldg., 400 S. 6th St.
Louisville 40203
502-587-3595

Owensboro

Consumer Affairs
Commission
101 E. 4th St.
Owensboro 42301
502-684-7251, ext. 208

LOUISIANA

State Offices

Governor's Office of
Consumer Protection
1885 Wooddale Blvd.,
1218
P. O. Box 44091, Capitol
Sta.
Baton Rouge 70804
504-389-7483
800-272-9868

Consumer
Protection/Commercial
Fraud Prosecution Unit
Office of Attorney
General
1885 Wooddale Blvd.,
1208
Baton Rouge 70806
504-389-7228

Branch Office

Consumer
Protection/Commercial
Fraud Prosecution Unit
234 Loyola Ave., 7th Fl.
New Orleans 70112
504-527-8371

Bureau of Marketing
Department of
Agriculture
P. O. Box 44302, Capitol
Sta.
Baton Rouge 70804
504-389-2111

LOUISIANA (cont.)

County Offices

East Baton Rouge Parish

Consumer Protection
Center
1779 Government St.
Baton Rouge 70802
504-344-8506

Jefferson Parish

Consumer Protection &
Commercial Frauds
Dept.
District Attorney's Office
1820 Franklin Ave., Suite
23
Gretna 70053
504-366-6611, ext. 441

City Offices

New Orleans

Mayor's Office of
Consumer Affairs
City Hall-1W12
New Orleans 70112
504-586-4441

MAINE

State Offices

Division of Consumer
Fraud and Protection
Office of Attorney
General
State House
Augusta 04330
207-289-3716

Bureau of Consumer
Protection
Dept. of Business
Regulation
51 Chapel St.
Augusta 04330
207-289-3731 (credit,
truth-in-lending,
collection agencies)

Bureau of Insurance
Dept. of Business
Regulation
State Office Annex
Western Ave.
Augusta 04330
207-289-3141 (insurance
only)

MARYLAND

State Offices

Consumer Protection
Division
Office of Attorney
General
One S. Calvert St.
Baltimore 21202
301-383-3713

Branch Offices

Metro. Branch Office
Md. Attorney General's
Cons. Prot. Division
5112 Berwyn Rd., 2nd Fl.
College Park 20740
301-474-3500

Western Md. Branch
Office
Md. Attorney General's
Cons. Prot. Division
138 E. Antietam St.
Hagerstown 21740
301-791-1150

Dealer Licensing &
Consumer Services
Motor Vehicle
Administration
6601 Ritchie Highway, NE
Glen Burnie 21061
301-768-7420

Peoples Counsel
Public Service Commission
301 W. Preston St.
Baltimore 21201
301-383-2375

Commissioner of
Consumer Credit
One S. Calvert St., Rm.
601
Baltimore 21202
301-383-3656

County Offices

Anne Arundel County

Board of Consumer
Affairs
Arundel Center, Rm. 403
Annapolis 21404
301-224-7300

MARYLAND (cont.)

Anne Arundel County (cont.)

Baltimore County

Consumer Fraud Division
State's Attorney's Office
316 Equitable Bldg.
Baltimore 21202
301-396-4997

Montgomery County

Office of Consumer
Affairs
24 Maryland Ave.
Rockville 20850
301-340-1010

Prince George's County

Consumer Protection
Commission
Courthouse
Upper Marlboro 20870
301-627-3000, ext. 561 or
589

MASSACHUSETTS

State Offices

Exec. Office of Consumer
Affairs
John W. McCormack
Bldg.
One Ashburton Pl.
Boston 02108
617-727-8000

Consumer Complaint
Division
(Same address as above)

Consumer Protection
Division
Department of Attorney
General
State House, Rm. 167
Boston 02133
617-727-7591

Branch Offices

Consumer Protection
Office of Attorney
General
235 Chestnut St.
Springfield 01103
413-785-1951

MASSACHUSETTS (cont.)

Branch Offices (cont.)

Mass. Consumers' Council
Leverett Saltonstall Bldg.
Government Center
100 Cambridge St., Rm.
2109
Boston 02202
617–727–2605; 2606

County Offices

Hampshire and Franklin Counties

Consumer Protection
Agency
District Attorney's Office
Courthouse
Northampton 01060
413–584–1597

Consumer Protection
Agency
Courthouse
Greenfield 01301
413–774–5102

City Offices

Boston

Boston Consumers'
Council
City Hall, Rm. 721
Boston 02201
617–722–4100, ext.
236–7–8

Branch Offices

14 maintained in Boston's
"Little City Hall"; to
contact phone
617–722–4100

Fitchburg

Consumer Protection
Service
455 Main St.
Fitchburg 01420
617–345–1946

Lowell

Consumer Advisory
Council
City Hall
Lowell 01852
617–454–8821

MASSACHUSETTS (cont.)

City Offices (cont.)

Weymouth

Weymouth Consumers'
Office
Town Hall
Weymouth 02189
617–335–2000, ext. 46

MICHIGAN

State Offices

Consumer
Protection/Antitrust
Division
Office of Attorney
General
670 Law Bldg.
Lansing 48913
517–373–1140
1–800–292–2431 (land
sales only)

Michigan Consumer
Council
414 Hollister Bldg.
Lansing 48933
517–373–0947

Consumer Services
Division
Insurance Bureau
Department of Commerce
111 N. Hosmer St.
Lansing 48913
517–373–0220 (insurance
only)

County Offices

Bay County

Consumer Protection Unit
Office of Prosecuting
Attorney
515 Center Ave.
Bay City 48706
517–893–3594

Genesee County

Consumer Fraud Unit
Office of Prosecuting
Attorney
105 Courthouse
Flint 48502
313–766–8768

MICHIGAN (cont.)

County Offices (cont.)

Ingham County

Consumer & Business
Affairs Division
Office of Prosecuting
Attorney
101 S. Washington
Lansing 48933
517–482–1517

Livingston County

Consumer Protection
Division
Office of
Prosecuting Attorney
211 E. Grand River Ave.
Howell 48843
517–546–1850

Macomb County

Consumer Fraud Unit
Office of Prosecuting
Attorney
Macomb Court Bldg., 6th
Fl.
Mt. Clemens 48043
313–463–7001

Oakland County

Consumer Fraud Division
Oakland County
Prosecuting Attorney
1200 N. Telegraph
Pontiac 48054
313–858–0650

Washtenaw County

Consumer Action Center
Consumer Protection
Division
Office of Prosecuting
Attorney
200 County Building
Main & Huron sts., Box
645
Ann Arbor 48107
313–994–2420

Wayne County

Consumer Protection
Agency
601 Lafayette Bldg.
144 W. Lafayette

MICHIGAN (cont.)

Wayne County (cont.)

Detroit 48226
313–224–2150

City Offices

Detroit

City Consumer Affairs
Dept.
10801 Curtis
Detroit 48221
313–224–3508 or
  313–342–6500

MINNESOTA

State Offices

Consumer Protection
Division
Office of Attorney
General
102 State Capitol
St. Paul 55155
612–296–3353

Office of Consumer
Services
Department of Commerce
Metro Square Bldg.
7th & Roberts sts., 5th Fl.
St. Paul 55101
612–296–4512

Branch Offices

Duluth Regional Office
332 W. Superior Rd.
Duluth 55802
218–723–4891

Commerce Commission
Consumer Advocacy
Program
5th Fl., Metro Square
Bldg.
St. Paul 55101
612–296–2488 (insurance
matters only)

County Offices

Hennepin County

Citizen Protection Division
County Attorney's Office
County Government
Center

MINNESOTA (cont.)

Hennepin County (cont.)

Minneapolis 55487
612–348–8105

City Offices

Minneapolis

Consumer Affairs Division
Dept. of Licenses &
Consumer Services
101A City Hall
Third Ave. & 4th St.
Minneapolis 55415
612–348–2080

MISSISSIPPI

State Offices

Consumer Protection
Division
Office of Attorney
General
Justice Bldg.,
P.O. Box 220
Jackson 39205
601–354–7130

Consumer Protection
Division
Dept. of Agriculture and
Commerce
High and President sts.
P. O. Box 1609
Jackson 39205
601–354–6586

MISSOURI

State Offices

Consumer Protection
Division
Office of Attorney
General
Supreme Court Bldg.
P. O. Box 899
Jefferson City 65101
314–751–3321

Branch Offices

Consumer Prot. Division
Office of Attorney
General
705 Olive St., Suite 1323

MISSOURI (cont.)

Branch Offices (cont.)

St. Louis 63101
314–241–2211

Consumer Protection Div.
Office of Attorney
General
615 E. 13th St.
Kansas City 64106
816–274–6686

Office of Consumer
Services
Dept. of Consumer
Affairs, Regulation and
Licensing
P. O. Box 1157
Jefferson City 65101
314–751–4996

Division of Insurance
515 E. High St., Box 690
Jefferson City 65101
314–751–4126

Branch Offices

615 E. 13th St.
Kansas City 64106
816–274–6381

225 S. Meramec
St. Louis 63105
314–863–7735

County Offices

Greene County

Consumer Fraud
Prosecution
County Prosecutor's
Office
County Courthouse, Rm.
206
Springfield 65802
417–869–3581

City Offices

Kansas City

Consumer Affairs
Specialist
Action Center
City Hall
Kansas City 64106
816–274–2222

MONTANA

State Offices

Consumer Affairs Division
Dept. of Business
  Regulation
805 N. Main St.
Helena 59601
406-449-3163

Montana Consumer
  Counsel
330 Fuller Ave.
Helena 59601
406-449-2771 or 2772
(utility and
transportation matters
only)

County Offices

Missoula County

Missoula County Attorney
County Courthouse
Missoula 58901
406-543-3111

NEBRASKA

State Offices

Assistant Attorney
  General
Department of Justice
State Capitol, 10th Fl.
Lincoln 68509
402-471-2682

Consumer Division
Dept. of Agriculture
P. O. Box 94844
Lincoln 68509
402-471-2341

Claims and Inquiries
Dept. of Insurance
Lincoln 68509

County Offices

Douglas County

Consumer Fraud Division
County Attorney's Office
Omaha-Douglas Civic
  Center
18th & Farnam sts., Rm.
  909
Omaha 68102
402-444-7625

NEVADA

State Offices

Consumer Affairs Division
Office of Attorney
  General
2501 E. Sahara Ave., 3rd
  Fl.
Las Vegas 89104
702-385-0344

Consumer Affairs Division
Department of Commerce
Bradley Bldg., 3rd Fl.
2501 E. Sahara Ave.
Las Vegas 89104
702-385-0344
800-992-0900

Branch Offices

Consumer Affairs Division
Department of Commerce
Nye Bldg., 201 S. Fall St.
Capitol Complex
Carson City 89710
702-885-4340

Division of Consumer
  Relations
Public Service Commission
Kinkead Bldg., 505 W.
  King St.
Carson City 89710
702-885-4180

County Offices

Clark County

Chief Deputy District
  Attorney
District Attorney's Office
Courthouse, 200 E.
  Carson
Las Vegas 89101
702-386-4011

Washoe County

Consumer Protection
  Division
District Attorney's Office
P. O. Box 11130
Reno 89510
702-785-5652

NEW HAMPSHIRE

State Offices

Consumer Protection
  Division
Office of Attorney
  General
Statehouse Annex
Concord 03301
603-271-3641

NEW JERSEY

State Offices

Division of Consumer
  Affairs
Dept. of Law & Public
  Safety
1100 Raymond Blvd., Rm.
  504
Newark 07102
201-648-4010; 3559

Division of Law
Dept. of Law & Public
  Safety
1100 Raymond Blvd., Rm.
  316
Newark 07102
201-648-2478

Public Advocate, Div. of
  Adminis.
Dept. of Public Advocate
P. O. Box 141
Trenton 08625
609-292-7087
800-792-8600 (state
  agency action only)

Consumer Services
Department of Insurance
201 E. State St.
Trenton 08625
609-292-5363

Bureau of Consumer
  Services
Dept. of Public Utilities
101 Commerce St., Rm.
  208
Newark 07102
201-648-2096

NOTE: Through its Consumer Affairs Local Assistance Program, the State Division of Consumer Affairs in New Jersey has established a network of Consumer Affairs Local Assistance Officers named to receive and mediate consumer complaints at the local level by their respective governments at the invitation of the State Division. Where fraud is evident, complaints are always referred to the State Division Office for intensive investigation with a view to litigation. Some of the designated CALA offices are, at the same time, county or city government-created consumer offices.

In the following listing, those serving as CALA offices ONLY are so indicated; those offices which ALSO function in the CALA program are so indicated. (*) Indicates office serves entire county.

Atlantic County

Northfield (also CALA) *
Atlantic County Office
of Consumer Affairs
25 Dolphin Ave.
Northfield 08232
609-646-6626

Pleasantville (CALA)
James Graziano
1 E. Lindley Ave.
Pleasantville 08232
609-641-7112

Bergen County

Englewood (CALA)
Lynn Theard
Municipal Bldg.
Box 228
Englewood 07631
201-567-1800, ext. 41

Fort Lee (also CALA) *
Cons. Prot. Board
Borough Hall,
309 Main St.
Fort Lee 07024
201-947-9400

Glen Rock (CALA)
Pat Hanscom
20 Cedar St.
Glen Rock 07452
201-652-0192

Hackensack (also CALA) *
Office of Consumer
Affairs
355 Main St.
Hackensack 07601
201-646-2650

Rocco Mazzo (CALA)
City Hall
65 Central Ave.
Hackensack 07602
201-342-3000

Bergen County (cont.)

Kearny-N. Arlington
(CALA)
Ruth Dangren
26 N. Midland Ave.
Kearny 07032
201-991-9282

Lodi (CALA)
Don DeMarco
Borough Hall
59 Main St.
Lodi 07644
201-779-0386

Lyndhurst (CALA)
Domenick Notte
390 Thomas Ave.
Lyndhurst 07071
201-438-5374

New Milford (CALA)
Fred Von Dettum
238 Linden Pl.
New Milford 07646

Paramus (CALA)
Josephine Norring
Paramus Borough Hall
Paramus 07652
201-265-2100

Anthony D'Ambrosio
Paramus High School
Paramus 07652

Ramsey (CALA)
Maxine Robins
44 Roandis Ct.
Ramsey

Rutherford (CALA)
Robert DiTommaso
176 Park Ave.
Rutherford 07070
201-939-1444

Teaneck (CALA)
George Haeuber

Bergen County (cont.)

Municipal Bldg.
Teaneck 07666
201-837-1600

Burlington County

Mt. Holly (also CALA) *
Burlington County Office
of Consumer Affairs
Grant Bldg., Rm. 101
54 Grant St.
Mt. Holly 08060
609-267-3300 ext. 259

Willingboro (CALA)
Theresa Mimm
Municipal Complex
Willingboro 08046
609-877-2201

Camden County

Camden (also CALA) *
Camden County Office of
Consumer Affairs
Suite 502 Parkade Bldg.
519 Federal St.
Camden 08101
609-757-8387

Oaklyn (CALA)
Bonnie Tyler
59 Hillcrest Ave.
Oaklyn 08107
609-854-8621

Westmont (Haddon
Township)
Barbara Horneff (CALA)
241 Strawbridge Ave.
Westmont 08108
609-667-6800

Cape May County

Wildwood (CALA)
Linda B. Foster, Chief
Community Dev. Agency

Cape May County (cont.)

Infor. & Complaint
Program
4400 New Jersey Ave.
Wildwood 08260
609–522–9245

Cumberland County

Bridgeton (also CALA) *
Dept. of Weights &
Measures and Consumer
Affairs
Court House
Broad & Fayette sts.
Bridgeton 08302
609–451–8000

Essex County

Belleville (also CALA) *
Municipal Bldg.
Belleville 07109
201–759–9100

Cedar Grove (CALA)
Eileen M. Murphy
3 Yorkshire Dr.
Cedar Grove 07009
201–239–9046

East Orange (CALA)
Toni Ross
Myrna Sims
Bureau of Consumer
Affairs
44 City Hall Plaza
East Orange 07109
201–266–5124

Irvington (CALA)
Carlo Tomasco
Municipal Bldg.
Civic Sq.
Irvington 07111
201–372–2100

Livingston (CALA)
Rayna Kleiman
28 Mt. Pleasant Pky.
Livingston 07039
201–992–5000

Marjorie Small
69 Elmwood St.
Livingston 07039

Maureen Bloom
8 W. Lawn Rd.
Livingston 07039

Essex County (cont.)

Newark (also CALA) *
Newark Office of
Consumer Affairs
24 Commerce St., 11th Fl.
Newark 07102
201–733–3808

Nutley (CALA)
Cecilia J. Sweeney
Town Hall
Nutley 07110
201–667–2800

Short Hills (CALA)
Judy Albers
8 Pinewood Ct.
Short Hills 07078

Judith Rivkin
473 Long Hill Rd.
Short Hills 07078

Millburn Township Town
Hall
Short Hills 07078
201–376–2030

Verona (CALA)
Esther Chernofsky
26 Lynwood Rd.
Verona 07044
201–239–6158

West Orange (CALA)
Robert M. Hilsen
66 Main St.
West Orange 07052
201–736–1500

Gloucester County

Woodbury (Deptford
Township
John Troxell (CALA)
542 Penn Blvd.
Woodbury 08096
609–227–5350

Hudson County

Bayonne (CALA)
Kevin Doyle
Dept. of Health
Municipal Bldg.
Bayonne 07602
201–823–1000, ext. 338

Hoboken (CALA)
Audrey Borg
City Hall

Hudson County (cont.)

Hoboken 07030
201–656–5580

Jersey City (CALA)
Judith Flaherty, Chairman
8 Erie St.
Jersey City 07302
201–434–3600, ext. 55–56

Kearny (CALA)
Ruth Dangren
26 N. Midland Ave.
Kearny 07032
201–991–9282

North Bergen (CALA)
Ken O'Grady
1215-46th St.
North Bergen 07047
201–863–8500, ext. 75

Secaucus (CALA)
G. Lichtenberger
729-9th St.
Secaucus 07094
201–867–6871

Union City (CALA)
Irma Africano
Vivian Geissler
No. Hudson Community
Action Corp.
507-26th St.
Union City 07087
201–866–2255

Weehawken (CALA)
Patricia Leonard
City Hall, Park Ave.
Weehawken 07087
201–867–1707

West New York (CALA)
Saul Blankstein, Chief
P. O. Box 361
West New York 07093
201–861–7000

Joseph Layton
Municipal Bldg.
West New York 07093
201–861–7000

Hunterdon County

Flemington (CALA)
Susan B. Miller
Borough Hall,
33 Park Ave.

Hunterdon County (cont.)

Flemington 08822
201–782–8840

Lebanon (Clinton
Township)
Rose Hanley (CALA)
Skyview Dr. R. D.
Lebanon 08833
201–735–4478

Olga Trimmer
Old Mountain Rd., R. D. 1
Lebanon 08833
201–236–6689

Mercer County

East Windsor (CALA)
Renee M. Kessler
5 Dover La.
East Windsor 08520
609–443–1659

Abby Miller
105 Hooverton Pl.
East Windsor 08520
609–443–3060

Princeton Junction (CALA)
Lorraine Baroody
23 Monterey Dr.
Princeton Junction
609–799–2054

Trenton (Hamilton
Township)
Pauline Raywood (CALA)
336 Lynwood Ave.
Trenton
609–586–7628

Mercer County Division of
Consumer Affairs (also
CALA) *
County Administration
Bldg.
640 S. Broad St., Rm. 116
Trenton 08607
609–989–8000

Middlesex County

East Brunswick (CALA)
Geri Webber
Municipal Bldg.
575 Ryders La.
E. Brunswick 08816
201–254–4600

Edison (CALA)
Sherrill Bressman

Middlesex County (cont.)

25 Tamarack Dr.
Edison 08817
201–494–1991

Lois Gelade
9 Dellview Dr.
Edison 08817
201–494–6037

Matawan (Madison
Township)
Barbara Cannon (CALA)
47 Lakeridge Dr.
Matawan 07747

Debra Romano
12 Haven Dr.
Matawan 07747

Consumer Affairs Office
Browntown School
Route 516
Old Bridge 08857
201–679—5577
Mon. & Wed. 9:30–11:30

Metuchen (CALA)
Everett L. Rich
Borough Hall
Metuchen 08840
201–549–3600

Middlesex (CALA)
Genevieve Ross
1200 Mountain Ave.
Middlesex
201–356–7400
201–356–8090

Perth Amboy (CALA)
Nathaniel Hutchins
City Hall
133 New Brunswick Ave.
Perth Amboy 08861
201–826–0290

Sayreville (CALA)
Joan Gullo
167 Main St.
Sayreville 08872
201–257–3200

Louise Marotta
39 Oakwood Dr.
Parlin 08559
201–727–5287

Woodbridge (CALA)
Teresa Thompson
City Hall
One Main St.

Middlesex County (cont.)

Woodbridge 07095
201–634–4195

Monmouth County

Asbury Park (CALA)
Hazel Samuels
Michael Furlong
Elsie Logan
Action Now
417 Bond St.
Asbury Park
201–775–2108

Freehold (Freehold
Township)
Ann White (CALA)
156 Randolph Rd.
Freehold 07728
201–462–8387

Margaret Radder
Stillwells Corner, R. D.
Freehold 07728
201–462–1364

Jean Moriarty
18 Village La.
Freehold 07728
201–462–8238

Freehold (Manalapan
Township)
Robert Weiss (CALA)
R. D. #1, Box 187
Freehold 07728
201–446–6804

Long Branch (CALA)
Ann Ryerson
72 Morris Ave.
Long Branch 07740
201–222–6752

Matawan Borough (CALA)
Mike Piperno
Borough Hall
Matawan Borough 07747
201–566–2113

Neptune (CALA)
William H. Berardi
4 Emerson Pl.
Neptune 07753
201–775–1615

Red Bank (CALA)
Carole Popper
Aubrey Bean
Office of Consumer
Affairs

Monmouth County *(cont.)*

32 Monmouth St.
Red Bank 07701
201–842–6110

Morris County

Boonton (CALA)
James Russell
325 Rexland Dr.
Boonton 07005
201–335–7280

Budd Lake (CALA)
Joan Phillips
29 Netcong Rd.
Budd Lake 07828
201–347–5389

Chatham (CALA)
Helen S. Hintz
Chatham 07928
201–635–6490

Denville (CALA)
Judith Lieberman
9 Aerie Wynde Dr.
Denville 07834
201–361–7809

Barbara Mufson
35 Kitchell Rd.
Denville 07834

Rena Thorsen
89 W. Glen Rd.
Denville 07834
201–625–4079

Morristown (CALA)
Joseph Gabriel
65 Spring St.
Morristown 07960
201–539–8130

Parsippany (also CALA) *
Office of Consumer
Affairs
120 Cherry Hill Rd.
Parsippany 07054
201–334–3600
201–335–0700

Randolph Township (CALA)
Marlene Padula
Donna Ostman
Municipal Bldg.
Randolph Township
07801
201–361–8200

Morris County *(cont.)*

Rockaway (CALA)
R. B. Feuchtbaum
28 Old Middletown Rd.
Rockaway 07866

Ocean County

Pine Beach (CALA)
Russell K. Corby
401 Buhler Ave.
Pine Beach 08741
201–349–6425

Toms River (also CALA) *
Dept. of Consumer Affairs
Adm. Bldg., Rm. 203-B
Hosper Ave.
Toms River 08753
201–224–2121 ext. 42′

Adrienne Cecere
54 Washington St.
Toms River 08753
201–341–1000, ext. 79, 49

Sophie Shomer
Max Shomer
1052 N. Maple Ave.
Toms River 08753

Passaic County

Clifton (CALA)
William J. Adelhelm
City Hall, Main Ave.
Clifton 07015
201–470–2600

Paterson (CALA)
Office of Consumer
Affairs
Adm. Bldg.
Railway Ave.
Paterson
201–525–5000
201–525–1736

Consumer Affairs
Dept. of Human
Resources
1 W. Broadway
Paterson 07505
201–881–8303

Wayne (CALA)
Ricky Trappe
Municipal Bldg.
Valley Rd.
Wayne 07470
201–694–1800, ext. 814

Somerset County

Somerset (also CALA) *
County Adm. Bldg.
Somerville 08876
201–725–4700, ext. 306

Sussex County

Sparta (CALA)
Anne M. Mesch
94 Hillside Rd.
Sparta 07871
201–729–6752

Union County

Clark (CALA)
Theresa M. Ward
60 Wheatsheaf Rd.
Clark 07066
201–382–2940

Cranford (CALA)
Debra Greenberg
2 Green Ct.
Cranford 07016
201–276–8900

Elizabeth (CALA)
Carmine Liotta
27 Prince St.
Elizabeth 07208
201–354–7530

(also CALA) *
City Hall
60 W. Scott Pl.
Elizabeth
201–353–6000, ext. 281

Fanwood (CALA)
Patricia Breuninger
85 Helen St.
Fanwood 07023
201–322–5587

Kenilworth (CALA)
533 Ridgefield Ave.
Kenilworth 07033
201–276–5802 (Town
Hall)

Mountainside (CALA)
Leon Greenberg
1441 Force Dr.
Mountainside 07092

Plainfield (CALA)
Glorid Crudup
City Hall
Plainfield 07061
201–753–3229

Somerset County (cont.)

Rochelle Park (CALA)
Anna Randazzo
10 E. Passaic St.
Rochelle Park 07662
201–843–1739

Scotch Plains (CALA)
Susan Stern
430 Park Ave.
Scotch Plains 07076
201–322–6700

Somerset County (cont.)

Springfield (CALA)
Ellen Bloom
Municipal Bldg.
Springfield 07081
201–376–5800

West Providence (CALA)
Nancy Krautter
285 Woodbine Cir.
West Providence 07974
201–665–0634

Warren County

Hackettstown (CALA)
Herbert Lewis
3 Herbert La.
Hackettstown 07840
201–852–3450

NEW MEXICO

State Offices

Consumer Protection
Division
Office of Attorney
General
P. O. Box 2246
Santa Fe 87501
505–827–2844 or 5237

County Offices

Bernalillo County

Consumer Protection
Division
District Attorney's Office
Courthouse, 415 Tijeras,
N. W.
Albuquerque 87101
505–766–4340

Eddy County

Consumer Affairs Division
District Attorney's Office
P. O. Box 1240
Carlsbad 88220
505–885–8822

Valencia County

District Attorney
Los Lunas 87031
505–865–9643

NEW YORK

State Offices

Consumer Protection
Board
99 Washington Ave., Rm.
1000
Albany 12210
518–474–8583

NEW YORK (cont.)

State Offices (cont.)

Branch Office

Two World Trade Center
Room 8225, 82nd Fl.
New York 10047
212–488–5666

Consumer Frauds &
Protection Bureau
Office of Attorney
General
Two World Trade Center
New York 10047
212–488–7530

Consumer Frauds &
Protection Bureau
Office of Attorney
General
State Capitol
Albany 12224
518–474–8686

*Branch Offices of the
Attorney General's
Consumer Frauds and
Protection Bureau*

Office of Attorney
General
403 Metcalf Bldg.
Auburn 13021
315–253–9765

Office of Attorney
General
19 Chenango St.
Binghampton 13901
607–773–7823

Office of Attorney
General
65 Court St.

NEW YORK (cont.)

Branch Offices (cont.)

Buffalo 14202
716–842–4385

Office of Attorney
General
48 Cornelia St.
Plattsburgh 12901
518–561–1980

Office of Attorney
General
65 Broad St.
Rochester 14614
714–454–4540

Office of Attorney
General
333 E. Washington St.
Syracuse 13202
315–473–8439, ext. 216

Office of Attorney
General
2 Catharine St.
Poughkeepsie 14301
914–452–7760

Office of Attorney
General
207 Genesse St., Box 528
Utica 13501
315–797–6120

Office of Attorney
General
317 Washington St.
Watertown 13001
315–782–0100

Consumer Complaint
Bureau
State Insurance
Department
Two World Trade Center

NEW YORK (cont.)

Branch Offices (cont.)

New York 10047
212–488–4005 (insurance
only)

Branch Office

Consumer Complaint
Bureau
State Insurance
Department
Albany 12210
518–474–4556 (insurance
only)

County Offices

Erie County

Consumer Fraud Bureau
District Attorney's Office
25 Delaware Ave.
Buffalo 14202
716–855–2424

Consumer Protection
Committee
Office of Erie County
Executive
95 Franklin Rd.
Buffalo 14202
716–846–6690

Greenburgh County

Greenburgh Consumer
Board
P. O. Box 205
Elmsford 10523
914–682–5245

Kings County

Consumer Frauds and
Economic Crimes
Bureau
District Attorney's Office
Municipal Bldg.
210 Joralemon St.
Brooklyn 11201
212–643–5100
(complaints of criminal
nature only)
(Ask for Complaint
Bureau)

Monroe County

Consumer Affairs Council
Rm. 410C, County Office
Bldg.

NEW YORK

Monroe County (cont.)

Rochester 14614
716–381–1833

Nassau County

Office of Consumer
Affairs
160 Old Country Rd.
Mineola 11501
516–535–3282

Commercial Frauds
Bureau
District Attorney's Office
262 Old Country Rd.
Mineola 11501
516–535–3340

Oneida County

Consumer Advocate
County Office Bldg.
800 Park Ave.
Utica 13501
315–798–5601

Onondaga County

Office of Consumer
Affairs
County Civic Center
421 Montgomery St.
Syracuse 13202
315–477–7911

Orange County

Dept. of Weights and
Measures and Consumer
Affairs
99 Main St.
Goshen 10924
914–294–5822

District Attorney's Office
of Consumer Affairs
County Government
Center
Main St.
Goshen 10924
914–294–5471

Rensselaer County

Citizen Affairs
Rensselaer County
Courthouse
Troy 12180
518–270–5360

NEW YORK (cont.)

County Offices (cont.)

Rockland County

Office of Consumer
Protection
County Office Bldg.
New Hempstead Rd.
New City 10956
914–638–0500, ext. 395

Steuben County

Dept. of Weights and
Measures and Consumer
Affairs
19 E. Morris St.
Bath 14810
607–776–4949

Suffolk County

Department of Consumer
Affairs
Suffolk County Center
Veterans Highway
Hauppauge, Long Island
11787
516–979–3100

Westchester County

Frauds Bureau
District Attorney's Office
County Courthouse
111 Grove St.
White Plains 10601
914–082–2100

Division of Weights and
Measures and Consumer
Affairs
County Office Bldg.
White Plains 10601
914–682–3300

City Offices

Colonie

Colonie Consumer
Protection Agency
Memorial Town Hall
Newtonville 12128
518–783–2700

Glen Cove

Office of Consumer
Affairs
City Hall, Rm. 203
Glen Cove 11542
516–676–2000, ext. 31

NEW YORK (cont.)

City Offices (cont.)

Huntington

Consumer Protection
Board
Town Hall, 227 Main St.
Huntington 11743
516–421–1000·

Islip

Consumer Protection
Section
Town Attorney's Office
655 Main St.
Islip 11751
516–581–8000

Mt. Vernon

Department of Weights
and Measures and
Consumer Affairs
Police Headquarters
Roosevelt Sq.
Mt. Vernon 10550
914–558–6000

New Rochelle

Consumer Affairs
Committee
City Hall
New Rochelle 10801
914–632–2021, ext. 218

Consumer Advisor
Office of Weights and
Measures
City Hall, 515 North Ave.
New Rochelle 10801
914–632–2021, ext. 324

New York City

Department of Consumer
Affairs
80 Lafayette St.
New York 10013
212–566–5456

Branch Offices

113-25 Queens Blvd.
Forest Hills 11375
212–261–2922

98-18 161st St.
Jamaica 11432
212–526–6600

NEW YORK (cont.)

Branch Offices (cont.)

144 W. 125th St.
(West Harlem)
New York 10026
212–222–9700

2838 Third Ave.
Bronx 11455
212–993–7770

227 E. 116th St.
(East Harlem)
New York 10029
212–348–0600

1468 Flatbush Ave.
Brooklyn 11210
212–434–1900

Niagara Falls

Sealer of Weights &
Measures
Division of Weights &
Measures
City Hall
Niagara Falls 14302
716–278–8360

Oswego

Office of Consumer
Affairs
City Hall, Rm. 104
Oswego 13126
315–342–2410

Ramapo

Consumer Protection
Board
Town Hall, Route 59
Suffern 10901
914–357–5100, ext. 57
or 58

Schenectady

Bureau of Consumer
Protection
City Hall, Rm. 206, Jay St.
Schenectady 12305
518–377–3381, ext. 314
or 357

Syracuse

Consumer Affairs Unit
City Hall, Rm. 421
233 E. Washington St.

NEW YORK (cont.)

Syracuse (cont.)

Syracuse 13202
315–473–3240

Yonkers

Yonkers Action Center/
Consumer Protection
Weights & Measures
City Hall, Rm. 316
Nepperhan Ave.
Yonkers 10701
914–965–0707, 963–3980

NORTH CAROLINA

State Offices

Consumer Protection
Division
Office of Attorney
General
Justice Bldg., P.O. Box
629
Raleigh 27602
919–829–7741
1–800–662–7925

Consumer Affairs
Administration Division
Department of Insurance
Wake County Courthouse
316 Fayetteville St.
Raleigh 27611
919–829–2032
1–800–662–7975
(insurance only)

Office of Consumer
Services
Department of
Agriculture
P. O. Box 27647
Raleigh 27611
919–829–7125

City Offices

Charlotte

Fraud Unit, Central
Investigations Bureau
Charlotte Police
Department
Law Enforcement Center
825 E. Fourth St.
Charlotte 28205
704–374–2311

NORTH DAKOTA

State Offices

Consumer Fraud Division
Office of Attorney
General
State Capitol
Bismarck 58501
701–224–2210

Consumer Affairs Office
State Laboratories
Department
Bank of North Dakota
Bldg.
Box 937
Bismarck 58505
701–224–2485

Claims Division
N. D. Insurance
Department
Capitol Bldg.
Bismarck 58505
701–224–2440 or 2451
(insurance only)

OHIO

State Offices

Consumer Frauds, Crimes
Section
Office of Attorney
General
State Office Tower, Suite
1541
30 E. Broad St.
Columbus 43215
614–466–8831

Consumer Protection
Division
Department of Commerce
180 E. Broad St. 13th Fl.
Columbus 43215
614–466–8760
800–282–1960 (all calls
except real estate and
insurance)

County Offices

Franklin County

Consumer Fraud Division
Office of Prosecuting
Attorney

OHIO (cont.)

Franklin County (cont.)

Hall of Justice, S. High St.
Columbus 43210
614–462–3248

Greene County

Consumer Protection and
Education Office
101 E. Church St.
Xenia 45385
513–372–4461

Lake County

Consumer Protection
Council
Office of Prosecuting
Attorney
Lake County Courthouse
Painesville 44077
216–352–6281, ext. 281

Montgomery County

Fraud Section
Office of Prosecuting
Attorney
County Courts Building
41 N. Perry St., Suite 308
Dayton 45402
513–228–5126 (criminal
fraud only)

City Offices

Akron

Division of Weights and
Measures and Consumer
Protection
69 N. Union St.
Akron 44314
216–375–2612

Canton

Commissioner of
Consumer Protection
919 Walnut Ave., N. E.
Canton 44704
216–455–8951, ext. 249

Cincinnati

Consumer Protection
Division
City Solicitor's Office
City Hall, Rm. 132

OHIO (cont.)

Cincinnati (cont.)

Cincinnati 45202
513–352–3971

Cleveland

Office of Consumer
Affairs
City Hall, Room 119
601 Lakeside Ave.
Cleveland 44114
216–694–3200

Columbus

Consumer Affairs
Department of
Community Services
720 E. Broad St.
Columbus 43215
614–461–7397

Dayton

Bureau of Consumer
Affairs
101 W. Third St.
Dayton 45402
513–225–5048 or 5574

Toledo

Consumer Protection
Agency
420 Madison Ave., Suite
1120
Toledo 43604
419–247–6191

Youngstown

Division of Consumer
Affairs
Youngstown Health
Department
Mill Creek Community
Center
496 Glenwood Ave.
Youngstown 44502
216–747–3561

OKLAHOMA

State Offices

Department of Consumer
Affairs
Jim Thorpe Bldg., Rm.
460

OKALHOMA (cont.)

State Offices (cont.)

Oklahoma City 73105
405-521-3653

Consumer Protection
Office of Attorney
General
State Capitol Bldg., Rm.
112
Oklahoma City 73105
405-521-3921

County Offices

LeFlore County

District Attorney for
LeFlore County
County Courthouse
Poteau 74953
918-647-2410, ext. 2411

OREGON

State Offices

Consumer Protection
Division
Office of Attorney
General
1133 S. W. Market St.
Portland 97201
503-229-5522

Consumer Service Division
Department of Commerce
Salem 97310
503-378-4320

Public Service
Insurance Division
Commerce Department
158-12th St., N. E.
Salem 97310
503-378-4271 (insurance
only)

Public Programs & Policy
Public Liability
Commission
300 Labor & Industries
Bldg.
Salem 97310
503-378-6600 (utilities
only)

Consumer Officer
Department of
Agriculture

OREGON (cont.)

State Offices (cont.)

Agriculture Bldg., Rm.
201
635 Capitol St. N. E.
Salem 97310
503-378-8298 (food,
sanitation, short weight,
agriculture products
only)

PENNSYLVANIA

State Offices

Bureau of Consumer
Protection
Office of Attorney
General
301 Market St.
Harrisburg 17101
717-787-9714

Branch Offices

Bureau of Consumer
Protection
Department of Justice
133 N. Fifth St.
Allentown 18102
215-821-0901

Spec. Asst. Attorney
General
Department of Justice
919 State St.
Erie 16501
814-454-7184

Deputy Attorney General
Harrisburg Regional
Office
Bureau of Consumer
Protection
Department of Justice
25 S. Third St.
Harrisburg 17101
717-787-7109

Deputy Attorney General
Bureau of Consumer
Protection
Department of Justice
342-44 N. Broad St.
Philadelphia 19102
215-238-6475

PENNSYLVANIA (cont.)

Branch Offices (cont.)

Deputy Attorney General
Bureau of Consumer
Protection
Department of Justice
300 Liberty Ave.
Pittsburgh 15222
412-565-5135

Deputy Attorney General
Bureau of Consumer
Protection
Department of Justice
1835 Centre Ave.
Pittsburgh 15219
412-566-1500, ext. 319

Deputy Attorney General
Bureau of Consumer
Protection
Department of Justice
402 Connell Bldg.
129 N. Washington Ave.
Scranton 18503
717-961-4582

Policy Holders Service and
Protection
Department of Insurance
Finance Bldg., Rm. 408
Harrisburg 17120
717-787-1131 (insurance
only)

Branch Offices

Erie Regional Office
P. O. Box 6142
Erie 16512
814-454-2818

Philadelphia Regional
Office
1400 Spring Garden St.
Philadelphia 19130
215-238-7240

Pittsburgh Regional Office
300 Liberty Ave.
State Office Bldg.
Pittsburgh 15222
412-565-5020

Consumer Affairs
Coordinator
Department of Banking
P. O. Box 2155

PENNSYLVANIA (cont.)

Branch Offices (cont.)

Harrisburg 17120
717-787-1854 (consumer credit companies, state savings and loans, state banks)

Division of Consumer Affairs
Department of Agriculture
2301 N. Cameron St.
Harrisburg 17120

Branch Offices

Consumer Services
Pa. Dept. of Agriculture
R. D. #4
Meadville 16335
814-724-1906

Consumer Services
Pa. Dept. of Agriculture
R. D. #1
Linden 17744

Consumer Coordinator
Pa. Dept. of Agriculture
Route 92 South
Tunkhannock 18657
717-836-2181

Consumer Services
Pa. Dept. of Agriculture
R. D. #1
Evans City 16033
412-776-1585

Consumer Coordinator
Pa. Dept. of Agriculture
615 Howard Ave.
Altoona 16601
814-943-1133

Consumer Coordinator
Pa. Dept. of Agriculture
Box 419
Summerdale 17093
717-787-3400

Consumer Coordinator
Pa. Dept. of Agriculture
100 W. Main St.
Lansdale 19446
717-368-3000

PENNSYLVANIA (cont.)

County Offices

Allegheny County

Bureau of Consumer Affairs
3rd Floor, Jones Law Bldg.
4th & Ross sts.
Pittsburgh 15219
412-355-5402

Armstrong County

Bureau of Consumer Affairs
342 Market St.
Kittaming 16201

Bucks County

Bucks County Department of Consumer Protection
Administration Annex
Broad and Union sts.
Doylestown 18901
215-348-2911

Butler County

Butler County Consumer Affairs Office
Court House
Butler 16001
412-285-4731

Cumberland County

Bureau of Consumer Affairs
Court House
Carlisle 17013

Delaware County

Consumer Affairs Division
Office of Public Information
Toal Bldg.
2nd and Orange sts.
Media 19063
215-891-2288

Indiana County

Indiana County Consumer Information and Referral Service
Indiana 15701

PENNSYLVANIA (cont.)

County Offices (cont.)

Lackawanna County

Department of Transportation, Environmental, Consumer Affairs
News Bldg., 8th Fl.
Scranton 18503
717-342-8366

Lancaster County

Lancaster County District Attorney
Consumer Protection Commission
County Courthouse
Lancaster 17602
717-299-4222

Montgomery County

County Consumer Affairs
County Courthouse
Norristown 19404
215-275-5000, ext. 228

Philadelphia County

Economic Crimes Unit
District Attorney's Office
No. 5 Penn Center Plaza
16th & Markets sts., 22nd Fl.
Philadelphia 19103
215-MU 6-2109, 2110

Washington County

Washington County Consumer Information and Referral Service
Washington, 15301

Westmoreland County

Bureau of Consumer Affairs
102 W. Otterman St., 3rd Fl., Box Q
Greenburg 15601
412-836-1002

City Offices

Monessen

Department of Consumer Affairs

PENNSYLVANIA (cont.)

Monessen (cont.)

Municipal Bldg.
Third and Donner
Monessen 15062
412-684-5087 or 4664

Philadelphia

Mayor's Office of
Consumer Services
City Hall, Rm. 143
Philadelphia 19107
215-MU6-2798

Pittsburgh

Office of Consumer
Advocate
City-County Bldg.
Pittsburgh 15219
412-281-3900, ext. 538

PUERTO RICO

State Offices

Department of Consumer
Affairs
Minillas Governmental
Center
Torre Norte Bldg.
De Diego Ave., Stop 22
P. O. Box 13934
Santurce 00908
809-726-6090 or 6190

Branch Offices

Bayamon, Arecibo,
Caguas, Mayaguez and
Ponce

RHODE ISLAND

State Offices

Rhode Island Consumers'
Council
365 Broadway
Providence 02902
401-277-2764

Division of Consumer
Protection
Department of Attorney
General
56 Pine St.
Providence 02903
401-277-3163

SOUTH CAROLINA

State Offices

Office of Citizens Service
Governor's Office
State House, P. O. Box
11450
Columbia 29211
803-758-3261

Department of Consumer
Affairs
Columbia Bldg., 6th Fl.
1200 Main, P. O. Box
11739
Columbia 29211
803-758-2040
800-922-1594

Consumer Protection
Office of Attorney
General
Hampton Office Bldg.
P.O. Box 11549
Columbia 29211
803-758-3970

Market Conduct Division
Department of Insurance
2711 Middleburg Dr.
P. O. Box 4067
Columbia 29204
803-758-2876 (insurance
only)

SOUTH DAKOTA

State Offices

Department of Commerce
and Consumer Affairs
State Capitol
Pierre 57501
605-224-3177

Branch Office

Department of Commerce
and Consumer Affairs
Division of Consumer
Prot.
Courthouse Plaza, Suite 2
Sioux Falls 57102
605-339-6691

TENNESSEE

State Offices

Div. of Consumer Affairs
Department of
Agriculture
Lab and Office Bldg.
Ellington Agricultural
Center
Hogan Rd., Box 40627
Melrose Sta.
Nashville 37204
615-741-1461
800-342-8385,

Consumer Protection
Office of Attorney
General
Supreme Court Bldg., Rm.
415
Nashville 37219
615-741-1671

TEXAS

State Offices

Consumer Protection
Division
Office of Attorney
General
P. O. Box 12548, Capitol
Sta.
Austin 78711
512-475-3288

Branch Offices

Assistant Attorney
General
4313 N. 10th
McAllen 78501
512-682-4547

Assistant Attorney
General
North Texas Regional
Office
2930 Turtle Creek Plaza
Dallas 75219
214-742-8944

Assistant Attorney
General
City-County Bldg.
El Paso 79901
915-533-3484

TEXAS *(cont.)*

Branch Offices (cont.)

Assistant Attorney
General
County Office Bldg.
806 Broadway
Lubbock 79401
806-747-5238

Assistant Attorney
General
200 Main Plaza, Suite 400
San Antonio 78205
512-224-1007

Assistant Attorney
General
Houston 77002

Consumer Center
201 E. Belknap St.
Forth Worth 76102
817-334-1788

Office of Consumer Credit
1011 San Jacinto Blvd.
P. O. Box 2107
Austin 78767
512-475-2111 (consumer
credit only)

Consumer Affairs Office
Department of
Agriculture
113 San Jacinto
Austin 78701
512-475-2154

County Offices

Bexar County
Consumer Fraud Division
Office of Criminal District
Attorney
San Antonio 78205
512-220-2323

*El Paso, Culberson and
Hudspeth Counties*
Consumer Fraud Division
Office of District Attorney
City-County Bldg., Rm.
401
El Paso 79901
915-543-2860

TEXAS *(cont.)*

County Offices (cont.)

Harris County
Consumer Fraud Division
Office of District Attorney
301 San Jacinto
Houston 77002
713-228-8311, ext. 7493

Tarrant County
Consumer Fraud Division
Office of District Attorney
New Criminal Courts
Bldg.
300 W. Belknap St.
Fort Worth 76102
817-334-1603 (criminal
consumer fraud)

Consumer Center of
Tarrant County
201 E. Belknap
Fort Worth 76102
817-334-1784

Travis County
Consumer and Housing
Office
307 W. 7th St.
Austin 78701
512-474-6554

*Waller, Austin and
Fayette Counties*
Office of District Attorney
County Courthouse, Box
171
Hempstead 77423
713-826-3335

City Offices

Austin
Consumer-Vendor Affairs
Office
City Attorney's Office
Municipal Bldg.
Austin 78767
512-477-6511

Dallas
Department of Consumer
Affairs
City Hall, Rm. 108
Dallas 75201
214-744-1133

TEXAS *(cont.)*

City Offices (cont.)

Fort Worth
Office of Consumer
Affairs
Weights and
Measures
1800 University Dr., Rm.
218
Fort Worth 76107
817-335-7211, ext. 209

San Antonio
Office of Consumer
Services
Department of Human
Resources
600 Hemisfair Way, Bldg.
249
San Antonio 78205
512-226-4301

UTAH

State Offices
Consumer Protection
Division
Office of Attorney
General
236 State Capitol
Salt Lake City 84114
801-533-6261

Uniform Consumer Credit
Code
Dept. of Financial
Institutions
10 W. Broadway, Suite 331
Salt Lake City 84101
801-533-5461 (consumer
credit only)

Division of Consumer
Affairs
Utah Trade Commission
Department of Business
Regulation
330 E. Fourth South
Salt Lake City 84111
801-533-6441

VERMONT

State Offices

Consumer Fraud Division
Office of Attorney
General
200 Main St., P. O. Box
981
Burlington 05401
802–862–6730
802–658–4353

Dept. of Banking and
Insurance
State Office Bldg.
120 State St.
Montpelier 05602
802–828–3301 (insurance
only)

Consumer Affairs Division
Vermont Public Service
Board
120 State St.
Montpelier 05602
802–828–2332

County Offices

Chittenden County

Economic Crime Division
County State's Attorney's
Office
39 Pearl St., P. O. Box 27
Burlington 05401
802–863–2865

VIRGIN ISLANDS

Consumer Services
Adminis.
Office of the Governor
Golden Rock Shopping
Center
Christiansted, St. Croix
00820
809–773–2226

Deputy Attorney General
Department of Law
P. O. Box 280, Charlotte
Amalie
St. Thomas 08801
809–774–1163

VIRGINIA

State Offices

Division of Consumer
Counsel
Office of Attorney
General
Supreme Court Bldg.
825 E. Broad St.
Richmond 23219
804–786–2042

Office of Consumer
Affairs
Dept. of Agriculture and
Commerce
825 E. Broad St.
Richmond 23219
804–786–2042
800–552–9963 (regarding
state agencies)

Branch Office

8301 Arlington Blvd.
Fairfax 22030
703–573–1286

Consumer Services &
Marketing
Department of Insurance
Blanton Bldg., 6th Fl.
Governor & Blank sts.
P. O. Box 1157
Richmond 23209
804–770–7691 (insurance
only)

County Offices

Arlington County

Office of Consumer
Affairs
2049 15th St., N.
Arlington 22201
703–558–2142

Fairfax County

Dept. of Consumer Affairs
Erlich Bldg., Suite 402
4031 University Dr.
Fairfax 22030
703–691–3214

Prince William County

Office of Consumer
Affairs
Garfield Adminis. Bldg.

VIRGINIA *(cont.)*

Prince William Cty. (cont.)

15920 Jefferson Davis
Hwy.
Woodbridge 22191
703–221–4156

City Offices

Alexandria

Office of Consumer
Affairs
405 Cameron St.
Alexandria 22314
703–750–6675 or 6697

Newport News

Office of Consumer
Affairs
City Hall, 2400 Wash. Ave.
Newport News 23607
804–247–8616 or 8618

Norfolk

Division of Consumer
Protection
City Hall Bldg., Rm. 804
Norfolk 23501
804–441–2821

Virginia Beach

Bureau of Consumer
Protection
Municipal Center, City
Hall
Virginia Beach 23456
804–427–4421

WASHINGTON

State Offices

Consumer Protection and
Antitrust Division
Office of Attorney
General
1266 Dexter Horton Bldg.
710 Second Ave.
Seattle 98104
206–464–7744
800–552–0700

Branch Offices

Consumer Prot. Division
Temple of Justice
Olympia 98504
206–753–6200

WASHINGTON (cont.)

Branch Offices (cont.)

Spokane Office of
Attorney General
1305 Old Nat'l Bank Bldg.
Spokane 99201
509–456–3123

Office of Attorney
General
116 South 9th St.
Tacoma 98402
206–593–2904

Office of Consumer
Services
Department of
Agriculture
406 General Adminis.
Bldg.
Olympia 98504
206–753–0929 (food,
agricultural products,
poison prevention only)

Branch Offices

2505 S. McClellan
Seattle 98144
206–464–6730

N. 811 Jefferson St.
Room 113
Spokane 99201
509–456–4057

County Offices

King County

Fraud Div.
County Prosecutor's
Office
C517 King County
Courthouse
516 Third Ave.
Seattle 98104
206–344–7350

City Offices

Everett

Weights and Measures
Dept.
City Hall, 3002 Wetmore
Ave.
Everett 98201
206–259–8845

WASHINGTON (cont.)

City Offices (cont.)

Seattle

Dept. of Licenses and
Consumer Affairs
Municipal Bldg., Rm. 102
600 Fourth Ave.
Seattle 98104
206–583–4346
206–583–6060 (complaint
line)

WEST VIRGINIA

State Offices

Consumer Protection
Division
Office of Attorney
General
State Capitol Bldg.
Charleston 25305
304–348–8986

Consumer Protection
Division
Department of Labor
1900 Washington St., E.
Charleston 25305
304–348–7890 (weights
and measures, bedding,
upholstery, mobile
homes, safety only)

Consumer Protection
Division
Department of
Agriculture
State Capitol, Rm. E-111
Charleston 25305
305–348–2226 (food,
agriculture products
only)

City Offices

Charleston

Consumer Protection
Dept.
P. O. Box 2749
Charleston 25330
304–348–8173

WISCONSIN

State Offices

Governor's Council for
Consumer Affairs
V29E Capitol
Madison 53702
608–266–3104

Attorney General
Office of Consumer
Protection
Department of Justice
State Capitol
Madison 53702
608–266–1852

Branch Office

Office of Consumer
Protection
Milwaukee State Office
Bldg.
819 N. 6th St., Rm. 520
Milwaukee 53203
414–224–1867

Bur. of Consumer Prot.
Trade Division
Dept. of Agriculture
801 W. Badger Rd.
Madison 53713
608–266–7228

Branch Offices

Central District Office
801 W. Badger Rd.
Madison 53713
608–266–7228

Northwest District Office
1727 Loring St.
Altoona 54720
715–836–2846

Northeast District Office
1181A Western Ave.
Green Bay 54303
414–494–4787

Southeast District Office
8500 W. Capitol Dr.
Milwaukee 53222
414–464–8580

County Offices

Kenosha County

District Attorney's Office
County Courthouse

WISCONSIN (cont.)

Kenosha County (cont.)

Kenosha 53140
414–657–5135

Marathon County

District Attorney's Office
Wausau 54401
715–842–2141, ext. 242

Milwaukee County

Consumer Fraud Division
District Attorney's Office
Safety Bldg., Rm. 406E
821 W. State St.
Milwaukee 53233
414–278–4792

WISCONSIN (cont.)

Portage County

Director, Consumer Fraud
Unit
District Attorney's Office
Stevens Point 54481
715–346–3393

Racine County

Consumer Fraud Division
District Attorney's Office
730 Wisconsin Ave.
Racine 53403
414–636–3125

WYOMING

State Offices

Office of Attorney
General
Capitol Bldg.
Cheyenne 82002
307–777–7384

Consumer Credit Code
Supreme Court Bldg.
Cheyenne 82002
307–777–7797 (consumer
credit only)

Source: U.S. Office of Consumer Affairs, Washington, D.C. 20201, September 1976.

DIRECTORY OF CALL FOR ACTION (CFA) OFFICES
AND OTHER BROADCAST MEDIA "ACTION" RESOURCES

City	Station*	Phone Number	Hours
Akron, Ohio	WAKR CFA	216–384–8888	11 A.M.–1 P.M.
Albany, N. Y.	WROW CFA	518–462–6445	11 A.M.–1 P.M.
Albuquerque, N. M.	KOB CFA	505–842–1224	11 A.M.–1 P.M.
Altoona, Pa.	WFBG CFA	814–944–9336	1 P.M.–3 P.M.; 7–9 P.M. Thurs.
Atlanta, Ga.	WGST CFA	404–231–1888	11 A.M.–1 P.M.
Baltimore, Md.	WBAL CFA	301–366–5900	11 A.M.–1 P.M.
Birmingham, Ala.	WYDE CFA	205–323–1668	10 A.M.–12 noon; 6–8 P.M. Wed.
Boston, Mass.	WBZ CFA	617–787–2300	11 A.M.–1 P.M.
Buffalo, N. Y.	WBEN CFA	716–876–1700	10 A.M.–12 noon
Chicago, Ill.	WIND CFA	312–644–0560	11 A.M.–1 P.M.
Cleveland, Ohio	WERE CFA	216–861–0235	10 A.M.–12 noon
Dallas/Fort Worth, Tex.	WBAP CFA		open 1977
Decatur, Ill.	WDZ CFA	217–428–1050	11 A.M.–1 P.M.
Denver, Colo.	KLZ CFA	303–759–2285	11 A.M.–1 P.M.
Detroit, Mich.	WJR CFA	313–873–8700	11 A.M.–1 P.M.
Durham, N. C.	WRAL-TV CFA	919–688–9306	11 A.M.–1 P.M.
Fort Wayne, Ind.	WOWO CFA	219–742–7277	10 A.M.–1 P.M.
Houston, Tex.	KHOU CFA		open 1977
Jacksonville, Fla.	WTLV-TV CFA	904–354–1858	11 A.M.–1 P.M.
Kansas City, Mo.	KCMO CFA		open 1977
Little Rock, Ark.	KARK-TV CFA	501–376–4441	9:30 A.M.–12 noon
Los Angeles, Calif.	KFWB CFA	213–461–4366	11 A.M.–1 P.M.
Memphis, Tenn.	WDIA CFA	901–278–6316	11 A.M.–1 P.M.
Miami, Fla.	WCIX-TV CFA	305–371–6566	11 A.M.–1 P.M.
Montreal, Quebec/Can.	CFCF CFA	514–273–1793	11 A.M.–1 P.M.
New Bedford, Mass.	WBSM CFA	617–997–2618	11 A.M.–1 P.M.
New Haven, Conn.	WELI CFA	203–281–1011	9:30 A.M.–11:30 A.M.
New York, N. Y.	WMCA CFA	212–586–6666	11 A.M.–1 P.M.
Niagara Falls/ St. Catherines, Ontario/Can.	CJRN CFA		open 1977
Oklahoma City, Okla.	KWTV CFA	405–848–2212	11 A.M.–1 P.M.
Omaha, Nebr.	WOW CFA	402–346–6300	11 A.M.–1 P.M.

City	Station*	Phone Number	Hours
Orlando, Fla.	WDBO CFA	305–841–8181	11 A.M.–1 P.M.
Peoria, Ill.	WRAU-TV CFA	309–699–7219	11 A.M.–1 P.M.
Philadelphia, Pa.	WFIL CFA	215–477–5312	11 A.M.–1 P.M.
Phoenix, Ariz.	KTAR-TV CFA	602–263–8856	24 hours/ 7 days a week
Pittsburgh, Pa.	KDKA CFA	412–333–9370	11 A.M.–1 P.M.
Providence, R. I.	WJAR CFA	401–274–2340	10 A.M.–12 noon
Raleigh, N. C.	WRAL-TV CFA	919–832–7578	11 A.M.–1 P.M.
Richmond, Va.	WLEE CFA		open 1977
St. Louis, Mo.	KMOX CFA	314–421–1975	11 A.M.–1 P.M.
Salt Lake City, Utah	KSL CFA	801–524–2555	11 A.M.–1 P.M.
San Diego, Calif.	KGTV CFA	714–263–2294	10 A.M.–1 P.M.
Suffolk County, N. Y.	WGSM CFA	516–423–1400	11 A.M.–1 P.M.
Syracuse, N. Y.	WHEN CFA	315–474–7441	11 A.M.–1 P.M.
Tucson, Ariz.	KTKT CFA	602–881–4440	10 A.M.–1 P.M.
Utica/Rome, N. Y.	WTLB CFA	315–797–0120	10 A.M.–2 P.M.
Washington, D.C.	WTOP CFA	202–686–6924	11 A.M.–1 P.M.
Wheeling, W. Va.	WWVA CFA	304–233–6060	11 A.M.–1 P.M.
Youngstown, Ohio	WFMJ CFA	216–744–5155	11 A.M.–1 P.M.

Source: Call for Action, 1785 Massachusetts Ave., N.W., Washington, D.C. 20036, April, 1977.
*Call letters indicate a radio station unless accompanied by the letters "TV."

STATIONS NOT AFFILIATED WITH CALL FOR ACTION THAT HAVE "ACTION" REPORTERS TO HELP INDIVIDUAL CONSUMERS

Mail your written complaint to the address listed and include a stamped, self-addressed envelope.

CALIFORNIA

KNBC–TV "Action 4"
P.O. Box 4444
Burbank 91505

KABC Ombudsman Service
3321 S. La Cienega Blvd.
Los Angeles 90016

KGFJ, Bob Howard and Bob Felix
5900 Wilshire Blvd., Suite 330
Los Angeles 90036

KNX Action Reporter
6121 W. Sunset Blvd.
Los Angeles 90028

CALIFORNIA (cont.)

Action Report
TV 8, 1405 Fifth Ave.
San Diego 92101

KCBS "File 74"
1 Embarcadero
San Francisco 94111
Phone: 415–982–7000

DISTRICT OF COLUMBIA

WRC–TV "Contact 4"
Box 4
Washington, DC 20044

GEORGIA

WAGA–TV Troubleshooter
1551 Briarcliff Rd. N.E.
P.O. Box 4207
Atlanta 30302
Phone: 404–876–4357—Calls accepted
  24–hour line

ILLINOIS

WLS–TV "Action 7"
190 N. State St.
Chicago 60601

LOUISIANA

Action Reporter
WVUE–TV
1025 S. Jefferson Davis Pky.
P.O. Box 13847
New Orleans 70185

MICHIGAN

Troubleshooter
WJBK–TV
#2 Storer Pl.
Southfield 48075

MINNESOTA

WCCO–TV "Action News"
50 S. Ninth St.
Minneapolis 55402

NEW YORK

WNBC–TV Action 4
Box 4000
Radio City Sta.
New York 10019

WNET–TV "Consumer Help"
356 W. 58th St.
New York 10019
Phone: 212–262–5555—Calls preferred
  (Mon.–Thur. 10 A.M.–1 P.M.)

WNEW–TV Action Reporter
Channel 5 News
205 E. 67th St.
New York 10021

TEXAS

KTRK–TV Action 13
P.O. Box 13
Houston 77001

UTAH

KSL–TV "Action Reporter"
145 Social Hall Ave.
Salt Lake City 84111
Phone: 801–524–2690—Calls accepted
  (Mon.–Fri. 9 A.M.–6 P.M.)

Source. Compiled by Kenneth Eisenberger, 1976, with prior assistance from Michael Mattice.

DIRECTORY OF
NEWSPAPER CONSUMER ACTION SERVICES

ALABAMA

"Action Line"
Birmingham Post Herald
2200 N. Fourth Ave.
Birmingham 35202

"Action Line"
Daily
P.O. Box 1527
Decatur 35601

"Action/Hot Line"
Mobile Press Register
304 Government St.
Mobile 36630

ALASKA

"Action Line"
Anchorage Times
820 Fourth Ave.
Anchorage 99501

ARIZONA

"Action Line"
Douglas Dispatch
530-11th St.
Douglas 85607

"Answer Line"
Phoenix Gazette
120 E. Van Euren St.
Phoenix 85004

"The Ombudsman"
Arizona Star
P.O. Box 26887
Tucson 85726

"Action Please!"
Tucson Daily Citizen
P.O. Box 26887
Tucson 85726

ARKANSAS

"Action Line"
Blytheville Courier News
P.O. Box 1108
Blytheville 72315

ARKANSAS (cont.)

"Answer Please"
Arkansas Democrat
Capitol Ave. & Scott
Little Rock 72203

"Action Line"
Newport Independent
308 Second St.
Newport 72112

"Action Line"
Commercial
300 Beech St.
Pine Bluff 71601

CALIFORNIA

"Barstow Briefs"
Desert Dispatch
130 Coolwater St.
Barstow 92313

"Probe"
Brawley News
617 Main St.
Brawley 92227

"Rap-Up"
Concord Transcript
P.O. Box 308
Concord 94522

"Action Line"
Corning Daily Observer
P.O. Box 558
Corning 96021

"Action Line"
Daily Pilot
330 W. Bay St.
Costa Mesa 93721

"Action Line"
Oakland Tribune
401 - 13th St.
Oakland 94612

"Fact Finder"
Fresno Bee
1559 Van Ness Ave.
Fresno 93721

"Action Line"

CALIFORNIA (cont.)

P.O. Box A
Garden Grove

"Question Box"
Hanford Sentinel
418 W. 8th St., P.O. Box 9
Hanford 93230

"Probe"
Daily News
45-14 Towne Ave.
P.O. Drawer NNN
Indio 92201

"Action Line"
Twin Coast Newspapers, Inc.
604 Pine Ave.
Long Beach 90844

"Answer Line"
Herald-Examiner
1111 S. Broadway
P.O. Box 2416
Los Angeles 90051

"Contact"
Daily Report
212 E. "B" St.
Ontario 91764

"Action"
Mercury-Register
P.O. Box 651
Oroville 95965

"Action Line"
Star-News
525 E. Colorado Blvd.
Pasadena 91109

"Action Line"
Progress-Bulletin
P.O. Box 2708
Pomona 91766

"Action Line"
Tribune
901 Marshall St.
Redwood Ctiy 94063

"Action Man"
Richmond Independent
164-10th St.
Richmond 94801

CALIFORNIA (cont.)

"Fact Finder"
Sacramento Bee
P.O. Box 15779
Sacramento 95813

"Action Line"
Californian
613 W. Main
El Cahon 92020

Pat Dunn
Orange Coast Pilot
P.O. Box 1875
Newport Beach 92663

"Action Desk"
Salinas Californian
123 W. Alisal St.
Salinas 93901

"Help"
Sun-Telegram
399 "D" St.
San Bernadino 92401

"Action Line"
Evening Tribune
350 Camino de la Reina
San Diego 92108

"Action Line"
San Jose Mercury News
750 Ridder Park Dr.
San Jose 95190

"Help"
Times & News Leader
1080 Amphlett Blvd.
San Mateo 94402

"The Trouble Shooter"
Santa Ana Register
625 N. Grand Ave.
Santa Ana 92711

"Trouble Shooter"
Evening Outlook
1540 Third St.
Santa Monica 90406

COLORADO

"Action Line"
Sun
103 W. Colorado Ave.
Colorado Springs 80902

"Slope Action"
Daily Sentinel
730 S. Seventh Street

COLORADO (cont.)

P.O. Box 668
Grand Junction 81501

"Action Line"
Times-Call
717 Fourth Ave.
Longmont 80501

"Around the Valley"
Reporter Herald
450 Cleveland
Loveland 80537

CONNECTICUT

"Action Line"
News-Times
333 Main St.
Danbury 06810

"Dear George"
Hartford Times
10 Prospect St.
Hartford 06101

DELAWARE

"Action Line"
Delaware State News
P.O. Box 737
Dover 19901

DISTRICT OF COLUMBIA

"Action Line"
Washington Post
1515 "L" St., N.W.
Washington, D.C. 20005

"Action Line"
Star-News
225 Virginia Ave., S.E.
Washington, D.C. 20061

FLORIDA

"The Helper"
News
34 S.E. Second St.
Boca Raton 33432

"Action Line"
Herald
401 - 13th St. W.
Bradenton 33505

"Help"
Cocoa Today
P.O. Box 1330
Cocoa 32922

FLORIDA (cont.)

"Reader's Line"
News-Press
Box 10
Fort Meyers 33902

"Action Line"
Sun
101 S.E. 2nd Pl.
Gainesville 32602

"Live Wire"
News Leader
P.O. Box 339
Homestead 33030

"Call Box"
Jacksonville Journal
P.O. Box 1949
Jacksonville 32201

"Action Line Reporter"
Ledger
P.O. Box 408
Lakeland 33802

"Action Line"
Miami Herald
Herald Plaza
Miami 33101

"For Your Information"
News
1075 Central Ave.
Naples 33940

"Independent Action"
Times
P.O. Box 1121
St. Petersburg 33731

"Hot Line"
Herald-Tribune/Journal
P.O. Box 1719
Sarasota 33578

"Action Line"
Democrat
277 N. Magnolia Dr.
Tallahassee 32302

"Troubleshooter"
Tribune & Times
507 East J. F. Kennedy
Blvd.
Tampa 33602

GEORGIA

"Action One"
Banner-Herald

GEORGIA *(cont.)*

One Press Pl.
Athens 30601

"Consumer Interest"
Journal-Constitution
72 Marietta St., N.W.
Atlanta 30303

"Action Line"
Enquirer-Ledger
17 W. 12th St.
Columbus 31902

"Action/Hot Line"
Journal
580 Fairground St.
Marietta 30060

"Action Line"
Macon News
120 Broadway
Macon 31201

"Times Line"
Times
Thompson Newspapers,
Inc.
Valdosta 31601

HAWAII

"Miss Fixit"
Advertiser
605 Kapiolani Blvd.
P.O. Box 3350
Honolulu 96801

"The Kokua Line"
Star Bulletin
605 Kapiolani Blvd.
P.O. Box 3350
Honolulu 96801

IDAHO

"Action Post"
Idaho Statesman
1200 N. Curtis Rd.
P.O. Box 40
Boise 83707

"Action Line"
South Idaho Press
230 E. Main St.
Burley 83318

"Action Forum"
Tribune
505 "C" St.
Lewiston 83501

IDAHO *(cont.)*

"Rap"
Idaho Free Press
316 - 10th Ave.
S. Nampa 83651

ILLINOIS

"Mr. Answer Man"
Evening Telegraph
111 E. Broadway
Alton 62002

"At Your Service"
Ledger
53 W. Elm St.
Canton 61520

"Action Line"
Chicago Tribune
435 N. Michigan Ave.
Chicago 60611

"Action Line"
Commercial News
17 W. North St.
Danville 61832

"Quest"
Herald & Review
365 N. Main St., P.O. Box
311
Decatur 62525

"Penny For Your
Thoughts"
Register-Mail
140 S. Prairie
Galesburg 61401

"For the Record"
Record
1209 State St., P.O. Box
559
Lawrenceville 62439

"Times Ticker"
Times
110 W. Jefferson St.
Ottawa 61350

"Help"
Register Public
99 E. State St.
Rockford 61105

"J-R Line"
State Journal-Register
313 S. 6th St.
Springfield 62705

INDIANA

"Hot Line"
Herald-Telephone
1900 S. Walnut St.
Bloomington 47401

"Times Line"
Times
119-121 E. National Ave.
Brazil 47834

"Truth Line"
Elkhart Truth
Communicana Bldg.
Elkhart 46514

"Action Line"
Journal-Gazette
701 S. Clinton St.
Fort Wayne 46802

"Monday Mini's"
Herald-Press
7 N. Jefferson
Huntington 46750

"Intercom"
Indianapolis Star
307 N. Pennsylvania St.
Indianapolis 46206

"Action Line"
Tribune
300 N. Union
Kokomo 46901

"Help"
Journal & Courier
217 N. 6th St.
Lafayette 47901

"H-Action Line"
Herald-Argus
701 State St.
La Porte 46350

"Live Wire"
Reporter
117 E. Washington
Lebanon 46052

"Answer Line"
Pharos-Tribune & Press
517 E. Broadway
Logansport 46947

"Do-Line"
News Dispatch
121 W. Michigan Blvd.
Michigan City 46360

"Action Line"
Tribune

INDIANA (cont.)

225 W. Colfax
South Bend 46626

IOWA

"Action Line"
Telegraph-Herald
W. 8th & Bluff sts.
P.O. Box 668
Dubuque 52001

"Survival Line"
Iowan
111 Communications
Center
University of Iowa
Iowa City 52240

"Action"
Journal
6th & Pavonia
Sioux City 51105

"Amblin"
Freeman Journal
720 Second St.
Webster City 50595

KANSAS

"Ask the Kansan"
Kansan
901 N. 8th St.
Kansas City 66101

"Needlepoint"
Times
416-22 Seneca
Leavenworth 66048

"Let's Ask"
Capitol-Journal
6th & Jefferson
Topeka 66607

KENTUCKY

"Line That Roars"
Park City News
813 College St.
Bowling Green 42101

"Lemme Doit"
Times
525 W. Broadway
Louisville 40202

"Hot Line"
Messenger
221 S. Main St.
Madisonville 42431

LOUISIANA

"Action Line"
Town Talk
Main at Washington sts.
P.O. Box 7558
Alexandria 71301

"Action, Please"
Advocate-State Times
525 Lafayette St.
Baton Rouge 70821

"Hot Line"
News
525 Ave. V
P.O. Box 820
Bogalusa 70427

"Hot Line"
Post-Herald
602 N. Parkerson Ave.
Crowley 70526

"The People's Choice"
Star
200 S. W. Railroad Ave.
P.O. Box 1319
Hammond 70401

"Action Corner"
Advertiser
219 Jefferson St.
Lafayette 70501

"Action Line"
Times-Picayune
3800 Howard Ave.
New Orleans 70140

"Hot Line"
World
127 N. Market St.
P.O. Box 1179
Opelousas 70570

"Action Line"
Journal
222 Lake St.
Shreveport 71130

MAINE

"Help"
Press Herald
390 Congress St.
Portland 04111

MARYLAND

"Mainline for Action"
News American

MARYLAND (cont.)

Lombard & South sts.
Baltimore 21203

"Direct Line"
Sun
Calvert & Centre sts.
Baltimore 21203

"Action Line"
News-Times
7-9 S. Mechanic St.
Cumberland 21502

"Action Line"
*Morning Herald & Daily
Mail*
25-31 Summit Ave.
Eagerstown 21740

MASSACHUSETTS

"Ask the Globe"
Boston Globe
Boston 02107

"Action Line"
Herald-American
300 Harrison Ave.
Boston 02106

"Sentry Line"
Sentinel
808 Main St.
Fitchburg 01420

"Open Ear"
Hyde Park Tribune
1205 Hyde Park Ave.
Hyde Park 02736

"Write-In"
Standard Times
555 Pleasant St.
New Bedford 02742

"You Asked For It"
Gazette
5-9 Cohannet St.
Taunton 02780

MICHIGAN

"Action Please!"
News
340 E. Huron St.
Ann Arbor 48106

"Action Line"
Enquirer & News.
155 W. Van Buren St.
Battle Creek 49016

MICHIGAN (cont.)

"Action Line"
Detroit Free Press
321 W. Lafayette Blvd.
Detroit 48231

"Hot Stuff"
Fenton Independent
125 S. Leroy St.
Fenton 48430

"Pinchhitter"
Press
Press Plaza
Vandenberg Center
Grand Rapids 49502

"Action, Please!"
Citizen Patriot
214 S. Jackson St.
Jackson 49204

"Oakland Hot Line"
Oakland Press
48 W. Huron St.
P.O. Box 9
Pontiac 48056

"Help"
Times Herald
907 Sixth St.
Port Huron 48060

"Community Action"
Press
20 E. Michigan Ave.
Ypsilanti 48197

MINNESOTA

"Question Mart"
Pioneer
Bemidji

"Action Editor"
Duluth Budgeteer
5807 Grand Ave.
Duluth 55807

"Action Line"
Dispatch & Pioneer Press
55 E. 4th St.
St. Paul 55101

MISSISSIPPI

"Bo"
Commonwealth
207-09 W. Market
Greenwood 38930

MISSISSIPPI (cont.)

"Ask Jack Sunn"
Clarion-Ledger News
P.O. Box 40
Jackson 39205

"Keeping Posted"
Post
920 South St.
Vicksburg 39181

MISSOURI

"Show Me"
Missourian
311 S. Ninth St.
Columbia 65201

"Action Line"
Tribune
4th & Walnut sts.
Columbia 65201

"Action Line"
Daily Dunklin Democrat
212-4 Main St.
Kennett 63857

"Action Line Answers"
Ledger
Love & Washington sts.
Mexico 65265

"Action Line"
News
1006 W. Harmony
Neosho 64850

"Action Line"
News
101 W. 7th
Rolla 65401

"Hot Line"
Capital Democrat
Seventh St., and
   Massachusetts Ave.
Sedalia 65301

"Action"
News, Leader & Press
651 Boonville
Springfield 65801

NEBRASKA

"Action Desk"
Tribune
P.O. Box 9
Fremont 68025

NEBRASKA (cont.)

"Action Line"
Telegraph
315 E. 5th
North Platte 69101

"Action Editor"
World Herald
14th & Dodge sts.
Omaha 68102

"Gripe Pipe"
News Times
327 Platte Ave.
Box 512
York 68467

NEW JERSEY

"Trouble Shooter"
Press
Press Plaza
Asbury Park 07712

"Mr. Action"
Press
1900 Atlantic Ave
Atlantic City 08401

"Gotta Gripe"
Courier-Post
Camden 08101

"Action Line"
Daily Advance
87 E. Blackwell St.
Dover 07801

"Action Line"
Record
150 River St.
Hackensack 07602

"Speak Up"
Herald-News
988 Main Ave.
Passaic-Clifton 07055

"Help!"
Courier-News
P.O. Box 3600
Somerville 08876

"Action Line"
Trenton Times
500 Perry St.
Trenton 08605

NEW MEXICO

"Action Line"
Journal
7th & Silver S.W.
Albuquerque 87103

"Quien Sabe?"
New Mexican
202 E. Marcy
. Santa Fe 87501

NEW YORK

"Action Line"
Albany Times-Union
645 Albany-Shaker Rd.
Albany 12201

"That's a Good Question"
Citizen-Advertiser
25 Dill St.
Auburn 13021

"Action Line"
Sun-Bulletin
Vestal Parkway East
Binghampton 13902

"NEWSpower
Buffalo Evening News
1 News Plaza
Buffalo 14240

"Courier Action"
Courier-Express
787 Main St.
Buffalo 14240

"Observer Hotline"
Observer
8-10 E. 2nd St.
Dunkirk 14048

"Help!"
Star-Gazette
201 Baldwin St.
Elmira 14902

"Action Line"
Newsday
550 Stewart Ave.
Garden City,
Long Island 11530

"Help!"
Journal
123 W. State St.
Ithaca 14850

"Action"
Times Herald-Record
40 Mulberry St.
Middletown 10940

NEW YORK (cont.)

"Help!"
Gazette
310 Niagara St.
Niagara Falls 14302

"Action"
Rockland-Journal-News
53-55 Hudson Ave.
Nyack 10960

"Action Line"
Oneonta Star
102 Chestnut St.
Oneonta 13820

"Action Line"
Press-Republican
55 Clinton St.
Plattsburgh 12902

"Help!"
Democrat & Chronicle
55 Exchange St.
Rochester 14614

"Track Down"
Saratogian-Tri-County News
20 Lake Ave.
Saratoga Springs 12866

"Mr. Fixit"
Advance
950 Fingerboard Rd.
Staten Island 10305

"Help!"
Observer Dispatch
221 Oriskany Plaza
Utica 13503

"Help!"
Reporter-Dispatch
One Gannett Dr.
White Plains 10604

NORTH CAROLINA

"Quest"
Observer
600 S. Tyron St.
P.O. Box 2138
Charlotte 28201

"Mr. Trib."
Tribune
125 Union St.
S. Concord 28025

NORTH CAROLINA (cont.)

"Sun Dial"
Herald Sun
115-19 Market St.
Durham 27702

"Hot Line"
News Record
200-04 N. Davie St.
Greensboro 27402

"Action Line"
Enterprise
210 Church Ave.
High Point 27261

"Action Line"
Robesonian
121 W. 5th St.
Lumberton 28358

"Public Eye"
Review
116 N. Scales St.
Reidsville 27320

"Hotline"
Times
215 S. McDowell St.
Raleigh 27601

"Open Line"
Telegram
150 Howard St.
Rocky Mount 27801

"Ask Us"
Post
131 W. Innes St.
Salisbury 28144

"Action Linc"
Star-News
P.O. Box 840
Wilmington 28401

"Whiz Line"
Times
117 N. Goldsboro
Wilson 27893

"Answer Man"
Twin City Sentinel
416-20 N. Marshall
Winston-Salem 27102

NORTH DAKOTA

"Action Line"
Journal
3rd & 4th Ave.
Devil's Lake 58301

NORTH DAKOTA (cont.)

"Action Line"
Herald
14 W. 4th St.
Williston 58801

OHIO

"Action Line"
Beacon Journal
44 E. Exchange St.
Akron 44328

"Question Mart"
Times Gazette
40 E. 2nd St.
Ashland 44805

"Action Line"
Cincinatti Enquirer
617 Vine St.
Cincinatti 45201

"PDQuickline"
Plain Dealer
1801 Superior Ave.
Cleveland 44114

"Action Line"
Press
901 Lakeside Ave.
Cleveland 44114

"Action Line"
Journal Herald
4th & Ludlow sts.
Dayton 45401

"Action Line"
Crescent-News
Cor. Perry & 2nd sts.
Defiance 43512

"Action Line"
Journal-News
Court & Journal Sq.
Hamilton 45012

"Ask"
Tribune
324-328 Railroad
Ironton 45638

"Here's the Answer"
Times
201 E. Columbus St.
Kenton 43326

"Hot Line"
News Journal
70 W. Fourth St.
Mansfield 44901

OHIO (cont.)

"Hot Line"
Times-Reporter
629 Wabash Ave.
New Philadelphia 44663

"Here's Your Answer"
Times
35 W. State St.
Niles 44446

"ZIP Line"
Times-Blade
541 Superior St.
Toledo 43660

"Action Line"
News
8 Willipic St.
Wapakoneta 45895

"Hot Line"
News-Herald
38879 Mentor Ave.
Willoughby 44094

OKLAHOMA

"Action Line"
Times
500 N. Broadway
P.O. Box 25125
Oklahoma City 73125

"Action Line"
Tulsa Daily World
P.O. Box 1770
Tulsa 74102

OREGON

"I'd Like to Know"
Mail Tribune
33 N. Fir St.
P.O. Box 1108
Medford 97501

PENNSYLVANIA

"Action Line"
Inquirer
400 N. Broad St.
Philadelphia 19101

"Action Line"
Globe-Times
202 W. Fourth St.
Bethlehem 18016

PENNSYLVANIA (cont.)

"Round the Square"
Era
43 Main St.
Bradford 16701

"Mirror of Public
  Opinion"
News
341 Chestnut St.
Columbia 17512

"Jottings"
Courier Express
Long at High sts.
DuBois 15801

"Action Express"
Express
30 N. Fourth St.
Easton 18042

"Action Line"
Ledger
835 Lawrence Ave.
Ellwood City 16117

"The Public Eye"
*Intelligencer Journal & New
  Era*
8 W. King St.
Lancaster 17604

"Mr. Fixit"
Bulletin
30th & Market sts.
Philadelphia 19101

"Action Line"
Pottsville Republican
111-113 Mahantongo St.
Pottsville 17901

"Action Line"
News-Item
701-709 N. Rock
Shamokin 17872

"Action Line"
Daily Item
200 Market St.
Sunbury 17801

"Action"
Observer-Reporter
122 S. Main St.
Washington 15301

RHODE ISLAND

"Ask Us"
Journal & Bulletin

RHODE ISLAND *(cont.)*

75 Fountain St.
Providence 02902

SOUTH CAROLINA

"Action Line"
Piedmont
305 S. Main St.
Greensville 29602

"Information Please"
Item
20 N. Magnolia St.
Sumter 29150

SOUTH DAKOTA

"Action Line"
Plainsman
49 E. 3rd
Huron 57350

"Action Line"
Journal
507 Main
Rapid City 57701

TENNESSEE

"DP Action Line"
Post-Athenian
320 S. Jackson St.
Athens 37303

"Searchlight"
Greenville Sun
200 S. Main St.
Greenville 33743

"Action Line"
Times-News
701 Lynn Garden Drive
P.O. Box 479
Kingsport 37662

"General Knox"
News Sentinel
208 W. Church Ave.
Knoxville 37901

"Action Line"
Times
307 E. Harper
Maryville 37801

"Action Please!"
Commercial Appeal
495 Union Ave.
Memphis 38101

TENNESSEE *(cont.)*

"Readers Ask, 'Help' "
Nashville Banner
1100 Broadway
Nashville 37202

TEXAS

"Action Line"
Reporter News
100 Block Cypress St.
Abilene 79604

"Action Line"
News
Box 1087
Arlington 76010

"High School Hot Line"
Herald
710 Scurry
Big Spring 79720

"Howdy Folks"
Times-Review
108 S. Anglin
Cleburne 76031

"Action Line"
Sun
405 E. Collin
Corsicana 75110

"Action Line"
Times
820 Lower Broadway
Corpus Christic 78401

"Action Line"
Dallas Times Herald
1101 Pacific
Dallas 75202

"Contact 33"
Record-Chronicle
314 E. Hickory
Denton 76201

"Action Desk"
Press
507 Jones
Fort Worth 76102

"Action Line"
Star-Telegram
P.O. Box 1870
Fort Worth 76101

"Open Line"
Register & Messenger
306 E. California
Gainesville 76240

TEXAS *(cont.)*

"Watchem"
Houston Chronicle
801 Texas St.
Houston 77002

"Action Line"
Houston Post
4747 Southwest Freeway
Houston 77001

"Duty Watch"
Times
P.O. Box 29
Laredo 78040

"Box 7-8-9"
News
549 - 4th St.
Port Arthur 77640

"Rumor Column"
Standard-Times
34 W. Harris
San Angelo 76901

"Express & Hot Line"
Express & Evening News
Ave. E & 3rd St.
San Antonio 78206

"Action Line"
Light
McCullough & Broadway
San Antonio 78206

"Hot Line"
Sun
P.O. Box 2249
Texas City 77590

UTAH

"Do-It Man"
Deseret News
Box 1257
Salt Lake City 84110

VIRGINIA

"Hot Line"
Herald Courier and
Virginia-Tennessean
320 Morrison Blvd.
Bristol 24201

"Action Line"
Progress
413 E. Market St.
Charlottesville 22902

VIRGINIA (cont.)

"Action Line"
Free Lance-Star
616 Amelia St.
P.O. Box 617
Fredericksburg 22401

"Question Line"
Times-Herald & Press
7505 Warwick Blvd.
Newport News 23607

"Action Line"
Ledger-Star
150 W. Brambleton Ave.
Norfolk 23501

"Action Dial"
Southwest Times
223 N. Washington Ave.
P.O. Box 391
Pulaski 24301

"Quick Line"
Times & World-News
201-09 W. Campbell Ave.
Roanoke 24010

"The Zip Line"
Virginia Gazette
Williamsburg 23185

WASHINGTON

"Ask Captain Clallam"
News
305 W. First
Port Angeles 98362

WASHINGTON (cont.)

"Action"
Post-Intelligencer
Sixth & Wall
Seattle 98111

"Troubleshooter"
Seattle Times
Fairview Ave N. & John
P.O. Box 70
Seattle 98111

"Action Corner"
Spokesman Review
W. 927 Riverside
Spokane 99253

"Action Line"
Herald Republic
114 N. Fourth St.
Yakima

WEST VIRGINIA

"Hotline"
Mail
1001 Virginia St., E.
Charleston 25301

"Action Line"
Huntington Advertiser
Box 2016
Huntington 25720

WEST VIRGINIA (cont.)

"Ridge Runner"
News
125 Wyoming St.
Welch 24801

WISCONSIN

"Action Line"
News
149 State St.
Beloit 53511

"Action Line"
Reporter
18 W. First St.
Fond du Lac 54935

"Ask the Journal"
Journal
333 W. State St.
Journal Square
Milwaukee 53201

"Speak Up"
Daily Herald
800 Scott St.
Wasau 54401

WYOMING

"Bob Peck's Column"
Ranger
Box 993
Riverton 82501

Source: Compiled, 1975, by Kenneth Eisenberger and Leora Brown, from *Editor & Publisher Year Book* (1975), 850 Third Avenue, New York City, and with prior assistance from Michael Mattice.

COMPARISON OF SMALL CLAIMS COURTS
IN THE UNITED STATES

The chart on the following eight pages compares Small Claims Courts in the United States. See page 363 for footnotes.

State	Name of Court	Maximum Amount of Claim	Filing Fees*
ALABAMA	Small Claims docket of District Court	$500	$10
ALASKA	District Court	$1,000	$15
ARIZONA	Justice of the Peace Court	$200 exclusive; $1,000 concurrent with Superior Court	$3
ARKANSAS	Municipal Court, Civil Div.	$100 personal property; $300 open accounts, contracts, etc.	$5.60 to $7.15
CALIFORNIA	Small Claims Div. of Municipal Court	$500	$2
COLORADO	Small Claims Court	$500	$9
CONNECTICUT	Small Claims Div. of Court of Common Pleas	$750	$6
DELAWARE	Justice of the Peace Courts or Magistrate Courts	$1,500	$15 to $35
FLORIDA	Small Claims or Civil Div. of County Courts	$2,500	$3.50 to $15
GEORGIA**	Small Claims Div. of Civil Court of Fulton County	$299.99	$7 for claim under $100; $13 for claim over $100
HAWAII	Small Claims Div. of District Court of the First Circuit	$300 (may be exceded in cases involving rental security deposits)	$5
IDAHO	Small Claims Depts. of District Courts	$500	$5
ILLINOIS	Small Claims Div. of Circuit Court	$300 to $1,000	7 to $10
INDIANA	Circuit or County courts, small claims dockets	$1,500	$10 plus expenses
IOWA	Small Claims Court	$1,000	$5 to $6
KANSAS	County Magistrate Court	$300	$5

May Attorney Represent?	Appeal By Defendant Possible?	Appeal By Plaintiff Possible?	On Appeal Attorney Is:	Appeal Claims Go to:
Yes	Yes	Yes	Preferable	Circuit Court
Yes	Yes	Yes	Preferable	Superior Court
Yes	Yes	Yes	Possible	Superior Court
Yes	Yes	Yes	Preferable	Circuit Court
No	Yes	No	Possible	Superior Court
Yes	No	No		
Yes	Only if case claimed for regular docket	No	Possible	Case may be transferred to civil docket by defendant
Yes	Yes	Yes	Preferable	Varies, usually to Superior Court
Yes	Yes	Yes	Preferable	Circuit Court
Yes	Yes	Yes	Possible	Appellate Div. of Civil Court
Yes (unless the disagreement concerns a rental security deposit)	No	No		
No	Yes	Yes	Possible	District Court
Yes (in Cook County, defendants only)	Yes	Yes	Preferable	Appellate Court
Yes	Yes	Yes	Preferable	Indiana Court of Appeals
Yes	Yes	Yes	Preferable	District Court
No	Yes	Yes	Preferable	

State	Name of Court	Maximum Amount of Claim	Filing Fees*
KENTUCKY (only one Small Claims Court in state)	Div. of Small Claims Jefferson Quarterly Court, Louisville	$500	$1.50 plus $5 sheriff's service fee (cases involving over $50 require additional $15 tax)
LOUISIANA	City Court, Justice of the Peace Court, State District Court	$300 in Justice of the Peace and city courts (except New Orleans—max. $25); $100 in State District Courts	$5 to $15 (higher in a few courts)
MAINE	District Court	$800	$5
MARYLAND	Small Claims Div. of District Court	$500	$2 to $5 for first defendant, $4 for ea. additional defendant
MASSACHUSETTS	District Courts of Mass. Boston Municipal Court, Boston Housing Court, Hampden County Housing Court	$400 (to be raised)	$3
MICHIGAN	Small Claims Div. of District Court or Municipal Court; Conciliation Div. of Common Please Court of Wayne Co.	$300	$5 to $10
MINNESOTA	Conciliation Court	$1,000	$3 to $19
MISSISSIPPI	Justice of the Peace Court	$500	$15
MISSOURI	Small Claims Div. of Magistrate Court	$500	$5

May Attorney Represent?	Appeal By Defendant Possible?	Appeal By Plaintiff Possible?	On Appeal Attorney Is:	Appeal Claims Go to:
Yes	Yes	Yes	Possible	Jefferson Quarterly Court
Yes	Yes	Yes	Possible	District Court if original case was filed in City Court for less than $100 or in Justice of the Peace Court; Appellate Court if original case was filed in City Court for more than $100 or in District Court
Yes	Yes	Yes	Preferable	Superior Court
Yes	Yes	Yes	Possible	Circuit Court
Yes	Yes	No	Preferable	
No	No	No		
Yes	Yes	Yes	Preferable	Municipal or County Court
Yes	Yes	Yes	Preferable	Circuit or County Court
Yes	Yes	Yes	Possible	Circuit Court

State	Name of Court	Maximum Amount of Claim	Filing Fees*
MONTANA†	Small Claims Court of the District Court	$1,500	$5
NEBRASKA	Small Claims Div. of County Court	$500	$3
NEVADA	Small Claims Div. of Justice's Court	$1,000 effective 7/77	$5 plus $5 service fee
NEW HAMPSHIRE	Small Claims Div. of District Court	$500	$3
NEW JERSEY	Small Claims Div. of County District Court	$500	$8
NEW MEXICO	Small Claims Court (only in countries with population of at least 100,000); Magistrate Court all other counties.	$2,000	Small Claims Court, $6.50; Magistrate Court, $10
NEW YORK	Small Claims Court	$1,000	$2
NORTH CAROLINA	Small Claims Court of District Court	$500	$8 plus $2 sheriff's fee
NORTH DAKOTA	Justice Court or Small Claims Div. of County Court	$200 in Justice Courts; $500 in County Courts	$3
OHIO	Small Claims Div. of Municipal Court	$300	$5
OKLAHOMA	Small Claims Div. of District Court	$600	$4 to $15
OREGON	Small Claims Dept. of Justice or District Court	$500	$8
PENNSYLVANIA	District Magistrate's Courts; in Philadelphia Municipal Court	$1,000	$7.50 to $12.50
RHODE ISLAND	Small Claims Div. of District Court	$500	$3 plus postage
SOUTH CAROLINA	Magistrate Court	$500	$ .35
SOUTH DAKOTA	Small Claims Div. of Magistrate Court	$500	$3 plus postage for certified mail
TENNESSEE	Metropolitan General Sessions Court	$3,000	$14.75 to $18.75

May Attorney Represent?	Appeal By Defendant Possible?	Appeal By Plaintiff Possible?	On Appeal Attorney Is:	Appeal Claims Go to:
Both parties must have an attorney or there will be *no* attorneys.	Yes	Yes	Possible	District Court
No	Yes	Yes	Possible	District Court
Yes	Yes	Yes	Preferable	District Court
Yes	Yes	Yes	Possible	County Superior Court
Yes	Yes	Yes	Possible	Superior Court, Appellate Div.
Yes	Yes	Yes	Possible	District Court
Yes	Yes	Yes	Preferable	County Court
Yes	Yes	Yes	Possible	District Court
Yes	No	No		
Yes	Yes	Yes	Possible	Municipal Court Judge
Yes	Yes	Yes	Possible	State Supreme Court
No	No	No		
Yes	Yes	Yes	Mandatory	Common Pleas Court
Yes (mandatory for corporations)	Yes	No	Possible	
Yes	Yes	Yes	Preferable	County or Common Pleas courts
Yes	No	No		
Yes	Yes	Yes	Mandatory	Circuit Court

State	Name of Court	Maximum Amount of Claim	Filing Fees*
TEXAS	Small Claims or Justice Court (Justice of the Peace of each co. acts as judge)	$150 $200 in wage disputes)	$5.15
UTAH	Small Claims Div. of City or Justice of the Peace courts	$200	$3
VERMONT	Small Claims Div. of District Court of Vermont	$250	$5 to $10 plus registered mail postage
VIRGINIA	District Court	$500 exclusive; $5,000 concurrent with Circuit Court	$4.25
WASHINGTON, D.C.	Small Claims and Conciliation Branch of Superior Court of the District of Columbia	$750	$1
WASHINGTON STATE	Small Claims Dept. of Justice's Court	$200 to $300	$1
WEST VIRGINIA	Magistrate Courts	$1,500	$10
WISCONSIN	Small Claims Div. of County Court	$1,000	$7.50 to $7.75
WYOMING	Small Claims Court; Justice of the Peace Court	$200	$5

May Attorney Represent?	Appeal By Defendant Possible?	Appeal By Plaintiff Possible?	On Appeal Attorney Is:	Appeal Claims Go to:
Yes	Yes	Yes	Preferable	County Court at Law
Yes	Yes	No	Possible	District Court
Yes, if both parties are represented	Yes	Yes	Preferable	Vermont Supreme Court
Yes	Yes	Yes	Preferable	Circuit Court
Yes	Yes, with consent of the court	Yes	Preferable	District of Columbia Court of Appeals
No, unless with judge's permission	Only if claim in excess of $100	No	Preferable	
Yes	Yes	Yes	Preferable	Circuit Court
Yes	Yes	Yes	Possible	Circuit Court
Yes	Yes	Yes	Possible	District Court

Source: Compiled through nationwide judicial survey by Kenneth Eisenberger, October 1976.

*Some amounts listed may include fees for serving papers on defendant(s).

**Georgia does not have a uniform statewide system of small claims courts. Information listed is for one small claims court in or near the capital city and may serve as an example. Other courts in the state may have the same or different procedures. Maximum amount of claim permissible varies statewide from $100 to $1,000, and the filing fees vary statewide from $7 to $20.

†A current Montana law set the uniform standards for small claims courts in that state. However, local jurisdictions have the choice of whether to establish a small claims court. As of September 1976, there were still no small claims courts in Montana.

AUTOCAPS OFFICIALLY RECOGNIZED BY OCA*

All AUTOCAPS officially recognized by OCA have one or more consumers on panel. Mail your complaints to AUTOCAP at the address of the association serving your area.

COLORADO

Metro Denver Automobile Dealers Assn. (L)
70 W. 6th Ave., Suite 101
Denver 80122
Phone: 303–222–1544

CONNECTICUT

Connecticut Automotive Trades Assn. (S)
18 N. Main St.
West Hartford 06107
Phone: 1–800–842–2276

DELAWARE

Delaware Automobile Dealers Assn. (S)
8 Hillvale Cir.
Wilmington 19808
Phone: 302–731–8475

FLORIDA

Central Florida Dealer Assn. (L)
3720 Silver Star Rd.
Orlando 32808
Phone: 305–647–5100

IDAHO

Idaho Automobile Dealers Assn. (S)
2230 Main St.
Boise 83706
Phone: 208–342–7779

INDIANA

Indianapolis Automobile Trade Assn. (L)
822 N. Illinois
Indianapolis 46204
Phone: 317–631–6301

KENTUCKY

Kentucky Automobile Dealers Assn. (S)
P.O. Box 498
Frankfort 40601
Phone: 502–583–4555

KENTUCKY (cont.)

Greater Louisville Auto Dealers Assn. (L)
1103 Heybrun Bldg., 332 W. Broadway
Louisville 40202
Phone: 502–583–0279

LOUISIANA

Louisiana Automobile Dealers Assn. (S)
P.O. Box 2863
Baton Rouge 70821
Phone: 504–343–8383

Greater New Orleans New Car Dealers Assn. (L)
811 International Bldg.
New Orleans 70130
Phone: 504–581–2777

MARYLAND

Automotive Trade Association (L)
National Capital Area
8401 Connecticut Ave., Suite 505
Chevy Chase 20015
Phone: 301–657–3200

NEVADA

Washoe Motor Car Dealers Assn. (L)
P.O. Box 7320
Reno 89510

NEW YORK

Niagara Frontier Automobile Dealers Assn. (L)
25 California Dr.
Williamsville 14221
Phone: 716–634–9611

OHIO

Cleveland Automobile Dealers Assn. (L)
310 Lakeside Avenue, West
Cleveland 44113
Phone: 216–241–2880

Toledo Automobile Dealers Assn. (L)
1811 N. Reynolds
Toledo 43615
Phone: 419–531–7154

OKLAHOMA

Oklahoma Automobile Dealers Assn. (S)
1601 City National Bank Tower
Oklahoma City 73102
Phone: 405–239–2603

OREGON

Oregon Automobile Dealers Assn. (S)
P.O. Box 14460
Portland 97214
Phone: 503–233–5044

TEXAS

Texas Automobile Dealers Assn. (S)
P.O. Drawer 1028
1108 Lavaca
Austin 78767
Phone: 512–476–2686

UTAH

Utah Automobile Dealers Assn. (S)
Newhouse Hotel, Box 1019
Salt Lake City 84101
Phone: 801–355–7473

Source: Compiled by Kenneth Eisenberger, with assistance from the National Automobile Dealers Association, 8400 Westpark Drive, McLean, Va. 22101, September 1976.

*I.e., Office of Consumer Affairs, U.S. Department of Health, Education, and Welfare.

Symbols: (L) = local association, (S) = state association.

Appendix 17

AUTOCAPS WITHOUT CONSUMER REPRESENTATION

ARIZONA

Arizona Automobile Dealers
  Assn. (S) (EC)
P.O. Box 5438
Phoenix 85010
Phone: 602–252–2386

ILLINOIS

Chicago Automobile Trade Assn. (L) (I)
O'Hare Plaza, 5725 E. River Rd.
Chicago 60631
Phone: 312–693–6630

IOWA

Iowa Automobile Dealers Assn. (S) (I)
405 E. First St.
Des Moines 50309
Phone: 515–244–2245

MICHIGAN

Detroit Automobile Dealers Assn. (L) (I)
6525 Lincoln Ave.
Detroit 48202
Phone: 313–873–2477

MISSISSIPPI

Mississippi Automobile Dealers
  Assn. (S) (I)
P.O. Box 137
Jackson 39205
Phone: 601–948–6868

MONTANA

Montana Automobile Dealers
  Assn. (S) (I)
501 N. Sanders
Helena 59601
Phone: 406–442–1233

NEW MEXICO

New Mexico Automobile Dealers
  Assn. (S) (I)
510 Second St., N.W., Rm. 202
Albuquerque 87102
Phone: 505–242–9365

NEW YORK

Greater New York, Long Island &
  Westchester Auto Dealers Assn. (L) (I)
One Hanson Pl., Rm. 1212
Brooklyn 11217
Phone: 212–783–2900

NORTH DAKOTA

Automobile Dealers Assn. of North
  Dakota (S) (I)
114 N. University Dr., Box 2524
Fargo 58102
Phone: 701–232–4455

OHIO

Columbus Automobile Dealers
  Assn. (L) (I)
209 S. High St.
Columbus 43215
Phone: 614–221–2544

PENNSYLVANIA

Pittsburgh Automobile Trade
  Assn. (L) (I)
400 Penn Center Blvd., Suite 417
Pittsburgh 15235
Phone: 412–661–4232

RHODE ISLAND

Rhode Island Automobile Dealers
  Assn. (S) (EC)
Regency West, 2 Jackson Walkway,
  Suite 5
Providence 02903
Phone: 401–421–3911

SOUTH DAKOTA

South Dakota Automobile Dealers
  Assn. (S) (I)
100 N. Phillips, Suite 912
Sioux Falls 57102
Phone: 605–336–2616

TEXAS

New Car Dealers Assn. of Tarrant
  Co. (L) (I)
Continental National Bank Bldg.
Suite 2618
Fort Worth 76102
Phone: 817–355–2107

VIRGINIA

Tidewater Automobile Dealers
  Assn. (L) (I)

VIRGINIA (cont.)

One Koger Executive Center, Suite 101
Norfolk 23502
Phone: 804–499–3725

WASHINGTON

King County Automobile Dealers
  Assn. (L) (I)
P.O. Box 21805
Seattle 98111
Phone: 206–623–2034

Source: Compiled by Kenneth Eisenberger, with assistance from the National Automobile Dealers Association, 8400 Westpark Drive, McLean, Va. 22101, September 1976.

Symbols: (EC) = program with "ethics committee" to mediate complaints, (I) = program with individual who mediates complaints, (L) = local association, (S) = state organization.

Appendix 18

NONGOVERNMENTAL CONSUMER ORGANIZATIONS

PART 1: STATE AND LOCAL ORGANIZATIONS

ALABAMA

*Alabama League of Aging
Citizens, Inc.*
837 S. Hull St.
Montgomery 36104
205–264–0229

*Elmore Community Action
Committee*
P.O. Drawer H
Wetumpka 36092
205–567–4361

*Federation of Southern
Cooperatives*
P.O. Box 95
Epes 35460
205–652–9676

*Minority Peoples Council on
the Tennessee-Tombigbee
Waterway*
P.O. Box 5
Gainesville 35464
205–652–9676

*Mobile Area Community
Action Committee*
850 Marion St.
Mobile 36603
205–432–3641

ALASKA

*Alaska Public Interest
Research Group, Inc.*
Box 1093
Anchorage 99510
907–278–3661

Fairbanks Consumer Group
P.O. Box 483
Fairbanks 99707

ARIZONA

Arizona Consumers Council
6480 Camino DeMichael
St.
Tucson 85718
602–884–2945

Human Action for Chandler
100 W. Boston
Chandler 85224
602–963–4321

ARKANSAS

*ACORN (Arkansas
Community Organizations for
Reform Now)*
523 W. 15th St.
Little Rock 72202
501–376–7151

Arkansas Consumer Research
1919 W. 7th St.
Little Rock 72202
501–374–2394

*Ark-Tex Chapter, American
Association Retired Persons*
Route 4, Box 325
Texarkana 75501
501–772–2136

*Urban League of Greater
Little Rock, Inc.*
600 W. 9th St.
Little Rock 72202
501–374–6431

CALIFORNIA

*Accountants for the Public
Interest*
351 California St., 16th Fl.
San Francisco 94104
415–956–3222

CALIFORNIA (cont.)

American Consumers Council
P.O. Box 24206
Los Angeles 90024
213–476–2888

*California Citizen Action
Group*
2315 Westwood Blvd.
Los Angeles 90064

*California Citizen Action
Group*
490 - 65th St.
Oakland 94609
415–841–9727

*California Citizen Action
Group*
909 - 12th St.
Sacramento 95814

California Consumer Club
403 W. 8th St., #303
Los Angeles 90014
213–624–3961

*California Public Interest
Research Group of the
Los Angeles Region*
University of California at
Los Angeles
321 A Kerckhoff Hall
308 Westwood Plaza
Los Angeles 90024
213–825–8461

*California Public Interest
Research Group/California
State University Northridge*
9520 Etiwanda
Northridge 91324
213–342–4664

CALIFORNIA (cont.)

*California Public Interest
Research Group*
334 Kalmia St.
San Diego 92101
714–236–1508

Citizens Action League
1161 Mission St.
San Francisco 94103
415–864–7510

*Coalition for Economic
Survival (CES)*
5889 W. Pico Blvd.
Los Angeles 90019
213–938–6241

Consumer Action
26 7th St.
San Francisco 94103
415–626–4030

*Consumer Federation of
California, Los Angeles-
Orange County Chapter*
621 S. Virgil Ave.
Los Angeles 90005
213–971–7722

*Consumer Federation of
California*
2200 L St.
Sacramento 95816
916–442–5340

Consumer Panel of America
1424 Windsor Dr.
San Bernardino 92404
714–885–5393

*Consumer Protection Project
Office of Environmental and
Consumer Affairs*
308 Westwood Plaza
University of California at
LA
Los Angeles 90024
213–825–2820

CALIFORNIA (cont.)

*Consumers Cooperative of
Berkeley, Inc.*
4805 Central Ave.
Richmond 94804
415–526–0440

*Consumers United of Palo
Alto, Inc.*
P.O. Box 311
Palo Alto 94302
415–494–1858

*Davis Consumer Affairs
Bureau*
364 Memorial Union, Rm.
373
University of California at
Davis
Davis 95616
916–752–6484

*El Concilio for the Spanish
Speaking*
126 H St.
Modesto 95351
209–521–2033

Fight Inflation Together
c/o Elaine Felsher
3635 Longridge Ave.
Sherman Oaks 91423

"The Group"
457 Haight St.
San Francisco 94115
415–861–6840

*Long Beach Commission on
Economic Opportunity*
853 Atlantic Blvd.
Long Beach 90813
213–436–3227

*Merced Action Agency
Merced Consumer Affairs
Office*
P.O. Box 2068
Merced 95340
209–722–3924

CALIFORNIA (cont.)

*Northern California Council
Against Health Fraud, Inc.*
426 17th St.
Oakland 94612
415–893–8446

*Northern California Public
Interest Research Group, Inc.*
P.O. Box 702
Santa Clara 95052
408–984–2777

Organize, Inc.
21115 Beverly Blvd.
Los Angeles 90057
213–483–6530

*Pasadena Community
Services Commission*
717 N. Lake Ave.
Pasadena 91106
213–798–0981

*Pasadena Consumer Action
Center*
1020 N. Fair Oaks
Pasadena 91104
213–794–7194

People's Action Research
1206 S. Gramercy Pl.
Los Angeles 90019
213–735–4969

People's Lobby
3456 W. Olympic Blvd.
Los Angeles 90019
213–731–8321

Public Media Center
2751 Hyde St.
San Francisco 94109
415–885–0200

*Sacramento Church Service
Bureau*
3720 Folsom Blvd.
Sacramento 95816
916–456–3815

CALIFORNIA (cont.)

St. Paul's Center for Urban
Work and Study
1012 - 15th St.
Sacramento 95814
916–448–5535

Self-Help for the Elderly
3 Old Chinatown La.
San Francisco 94108
415–982–9171

Senior Citizens Association of
Los Angeles County, Inc.
427 E. 5th St.
Los Angeles 90013
213–624–6467

Stanislaus County
Commission on Aging
Staff Coordinator
P.O. Box 3404
Modesto 95353
209–526–6339

Toward Utility Rate
Normalization
2209 Van Ness Ave.
San Francisco 94109

Watts Labor Community
Action Committee
11401 S. Central Ave.
Los Angeles 90059
213–564–5945

COLORADO

Associated Students Consumer
Protection Office
Student Center
Colorado State University
Fort Collins 80523
303–491–5931

Associated Students Renter's
Information Office
Student Center
Colorado State University
Fort Collins 80523
303–491–5931

COLORADO (cont.)

Colorado Consumers
Association
P.O. Box 471
Boulder 80302
303–441–3700

Colorado League for
Consumer Protection
8230 W. 16th Pl.
Lakewood 80215
303–233–5891

Colorado Public Interest
Research Group
1711 Pennsylvania
Denver 80203
303–861–1973

Colorado Public Interest
Research Group
Box 208, Student Center
Colorado State University
Fort Collins 80523
303–491–7417

Colorado Public Interest
Research Group, Inc.
Director, Consumer
  Division
University Center, Rm.
  207
University of Northern
  Colorado
Greeley 80639
303–351–4504

Crusade for Justice
P.O. Box 18347
Denver 80218
303–832–1145

East-Side Action Movement
2855 Tremont Pl., Rm.
  201
Denver 80205
303–534–6228

Environmental Action of
Colorado
2239 E. Colfax Ave.
Denver 80206
303–321–1645

COLORADO (cont.)

Health Insurance Mediators,
Inc.
P.O. Box 4345
Colorado Springs 80930
303–632–6153

Mt. Plains Congress of Senior
Citizens
820 Sixteenth St., #617
Denver 80202
303–629–7270

CONNECTICUT

Connecticut Citizen Action
Group
130 Washington St.
P.O. Box G
Hartford 06106
203–527–7191

Connecticut Consumers'
Group
53 Wildwood Ave.
Milford 06460
203–878–0414

Connecticut Public Interest
Research Group
P.O. Box 1571
Hartford 06101
203–486–4525

Connecticut Public Interest
Research Group
Trinity College
Summit St.
Hartford 06106
203–527–3151, ext. 292

Connecticut Public Interest
Research Group
Box U-8
Storrs 06268
203–486–4525

Consumer Information
Services
One Landmark Sq., Suite
  100
Stamford 06901
203–359–2112

DISTRICT OF COLUMBIA

Auto Owners Action Council
733 15th St., N.W., Suite 236
Washington, D.C. 20005
202-638-5550

Aviation Consumer Action Project
P.O. Box 19029
Washington, D.C. 20036
202-223-4498

Consumer Affairs Committee of the Americans for Democratic Action
3005 Audubon Terr., N.W.
Washington, D.C. 20008
202-244-4080

Consumer H-E-L-P
2000 H Street, N.W., Suite 100
Washington, D.C. 20052
202-676-7585

Consumer Protection Center
National Law Center
George Washington University
Washington, D.C. 20052
202-785-1001

D. C. Citywide Consumer Council
1027 Girard St., N.E.
Washington, D.C. 20001
202-724-4946

D. C. Community Research Foundation
P.O. Box 19542
Washington, D.C. 20036
202-331-7270 or 676-7388

D. C. Power
2436 1/2 18th St., N.W.
Washington, D.C. 20009
202-667-6461

DIST. OF COLUMBIA (cont.)

D. C. Public Interest Research Group
P.O. Box 19542
Washington, D.C. 20036
202-676-7388

D. C. Public Interest Research Group
Box 19542
Washington, D.C. 20036
202-333-0844

National Consumer Information Center
3005 Georgia Ave., N.W.
Washington, D.C. 20001
202-723-8090

National Consumers Committee for Research and Education
1411 Hopkins St., N.W.
Washington, D.C. 20036
202-785-1438

Neighborhood Legal Services
635 F St., N.W.
Washington, D.C. 20004
202-628-9161

Protection for Elderly Persons (P.E.P.)
1806 Adams Mill Rd., N.W.
Washington, D.C. 20009
202-265-4900

RUCAG
1832 M St., N.W.
Washington, D.C. 20036
202-833-3935

United Planning Organization Consumer Protection Branch
1021 14th St., N.W.
Washington, D.C. 20005
202-638-7300

UNWRAP (United We Resist Additional Packaging)
Suite 301, Bacon Hall
2000 H St., N.W.
Washington, D.C. 20006
202-659-4310

FLORIDA

American Consumer Association, Inc.
P.O. Box 24141
Fort Lauderdale 33307
305-772-5198

Consumer Committee on Utility Rates and the Environment
P.O. Box 10578
St. Petersburg 33733
813-393-1106

Consumers Cure Inc. of Florida
P.O. Box 10578
St. Petersburg 33733
813-393-1106

Florida Consumers Federation
Clematis Building, Suite 600
208 Clematis St.
West Palm Beach 33401
305-659-5133

Florida Public Interest Research Group
University Union, Rm. 331
Florida State University
Tallahassee 32306

Greater Jacksonville Economic Opportunity, Inc.
P.O. Box 52025
Jacksonville 32201
904-355-3651

Leon County CAP, Inc.
P.O. Box 1775
Tallahassee 32301
904-222-2043

Student Consumers Union
University Union, Rm. 334
Florida State University
Tallahassee 32306
904-644-1811

GEORGIA

Georgia Citizens' Coalition on Hunger, Inc.
201 Washington St., SW
Atlanta 30303
404–659–0878

The Georgia Conservancy, Inc.
3376 Peachtree Rd., Suite 414
Atlanta 30326
404–262–1967

HAWAII

Citizens Against Noise
205 Merchant St., Rm. 18
Honolulu 96813
808–537–3490

Kokua Council
2535 S. King St.
Honolulu 96814
808–732–0455 or 373–3879

Life of the Land
404 Piikoi St., Rm. 209
Honolulu 96814
808–521–1300

IDAHO

The Consumer-Business Association, Inc.
428 Park Ave., Rms. 200 and 201
Idaho Falls 83401
208–523–6660

Idaho Consumer Affairs, Inc.
Suite 209
817 W. Franklin St.
Boise 83702
208–343–3554

ILLINOIS

Business and Professional People for the Public Interest
109 N. Dearborn St., Suite 1001
Chicago 60602
312–641–5570

ILLINOIS (cont.)

Chicago Consumer Coalition
Loop College
64 E. Lake St.
Chicago 60601
312–269–8101

Citizens for a Better Environment
59 E. Van Buren St., #2610
Chicago 60605
312–939–1984

Community Action Program
2200 N. Lincoln
Chicago 60614
312–929–2922

Consumer Coalition
P.O. Box 913
Highland Park 60035
312–679–8735

Consumer Information for Low Income Consumers
Southern Illinois University
Edwardsville 62025
618–692–2420

Food and Cooperative Project
64 E. Lake
Chicago 61601
312–269–8101

Illinois Public Interest Research Group
Southern Illinois University
Carbondale 62901
618–536–2140

Midwest Academy
600 W. Fullerton
Chicago 60614
312–953–6525

Pollution and Environmental Problems
President, Box 309
Palatine 60067
312–381–6695

ILLINOIS (cont.)

Public Action
59 E. Van Buren, Suite 2610
Chicago 60605
312–427–6262

PUSH
930 E. 50th St.
Chicago 60615
312–373–3366

INDIANA

Citizens Energy Coalition
Executive Director
1606 N. Delaware St.
Indianapolis 46205
317–923–2494

Indiana Consumer Center
730 E. Washington Blvd.
Ft. Wayne 46802
219–422–7630

Indiana Public Interest Research Group
703 E. 7th St.
Bloomington 47401
812–337–7575

Indiana Public Interest Research Group
1825 Northside
South Bend 46624

New World Center
428 E. Berry St.
Fort Wayne 46202
219–422–6821

IOWA

Citizens United for Responsible Energy (CURE)
500 E. 6th St.
Des Moines 50309
515–282–8191

Iowa Consumers League
Box 189
Corydon 50060
515–872–2329

IOWA *(cont.)*

Iowa Public Interest Research Group
Ames 50010
315–294–8094

Iowa Public Interest Research Group
Student Activities Center
Iowa Memorial Union
Iowa City 52242
319–353–7049

KANSAS

Action News
KAKE-TV, Box 10
Wichita 67201
316–943–4221

CAN HELP
P.O. Box 4253
Topeka 66616
913–235–3434

Consumer Assistance Center
North Central Kansas
  Libraries
Juliette & Poyntz
Manhattan 66502
913–776–7776

Consumer United Program
8410 West Highway #54
Wichita 67209
316–722–4251

El Centro De Servicios Para Mexicanos, Inc.
1117 Seward Ave.
Topeka 66616
913–232–8207

Kansas Home Economics Association Consumer Interest Committee
21 E. Des Moins Ave.
South Hutchinson 67505
316–663–5491

Kansas National Consumer Information Center
315 N. 20th St.
Kansas City 66102
913–342–4574

IOWA *(cont.)*

Manhattan Consumer-Business Relations Center
c/o KSU Consumer
  Relations Board
S. G. A.
Kansas State Union
Manhattan 66506
913–532–6541

MIDKAP, Inc.
P.O. Box 1034
Eldorado 67042
316–321–6373

Older Citizens Information Center
1122 Jackson
Topeka 66616
913–232–9037

People's Energy Project
P.O. Box 423
Lawrence 66044
913–843–7592

Shawnee County Community Assistance and Action
603 Topeka Ave.
Topeka 66603
913–235–9561

Topeka Housing Complaint Center
3120 E. 6th St.
Topeka 66603
913–234–0217

Women's Center of Topeka
1268 Western
Topeka 66603
913–357–7650

KENTUCKY

Budget Counseling Club
1730 S. 13th St.
Louisville 40210
502–635–2723

Community Incorporated
222 N. 17th St.
Louisville 40203
502–583–8385

KENTUCKY *(cont.)*

Concerned Consumers
P.O. Box 325
747 Liberty St.
Newport 41071
606–491–4444

Concerned Consumers of Electric Energy
Route 2, Box 468
Shepherdsville 40165

Consumer Association of Kentucky, Inc.
P.O. Box 111
Frankfort 40601
502–875–2207 or
  587–0772

Kentucky Joint Legislative Committee NRTA/AARP
Route 2, Box 468
Shepherdsville 40165

The Kentucky Organization (T.K.O.)
3113 Johnston Blvd.
Lexington 40503

Kentucky Public Interest Research Group
65 Echo Trail
Louisville 40299
802–588–5809

Louisville and Jefferson County Community Action Agency
1347 S. Third St.
Louisville 40208
502–634–4711

Public Bus for Bullitt County
Route 4
Shepherdsville 40165
502–543–6841

LOUISIANA

Gulf Coast Area NCIC
P.O. Box 5122
Alexandria 71301
318–442–1614

LOUISIANA (cont.)

Louisiana Center for the Public Interest

Suite 700
Maison Blanche Bldg.
New Orleans 70112
504-524-1231 or 8182

Louisiana Consumers' League

Capital Area Chapter
P.O. Box 14301
Baton Rouge 70808
504-293-3088

Louisiana Consumers' League, Inc.

P.O. Box 1332
Baton Rouge 70821
504-581-9322

New Orleans Council on Aging

705 Lafayette St.
Rm. 103, Gallier Hall
New Orleans 70130
504-586-1221

New Orleans Legal Assistance Corp.

226 Carondelet St., Suite 605
New Orleans 70130
504-523-1297

Opportunities Industrialization Center

315 N. Broad St.
New Orleans 70119
504-821-8222

SER - Jobs for Programs, Inc.

421 S. Roman St.
New Orleans 70112
504-524-0208

Tulane Consumer Center

308 Alcee Fortier Hall
Tulane University
New Orleans 70115
504-866-0849

MAINE

Citizens Committee on the Maine Economy (CCME)

Box 2066
Augusta 04330

Consumer Affairs Program Task Force on Human Needs

240 Main St.
Lewiston 04240
207-783-0720

Maine Public Interest Research Group

2 Stone St.
Augusta 04330
207-622-9411

Maine Public Interest Research Group

Colby College
Waterville 04901

Northeast COMBAT, Inc.

33 Idaho Ave.
Bangor 04401
207-947-3331

Pine Tree Legal Assistance

178 Middle St.
Portland 04111
207-784-1558

Safe Power for Maine

12 Main St.
Camden 04843
207-236-3610

MARYLAND

Baltimore Urban League Consumer Services Department

1150 Mondawmin Concourse
Baltimore 21215
301-523-8150

Cambridge Park East Tenants Assn.

600 Greenwood Ave., Apt. 201
Cambridge 21613
301-228-8581

MARYLAND (cont.)

Dorchester Community Development Corp.

P.O. Box 549
445 Race St.
Cambridge 21613
301-228-3600

Garrett County Community Action Committee, Inc.

P.O. Box 149
Oakland 21550
301-334-9431

Maryland Action, Inc.

8120 Fenton St., Suite 300
Silver Spring 20910
301-585-4482

Maryland Association of Housing Counselors

P.O. Box 549
Cambridge 21613
301-228-3600

Maryland Citizens Consumer Council

P.O. Box 34526
Bethesda 20034
Wash., D.C. area:
301-365-5095
Baltimore area:
301-448-9552

Maryland Public Interest Group

3110 Main Dining Hall
University of Maryland
College Park 20742
301-454-5601

Neighborhoods Uniting Project, Inc.

4300 Rhode Island Ave.
Brentwood 20722
301-277-7085

North Arundel Consumers Association

106 Thomas Rd.
Glen Burnie 21061
301-761-0106

MARYLAND (cont.)

St. Ambrose Housing Aid Center, Inc.
319 E. 25th St.
Baltimore 21218
301–235–5770

Southeast Community Organization
10 S. Wolfe St.
Baltimore 21231
301–327–1626

United Communities Against Poverty, Inc.
6001 Sheriff Rd., 2nd Fl.
Fairmount Heights 20027
301–925–9800

MASSACHUSETTS

Berkshire County Consumer Advocates, Inc.
54 Wendell Ave.
Pittsfield 01201
413–442–7439

Consumer Action Center
721 State St.
Springfield 01109
413–736–3210

Massachusetts Community School
107 South St.
Boston 02111
617–266–7505

Massachusetts Consumer Association
c/o Boston College
140 Commonwealth Ave.
Chestnut Hill 02167
617–969–0100

Massachusetts Public Interest Research Group
233 N. Pleasant St.
Amherst 01002
413–256–6434

MASSACHUSETTS (cont.)

Massachusetts Public Interest Research Group
120 Boylston St., Rm. 320
Boston 02116
617–423–1796

National Consumer Law Center, Inc.
11 Beacon St.
Boston 02108
617–969–1576

Springfield Action Commission
721 State St.
Springfield 01109
413–736–3210

MICHIGAN

The Calhoun Community Action Agency
P.O. Box 1026
Battle Creek 49016
616–965–7766

Citizens for Better Care
960 E. Jefferson
Detroit 48207
313–568–0513

Consumer Affairs Bureau Kalamazoo County Chamber of Commerce
500 W. Crosstown
Kalamazoo 49008
616–381–4004

Consumer Alliance of Michigan
14382 Glastonbury Rd.
Detroit 48223
313–868–5400

Consumer Research Advisory Council
51 W. Warren Ave. #310
Detroit 48201
313–831–2290

MICHIGAN (cont.)

Consumer Research Advisory Council East Side, Coordinating Center
Wayne State University, Extension Center
3127 E. Canfield
Detroit 48209
313–554–1223

Consumer Research Advisory Council West Side Coordinating Center La Sed.
4138 W. Vernon Hwy.
Detroit 48209
313–554–1223

Greater Lansing Area Citizens for Better Care
855 Grove St.
East Lansing 48823
517–337–1676

Greater Lansing Legal Aid Bureau
300 N. Washington Ave.
P.O. Box 14171
Lansing 48901
517–485–5411

Housing Assistance Foundation Consumer Services Project
935 N. Washington Ave.
Lansing 48906

Kent County Legal Aid
1208 McKay Tower
Grand Rapids 49502
616–774–9672

Landlord Tenant Clinic
144 W. Lafayette, 2nd Fl.
Detroit 48226
313–963–1375

Mediation Services
2205 Michigan Union
University of Michigan
Ann Arbor 48104
313–763–1071

MICHIGAN (cont.)

Memorial Society of Greater Detroit

4605 Cass
Detroit 48202
313–TE 3–9107

Michigan Citizens Lobby

105 Fairfax Office Plaza
15660 W. 10 Mile Rd.
Southfield 48075
313–559–9260

Michigan Consumer Council

414 Hollister Bldg.
Lansing 48933
517–373–0947

Michigan Consumer Education Center

217-A University Library
Eastern Michigan
University
Ypsilanti 48197
313–487–2292

Michigan Tenant Rights Coalition

745 Eastern, S.E.
Grand Rapids 49503
616–241–6429

Oakland/Livingston Human Services Agency

196 Oakland Ave.
Pontiac 48020
313–858–5134

Public Interest Research Group in Michigan

590 Hollister Bldg.
Lansing 48933
517–487–6001

Tenants Resource Center

855 Grove St.
East Lansing 48823
517–337–9795

Upper Penninsula Chapter–Citizens for Better Care

107 Tenth Ave.
Menominee 49858
906–864–2385

MICHIGAN (cont.)

West Michigan Environmental Action Council

1324 Lake Dr., SE
Grand Rapids 49506
616–451–3051

MINNESOTA

Alternative Sources of Energy Magazine

Route 2, Box 90A
Milaca 56353
612–983–6892

Minnesota Consumer Alliance

3410 University Ave., SE
Minneapolis 55414
612–331–7770

Minnesota Public Interest Research Group

University of Minnesota
Kirby Student Union
Duluth 55802

Minnesota Public Interest Research Group

3036 University Ave., SE
Minneapolis 55414
612–376–7554

Northeastern Minnesota Consumer's League

206 W. 4th St.
Duluth 55806
218–727–8973, ext. 5

United Handicapped Federation, Inc.

1951 University Ave.
St. Paul 55104
612–646–1515

MISSISSIPPI

Harrison County Neighborhood Service Center/Consumer Awareness and Action Agency

P.O. Box 519
Gulfport 39501
601–864–3421

MISSISSIPPI (cont.)

Mississippi Consumers Association

375 Culley Dr.
Jackson 39206
601–362–6643

MISSOURI

Community Services, Inc.

214 W. Third
Maryville 64468
816–582–3114

Human Resources Corporation

3205 Woodland
Kansas City 64109
816–923–7907

HRC–Education Center

3210 Michigan
Kansas City 64109
816–921–9000

Greater Kansas City Consumer Association

320 E. 10th St.
Kansas City 64106
816–471–8030, ext. 49

Housewives Elect Lower Prices

631 East Polo Dr.
Clayton 63105
314–727–0222

Legal Aid Society of the City and County of St. Louis

607 N. Grand
St. Louis 63103
314–533–3000

Missouri A.C.O.R.N.

2335 S. Grand
St. Louis 63104
314–865–3835

Missouri Association of Consumers

Box 514
Columbia 65201
816–454–6333

MISSOURI *(cont.)*

Missouri Public Interest Research Group

Box 8276
St. Louis 63156
314–361–5200

Tax Reform Group

2335 S. Grand
St. Louis 63104
314–865–3835

Utility Consumers Council of Missouri, Inc.

Suite 503
7710 Carondelet
Clayton 63105
314–726–2500

MONTANA

Center for Public Interest

P.O. Box 931
Bozeman 59715
406–587–0906

Montana Consumer Affairs Council, Inc.

P.O. Box 414
Helena 59601
406–792–3981

Montana State Low Income Organization

436 N. Jackson
Helena 59602
406–442–9127

Student Action Center

University Center
University of Montana
Missoula 59801
406–243–2451

NEBRASKA

Consumer Alliance of Nebraska

Nebraska Center
33rd and Holdrege
Lincoln 68583
402–472–2844

NEBRASKA *(cont.)*

Nebraska Public Interest Research Group

Nebraska Union #336
University of Nebraska
Lincoln 68508
402–472–2448

NEVADA

Citizen Alert

Box 5731
Reno 89513
702–747–5053

Citizens For Survival, Inc.

6325 Factor Ave.
Las Vegas 89107
702–878–7422

Consumers League of Nevada

3031 Garnet Ct.
Las Vegas 89121
702–457–1953

KOLO-TV

News Department
770 E. 5th St.
Reno 89502
702–786–2932

Poor People Pulling Together

1285 W. Miller
Las Vegas 89106
702–648–4645

NEW HAMPSHIRE

New Hampshire Public Interest Research Group

Dartmouth College
Hanover 03755
603–643–2473

Newmarket Health Center, Inc.

84 Main St.
Newmarket 03857
603–659–3106

NEW JERSEY

Action Now

City Hall
Plainfield 07061
201–753–3229

NEW JERSEY *(cont.)*

Community Union Project

116 N. Oraton Pky.
East Orange 07017
201–675–8600

Consumers League of New Jersey

20 Church St., Rm. 11
Montclair 07042
201–744–6449

Gray Panthers of South Jersey

408 Cooper St.
Camden 08102

National Consumer Advisory Council

217 13th Ave.
Belmar 07719
201–681–7494

Newark Consumer Project

14 Sayre St.
Newark 07103
201–248–1997

New Jersey Public Interest Research Group

Rutgers Law School
5th and Penn sts.
Camden 08102

New Jersey Public Interest Research Group

Douglass College, DPO 23
New Brunswick 08903
201–745–1100

New Jersey Public Interest Research Group

32 W. Lafayette St.
Trenton 08608
609–393–7474

Ocean Community Economic Action Now, Inc.

40 Washington St.
P.O. Box 1029
Toms River 08753
201–244–5337

NEW JERSEY (cont.)

Office of Economic Opportunity
515 Broadway
Camden 08103
609–541–7675

Paterson Task Force for Community Action, Inc.
240 Broadway
Paterson 07501
201–271–7400

NORTH CAROLINA

Carolina Action
Box 1985
Durham 27702
919–682–6076

Consumers Center of North Carolina
19 Hargett St.
Raleigh 27601
919–832–8111

I CARE, INC.
Consumer Affairs
P.O. Box 349
502 S. Center St.
Statesville 28677
704–872–8141

Institute for Southern Studies
P.O. Box 230
Chapel Hill 27514
919–929–2141

The North Carolina Consumers Council, Inc.
P.O. Box 6434
Raleigh 27608
919–834–6749

National Carolina Public Interest Research Group
P.O. Box 2901
Durham 27705
919–286–2275

North Carolina Senior Citizens Federation
P.O. Box 1453
Henderson 27536
919–492–6031

NORTH CAROLINA (cont.)

Operation Breakthrough, Inc.
P.O. Box 1470
Durham 27702
919–477–7327

NEW MEXICO

All Indian Pueblo Council, Inc.
1015 Indian School Rd., NW
P.O. Box 6507, Station B
Albuquerque 87102
505–843–7048

Consumer Action and Education Jicarilla Apache Tribe
Box 272
Dulce 87528
505–759–3493 or 759–3494

Economic Opportunity Council Legal and Consumer Assistance Program
206 S. Millen
Farmington 87401
505–325–8886

New Mexico Public Interest Research Group
P.O. Box 4564
Albuquerque 87106
505–277–2757

Senior Citizens Law Office–Legal Aid Society of Albuquerque, Inc.
1121 Kent St., NW
Albuquerque 87102
505–243–3779

Southwest Research and Information Center
Box 3524
Albuquerque 87106
505–265–0461

NEW YORK

A.C.C.O.R.D.
264 E. Onondaga St.
Syracuse 13202
315–422–2331

NEW YORK (cont.)

Bi-County Consumer Coalition of Long Island
23 Roberts St.
Farmingdale 11735

Brinkerhoff Action Association. Inc.
President
174-16 110th Ave.
St. Albans 11433
212–739–8281

Citizens Energy Council of Western New York
P.O. Box 312
Wilson 14172
716–751–6227

Consumer Action Now, Inc.
49 E. 53rd St.
New York 10022
212–752–1220

Consumer Action Program
270 Pulaski St.
Brooklyn 11206
212–453–7602

Consumer Education Project
977 Bedford Ave.
Brooklyn 11216
212–857–4521

Council on Environmental Alternatives
49 E. 53rd St.
New York 10022
212–838–3828

Empire State Consumer Association, Inc.
109 Heather Dr.
Rochester 14625
716–381–2758

Flatbush Tenants' Council
1702 Church Ave.
Brooklyn 11226
212–287–0242

GET Consumer Protection
P.O. Box 355, Ansonia Sta.
New York 10023

NEW YORK (cont.)

Harlem Consumer Education Council, Inc.
1959 Madison Ave.
New York 10035
212–926–5300

Institute for Consumer Education
300 Dun Bldg.
110 Pearl St.
Buffalo 14202
716–834–4236 or
854–0300

Irate Consumers of Ulster County
Box 419
Saugerties 12477
914–246–4021

National Coalition to Fight Inflation
160 Fifth Ave.
New York 10011
212–924–7871

Neighborhood Council Action Services Economic Development
105-19 177th St.
Jamaica 11433
212–291–8115

New Frontier Consumer Council
723 Steven Ct.
East Meadow 11554

New York City Community Development Agency
349 Broadway
New York 10013
212–433–2238

New York Consumer Assembly
465 Grand St.
New York 10002
212–674–5990

New York Public Interest Research Group, Inc.
1 Columbia Pl.
Albany 12207
518–436–0876

NEW YORK (cont.)

New York Public Interest Research Group
University Union
SUNY at Binghamton
Binghamton 13901
607–798–4971

New York Public Interest Research Group, Inc.
Brooklyn College Chapter
1479 Flatbush Ave.
Brooklyn 11210
212–338–5906

New York Public Interest Research Group
153-11 61st Rd.
Flushing 11367
212–520–8616

New York Public Interest Research Group, Inc.
5 Beekman St.
New York 10038
212–349–6460

New York Public Interest Research Group
1004 E. Adams St.
Syracuse 13210
315–476–8381

Oswego Consumer Protection League
Route 8
Oswego 13126
315–342–3850

Store Front
140 W. State St.
Ithaca 14850
607–273–9012

Suffolk Citizens for Consumer Protection
Southhaven Ministries
Southhaven Mall
Lake Grove 11755
516–724–8273

NORTH DAKOTA

Area Low Income Council
1219 College Dr.
Devils Lake 58301
701–662–5388

Quad County Consumer Action
2 N. 3rd, 2nd Fl. Annex
Grand Forks 58201
701–772–8989

OHIO

Active Clevelanders Together
11628 Madison
Cleveland 44102
216–221–8300

Cleveland Citizen Action Foundation, Inc. and Cleveland Consumer Action, Inc.
532 Terminal Tower
Cleveland 44113
216–687–0525

Community Action Commission of the Cincinnati Area
801 Linn St.
Cincinnati 45203
513–241–1425

Consumer Conference of Greater Cincinnati
7432 Clovernook Ave.
Cincinnati 45231
513–521–3498

Consumer Protection Agency
5 E. Buchtel Ave., Rm. 202
Akron 44308
216–376–1666

Consumer Protection Agency
420 Madison Ave., Suite 1120
Toledo 43604
419–247–6191

Consumer Protection Association
118 St. Clair Ave. #405
Cleveland 44114
216–241–0186

OHIO (cont.)

Consumers League of Ohio
940 Engineers Bldg.
Cleveland 44114
216–621–1175

Free Stores, Inc.
76 E. McMicken St.
Cincinnati 45210
513–241–1064

Humanity House
475 W. Market St.
Akron 44303
216–253–7151

Lake County Branch, NAACP
Suite B-3-3, New Market Mall
Painesville 44077
216–354–2148

Montgomery County CAA
3304 N. Main
Dayton 45405
513–276–5011

Ohio Consumer Association
P.O. Box 1559
Columbus 43216
614–422–0321

Ohio Public Interest Research Group
Box 25, Wilder Hall
Oberlin 44074
216–775–8137

Ohio Public Interest Research Group
Box 577
University of Dayton
Dayton 45469
513–229–2229

Ohio Tea Party
475 W. Market St.
Akron 44303
216–253–5114

OHIO (cont.)

Spanish Speaking Information Center
7118 Jackson Ave.
Toledo 43624
419–243–5958

Student Consumer Union
Bowling Green State University
405C Student Services Bldg.
Bowling Green 43403
419–372–0248

OKLAHOMA

Delta Community Action Foundation, Inc.
1024 Main St.
Duncan 73533
405–255–3222

OREGON

Community Care Association, Inc.
2022 N.E. Alberta St.
Portland 97211
503–228–8787

Consumers' Food Council
Route 1, Box 842
Beaverton 97005
503–628–1227

Multnomah County Legal Aid Service
310 S.W. 4th Ave., Rm. 1100
Portland 97204
503–224–4086

Oregon Consumer League
3131 N.W. Luray Terr.
Portland 97210
503–228–8787

Oregon Student Public Interest Research Group
Hughes Bldg., 4th Fl.
115 S. W. 4th Ave.
Portland 97204
503–222–9641

OREGON (cont.)

Portland Neighborhood Services
9 Chatham Ct.
Portland 97217
203–392–3444

RAIN
2270 N. W. Irving
Portland 97210
503–227–5110

PENNSYLVANIA

Action Alliance of Senior Citizens of Greater Philadelphia
401 N. Broad, Rm. 800
Philadelphia 19108
215–574–9050

Alliance for Consumer Protection
P.O. Box 1354
Pittsburgh 15230
412–243–0163

Areas of Concern
P.O. Box 47
Bryn Mawr 19010
215–525–1129

Bucks County Consumer Organization
30 Spice Bush Rd.
Levittown 19056
215–945–3373

Bucks County Opportunity Council
Nesshaminy Manor Center
Doylestown 18901
215–343–2800, ext. 360

Carlisle Consumer Protection Agency
Dickinson College
Denny Hall, 1st Fl.
Carlisle 17013
717–243–5121

PENNSYLVANIA (cont.)

Citizens Choice Coalition of
Luzenne County
186 Barney St.
Wilkes Barre 18702
717–825–6049

Concerned Citizens of The
Delaware Valley
P.O. 47
Bryn Mawr 19010
215–LA 5–1129

Consumer Action Bureau of
Berks County
YWCA Building
8th and Washington sts.
Reading 19601
215–376–7317

Consumer Education and
Protective Assn.
6048 Ogontz Ave.
Philadelphia 19141
215–424–1441

Consumers United Together
(CUT)
1022 Birch St.
Scranton 18505
717–346–5642

Council of Spanish Speaking
Organizations
2861 N. Fifth St.
Philadelphia 19133
215–574–3535

Institute for Community
Services
Edinboro State College
Edinboro 16412
814–732–2451

Legal Educational Assistance
Program
Temple University
1719 N. Broad St.
Philadelphia 19122
215–787–8953

PENNSYLVANIA (cont.)

Lehigh Valley Committee
Against Health Fraud, Inc.
P.O. Box 1602
Allentown 18105
215–437–1795

National Students Consumer
Protection Council
328 Bartley Hall
Villanova University
Villanova 19085
215–527–2100, ext. 331

North West Consumer
Council
Box 725
Edinboro 16412
814–732–2451

Northwest Tenants
Organization
5622 Germantown Ave.
Philadelphia 19144
215–849–7111

Pennsylvania Public Interest
Research Group
20 Hetzel Union Bldg.
University Park 16802
814–865–6851

Pennsylvania Consumers
Board
Houston Hall
3417 Spruce St.
Philadelphia 19174
215–243–6000

Pennsylvania Consumers
Council
Box 17019
Pittsburgh 15235
412–355–5405

Pennsylvania League for
Consumer Protection
2929 N. Front St.
Harrisburg 17110
717–233–5704

PENNSYLVANIA (cont.)

Philadelphia Area Consumer
Organization
1410 Chestnut St.
Philadelphia 19102
215–763–1744

Philadelphia Consumer
Services Cooperative
1008 River Park House
3600 Conshohocken Ave.
Philadelphia 19131
215–GR 3–0482

Philadelphia Tenants
Information Service
5622 Germantown
Philadelphia 19144
215–849–4344

South Wilkes Barre Council
of Organizations
186 Barney St.
Wilkes Barre 18702
717–822–5173

State Tenants Organization
of Pennsylvania
1415 Peterson
Chester 19013
215–494–7659

Taxpayers Information
Project
330 Race St.
Philadelphia 19106
215–922–6890

Tenant Action Group
5710 Germantown Ave.
Philadelphia 19144
215–849–8877

United Consumers of the
Alleghenies, Inc.
P.O. Box 997
Johnstown 15907
814–535–8608

PUERTO RICO

Committee for Consumer Action
W-3 Loma Alta
Garden Hills
Guaynabo 00657

RHODE ISLAND

Coalition for Consumer Justice
428 Dexter St.
Central Falls 02863
401-723-3147

Rhode Island Public Interest Research Group
University of Rhode Island
232 Gorham Hall
Kingston 02881
401-792-5444

Rhode Island Public Interest Research Group
Brown University, Box 2145
Providence 02912
401-863-4343

Rhode Island Workers Association
212 Union St., Rm. 206
Providence 02903
401-751-2008

Urban League of Rhode Island
131 Washington St.
Providence 02903
401-351-5000

SOUTH CAROLINA

Midlands Community Action Agency
2000 Washington St.
Columbia 29204
803-779-7250, ext. 68

South Carolina Public Interest Research Group
Furman University
Greenville 29613
803-294-2174

SOUTH DAKOTA

ACORN
611 S. 2nd Ave.
Sioux Falls 57104
605-332-2328

Consumers League
Rapid City 57701
605-343-6836

NE South Dakota Community Action Program
323 Jot Ave., East
Sisseton 57262
605-698-7654

South Dakota Consumers League
P.O. Box 106
Madison 57042
605-256-4536

TENNESSEE

Community Services Administration
444 James Robertson Pky.
Nashville 37219
615-741-2615

Elk and Duck Rivers Community Association
701 S. Lincoln Ave.
Fayetteville 37334
615-433-7182

The Highlander Center
Route 3, Box 370
New Market 37820
615-933-3443

TEXAS

Community Action Resource Services
1510 Plum St.
Texarkana 75501
214-794-3386 or
    501-921-4608

Dallas Community Action
Consumer Education Dept.
2208 Main
Dallas 75201
214-742-2500

TEXAS (cont.)

Dallas County Community Action Center
2208 Main St.
Dallas 75201
214-742-2500

Low Income Consumer Club
1510 Plum St.
Texarkana 75701
214-794-3386 or
    501-774-5259

Senior Citizens Service, Inc., of Texarkana
P.O. Box 619
Texarkana 75501
214-792-5131

Tarrant County Legal Services
201 E. Belknap
Ft. Worth 76102
817-334-1435

Texas Citizen Action Group
2226 Guadalupe
Austin 78705

Texas Consumer Association
P.O. Box 12542
Houston 77017
713-228-1521

Texas Public Interest Research Group
Box 237-UC
University of Houston
Houston 77004
713-749-3130

UTAH

League of Utah Consumers
2096 N. 220 East
Provo 84601
801-375-6726

Ogden Area Community Action Center
206 24th St.
Ogden 84401
801-399-9281

UTAH (cont.)

Salt Lake Community Action Agency
2033 S. State
Salt Lake City 84115
801–487–3641

Utah Consumer Advisory Committee
147 N. Second West
Salt Lake City 84103
801–533–5421

Utah Consumers Organization
203 E. 7th South
Salt Lake City 84111
801–531–9039

Utah Home Economics Association
7 E. State St.
Farmington 84025
801–867–2211

Utah Issues and Information
2024 Annex, University of Utah
Salt Lake City 84114
801–581–7208

Utah Nutrition Council
College of Family Life
Utah State University
Logan 84322
801–752–4100, ext. 7681

Utah State Coalition of Senior Citizens
110 W. 2950 South
Salt Lake City 84115
801–467–1273

Utility Consumer Action Group
Chairman, Box 8195
Salt Lake City 84108
800–662–5431

VERMONT

Consumer Association for the Betterment of Living (CABOL)
Box 77
Danby 05739
802–293–5462

Vermont Alliance
5 State St.
Montpelier 05602
802–229–9104

Vermont Public Interest Research Group, Inc.
26 State St.
Montpelier 05602
802–223–5221

Vermont Public Interest Research and Education Fund (VPIREF)
26 State St.
Montpelier 05602
802–223–5221

Vermont Workers Rights Project
5 State St.
Montpelier 05602
802–229–9104

VIRGINIA

Church Hill Multi-Service Center, Inc.
800 N. 21st St.
Richmond 23223
804–649–8673

Concerned Citizens for Justice, Inc. (CCJ)
P.O. Box 1409
Wise 24293
703–328–9239

Consumer Congress of the Commonwealth of Virginia
710 E. Franklin St.
Richmond 23219
804–649–7664

VIRGINIA (cont.)

Consumers Organized for Fairness
c/o Lord Fairfax Community College
P.O. Drawer E
Middletown 22645
703–869–1120

North Anna Environmental Coalition
P.O. Box 3951
Charlottsville 22903
804–293–6039

Office of Appalachian Ministry
Catholic Diocese of Richmond
Box 1376
Wise 24293
703–328–6800

Pittsylvania County Community Action Agency
P.O. Box 936
Chatham 24531
804–432–8250

Southwest Virginia Black Lung Assn.
Box 1409
Wise 24293
703–328–9147

Tidewater Citizens Coalition
4801 Peachcreek La.
Virginia Beach 23455
804–499–0845

Total Action Against Poverty Consumer Education Program
P.O. Box 2868
Roanoke 24001
702 Shenandoah Ave., NW
Roanoke 24016
703–345–6781, ext. 319

Virginia Citizens Consumer Council
P.O. Box 777
Springfield 22150
703–941–1441

VIRGINIA (cont.)

Virginia Citizens Consumer
Council Northern Virginia
Chapter
P.O. Box 777
Springfield 22150
703–941–1441

Virginia Citizens Consumer
Council, Richmond Chapter
P.O. Box 5462
Richmond 23220
804–266–2534

Virginia Citizens Consumer
Council, Roanoke Chapter
702 Shenandoah Ave.,
  NW
Roanoke 24016
703–345–6781, ext. 319

Virginia Home Economics
Association
706 N. Frederick St.
Arlington 22203

VIRGIN ISLANDS

Consumer Cooperative of the
Virgin Islands
President
809–774–8689

WASHINGTON

Blue Mountain Action
Council
19 E. Poplar St.
Walla Walla 99362
509–529–4980

Central Area Motivation
Program Consumer Action
105 14th, Suite D
Seattle 98122
206–324–1166

Central Seattle Community
Council Federation
810 18th Ave.
Seattle 98122
206–322–7100

WASHINGTON (cont.)

Community Action Council
P.O. Box 553
Port Townsend 98368
206–385–0776

Consumer Action Project
(CAMP)
105 - 14th Ave., Suite D
Seattle 98122
206–324–1166

Hunger Action Center
Olympia 98505
206–866–6695

Hunger Action Center
323 2nd and Cherry Bldg.
Seattle 98104

Hunger Action Center
c/o Spokane Office of
  Legal Services
W. 246 Riverside
Spokane 99201
509–838–3671

KGY (Radio) Action Line
1240 N. Washington
Olympia 98501
206–943–1240

Seattle Consumer Action
Network (SCAN)
P.O. Box 22455
Seattle 98122
206–324–1196

Spokane Dietetic Association
West 327 8th Ave.
Spokane 98204
509–325–1201

The Spokane Food Bank
S. 157 Howard
Spokane 99204
509–747–4332

Washington Committee on
Consumer Interests
2701 First Ave., Suite 300
Seattle 98121
206–682–1174

WASHINGTON (cont.)

Washington Public Interest
Research Group
Box 225 FK-10
University of Washington
Seattle 98195
206–543–8700

WEST VIRGINIA

Appalachian Research and
Defense Fund
1116 B Kanawha Blvd., East
Charleston 25301
304–344–9687

Council of the Southern
Mountains West Virginia
Branch
125 McDowell St.
Welch 24801
304–436–2185

Multi-County Community
Against Poverty
P.O. Box 3228
Charleston 25332
304–343–4175

North-Central West Virginia
Community Action
Association, Inc.
208 Adams St.
Fairmont 26554
304–363–2170

West Virginia Citizens Action
Group, Inc.
1324 Virginia St., East
Charleston 25301
304–346–5891

West Virginia Public Interest
Research Group
Box 198
Wesleyan College
Buchhannon 26201

West Virginia Public Interest
Research Group
S.O.W. Mountainlair
West Virginia University
Mortantown 26506
304–293–2108

WISCONSIN

Center for Consumer Affairs
University of Wisconsin
Extension
929 N. 6th St.
Milwaukee 53203
414–224–4177

**Center for Public
Representation**
520 University Ave.
Madison 53703
608–251–4008

**Central Wisconsin
Community Action Council,
Inc.**
211 Wisconsin Ave.
P.O. Box 448
Wisconsin Dells 53965
608–254–8353

**Coalition for Balanced
Transportation**
114 N. Carroll St., Rm.
208
Madison 53703
608–256–6647

WISCONSIN (cont.)

**The Concerned Consumers
League, Inc.**
524 W. National Ave.
Milwaukee 53204
414–645–1808

Forest Community
RPI, Box 86
Marengo 54855

**Greater Milwaukee
Consumers League**
314 N. 116 St.
Milwaukee 53226
414–645–8213

**People United for Responsible
Energy (PURE)**
P.O. Box 3482
Madison 53704
608–255–9978

**Racine County Community
Action Committee, Inc.**
Memorial Hall
72 7th St.
Racine 53402
414–633–1883

WISCONSIN (cont.)

Wisconsin Consumers League
P.O. Box 1531
Madison 53701
608–238–8153

**Wisconsin's Environmental
Decade**
114 E. Mifflin St.
Madison 53703
608–251–7020

**Wisconsin Peoples'
Bicentennial Commission**
306 N. Brooks St.
Madison 53715
608–251–7954

**Wisconsin Peoples'
Information Exchange**
Room 532, Lowell Hall
610 Landon St.
Madison 53703
608–262–9960

WYOMING

**Wyoming Consumers United
Program**
864 S. Spruce St.
Casper 82601
307–234–6060

PART 2: NATIONAL AND INTERNATIONAL ORGANIZATIONS

**American Association of
Retired Persons**
1909 K St., N.W.
Washington, D.C. 20049
202–872–4700

**American Council on
Consumer Interests**
162 Stanley Hall
University of Missouri
Columbia, Mo. 65201
314–882–4450

**C.O.C.O.–Conference of
Consumer Organizations**
Box 4277
Tucson, Ariz. 85717
602–884–2945

**Consumer Federation of
America**
1012 14th St., N.W., Suite
901
Washington, D.C. 20005
202–737–3732

**Consumers Union of the
United States, Inc.**
256 Washington St.
Mount Vernon, N.Y. 10550
914–664–6400

**Consumers Union of the
United States, Inc.–Regional
Office**
1714 Massachusetts Ave.,
N.W.
Washington, D.C. 20036

**Consumers Union of the
United States, Inc.–Regional
Office**
433 Turk St.
San Francisco, Calif. 94104

**International Organization of
Consumers Unions**
9 Emmastraat
The Hague
The Netherlands
83.49.04 Cables: Interocu

**National Center on the Black
Aged**
1730 M St., N.W., Suite 811
Washington, D.C. 20036
202–785–8766

National Consumers Congress
1346 Connecticut Ave.,
  N.W., Rm. 209
Washington, D.C. 20036
202–833–9704

National Consumers League
1785 Massachusetts Ave.,
  N.W.
Washington, D.C. 20036
202–797–7600

*National Council on the
Aging*
  1828 L St., N.W.
Washington, D.C. 20036
202–223–6250

*National Council on Senior
Citizens*
  1511 K St., N.W.
Washington, D.C. 20005
202–638–4351

*National Retired Teachers
Association*
1909 K St., N.W.
Washington, D.C. 20049
202–872–4700

Source: U.S. Office of Consumer Affairs, Washington, D.C. 20201, October 1976.

ADDITIONAL REFERENCES

BOOKS

BITTINGER, MARVIN L., *The Consumer Survival Book*. Danvers, Mass.: Book Production Services, Inc., 1974.

BRUCE, RONALD, *The Consumer's Guide to Product Safety*. Hauppauge, N.Y.: Award Books, Universal Publishing and Distribution Corp., 1971.

CENTER FOR AUTO SAFETY, *Mobile Homes*. New York: Grossman Publishers, Inc., distributed by Viking Press, 1975.

CHARELL, RALPH, *How I Turn Ordinary Complaints into Thousands of Dollars: The Diary of a Tough Customer*. Briarcliff Manor, N.Y.: Stein and Day, 1973.

CHERNIK, VLADIMIR P., *The Consumer's Guide To Insurance Buying*. Los Angeles: Sherbourne Press, 1970.

Consumer Guide—How It Works and How To Fix It. New York: New American Library, 1974.

Consumer's Almanac and Calendar. Washington, D.C.: National Consumers League.

CO-OP HANDBOOK COLLECTIVE, *The Food Co-op Handbook: How To Bypass Supermarkets To Control the Quality and Price of Your Food*. Boston: Houghton Mifflin Co., 1975.

DENNENBERG, HERBERT, *How to Protect Yourself Against Con-Men, Thieves, Bilko Artists, Dentists, Lawyers, Surgeons and Insurance Agents*. Philadelphia: Running Press, 1976.

————, *The Shopper's Guidebook to Life Insurance, Health Insurance, Auto Insurance, Homeowner's Insurance, Doctors, Dentists, Lawyers, Pensions, Etc.* Washington, D.C.: Consumer News, Inc., 1974.

DORFMAN, JOHN, *A Consumer's Arsenal.* New York: Praeger Publishers, 1976.

————, *Consumer Survival Kit.* New York: Praeger Publishers, 1975.

DRURY, TERESA, AND WILLIAM L. ROPER, *Consumer Power.* New York: Nash Publishing Corp., distributed by E.P. Dutton and Co., Inc., 1974.

FARGIS, PAUL, *The Consumer's Handbook.* New York: Hawthorn Books, Inc., 1974.

GARDNER, JOHN W., *In Common Cause.* New York: W.W. Norton and Company, Inc., 1973.

LADSTONE, BERNARD, *New Complete Guide to Home Repair.* New York: Quadrangle/The New York Times Book Co., Inc., 1974.

Guide To Federal Consumer Services. Washington, D.C.: Superintendent of Documents, U.S. Government Printing Office, 1976; revised periodically.

HESS, NANCY R., *The Home Buyer's Guide.* Englewood Cliffs, N.J.: Prentice-Hall, Inc., Spectrum Books, 1976.

How Things Work in Your Home (and What To Do When They Don't). Chicago: Time-Life Books, 1975.

MCLEOD, STERLING, AND SCIENCE BOOK ASSOCIATION EDITORS, *Careers in Consumer Protection.* New York: Julian Messner, distributed by Simon and Schuster, Inc., 1974.

MASSEY, CARMEN, AND RALPH WARNER, *Sex, Living Together and the Law.* Berkeley, Calif.: Nolo Press, 1974.

NADER STUDY GROUP, *Unsafe at Any Speed.* Des Plaines, Ill.: Bantam Books, Inc., 1973.

PETERSON, FRANKLYNN, *How to Fix Damn Near Everything.* Englewood Cliffs, N.J.: Prentice-Hall, Inc., Spectrum Books, 1977.

STANTON, DOUGLAS R., *Your Consumer Credit Rights.* Chatsworth, Calif.: Major Books, 1975.

TEEMAN, L., ed., *Consumer Guide—Do It Yourself Product Test Report.* New York: New American Library, 1974.

WEIL, GORDON L., *The Consumer's Guide to Banks.* Briarcliff Manor, N.Y.: Stein and Day, 1975.

WEINSTEIN, GRACE W., *Children and Money: A Guide for Parents.* New York: Schocken Books, 1976.

WHITE, JACK, et al., *The Angry Buyer's Complaint Directory.* New York: Peter H. Wyden, distributed by David McKay Co., Inc., 1974.

MAGAZINES AND JOURNALS

Consumer Newsweek, Consumer News, Inc., 813 National Press Building, Washington, D.C. 20045.

Consumer Reports, Consumers Union of the United States, Inc., 256 Washington Street, Mount Vernon, N.Y. 10550.

Consumers Digest, Arthur Weber, Publisher, 6316 No. Lincoln Ave., Chicago, Ill. 60659.

Consumers Union News Digest, Consumers Union of the United States, Inc., 256 Washington Street, Mount Vernon, N.Y. 10550.

Consumers' Research Magazine, Consumers' Research, Inc., Bowerstown Road, Washington, N.J. 07882.

Everybody's Money, Credit Union National Association, Inc., P.O. Box 431, Madison, Wis. 53701.

The Journal of Consumer Affairs, The American Council on Consumer Interests, 238 Stanley Hall, University of Missouri, Columbia, Mo. 65201.

NEWSLETTERS AND NEWSPAPERS

The ACCI Newsletter, The American Council on Consumer Interests, 238 Stanley Hall, University of Missouri, Columbia, Mo. 65201. (Write for free copy.)

Consumer News, published by Office of Consumer Affairs, Department of Health, Education and Welfare; sold by Superintendent of Documents, U.S. Government Printing Office, Washington, D.C. 20402.

Moneysworth, Ralph Ginzburg, Publisher, 251 West 57th Street, New York, N.Y. 10019.

A Report to the Consumer, Ida Honorof, P.O. Box 5449, Sherman Oaks, Calif. 91403.

Vector Consumer Newsletter, Vector Enterprises, Inc., P.O. Box 512, Arcadia, Calif. 91006. (Emphasis on California consumer needs.)

PAMPHLETS

Those marked with an asterisk (*) may be obtained free by sending a self-addressed, stamped envelope to the address indicated.

Career and Educational Opportunities in the Consumer Field, by John R. Burton, Ph.D., Consumer Research Project, Manchester Community College, Manchester, Conn. 06040.

Consumer Information, index and order form for selected federal publications of consumer interest, Consumer Information Center, Public Documents Distribution Center, Pueblo, Colo. 81009.

*Consumer Satisfaction With Food Products and Marketing Services, Publications Division, Economic Research Service, Room 0054 S, Agriculture Department, Washington, D.C. 20250.

*Freedom of Information Act, Freedom of Information Clearinghouse, P.O. Box 19367, Washington, D.C. 20036.

Insurance Reprints, prepared by staff of *Everybody's Money,* Credit Union National Association, Inc., Box 431, Madison, Wis. 53701.

*Public Citizen Action Projects, P.O. Box 19404, Washington, D.C. 20036.

*Public Citizen Health Research Group, list of reports and publications, P.O. Box 19404, Washington, D.C. 20036.

*Public Citizen, Reports and Publications, P.O. Box 19404, Washington D.C. 20036.

Touring With Towser, directory of hotels and motels in the United States and Canada that accept reservations for guests with dogs, Gaines TWT, CG 11, P.O. Box 1007, Kankakee, Ill. 60901.

Universal Solar Kitchen, details on building one, National Technical Service, 5285 Port Royal Road, Springfield, Va. 22150.

*Utility Rates, Residential Utility Consumer Action Group, Public Citizen, P.O. Box 19404, Washington, D.C. 20036.

INDEX